# i-Net+™ Test Yourself Practice Exams

# i-Net+™ Test Yourself Practice Exams

Syngress Media, Inc.

Osborne McGraw-Hill

Berkeley  New York  St. Louis  San Francisco  Auckland  Bogotá  Hamburg  London  Madrid  Mexico City
Milan  Montreal  New Delhi  Panama City  Paris  São Paulo  Singapore  Sydney  Tokyo  Toronto

Osborne McGraw-Hill
2600 Tenth Street
Berkeley, California 94710
U.S.A.

For information on translations or book distributors outside the U.S.A., or to arrange bulk purchase discounts for sales promotions, premiums, or fund-raisers, please contact Osborne/**McGraw-Hill** at the above address.

**i-Net+™ Test Yourself Practice Exams**

1234567890 AGM AGM 019876543210

ISBN 0-07-212413-X

| | |
|---|---|
| **Publisher**<br>Brandon A. Nordin | **Technical Editor**<br>Patrick Santry |
| **Associate Publisher and**<br>**Editor-in-Chief**<br>Scott Rogers | **Copy Editors**<br>Beth Roberts<br>Adaya Henis |
| **Acquisitions Editor**<br>Gareth Hancock | **Proofreader**<br>Tandra McLaughlin |
| **Associate Acquisitions Editor**<br>Timothy Green | **Computer Designers**<br>Jani Beckwith<br>Dick Schwartz |
| **Editorial Management**<br>Syngress Media, Inc. | **Illustrators**<br>Robert Hansen<br>Michael Mueller<br>Beth Young |
| **Project Editor**<br>Eva Banaszek | |
| **Acquisitions Coordinator**<br>Tara Davis | **Series Design**<br>Roberta Steele |
| **Series Editor**<br>Maxwell Miller, PhD. | **Cover Design**<br>Matthew Willis |

# FOREWORD

## From Global Knowledge

At Global Knowledge we strive to support the multiplicity of learning styles required by our students to achieve success as technical professionals. In this series of books, it is our intention to offer the reader a valuable tool for successful completion of the i-Net+ Certification Exam.

As the world's largest IT training company, Global Knowledge is uniquely positioned to offer these books. The expertise gained each year from providing instructor-led training to hundreds of thousands of students worldwide has been captured in book form to enhance your learning experience. We hope that the quality of these books demonstrates our commitment to your lifelong learning success. Whether you choose to learn through the written word, computer-based training, Web delivery, or instructor-led training, Global Knowledge is committed to providing you the very best in each of those categories. For those of you who know Global Knowledge, or those of you who have just found us for the first time, our goal is to be your lifelong competency partner.

Thank you for the opportunity to serve you. We look forward to serving your needs again in the future.

Warmest regards,

Duncan Anderson
President and Chief Executive Officer, Global Knowledge

# The Global Knowledge Advantage

Global Knowledge has a global delivery system for its products and services. The company has 28 subsidiaries, and offers its programs through a total of 60+ locations. No other vendor can provide consistent services across a geographic area this large. Global Knowledge is the largest independent information technology education provider, offering programs on a variety of platforms. This enables our multi-platform and multi-national customers to obtain all of their programs from a single vendor. The company has developed the unique CompetusTM Framework software tool and methodology which can quickly reconfigure courseware to the proficiency level of a student on an interactive basis. Combined with self-paced and on-line programs, this technology can reduce the time required for training by prescribing content in only the deficient skills areas. The company has fully automated every aspect of the education process, from registration and follow-up, to "just-in-time" production of courseware. Global Knowledge, through its Enterprise Services Consultancy, can customize programs and products to suit the needs of an individual customer.

# Global Knowledge Classroom Education Programs

The backbone of our delivery options is classroom-based education. Our modern, well-equipped facilities staffed with the finest instructors offer programs in a wide variety of information technology topics, many of which lead to professional certifications.

# Custom Learning Solutions

This delivery option has been created for companies and governments that value customized learning solutions. For them, our consultancy-based approach of developing targeted education solutions is most effective at helping them meet specific objectives.

# Self-Paced and Multimedia Products

This delivery option offers self-paced program titles in interactive CD-ROM, videotape and audio tape programs. In addition, we offer custom development of interactive multimedia courseware to customers and partners. Call us at 1 (888) 427-4228.

# Electronic Delivery of Training

Our network-based training service delivers efficient competency-based, interactive training via the World Wide Web and organizational intranets. This leading-edge delivery option provides a custom learning path and "just-in-time" training for maximum convenience to students.

# ARG

American Research Group (ARG), a wholly-owned subsidiary of Global Knowledge, one of the largest worldwide training partners of Cisco Systems, offers a wide range of internetworking, LAN/WAN, Bay Networks, FORE Systems, IBM, and UNIX courses. ARG offers hands on network training in both instructor-led classes and self-paced PC-based training.

# Global Knowledge Courses Available

## Network Fundamentals
- Understanding Computer Networks
- Telecommunications Fundamentals I
- Telecommunications Fundamentals II
- Understanding Networking Fundamentals
- Implementing Computer Telephony Integration
- Introduction to Voice Over IP
- Introduction to Wide Area Networking
- Cabling Voice and Data Networks
- Introduction to LAN/WAN protocols
- Virtual Private Networks
- ATM Essentials

## Network Security & Management
- Troubleshooting TCP/IP Networks
- Network Management
- Network Troubleshooting
- IP Address Management
- Network Security Administration
- Web Security
- Implementing UNIX Security
- Managing Cisco Network Security
- Windows NT 4.0 Security

## IT Professional Skills
- Project Management for IT Professionals
- Advanced Project Management for IT Professionals
- Survival Skills for the New IT Manager
- Making IT Teams Work

## LAN/WAN Internetworking
- Frame Relay Internetworking
- Implementing T1/T3 Services
- Understanding Digital Subscriber Line (xDSL)
- Internetworking with Routers and Switches
- Advanced Routing and Switching
- Multi-Layer Switching and Wire-Speed Routing
- Internetworking with TCP/IP
- ATM Internetworking
- OSPF Design and Configuration
- Border Gateway Protocol (BGP) Configuration

## Authorized Vendor Training
### Cisco Systems
- Introduction to Cisco Router Configuration
- Advanced Cisco Router Configuration
- Installation and Maintenance of Cisco Routers
- Cisco Internetwork Troubleshooting
- Cisco Internetwork Design
- Cisco Routers and LAN Switches
- Catalyst 5000 Series Configuration
- Cisco LAN Switch Configuration
- Managing Cisco Switched Internetworks
- Configuring, Monitoring, and Troubleshooting Dial-Up Services
- Cisco AS5200 Installation and Configuration
- Cisco Campus ATM Solutions

### Bay Networks
- Bay Networks Accelerated Router Configuration
- Bay Networks Advanced IP Routing
- Bay Networks Hub Connectivity
- Bay Networks Accelar 1xxx Installation and Basic Configuration
- Bay Networks Centillion Switching

### FORE Systems
- FORE ATM Enterprise Core Products
- FORE ATM Enterprise Edge Products
- FORE ATM Theory
- FORE LAN Certification

## Operating Systems & Programming
### Microsoft
- Introduction to Windows NT
- Microsoft Networking Essentials
- Windows NT 4.0 Workstation
- Windows NT 4.0 Server
- Advanced Windows NT 4.0 Server
- Windows NT Networking with TCP/IP
- Introduction to Microsoft Web Tools
- Windows NT Troubleshooting
- Windows Registry Configuration

### UNIX
- UNIX Level I
- UNIX Level II
- Essentials of UNIX and NT Integration

### Programming
- Introduction to JavaScript
- Java Programming
- PERL Programming
- Advanced PERL with CGI for the Web

## Web Site Management & Development
- Building a Web Site
- Web Site Management and Performance
- Web Development Fundamentals

## High Speed Networking
- Essentials of Wide Area Networking
- Integrating ISDN
- Fiber Optic Network Design
- Fiber Optic Network Installation
- Migrating to High Performance Ethernet

## DIGITAL UNIX
- UNIX Utilities and Commands
- DIGITAL UNIX v4.0 System Administration
- DIGITAL UNIX v4.0 (TCP/IP) Network Management
- AdvFS, LSM, and RAID Configuration and Management
- DIGITAL UNIX TruCluster Software Configuration and Management
- UNIX Shell Programming Featuring Kornshell
- DIGITAL UNIX v4.0 Security Management
- DIGITAL UNIX v4.0 Performance Management
- DIGITAL UNIX v4.0 Intervals Overview

## DIGITAL OpenVMS
- OpenVMS Skills for Users
- OpenVMS System and Network Node Management I
- OpenVMS System and Network Node Management II
- OpenVMS System and Network Node Management III
- OpenVMS System and Network Node Operations
- OpenVMS for Programmers
- OpenVMS System Troubleshooting for Systems Managers
- Configuring and Managing Complex VMScluster Systems
- Utilizing OpenVMS Features from C
- OpenVMS Performance Management
- Managing DEC TCP/IP Services for OpenVMS
- Programming in C

## Hardware Courses
- AlphaServer 1000/1000A Installation, Configuration and Maintenance
- AlphaServer 2100 Server Maintenance
- AlphaServer 4100, Troubleshooting Techniques and Problem Solving

## About Syngress Media

**Syngress Media** creates books and software for Information Technology professionals seeking skill enhancement and career advancement. Its products are designed to comply with vendor and industry standard course curricula, and are optimized for certification exam preparation. Visit the Syngress Web site at www.syngress.com.

## Contributors

**André Paree-Huff** (CCNA, MCSE+I, ASE, A+, Network+, i-Net+) has been working in the computer field for over seven years. He is currently working for Compaq Computer Corporation as a Network Support Specialist, level III, for the North America Customer Support Center in Colorado Springs, Colorado. André handles troubleshooting network hardware, specializing in Layers 2 and 3 of the OSI model. André has co-authored two network-related technical manuals and has been a technical editor on many others. He is currently working toward his CCIE.

**Amy Thomson** (A+, MOUS Master) is a software and A+ instructor in Halifax, Nova Scotia, and she has over ten years of experience in dealing with computer hardware and applications. Amy has taught computer classes from one end of Canada to the other and back again. She holds an Honours B.Sc. in Psychology and is currently preparing for certification as an MCSE.

**Tien Nguyen** (MCSD, MCT) is a Principal Consultant with Cotelligent, a national information technology consulting firm. He is involved in various e-Business projects that need multi-tier architecture. He also teaches Visual Basic 6 and Web Development at Cotelligent. He has been designing and developing business applications for more than 17 years and is a Chartered Microsoft Certified Solution Developer (and Site Builder) and a Microsoft Certified Trainer.

## About the Technical Editor

**Patrick Santry** (MCT, MCSD, MCP+SB, i-Net+) has been involved in Web development and management for over five years. He specializes in systems integration for business-to-business e-commerce applications. Patrick currently works as a Senior Information Systems Specialist for a large chemical and mechanical products manufacturer in Erie, Pennsylvania. His responsibilities include Web server management, Web development and integration. In his spare time he runs a Web site devoted to Web professionals located at http://www.santry.com. Patrick dedicates his writing efforts to his family: his wife Karyn, daughters Katie and Karleigh, and his son Patrick Jr. (aka PJ).

## About the Series Editor

**Maxwell Miller** (PhD, CIW, CIT, i-Net+) is a consultant specializing in e-business and IT training and certification. Max provides consulting services in the areas of instructional systems design, competency management, distance learning, curriculum architecture, and psychometrics. Formerly, Max was the Chief Content Architect of ProsoftTraining.com and co-led the development of the IBM-Certified Internet Webmaster (CIW) Internet certification program. He has managed the development of numerous commercial IT training products, including software and courseware, CBT, WBT, and distributed learning solutions for customers, including the Gartner Group, Netscape Communications, IBM, Citibank, and GE. Max began his career as a Telecommunications Systems Engineer at AT&T Bell Labs in Holmdel, New Jersey, and has served as a Senior Scientist consultant to the Federal government in the areas of IT systems architecture, imagery analysis, and sonar classification for automatic target recognition. Max completed his doctorate in Applied/Cognitive Science and Acoustics at the Catholic University of America in Washington, D.C., and holds a masters degree in Human Factors Engineering. He can be contacted at mail24558@pop.net. In addition to technically reviewing the material, Max authored portions of this book.

# ACKNOWLEDGMENTS

We would like to thank the following people:

- Richard Kristof of Global Knowledge for championing the series and providing access to some great people and information.

- All the incredibly hard-working folks at Osborne/McGraw-Hill: Brandon Nordin, Scott Rogers, and Gareth Hancock for their help in launching a great series and being solid team players. In addition, Lisa Theobald, Tim Green, and Tara Davis for their help in fine-tuning the book.

# CONTENTS

## Part 2
### Test Yourself: i-Net+ Certification Practice Exams

This book's primary objective is to help you prepare for and pass the required i-Net+ Certification Exam so you can begin to reap the career benefits of certification. Every time we asked CompTIA and i-Net+ certification candidates what they wanted in their study materials, they answered "More questions!" We believe that the only way to do this is to help you increase your knowledge and build your skills by the ability to test yourself to your heart's content. After completing this book, you should feel confident that you have thoroughly prepared yourself for all of the objectives that CompTIA has established for the i-Net+ exam.

## In This Book

This book is organized in parts or modules, according to topics covered within the i-Net+ exam administered at Sylvan Prometric Testing Centers. We cover each of the exam topics in a separate section or module of questions and answers, and we also have a separate "Test Yourself" module of stand-alone practice exams. CompTIA has specific objectives for its exams: we've followed its list carefully, so you can be assured you're not missing anything.

## The Q&A Modules

The Q&A modules in this book contain a question section followed by an answer section that has full explanations of both the correct and incorrect choices.

The modules are divided into categories, so you will cover every topic tested by CompTIA. Each exam topic is a module within the Q&A section, so you can study by topic if you like. Should you find you need further review on any particular topic, you will discover that the topic headings correspond to the chapters of Osborne/McGraw-Hill's *i-Net+ Certification Study Guide*. Want to simulate an actual exam? The section "The Test Yourself Module" explains how.

## The Test Yourself Module

If you have had your fill of exam questions, answers, and explanations, the time has come to test your knowledge. Or maybe, you want to start with a practice exam in the Test Yourself module to see where your strengths and weaknesses are, and then review only certain topics. Either way, turn to Part 2 of the book, the Practice Exams. Here we actually simulate the exams. Lock yourself in your office or clear the kitchen table, set a timer, and jump in.

## The Global Knowledge Web Site

*Check out the Web site.* Global Knowledge invites you to become an active member of the Access Global Web site. This site is an online mall and an information repository that you'll find invaluable. You can access many types of products to assist you in your preparation for the exams, and you'll be able to participate in forums, on-line discussions, and threaded discussions. No other book brings you unlimited access to such a resource.

# How to Take the i-Net+ Certification Examination

### By André Paree-Huff, ASE, A+, CCNA, i-NET+, MCSE+I, Network+

CompTIA has again created a certification to help you stand out professionally. The new i-Net+ certification follows in the footsteps of its predecessors, and it is quickly proving to be a highly accepted, great benchmark for Internet knowledge.

CompTIA has developed the i-Net+ certification to give IT professionals a chance to prove their knowledge to their employers and customers in the area of Internet, Extranet and Intranet technologies. Similarly to the Network+ and A+, i-Net+ certification is vendor-neutral; it was developed with help from people representing various companies to make sure that it remains a neutral certification.

More than 6,000 people in over 20 countries signed up to take the beta version of the test, proving that this certification may quickly become a standard for knowledge and experience baseline assessment. Presently, the test is being offered in English in 22 countries.

# Why Choose the CompTIA i-Net+ Certification?

There are several reasons why you should choose the CompTIA i-Net+ certification. Some of them are:

- **Recognition** of your knowledge and experience
- **Customer satisfaction** Customers are more satisfied with the service received from a certified professional.

- **Confidence** You will feel more confident with your knowledge in front of your customers after passing the certification exam.

- **Career Advancement** Many companies reward or promote employees who have proved their knowledge with certification.

# Computerized Testing

Considering the popularity of CompTIA's certifications, and the fact that certification candidates are spread around the world, the only practical way to administer tests for the certification program is through Sylvan Prometric testing centers. Sylvan Prometric provides proctored testing services for Microsoft, Oracle, Novell, Lotus, and CompTIA's other certifications, the A+ computer technician certification, Network+, and the CDIA certifications. In fact, most companies that need secure test delivery over a wide geographic area use the services of Sylvan Prometric. In addition to delivery, Sylvan Prometric also scores the tests and provides statistical feedback on performance on each test question directly to the companies and organizations that use their services.

Typically, several hundred questions are developed for each new certification examination. The questions are first reviewed by a number of subject matter experts for technical accuracy and then are presented in a beta test. The beta test usually lasts two to three hours due to the large number of questions. After a few weeks, CompTIA uses the statistical feedback from Sylvan to check the performance on the beta questions.

Questions are discarded as too easy if the majority of the test takers gets them right, or as too difficult if the majority gets them wrong. A number of other statistical measures are taken for each question. Although the scope of our discussion precludes a rigorous treatment of question analysis, you should be aware that CompTIA and other vendors spend a great deal of time and effort making sure their examination questions are valid. In addition to the obvious desire for quality, the fairness of a vendor's certification program must be legally defensible.

The questions that survive statistical analysis form the pool of questions for the final certification examination. This pool is what the questions for the actual test are drawn from. Each time you take the exam you will receive a new set of questions; you might see some of the same questions but don't count on memorization of questions for a retake.

## Exam Information

The i-Net+ Certification Exam is a Sylvan Prometric delivered exam. The test comprises a question pool with each tester receiving 72 questions. Each test question weighs exactly the same, no matter if the question is true/false, single-answer, or multiple choice. To receive a passing grade, you must answer 53 questions correctly. This will give you the required 73% needed to achieve the certification.

You will be given 90 minutes to complete 72 questions; you will have, therefore, 1.25 minutes for each question. If you do not know the answer within 30 seconds of looking at the test, you are advised to make an educated guess, mark the question, and move on quickly. Once you have finished the last question, return to the questions you marked for a more in-depth look. Use your time wisely and remember that an unanswered question is always wrong; thus, if you have no idea of the correct answer, take your best guess.

The test is in a non-adaptive form, which means that you can move forward and backward to rethink your answers. Many times a test question will be answered later in the test in the form of a question.

### Example:

**10.** Which of the following is considered a fruit?

A. Apple

B. Potato

C. Cow

D. Garlic

**21.** An apple is a _____?

A. Animal

B. Mineral

C. Building supply

D. Fruit

CompTIA might soon start following the testing practice of Cisco, Microsoft, and Novell and change its tests to an adaptive form, in which each next question is based on the previous question. Thus, if you get two questions in a row correct, you will not be asked any additional questions in that category, but if you miss two out of three, you will automatically be asked an additional three questions in that category. Adaptive tests are better for both Sylvan and the vendor because you can get more test subjects in the same period, as most adaptive test takers rarely take more than 30 minutes to either pass or fail a test. For the vendor, it assures greater security, as the test taker receives fewer questions to remember when leaving.

## Questions on a Computerized Certification Exam

Computerized test questions can be presented in a number of ways. Some of the possible formats are used in CompTIA certification examinations, and some are not.

### True/False

Think back to school and the test you forgot to study for. What was the one type of question you hoped for? True/false! CompTIA does not use this type of question, because you always have a 50 percent chance of guessing the correct answer.

### Multiple Choice

The majority of the i-Net+ certification questions are in the multiple-choice format, with either one correct answer or more than one correct answer. In the case of multiple-choice questions with more than one correct answer, the candidate may or may not be told how many answers are correct.

### Example:

1. Which networking protocols are routable? (Choose two.)

   or

2. Which networking protocols exist in the Network Layer of the OSI model? (Choose all that apply.)

   You may see both variations on CompTIA certification examinations, but the trend seems to be toward the first type, in which candidates are told explicitly how many answers are correct. Questions of the "Choose all that apply" variety are more difficult and can be confusing, so you will not see as many of this type, as CompTIA does not intend to trick you.

### Graphical Questions

Graphics are sometimes used as exhibits to help present or clarify an exam question. These may be network diagrams or pictures of networking components. It is often easier to present the concepts required for a complex performance-based scenario with a graphic than it is with words. Expect only a couple of graphical questions on your i-Net+ exam.

Test questions known as "hotspots" actually incorporate graphics as part of the answer. These questions ask the certification candidate to click a location or graphical element to answer the question. For example, you might be shown the diagram of a network and be asked to click an appropriate location for a bridge. Your answer would be correct if you clicked within the hotspot that marked the correct location. The i-Net+ exam may have a few of these graphical hotspot questions. Expect only a couple of hotspot questions on your exam.

### Free Response Questions

The free response question requires a free response, type-in answer. This type of question might present a TCP/IP network scenario and ask you to calculate and enter the correct subnet mask in dotted decimal notation. This type of question is not often used; the beta i-Net+ exam I took recently does not contain any free response questions.

### Testing Job Performance

CompTIA certification focuses on timeliness and the ability to perform job tasks. Even performance-based multiple-choice questions do not really measure performance. Another strategy is needed to test job skills.

With unlimited resources, it would not be difficult to test job skills. In an ideal world, CompTIA would fly i-Net+ candidates to a test facility (much as Cisco does for the CCIE), place them in a controlled environment with a team of experts, and ask them to plan, install, maintain, and troubleshoot an Internet, intranet, and extranet and to design and implement a Web server and pages. In a few days at most, the experts could decide whether each candidate should or should not be granted i-Net+ certification status. Needless to say, this is not likely to happen. The cost would be prohibitive, and it would be impossible to test more than one person on a set of equipment at a time.

Another more practical way to test performance is to use the actual software and create a testing program to present tasks and automatically grade a candidate's performance when the tasks are completed. This cooperative approach would be practical in some testing situations, but the same test that is presented to I-Net+ candidates in Boston must also be available in Bahrain and Botswana. Many Sylvan Prometric testing locations around the world cannot run 32-bit applications, much less provide the complex networked solutions required by cooperative testing applications.

The most workable method of measuring performance in today's testing environment is a simulation program. When the program is launched during a test, the candidate sees a simulation of the actual software that looks and behaves just like the real thing. When the testing software presents a task, the simulation program is launched and the candidate performs the required task. The testing software then grades the candidate's performance on the required task and moves to the next question. In this way, a 16-bit simulation program can mimic the look and feel of 32-bit operating systems, a complicated network, or even the entire Internet.

Simulation questions provide many advantages over other testing methodologies, and simulations are expected to become increasingly important in computer certification programs. Studies have shown that there is a very high correlation between the ability to perform simulated tasks on a computer-based test and the ability to perform the actual job tasks. Thus, simulations enhance the validity of the certification process.

Another benefit of simulations is in the area of test security. It is just not possible to cheat on a simulation question. In fact, you will be told exactly what tasks you are expected to perform on the test. How can a certification candidate cheat? By learning to perform the tasks? What a concept!

## Knowledge-Based and Performance-Based Questions

CompTIA Certification develops a blueprint for each certification examination with input from subject-matter experts. This blueprint defines the content areas and objectives for each test, and each test question is created to test a specific objective. The basic information from the examination blueprint can be found on CompTIA's Web site at http://www.comptia.org.

Psychometricians categorize test questions as knowledge-based or performance-based. As these terms imply, knowledge-based questions are designed to test knowledge, and performance-based questions are designed to test performance.

Some objectives demand a knowledge-based question. For example, objectives that use verbs such as "list" and "identify" tend to test only what you know, not what you can do.

### Example:
Objective: Types of URLs to access a given type of server.

1. Which two transport protocols can be used to display a HTML document on a Web browser? (Choose two.)

   A. FTP

   B. HTTPS

   C. mailto

   D. HTTP

   Correct answers: **B, D**.

The i-Net+ exam consists primarily of straightforward, knowledge-based, multiple-choice questions that can be answered fairly quickly if you know your stuff. These questions do not present complex scenarios to confuse you.

Other objectives use action verbs such as "install," "configure," and "troubleshoot" to define job tasks. These objectives can often be tested with either a knowledge-based question or a performance-based question.

### Example:
Objective: Cookies
Here's an example of a knowledge-based question:

1. Where do you configure an Internet Explorer 5.x Web browser to accept cookies?

   A. File | Properties Cookies

   B. Tools | Internet Options | Security tab

C. Options | Cookies

D. View | Options | Security | Cookies

Correct answer: **B.**

Here's an example of a performance-based question:

1. You want to ensure that you have a reliable tape backup scheme that is not susceptible to fire and water hazards. You are backing up three Windows NT servers and would like to completely back up the entire system. Which of the following is the most reliable backup method?

A. Configure the backup program to back up the user files and operating system files: Complete a test restore of the backup; and store the backup tapes offsite in a fireproof vault.

B. Configure the backup program to back up the entire hard drive of each server, and store the backup tapes offsite in a fireproof vault.

C. Copy the user files to another server; configure the backup program to back up the operating system files; and store the backup tapes offsite in a fireproof vault.

D. Configure the backup program to back up the user files and operating system files, and store the backup tapes offsite in fireproof vault.

Correct answer: **A.**

Even in this simple example, the superiority of the performance-based question is obvious. The knowledge-based question asks for a single fact, but the performance-based question presents a real-life situation and requires that you make a realistic decision. Thus, performance-based questions give more "bang" (validity) for the test author's buck (individual question).

# Study Strategies

There are appropriate ways to study for the different types of questions you will see on a CompTIA certification examination.

## Knowledge-Based Questions

Knowledge-based questions require that you memorize facts. There are hundreds of facts inherent in every content area of every certification examination. There are several tricks to memorizing facts:

- **Repetition** The more times your brain is exposed to a fact, the more likely you are to remember it. Flash cards are a wonderful tool for repetition. Either make your own flash cards on paper or download a flash card program and develop your own questions.

- **Association** When facts are connected within a logical framework, they are easier to remember. Try using mnemonics, such as "All People Seem To Need Data Processing" to remember the seven layers of the OSI model in order.

- **Motor Association** It is often easier to remember something if you write it down or perform some other physical act, such as clicking a practice test answer. You will find that hands-on experience with the product or concept being tested is a great way to develop motor association.

The emphasis of CompTIA certification is job performance, so there are very few knowledge-based questions on CompTIA certification exams. There are important reasons that you should you spend time learning file names, IP address formulas, and other minutiae.

## Performance-Based Questions

Most of the questions you will face on a CompTIA certification exam are performance-based scenario questions. These questions are superior to simple knowledge-based questions, but the job task orientation of CompTIA certification extends the knowledge you need to pass the exams; it does not replace this knowledge. Therefore, the first step in preparing for scenario questions is to absorb as many facts relating to the exam content areas as you can. In other words, go back to the previous section and follow the steps to prepare for an exam composed of knowledge-based questions.

The second step is to familiarize yourself with the format of the questions you are likely to see on the exam. This book is a useful tool to directly test your skills and knowledge of the exam objectives. The day of your test is not the time to be surprised by the complicated construction of some exam questions.

For example, one of CompTIA Certification's favorite formats of late takes the following form found on Microsoft exams:

Scenario: You have a network with...
Primary Objective: You want to...
Secondary Objective: You also want to . . .
Proposed Solution: Do this...

1. What does the proposed solution accomplish?

   A. It achieves the primary and the secondary objective.
   B. It achieves the primary but not the secondary objective.
   C. It achieves the secondary but not the primary objective.
   D. It achieves neither the primary nor the secondary objective.

   This kind of question, with some variation, is seen on many Microsoft Certification examinations and will be present on your i-Net+ Certification Exam.

   At best, these performance-based scenario questions really do test certification candidates at a higher cognitive level than knowledge-based questions do. At worst, these questions can test your reading comprehension and test-taking ability rather than your ability to administer networks. Be sure to get in the habit of reading each question carefully to determine what is being asked.

   The third step in preparing for CompTIA scenario questions is to adopt this attitude: Multiple-choice questions aren't really performance-based. These scenario questions are just knowledge-based questions with little stories wrapped around them.

   To answer a scenario question, you have to sift through the story to determine the underlying facts of the situation and apply your knowledge to determine the correct answer. This may sound silly at first, but the process we go through in solving real-life problems is quite similar. The key concept is that every scenario question (and every real-life problem) has a fact at its center, and if we can identify that fact, we can answer the question.

## Exam Blueprint

The i-Net+ exam is divided into six major areas. These areas are broken down here to show you the areas that will be covered. Each area is further broken down into objectives on the test. You will be tested extensively in each of these areas, so prepare as well as you can for each section.

| Testing area | % of Examination (approximately) |
|---|---|
| i-Net+ Basics | 10% |
| i-Net+ Clients | 20% |
| Development | 20% |
| Networking | 25% |
| i-Net+ Security | 15% |
| Business Concepts | 10% |

The objectives for the test, as well as other information about the CompTIA certification exams, can be found on CompTIA's Web site at http://www.comptia.org.

## Scheduling the Test

To take the i-Net+ certification test, you will need to contact Sylvan at 1-877-803-6867, in the United States. Not all testing centers offer all tests, so you may not be able to take the test at the center closest to you. You can also schedule a test by using Sylvan's online registration system at http://www.2test.com.

If for some reason you are unable to keep your test appointment, you must cancel your appointment by 7:00 P.M. central time on the day before your scheduled exam date. You can reschedule your exam at that time or wait until later to do so. Your test must be rescheduled within one year of the original test date, or all monies paid are forfeited.

A fee of $185.00 (price at the time this book went to press) is required for each attempt at the test. Payment must be made prior to scheduling the test, in the form of voucher, credit card, bank transfer, or check. If you pay by personal check, Sylvan will bill you or your company by invoice for the cost and must receive the check before you schedule your testing time.

When you have scheduled your test, you will be given some important information. You should make note of this information so that in case of any problems on your test day, you will have all information ready to give to the proctor. This information will be:

- Test number
- Date of test
- Location
- Seat number
- Confirmation number

## Taking the Test

On the day of the test, try to arrive at the testing center about 10 to 15 minutes early to sign in and get your paper and pencil. Make sure you bring two forms of ID; one must include a photograph, and both must include a signature.

The picture ID may be any of the following:

- Driver's license
- State ID
- Work ID
- Military ID
- Passport

Please remember not to bring any cell phones, pagers, or study material into the testing center, as they are not allowed in the testing area.

## The Stress Is Over

After you end the test you will immediately receive on your monitor a report of your score as well as notification whether you passed or failed the exam. You will need to stop by the proctor's desk to pick up a hard copy of your test results for your records. If you passed the exam, you will receive a packet in the mail in approximately four to six weeks with your certification certificate and a letter of congratulations from CompTIA.

Good luck!

# Part I

## i-Net+ Certification Exam Q&As

### EXAM TOPICS

i-Net+ Basics

Indexing and Caching

i-Net+ Clients

Client Security, Troubleshooting, and MIME

HTML

Multimedia

i-Net+ Languages

Networking and Infrastructure

Protocols

Hardware and Software

Servers and Bandwidth Technologies

i-Net+ Security

Business Concepts

E-Commerce

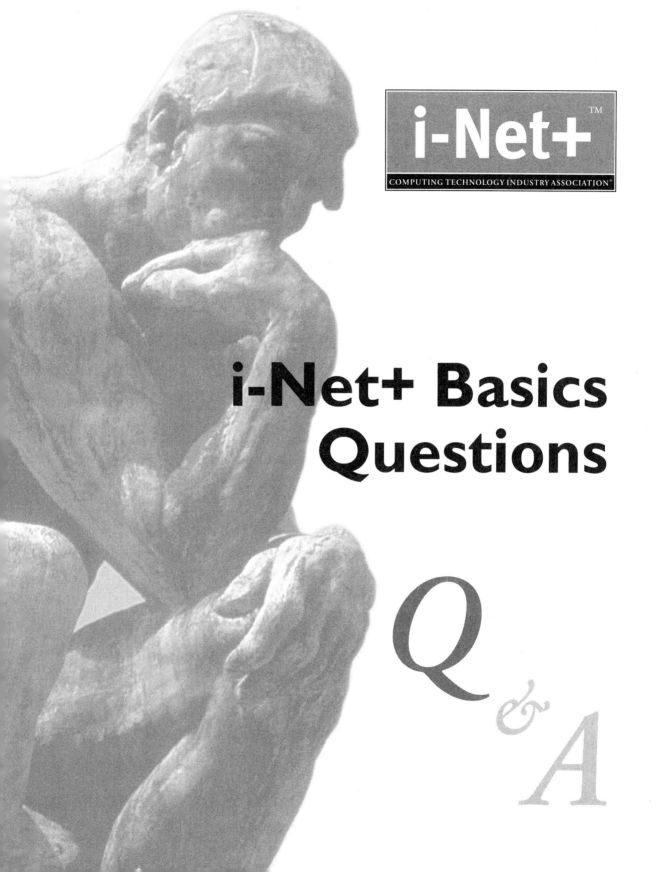

# i-Net+ Basics
# Questions

# i-Net+ Basics

1. You are working as a network security specialist at a small company. They are concerned with people accessing their information from the Internet. You have blocked just about everything you can think of on the firewall except FTP. What port should you block to keep people on the Internet from FTPing into your company?

   A. 21

   B. 23

   C. 25

   D. 80

2. The URL NNTP:\\www.ourcompany.com would take you to what?

   A. A Web page located at www.ourcompany.com

   B. A news server located at www.ourcompany.com

   C. A mail server located at www.ourcompany.com

   D. This is not a valid URL

3. What we know now as the World Wide Web was born in 1992 at what research center?

   A. CERN

   B. UCLA

   C. MIT

   D. NCSA

4. NSF turned over the distribution and maintenance of domain names to one organization that controlled all distribution until mid 1999. What organization did NSF designate to do this?

   A. World-Wide Web Consortium

   B. Network Solutions, Inc.

   C. Internet Engineering Task Force

   D. Internet Society

**5.** You are responsible for connecting your company's network to the Internet via a local ISP. What protocols can you run on the Internet?

A. TCP/IP only

B. TCP/IP and IPX

C. IPX only

D. Any routable protocol can be run on the Internet

**6.** When accessing information on an Internet server, you need some type of application to connect to the server and view the requested information. What computer platforms are able to connect to an Internet server?

A. Windows

B. UNIX

C. Macintosh

D. VMS

**7.** You decide to start designing Web pages as a part-time job for some small companies that are starting up in your area. You do not know much about Web design, and need to know what language to learn to be able to code the pages. What is the language that most Web pages are written in?

A. C++

B. Java

C. CGI

D. HTML

**8.** When connecting to a secured Web site, such as a page requesting credit card information for an e-purchase, what URL would you use if the site were www.buybooks.com\purchase?

A. HTTP:\\www.buybooks.com\purchase

B. HTTP:\\www.buybooks.com\purchase\secured

C. SHTPP:\\www.buybooks.com\purchase

D. HTTPS:\\www.buybooks.com\purchase

**9.** As a rule, you as the Internet Service Provider are responsible for providing what for your customers?

    A. Serve as their connection to another LAN

    B. Serve as a gateway for their data to the Internet

    C. Provide the client-side hardware needed to access the Internet

    D. Provide the bandwidth purchased by the end user

**10.** When you make a connection to a Web page, what happens once the page has been downloaded to your system?

    A. The connection is maintained until you close the browser or click on a new page.

    B. The connection is maintained until you click on a link on the page.

    C. The connection is maintained until the keep-alive counter expires—usually 1.5 minutes.

    D. The connection is dropped, and any further request from the page requires a new connection.

**11.** When embedding graphics in a Web page, performance is always an issue. If the page loads too slowly, users will get frustrated and may not come back to the site. On the other hand, if the graphics are very poor, users might not want to return because they will think it's a poorly designed site. If your page seems to have a performance issue with the graphics, what are some steps you can take to make the page and graphics download more quickly?

    A. Convert all your JPEG files to GIF files to make them smaller.

    B. Reduce the size of the picture.

    C. Replace a very large graphic with two or three smaller graphics.

    D. Reduce the number of colors in the image.

**12.** An intranet is _____?

    A. The term used for a company's network that is housed entirely behind a firewall.

    B. The term used for a company's network that has no connection to the Internet.

    C. The term used for the idea of connecting two separate corporate networks together using the Internet.

    D. Just another term for the Internet.

**13.** In what way did first-generation Web browsers differ from today's browsers?

    A. They could only display graphics in eight colors.

    B. They could not display graphics.

    C. They could not include embedded links to other sites.

    D. They were available only for Windows 3.*x* systems.

**14.** You design a large, detailed Web page for a company, with lots of graphics showing the products they sell. The owner of the company calls and complains that when he's at home, the Web page "takes forever to load." He does not notice this when he is in the office and connects to the company's Web page or any other Web page on the Internet. What is the most likely problem?

    A. The connection from the Web server to the Internet is too slow.

    B. The processor on the Web page is too slow to handle the large amount of graphics on the page.

    C. His home system is slower than the system he uses at the office.

    D. He is on a LAN in the office with a fast connection to the Internet; at home, he is using a dial-up connection that at best is 56K.

**15.** You are setting up Internet access for your company. They would like to be able to be kept up to date on information by monitoring messages posted by users on the Internet. Which protocol would allow them to do this?

    A. HTTP

    B. POP3

    C. SMTP

    D. NNTP

**16.** When you enter a URL in your browser's location field, what port on the Web server is it going to contact for a connection to retrieve the requested information?

    A. Port 21

    B. Port 23

    C. Port 25

    D. Port 80

**17.** What is the device used to connect two networks that run different protocols?

A. Switch

B. Bridge

C. Gateway

D. Translator

**18.** What was the original purpose of the Internet?

A. It was developed for the Department of Defense for use as a military network.

B. It was developed as a way to connect universities together to share educational issues.

C. It was developed as a replacement for the United States Postal Service.

D. It was developed to connect all medical facilities together to better serve their patients.

**19.** Which one body is responsible for management of the Internet?

A. CERN

B. Internet Society

C. W3C

D. None of the above

**20.** You were the person who did the research for your company's Internet connection. Based on your recommendations for the speed of the connection, your company purchased a T1 connection to the Internet. What speed is this connection?

A. 128 K

B. 1.544 Mbps

C. 3 Mbps

D. 45 Mbps

**21.** Your company has decided that they will no longer allow the use of ISDN connection for their employees to connect from home. They have found some advantages to using dial-up connection instead of dedicated connections. What are the advantages of using a dial-up connection to your ISP?

A. You are always connected.

B. You can run voice and data at the same time on the same wire. Talk while you surf.

C. Better security; when you're not dialed in, no one can connect to your system.

D. It is inexpensive.

**22.** You have been hired to develop a Web page for a new customer. You are told that the page will be used by both in-house personnel and customers connecting via the Internet. When designing a Web page, what is one of the biggest things you need to keep in mind about the page and those using it?

A. The better the pictures, the more the users will like it.

B. A plain and fast page will bring users back faster than a great page that takes considerable time to download.

C. Find the lowest common denominator between the speeds of those who will access the site. Do not design for those on the local network if the majority of users will be connecting at 28.8K.

D. You're the designer, so it's up to you to make the page the way you want it.

**23.** A thin client is also known as:

A. A personal digital assistant

B. A station on a slow connection

C. A Web browser

D. A high-end system loaded with memory

**24.** Which of the following Fully Qualified Domain Names (FQDNs) represents a not-for-profit business?

A. www.helpthepeople.com

B. www.helpthepeople.net

C. www.helpthepeople.org

D. www.helpthepeople.edu

# i-Net+ Basics

1. ☑ **A.** FTP uses TCP port 21. To block all FTP, you would need to block port 21 on your firewall. If your company's users need to FTP in from the outside, you can assign a new port for FTP; for example, 4021 or something similar.

   ☒ **B** is incorrect. Port 23 is used for Telnet. **C** is incorrect. Port 25 is used for SMTP. **D** is incorrect. Port 80 is used for HTTP traffic.

2. ☑ **D.** This is not a valid URL, because News Server URLs begin with news, not NNTP.

   ☒ **A** is incorrect; a Web page would be listed as HTTP:\\. **B.** Although NNTP is the protocol by which you connect to a News Server, this is not the correct syntax for entering the transfer protocol in the URL. **C** is incorrect; a mail server URL would begin with MAILTO:\\.

3. ☑ **A.** The WWW was created at CERN in Geneva, Switzerland, in 1992.

   ☒ **B, C,** and **D** are incorrect; they in their own right have made major contributions to the WWW, but not in its infant stage.

4. ☑ **B.** Until 1999, Network Solutions, Inc. was the sole holder of all domain names in the word. In mid 1999, several global organizations came together and decided that the distribution and maintenance of domain names should not be held in the hands of one organization and opened it up to many different organizations spread across the globe.

   ☒ **A, C,** and **D** are all incorrect; these are all global Internet standards bodies that help maintain and standardize the use of the Internet.

5. ☑ **A.** The Internet is a TCP/IP network, meaning it only runs TCP/IP. Other protocols can be encapsulated in a TCP/IP packet to transverse the Internet, but cannot do it alone.

   ☒ **B, C,** and **D** are incorrect. TCP/IP, IPX, and other protocols can be run on a LAN, but not on the Internet.

**6.** ☑ **A, B, C,** and **D.** You can access an Internet server from any of these platforms. The applications that run on each of them are a little different, but are pretty much standard across all operating systems.

**7.** ☑ **D.** The majority of all Web-based pages are written in HTML, or HyperText Markup language.
☒ **A** is incorrect. C++ can be used to write programs that will interact with Web pages but not to write the actual Web page. **B** and **C** are also incorrect. Java and CGI are used to write applets that will be called by the Web page.

**8.** ☑ **D.** To connect to a secured Web page, the HTTPS or secured socket connector is needed. You should also make certain that the "SSL indicator " on the browser has changed to indicate that the site is secure.
☒ **A** is incorrect as it is a nonsecured site. If you give private information such as credit card numbers on a site with only an HTTP:\\ prefix, you are sending it in plain text that can be viewed by anyone with a network sniffer. **B** is incorrect. The URL given was just www.buybooks.com\purchase. By adding \secured to the end, you have changed the location of the page. **C** is incorrect; the S goes after the HTTP on the URL command.

**9.** ☑ **B** and **D.** As the ISP, you are the gateway for the end user to the Internet, and you have a responsibility to provide the bandwidth purchased by the end. If you sell them a 128K connection, you are responsible for making sure that they are getting a 128K connection at all times. You cannot sell bandwidth you do not have; for example, you can't sell T3s if your connection to the Internet is only a T1.
☒ **A** is incorrect. Your responsibility is to connect them to the Internet, not to another LAN. **C** is also incorrect. Ninety-nine percent of the time, the ISP is not responsible for providing hardware.

**10.** ☑ **D.** A connection to a Web page is maintained while data is being downloaded. Once the data is displayed in the browser, the connection is no longer needed and is terminated until a new request is made. At that point, a new connection to the page is needed.

☒  A, B, and C are all incorrect. Connections to a Web page are broken as soon as all the data is downloaded.

11. ☑  B and D. Reducing both the size of a graphic and the number of colors used will allow it to download much faster. This will especially help users who are on slow modems.
☒  A is incorrect. JPEG files are almost always more compressed/smaller than GIF files, so doing this will cause them to be larger and slower in download. C is incorrect. You will not gain performance by adding more graphics to a page, even if they are smaller than the original. The more graphics on a page, the slower it will load.

12. ☑  A. An intranet is a network that is usually behind a firewall that allows limited connection to the inside via the Internet. The network must have an internal Web site and use TCP/IP.
☒  B is incorrect. A network that has no connection to the Internet would just be considered a LAN. C is incorrect, as this would be an extranet. D is also incorrect; there is a difference between the Internet and an intranet.

13. ☑  B. First-generation Web browsers could not display graphics.
☒  A is incorrect. There were no capabilities for displaying graphics. C is incorrect. The browsers were able to embed links to other sites in the pages. D is incorrect. First-generation browsers were for test-based systems only; browsers for Windows 3.*x* weren't available until around 1993 when Mosaic was released.

14. ☑  D. A LAN connection can range from 10 Mbps to 1000 Mbps, whereas a connection from home is at best 56K on a dial-up connection. You can get faster connection speeds by using ISDN or xDSL.
☒  A is incorrect. The Web server is using the same Internet connection that the owner uses in the office, and Web pages on the Internet are not slow from the office. B is incorrect. If this were the case, the Web page would be slow to display both in the office and at home. C is incorrect. The speed of the computer has little to do with the speed at which a Web page is displayed. The modem is the major player in the connection and downloading of information from the Internet.

**15.** ☑ **D.** NNTP is the Network News Transfer Protocol, which allows a user to connect to a news server to monitor news threads or discussions. There are thousands of news groups, and each server offers a subset of the total.

☒ **A** is incorrect. HTTP is used for accessing the Web. It can be used to connect to a news server, but NNTP is the protocol that is in play at that point. **B** is incorrect. POP3 is used to access a mail server to retrieve mail. **C** is also incorrect. SMTP is used to send mail.

**16.** ☑ **D.** HTTP uses port 80 for connections. This can be modified and another port can be used in its place; many times this is done for security reasons.

☒ **A** is incorrect. Port 21 is used to retrieve or send files to a remote site via FTP. **B** is incorrect. Port 23 is used to establish a Telnet connection to a remote host. **C** is also incorrect. Port 25 is used for SMTP connections.

**17.** ☑ **C.** A gateway is the device used to connect networks running different protocols. It can also be the connector between a network and the Internet or an ISP.

☒ **A** and **B** are incorrect. They are level-2 network devices and move packets based on destination address only, not protocol. **D** is incorrect and has nothing to do with a network.

**18.** ☑ **A.** The Internet was originally developed to be used for conducting research and development for advanced military technologies.

☒ **B** is incorrect. It wasn't until later that universities were connected to the Internet. **C** is incorrect. The Internet was never intended as a replacement for the USPS. **D** is also incorrect. The Internet had no medical attachments at all. It wasn't until recently that medical facilities started to share patient data via the Internet.

**19.** ☑ **D.** There is no set body that manages the Internet. It is managed by several groups spread throughout the world; IETF, W3C, and ISOC are just three of the managing bodies.

☒ **A**, **B**, and **C** are incorrect. They are together responsible for the management of the Internet, but no one group/body has any more power than the other.

**20.** ☑  **B.** A T1 connection has a connection speed of 1.544 Mbps.
☒  **A** is incorrect. 128K is the standard for an ISDN consisting of two B channels and one D channel. **C** is incorrect. 3 Mbps is the bottom-end rate for a T3. **D** is also incorrect. 45 Mbps is the top connection speed for a T3 connection.

**21.** ☑  **C** and **D.** Dial-up connections are inexpensive compared to ISDN or T1 connections. In a sense, they offer better security than direct connect because when you disconnect the session from your ISP, you have no fear of someone hacking into your system.
☒  **A** is incorrect. A dial-up connection is only connected when you have created a session. **B** is incorrect. You cannot have a voice conversation while using the same telephone line for data.

**22.** ☑  **C.** When designing a page, you need to take into account the slowest speed that the majority of users will use to connect to your site. If the majority of users are on a LAN, you can put in more graphics and "high tech" items. If the majority of users are connecting via dial-up modems at 28 K or even 56 K, you have to scale down the graphics because of the download time.

**23.** ☑  **A, B, C,** and **D.** These items are all considered thin clients. Any device that is capable of displaying an HTML document is a thin client.

**24.** ☑  **C.** An .org suffix usually indicates a not-for-profit organization.
☒  **A** is incorrect; .com suffixes indicate a business or commercial Web site. **B** is incorrect; .net suffixes generally indicate an ISP. **D** is also incorrect; the .edu suffix is used for educational networks.

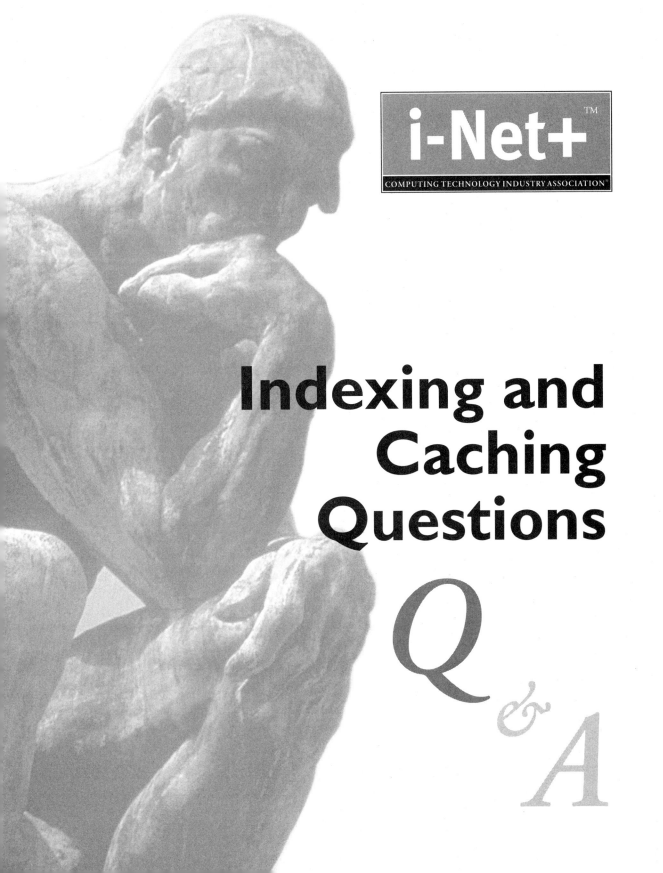

# i-Net+™

COMPUTING TECHNOLOGY INDUSTRY ASSOCIATION®

# Indexing and Caching Questions

*Q & A*

# Indexing and Caching

1. You are building an intranet application for your company that will allow store clerks to know inventory level at any time in order to serve clients. A heavily used page lists all items for a store and its stock quantity. The stock quantities are updated throughout the day at any time as a result of shipping and supply. What are the options for improving performance? (Choose two.)

   A. Use the caching mechanism of the Web server.
   B. Use the browser cache.
   C. Improve database server capacity (CPU speed, number of processors, memory).
   D. Use the database cache for heavily used queries.

2. You access regularly your local newspaper Web site. The home page contains a large amount of information organized into various sections, as well as small graphics and small photos. You notice that when you stay inside the newspaper Web site, performance seems to be good. But when you leave the site and go to other sites during the day and come back to the newspaper Web site, the page seems to take longer to load. You know that the information does not change, and you set the browser to get new versions of the pages only when the browser is open. What could be the problem?

   A. The newspaper Web server is under heavier load.
   B. The network is under heavier load.
   C. The cache folder may be too small.
   D. The history folder may be too small.

3. You maintain an intranet Web site that allows Product Managers of your company to update the catalog of products. They can select the set of products by entering selection criteria and get a list of products that satisfy the selection criteria. The products are displayed in a tabular format. Each line on the page contains the picture of the product displayed as a

thumbnail picture, the name, and the price. The users can select a specific product on that list and bring up the data entry page to modify the characteristics of the products. When users are finished entering data, they click on a hyperlink to go back to the list of products. You want the list of products to show the new data; what is the best way to accomplish this?

A. Ask the users to set the browser option to get the new version of the page every time the page is accessed.
B. Ask the users to click the Refresh button of the browser.
C. Use the HTTP Expires header to specify that the Product List page expires immediately.
D. None of the above.

**4.** You build a Web site for a car dealer that allows users to view available used cars. The users select the make and model to get a list of cars by first selecting the make from a drop-down box; the model can be selected on the next page from another drop-down box. The application then can run the search against a database that is updated every night to refresh the inventory. You do not want to show the makes and models that are not available (not in stock). How would you optimize the performance of the search page (show only the makes and models that are available in the drop-down boxes without fetching them from the database each time)?

A. Dynamically turn on browser cache using the Expires Header of HTTP 1.1 protocol.
B. Build the HTML search pages that contain the list of makes and models every night after update.
C. Use database cache.
D. Implement a Web server caching mechanism to cache the page created dynamically through server script or CGI.

**5.** You build a Web site for a group of car dealers that allows users to view used cars available. To get a list of used cars available at the car dealers group, the users select the make of the car from a drop-down box. The model can be selected on the next page from another drop-down box. The application then can run the search against a database that is updated every night (to refresh the inventory) to retrieve the list of cars. All dealers can sell each other's cars, so the available cars are common to all dealers. Each dealer has its own layout and logo and specific information such as office hours, etc.; the search pages are specific to each dealer. You do not want to show the makes and models that are not available (not in stock). How would you optimize the performance of the search pages (show only the makes and models that are available in the drop-down boxes without fetching them from the database each time) while observing the custom layout and information specific to each dealer?

A. Build the HTML search pages that contain the list of makes and models every night after update for all dealers.

B. Use database cache.

C. Implement Web server caching mechanism to cache the page created dynamically through server script or CGI.

D. Build flat files containing HTML code for showing the makes and models every night. Include these files in the specific HTML search pages for each dealer.

6. You use an intranet Human Resources application that has restricted use because of the confidentiality of the data. You can access it as the Manager of the Manufacturing and Planning Department and have to log in to the application using a login name and a password. As a user, how would you protect the confidentiality of the data?

A. Clear the cache after you access the application.

B. Set the browser to check for new versions of the cached pages every time the page is accessed.

C. Use Secure Socket Layer (SSL) to encrypt the data.

D. Set browser security to the highest level (no download and execution of code).

7. You just made some significant enhancements to the intranet Web site of your company, and you are ready to deploy the new application. The home page of the site has important information that you would like to convey to the users as soon as it is in place. You know that the previous version of the

home page did not specify any cache control directives. How can you make sure that all users get the new home page?

A. Use the Expires header in the new page.
B. Nothing has to be done. The browsers automatically detect the new version since the page uses the default cache-control mechanism.
C. Inform the users by telephone or e-mail to refresh the page using the Refresh or Reload button of the browser. Also place a message on the page asking the users to refresh the page for the latest information.
D. Clear the Web server cache before putting out the new home page.

**8.** You just made some changes to your company's intranet Web site. There are now two separate sites to accommodate different departments. The URL the users have been using now points to a different site, and the users should from now on use a new URL. You want the users to use the new URL and decide to deploy the new Web site during off-hours to minimize impact on the users and simplify the deployment process. You have to go to each user's computer and prepare it for the new configuration to make this change transparent to the users when they come back the next day. What browser options should you change? (Choose all that apply.)

A. Clear the cache.
B. Clear the History list.
C. Change the Bookmarks (or Favorite items) to point to the new URL.
D. Change the Connection information of the browser to reflect the new URL.

**9.** You maintain a Web server that hosts a public Web site. The site allows users to view technical documentation on various FAX machines that your company manufactures. The number of documents has been increasing steadily, and you received recently through the Help Desk feedback from the users that the site performance is degrading. You investigated and used a performance-monitoring tool to monitor the Web server on a daily basis for about a week. You noticed that the only factor that has increased significantly is the number of users; all other indicators and ratios stay about the same. What could be the performance bottleneck?

    A. The cache size on the Web server

    B. The network capacity

    C. The Web server processor

    D. The amount of memory on the Web server

**10.** You maintain a Web site that allows customers to order fashion accessories online. The customers can see thumbnail pictures of the products when they go to the shopping area. To improve the user shopping experience, you show only 10 product pictures at a time on one page, and set up navigational buttons as links so the customers can browse the catalog by moving back and forth between the pages. The pages are static HTML pages and the catalog is updated only once a year. What features of the browser should you recommend to your customers for optimum performance?

    A. Set the browser not to accept cookies.

    B. Set the browser to check for new versions of the cached pages every time you open the browser.

    C. Set the browser to check for new versions of the cached pages every time the page is accessed.

    D. Increase the size of the cache folder.

**11.** You have to do research for your project and have to access various academic Web sites to look for various surveys. You know that a few surveys are updated frequently, probably every day or even more frequently. In browsing the pages, you often have to use the Back button of the browser to go back to previous pages, since most surveys are simple text and lack navigational buttons. How do you make sure that you get the latest information when reading those specific surveys?

    A. Set the browser cache option to "Check for new version every time the page is accessed."

    B. Set the browser cache option to "Check for new version when the browser is open."

    C. Set the browser cache option to "Never check for new version."

    D. Use the Refresh button.

**12.** You maintain a Web site for a local newspaper that also displays on the home page various Stock Market index averages. The home page contains a lot of information organized into various sections, as well as small graphics and small photos. The Web site is updated daily during off-hours, and all the pages of the Web site have a hyperlink to the home page. The stock data is fed to the Web server every five minutes from a third-party source. How would you design the page, and what browser options would you recommend to the users for best performance? (Choose all that apply.)

A. Set the browser to check for new versions of the cached pages every time you open the browser, and tell the users to use the Refresh (or Reload) button to get new stock market data.

B. Set the browser to check for new versions of the cached pages every time the page is accessed, and tell the users to use the Refresh (or Reload) button to get new stock market data.

C. Set the browser to check for new versions of the cached pages every time you open the browser, and put a Refresh Data button in the Stock Market index section that refreshes the page.

D. Set the browser to check for new versions of the cached pages every time the page is accessed, and put a Refresh Data button in the Stock Market index section that refreshes the page.

**13.** You have a few Web pages that contain a large number of medical terms. You want the users to find them if they use major search engines. What type of search index is most appropriate?

A. Static index or site map

B. Keyword index

C. Full-text index

D. All of the above

**14.** You are building a Web site for your company that allows customers to view and order automobile parts. The parts are organized into categories such as Engine, Body, Accessories, Logo merchandise, etc. The Web site also offers other types of marketing information such as "About Us," Business Hours, Shipping and Delivery, etc. All the pages are static, except the order and confirmation pages that use server scripting. Since the number of categories are quite large (more than 50), you cannot show them all on the home page, and have to show only the top-level categories such as Parts, Shipping and Delivery, etc. You want to offer the users a way to have an overview of all the different categories of information that are available, so you decide to build a site map page and have a hyperlink entitled "Site Map" on the home page. What are the possible ways to build one? (Choose all that apply.)

A. Use an HTML authoring tool that has an automatic site map building feature.
B. Follow all the links from the home page and build the site map.
C. Use a text processor and launch a search on the HTML tag <A> to detect all the links and build the site map.
D. Use a text processor and launch a search on the HTML tag <LINK> to detect all the links and build the site map.

15. You design a public Web site that sells food supplements online. You also want the prospective customers to find your pages easily if they use the various search engines to look for certain keywords. You have a page that contains herbal products for arthritis and want the search engines to index the page on the words Arthritis, Joints, Pain. What HTML code is appropriate? (Choose all that apply.)

A. ```
<BODY>
<META KEYWORDS=" Arthritis, Joints, Pain">.
...
</BODY>
```
B. ```
<HEAD>
<META KEYWORDS=" Arthritis, Joints, Pain">.
...
</HEAD>
```
C. ```
<HEAD>
<META NAME="keywords" CONTENT=" Arthritis, Joints, Pain">.
...
</HEAD>
```
```

D. `<BODY>`
`<META NAME="keywords" CONTENT=" Arthritis, Joints, Pain">.`
...
`</BODY>`

**16.** You design a public Web site that sells food supplements online to international customers. The site is translated into many different languages. You also want the prospective customers to find your pages easily if they use the various search engines to look for certain keywords. The pages that are returned as a result of the search should be in the local language of the user. What HTML elements (tag and attribute) should you use?

A. The META tag and the attribute LANG

B. The LINK tag and the attribute LANG

C. The LINK tag and the attribute HREFLANG

D. The META tag and the attribute LANGUAGE

**17.** You are building a Web site that allows your sales force to view product price information online. This is confidential data, so you require the account representatives to log in using a username and password to get to the Web site. The home page contains a list of the products that can be sold, and you want it to be accessible to the customers through search engines because the customers may want to see the features of the products. The number of products and product-related technical terms are large (over 100 on the home page). You want to take advantage of full-text indexing that many search engines offer. You submitted the Web site to a number of them, but found out later that you cannot find your home page through major search engines. What would be the appropriate action to take?

A. Build another Web site with the unprotected home page for the users.

B. Remove the login process.

C. Use keyword index through appropriate HTML tags on the home page.

D. Do not protect the home page, protect only the product price pages by requiring a login name and password.

**18.** You design a public Web site for a private school that allows users to view information about the school and the classes that it offers. The class information page also has an enrollment form that the user can print out and mail back with his or her signature. You provide a printable version of the pages in a proprietary document format (such as word processing). The HTML pages then have a hyperlink to their printable version. You want the search engines to find the printable version of the class information pages. What would be the best solution?

A. Use the META tag to tell the search engines where to find the printable version on the HTML page.

B. Use the META tag to tell the search engines where to find the printable version on the printable document.

C. Use the LINK tag to tell the search engines where to find the printable version on the HTML page.

D. Use the LINK tag to tell the search engines where to find the printable version on the printable document.

**19.** You are building a Web site for your company that allows customers to view user manuals online. The manuals contain instructions for the assembly of the model cars that your company sells. Since the customers have been asking for online manual viewing, you want the Web site to be up quickly. You do not have the soft copy of the manuals and have to scan them as pictures and put them on the pages. You submitted your Web site to many search engines, tried some of them a few weeks later, and noticed that you cannot find the technical terms, especially the model numbers that are printed on the original manuals. What would be the problem?

A. Most search engines take longer than that to visit the Web sites.

B. The search engine robots cannot read text inside images.

C. There is no META tag on the pages to help the search engine robots.

D. None of the above.

**20.** You design a public Web site that sells sporting goods online. You want to offer articles written by various sports authorities as marketing material on your Web site. You also want the prospect customers to find your pages if they use the various search engines. What is the most efficient feature you should consider when designing your Web site?

A. Build indexes on all your pages and offer the users a Search page.

B. Use the <META> tag and use the attribute NAME and CONTENT to specify the description and keywords of all the HTML pages of your site.

C. Register your pages with all the search engines.

D. You have nothing to do. The search engines robots can find your pages and index them.

**21.** You design a public Web site that allows international users to book cruises online. You also want the prospective customers to find your pages easily if they use the various search engines to look for certain keywords. However, you want to get the largest exposure by allowing users to run searches in their local language. You are ready to translate the keywords into the different languages. What HTML element (tag) and attributes are appropriate? (Choose all that apply.)

A. Element: META

B. Attributes: LANGUAGE

C. Attributes: NAME

D. Attributes: CONTENT, LANG

i-Net+ ™

COMPUTING TECHNOLOGY INDUSTRY ASSOCIATION®

# Indexing and Caching Answers

Q & A

# Indexing and Caching

1. ☑  **C, D.** This is a transaction-heavy application with frequent updates, and is not a good application for the caching mechanism on the Web server or the browser. The database server can be improved, especially the number of processors and memory can be increased to handle multiple transactions if need be. Database cache can store heavily used queries to speed up their processing, and can also store data that is accessed frequently.

   ☒  **A** is incorrect because the Web server cache stores frequently requested pages to improve performance and is suitable for static pages. This is not the case here; we have pages that are very dynamic and change frequently (the Web server cache can store heavily used script or code, but the performance gain is not as significant as on the database side). **B** is incorrect because the browser cache can be used to speed up display of previously accessed pages, but if the pages change frequently, caching does not really improve performance because we have to refresh them.

2. ☑  **C.** The symptom indicates that the cached pages of the newspaper Web site were flushed and the pages are being reloaded from the Web server. This may be due to the insufficient capacity of the cache folder; the pages of other Web sites replaced the ones of the newspaper Web site.

   ☒  **A** is incorrect because when the browser is set to get the new version only when it is open, it gets the page from the cache, so the Web server load is not relevant. **B** is incorrect because when the browser is set to get the new version only when it is open, it gets the page from the cache, so the network load is not relevant. **D** is incorrect because the history folder contains the links to the pages previously visited; it has nothing to do with the performance of the browser when it loads a page.

3. ☑  **C.** The HTTP Expires header is used to specify the amount of time the browser can use the cache version. If it is set to expire immediately (usually with a past date, or sometimes the value $-1$), then the browser has to contact the Web server for update. Note: The Back button of the browser uses the cache version, so the users should be told not to use the Back button.

☒  **A** is incorrect because although this will give the desired result, it is not a reliable way to accomplish this; the users may want to set the option to other values for other Web sites and forget to switch back to this specific value. **B** is incorrect because although this achieves the desired result, the users may forget to do so; besides, this is cumbersome for the users. **D** is incorrect because we can use the HTTP Expires header.

4.  ☑  **B.** The makes and models are not changed during the day, so HTML pages can be built every night that contain only the makes and models available in stock. Since the HTML pages are static, there is no processing on the server to fetch the data and build them each time; this reduces the workload on the server, and takes advantage of browser cache. This is also referred to as "output caching," where the final output HTML page is created to avoid running server code.
☒  **A** is incorrect because the cache is effective for subsequent requests for the page; the first time the page is accessed (for each user), the server code still has to run to fetch data. **C** is incorrect because database caches are effective if the data is very often used; it may be swapped out as new data is needed, thus reducing the reliability of the caching scheme. In this situation, we want to have the fastest page for all users during the day. **D** is incorrect because Web server cache has the same disadvantage as database cache in this scenario. The page may be cached, but as new pages are needed, the page may be flushed out of the cache, thus reducing the reliability of the caching scheme.

5.  ☑  **D.** The makes and models are not changed during the day; the flat files (include files) can be built every night that contain only the makes and models available in stock. The HTML search pages can include these flat files using the <!— #include file ... —> tag. This is also referred to as "input caching," where the data is cached as static on the server, and is used in many different pages. Since the HTML pages are static, there is no processing on the server to fetch the data and build them each time; this reduces the workload on the server and takes advantage of browser cache.
☒  **A** is incorrect because although this will work, it is not efficient to create many different pages; the number may be large and the code may be

complex. **B** is incorrect because database caches are effective if the data is very often used; it may be swapped out as new data is needed, thus reducing the reliability of the caching scheme. In this situation, we want to have the fastest page for all users during the day. **C** is incorrect because Web server cache has the same disadvantage as database cache in this scenario. The page may be cached, but as new pages are needed, the page may be flushed out of the cache, thus reducing the reliability of the caching scheme.

6. ☑  **A.** For performance reasons, browsers may cache pages locally, and when we close the browser, the cache is still on the local hard disk, which compromises confidentiality of the data. The safest way is to clear the cache of the browser when we exit the application.
   ☒  **B** is incorrect because the cache is still there when the browser is closed. This option only gets the latest version of the page. **C** is incorrect because as users, we do not have control over the use of SSL; SSL is a protocol that must be supported by both the Web server and the browser. SSL does not affect the browser cache, it only encrypts the data that is transferred over the network. **D** is incorrect because browser security in this sense does not affect the browser cache, it only prevents code from being downloaded and run within the browser; this has nothing to do with data security.

7. ☑  **C.** Users may have different cache settings for their browser. If they are still browsing and go back to the home page using the BACK button or get back to it through the History list, the page is not necessarily refreshed to show the latest information. In this case, clearing the browser cache or manually refreshing the page is the most reliable action.
   ☒  **A** is incorrect because this will affect future versions of the page. If the users use the Back button or the History list, they still get the cached version of the page. **B** is incorrect because the browser does not automatically detect the new version of every page if the correct setting is not used. Also, for best performance, other settings may be used that take advantage of the browser cache. **D** is incorrect because the Web server cache is not the browser cache. We have to deal with the browser cache that is holding an old version of the page we are putting out.

**8.** ☑ **B, C.** The History list allows users to get back to a visited page, and if the page is in the cache, the user will get the old version of the page and will be confused later on when navigating within the new site. Therefore, we have to clear the History list to make sure that the users do not get back to the old version. Also, Bookmarks that point to the outdated URL should be changed so when the users use the Bookmarks, they go to the new site.

☒ **A** is incorrect because clearing the cache only is not enough. The users can still use the History list or the Bookmarks to get to the old URL and may get an error if the page does not exist in the new site. The users may even get wrong information if the page name stays the same because they go to a wrong site. Besides, clearing the cache may affect performance for other Web sites. **D** is incorrect because connection information specifies the type of the connection to the Internet and related information such as modem or local area network, phone number if a modem is used, speed, etc. It does not pertain to site address or URL.

**9.** ☑ **B.** All performance indicators measured on the Web server stay about the same. The increase of the number of users most likely affected the network capacity.

☒ **A** is incorrect because there is no indication that the server cache is the performance bottleneck. **C** is incorrect because there is no indication that the server processor is the performance bottleneck. **D** is incorrect because there is no indication that the server memory is the performance bottleneck.

**10.** ☑ **B.** Since the pages are static and are not updated frequently, the browser local cache will speed up their display when the users go from page to page. When the pages are updated on the server during off-hours, the users will get the new version the next day.

☒ **A** is incorrect because the use of cookies does not affect performance in this case. Cookies are used to store information locally for the server's use. **C** is incorrect because there is no need to check for the new version every time the pages are accessed; they do not change for the entire year until the next catalog yearly update. **D** is incorrect because the size of the cache folder does not affect performance in this case. Increasing the folder size means we can cache more elements, but the determining factor is the browser's use of the cache: The browser must use the cache to improve performance.

11. ☑ **D.** The Back button (or the History list) uses the cached version of the page. This is the behavior recommended by the HTTP protocol and implemented by most major browsers: The Back button should show the version the user last saw. So, to get the new version of a page, we should use the Refresh button.
☒ **A, B,** and **C** are incorrect because regardless of the Cache Option settings, the Back button (or the History list) uses the cached version of the page. If we use the Back button, we are not getting a new version of the page.

12. ☑ **A, C.** The Refresh (or Reload) button gets the new version of the page. Having a Refresh Data button on the page also gives a visual clue and an indication to the users so they can refresh the data when necessary. There is no need for the users to see the latest Stock Market data at all times, so there is no need to have the latest version every time.
☒ **B** and **D** are incorrect because there is no need to get the latest version of the stock data every time the users come to the page.

13. ☑ **C.** Most search engines can do a full-text index on your Web pages and index all the medical terms without intervention on your part.
☒ **A** is incorrect because the site map helps when the user already finds your Web site. Here we want them to find your Web site by running a search engine to search Web sites. **B** is incorrect because although we can use a keyword index with the appropriate HTML tags, this is not an appropriate use of a keyword index since there are a large number of keywords. **D** is incorrect because only **C** is correct.

14. ☑ **A, B, C.** We are building a custom site map and we need all the hyperlinks information. We can achieve this with the help of an authoring tool that offers this feature (the tool will give us the list of all hyperlinks

found), or do this manually by following all the links from the home page. This can also be achieved by searching all occurrences of the HTML tag <A>. Once we have all the links, we can build the site map that consists of the description of all the categories and the link to the corresponding start pages.

☒ **D** is incorrect because the <LINK> tag is not used to build hyperlinks.

**15.** ☑ **C.** This is the correct syntax for the META tag with the NAME and CONTENT attributes. The META element is used within the HEAD element to embed document meta-information. Robots (or Web Spiders) often look at two META attributes, NAME and CONTENT, to extract the description of the document and the keywords.

☒ **A** and **B** are incorrect because there is no attribute KEYWORDS. **D** is incorrect because the META element must be inside the HEAD element.

**16.** ☑ **C.** The LINK element and the attribute HREFLANG allow an indexing engine to offer users search results in the users' preferred language, regardless of how the query was written (the attribute REL = "alternate" should also be used).

☒ **A** is incorrect because the META tag and the attribute LANG allow search engines to index the keywords in the specified language and can be used to allow users to search for keywords translated into the local language. However, they do not provide an alternate document to search engines as is required; they show the document where the index comes from, which is not necessarily in the preferred language. **B** is incorrect because the attribute LANG of the LINK element applies to the attribute TITLE to specify the language of the title. The correct attribute to use here is HREFLANG. **D** is incorrect because there is no attribute LANGUAGE for the element META.

**17.** ☑ **D.** Search engine robots cannot read a page if it is behind a firewall or protected by a password. This is the case with the home page; the solution is to make it public (no password) but protect the product price pages.

☒ **A** is incorrect. This is possible, but this solution involves more cost.

Besides, we will have to solve the problem of duplicate pages in two different sites. **B** is incorrect because we want to keep the product prices confidential. **C** is incorrect because keyword index is not appropriate in this case due to the large number of products and technical terms.

18. ☑   **C.** The LINK tag can be used to tell search engines where to find alternate versions of a document such as documents designed for different media; for instance, a version especially suited for printing.
☒   **A** is incorrect because the META tag does not tell the search engines where to find the alternate version of a document. **B** and **D** are incorrect because we cannot change the document in proprietary format to include HTML tags.

19. ☑   **B.** Search engine robots cannot read text inside images, nontext files, multimedia files, extremely long text files, or dynamic content.
☒   **A** is incorrect because this may apply to some search engines, but generally speaking, once we submit the pages, search engines can index them very quickly. **C** is incorrect because even without META tags, most major search engines can do a full-text index on Web pages and build indexes from the page. If the technical terms had been written in plain text in the pages, they would have been indexed. **D** is incorrect because the correct answer is B.

20. ☑   **B.** The META element is used within the HEAD element to embed document meta-information. This embedded information can be extracted to identify, index, and catalog specialized document meta-information. Robots (or Web Spiders) often look at two META attributes, NAME and CONTENT, to extract the description of the document and the keywords. Using the META element will increase the chance of the page being indexed by a larger number of search engines.
☒   **A** is incorrect because although this is possible, this solution involves some development and maintenance costs. Also, the requirement is to get exposure through search engines, and this solution is applicable when the users already get to the Web site. **C** is incorrect because this process may be

costly. The number of search engines can be quite large, and this is a manual process that is time consuming. **D** is incorrect because although most search engines are sophisticated enough to automatically index all the pages found, we still need to cover the widest range of engines to make sure that we have the greatest chance of being found. Most search engines exploit the HTML META tag to build their indexes, so we should help them by using the META tag.

**21.** ☑ **A, C, D.** The META element is used to specify keywords that should be indexed on the page. The attributes NAME and CONTENT are set to "keywords" and the list of the keywords (separated by comma), respectively. The attribute LANG is used to specify the language code. For example:

```
<META NAME="keywords" CONTENT="Greece, island, sunshine"
LANG="en-us">
<META NAME="keywords" CONTENT="Gr&egrave;ce, ile, soleil"
LANG="fr">
```

☒ **B** is incorrect because there is no attribute LANGUAGE for the element META.

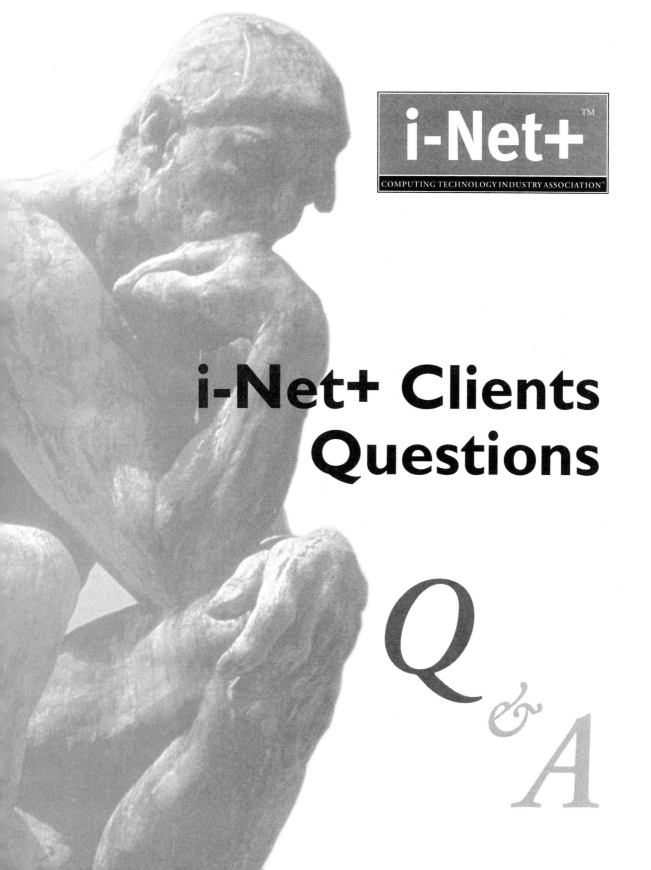

i-Net+

COMPUTING TECHNOLOGY INDUSTRY ASSOCIATION

# i-Net+ Clients
# Questions

Q & A

# i-Net+ Clients

1. You work on a Windows NT 4.0 system running Service Pack 6. You notice that often after reboot, you have a different IP address than you had before. This doesn't happen all the time, but mostly when you shut down on Friday and reboot on Monday morning. You notice that the WINS server, DNS server, and other IP-related information are still the same, only your address changes. What is the reason for this?

   A. Someone is changing the IP address on your system while you are away from your desk and it doesn't take effect until after you reboot. At that point, the IP address that someone entered for you is current.

   B. You are mistaken. The IP address is the same as it was before and there is no problem.

   C. This is normal on a network. IP addresses change randomly, they are not a permanent setting on a system. The system or computer name is what is important and thus does not change.

   D. You are running DHCP on your network, and after you shut down, someone else acquired the IP address that you had. Therefore, the next time you booted your system, you were assigned a new one.

2. You need to access a directory on a remote system that runs UNIX. You are on a Windows 95 system. You will need to run a program on the UNIX system once you access the directory. What would be your best option for completing this task?

   A. FTP to the UNIX system and download the program. Once it is downloaded, you can run it from your local system.

   B. Telnet to the UNIX system and log in with the Anonymous access that you use for FTPing. Access the directory and run the program.

   C. Telnet to the UNIX system and log in with the username and password that was assigned to you. Access the directory and run the program.

   D. FTP to the UNIX system, and log in using the username and password assigned to you. Access the directory and run the program.

**3.** You are looking for a game to play to lower your stress from studying for your certification test. You have been told that there is a games server in a domain called play.com. You have accessed your FTP program under a command prompt in Windows NT. What command would you use at the ftp> prompt to access a system named games in the domain play.com?

A. FTP games

B. Open games.play.com

C. Open play.com

D. FTP games.play.com

**4.** You are debating on a new PC and Internet Service Provider. You want something that is easy to operate, will allow you to surf the Web, and will make it easier for you to monitor what your children are doing online. You come across an ad that reads "send and read e-mail, browse the Web, play games, and interact with TV shows all at the same time." What is the ad representing?

A. A desktop system

B. A handheld PC

C. A WebTV system

D. A laptop

**5.** What would allow you to access information sent to you from users and allow you to respond to their information without giving them access to your system or giving you access to theirs? Privacy and confidentiality of the information being sent are major concerns.

A. FTP

B. E-mail

C. Telnet

D. WWW

**6.** Software that allows you to view documents sent via SMTP are all forms of what?

    A. FTP clients

    B. Telnet clients

    C. E-mail clients

    D. Web browsers

**7.** Host files are used on a PC in place of, or along with, a DNS server to access other systems. They are used by Ping, Finger, and other TCP/IP clients and utilities for resolving names to IP addresses. Which of the following would be the correct Host file configuration?

| | | |
|---|---|---|
| A. Sales_ PC | 192.168.101.101 | #PC in sales |
| B. Sales_PC | #PC in sales | 192.168.101.101 |
| C. #PC in sales | Sales_PC | 192.168.101.101 |
| D. 192.168.101.101 | Sales_PC | PC in sales |

**8.** You are given an address of accounts.ourcompany.com and told that a file named accounts-receivable.html is there and needs to be printed. What product would you use to access this file?

    A. FTP

    B. Telnet

    C. A Browser

    D. E-mail

**9.** When using an e-mail client that downloads the e-mail from the server to your system (such as Outlook Express), to what folder are the new messages downloaded?

    A. Mail

    B. Personal Mail

    C. Hold

    D. Inbox

**10.** You are new to your company and working as a level-1 computer technician. You are handed a work order to install a network interface card (NIC) in a system for one of the people in administration. What is this?

A. A removable hard drive

B. A network connection

C. A link to a printer

D. Memory

**11.** You have a salesperson in your company who currently carries around a very large organizer to keep track of meetings, to-do lists, contacts, and orders. He would like to get rid of this organizer, but needs to find something to replace it that is quick, easy to operate, and requires a very short boot-up time. This salesperson was assigned a laptop about five years ago that runs Workgroup for Windows, but it was extremely slow and cumbersome. He has come to you, the IS director, for help in this matter. What would be the best recommendation for this person?

A. A laptop with a Pentium 366mhz chip running Windows 98, 128MB memory, and a 2G hard drive. The high-speed chip along with the large amount of RAM would cut the boot time down. The 2G drive would allow for all the information to be stored.

B. A handheld PC running Windows 98. The boot time is minimal, and it is easy to operate and learn, and the salesperson can sync with his desktop PC for order and e-mail transfer.

C. An electronic voice recorder to store important information until he can get back to the office and enter the information in his desktop system.

D. The organizer is the best option for him; you tell him you can't make a better recommendation.

**12.** You have just signed a contract with eight new suppliers. These suppliers are offering same-day shipping when you order using their order pages on secured servers. You are not familiar with a secured server and have to do some reading to find out more about this, including what it requires in client software to access things such as Telnet or FTP. What client software do you need for accessing the clients' secured server order pages?

A. Telnet

B. FTP

C. Web browser

D. Gopher

13. You are working a customer support issue and have a customer who has two systems completely down due to a corrupt file. They still have several systems up and running, but need to get the other two systems up in the next couple of hours before the rest of the shift comes to work. You need to get a copy of the corrupted file to the customer. The file is 25MB. What would be your best option?

A. Telnet to the customer's site and then issue the put command to place the file on the customer's system.

B. FTP to the customer's site, issue the put command, and place the file on the customer's system.

C. Attach the file to an e-mail message and send it to the customer's e-mail address.

D. Copy the file to a backup tape and ship the package to the customer.

14. You want to purchase the latest version of a popular Web browser at the computer store. When you get there, you notice that there are four variants of the same version. What is your main concern when deciding which variant of the product you should purchase?

A. Operating system

B. ISP connection speed

C. Different ones have different options that you must consider

D. The amount of memory you have in the system you wish to install it on

15. You have decided to purchase a new system for your home. At work you use MS office products to send e-mail, type letters, and access spreadsheets. You would like to be able to use the same products at home as you do in the

office since you will be working there 25% of the time. You head out to the computer stores and look at all the different types, models, and makes of computers. Which option would be the best choice to make so that there would be very little "relearning" to do?

A. Purchase an Apple MAC

B. Purchase a Intel-based personal computer

C. Purchase an Alpha running UNIX

D. Purchase a WebTV system

16. When configuring a PC for the first time for TCP/IP, assuming you are doing static entries and not DHCP, what is the minimum required information that needs to be entered? This PC will never need to access the Internet, but will need to access servers on another subnet.

A. TCP/IP address

B. Gateway address

C. DNS server

D. Subnet mask

17. Your company has just installed a firewall and Proxy server. You notice that you can no longer access Web pages outside of your company. You received an e-mail stating that you will need to enter proxy1.ourcompany.com into your browser to access the Web. How do you go about doing so?

A. Enter proxy1.ourcompany.com on the address line and it will take you to a new page where you can enter the page you wish to view.

B. Enter the proxy address in front of the address you wish to access (e.g., Proxy1.ourcompany.com/www.toys.com/cars.html).

C. Enter the Proxy information under the configuration section of your browser.

D. Add a file proxy.html in the directory in which your browser program resides, with the proxy1.ourcompany.com address as the only line in it. Each time your browser opens, it will read this file and be configured for Proxy access.

**18.** You have just received your new system at work. It is an Intel-based processor running Windows NT 4.0 Service Pack 5. When you boot it up and sign in, you notice that the icons on your screen are much larger than what appeared on your previous system. You also notice that when you open a file in MS Word, you cannot see as much on the screen as you did before. You call the helpdesk and they tell you to change the desktop area settings to something more comfortable for you. How do you do this?

A. Click Start | Programs | Administrative Tools | Desktop and change it in the Settings window that pops up.

B. Right-click on the desktop and choose Options, then click on the Settings tab and change the settings via the drop-down menu for the desktop area.

C. Click Start | Settings | Control Panel. Choose Console and make your changes.

D. Right-click on the desktop, choose Properties, click on the Settings tab, and make your changes using the slide bar for the desktop area.

**19.** You have been hired to design and set up a new network for a company. They will have 25 servers in the control room, 350 desktop PCs (one per office), and 50 people using laptops who will need access to the network from many points, including conference rooms, dial-up, and the control room. The office is housed across three floors of a building and you have decided to break it up into seven segments: one for the control room and two for each floor indicated as North and South. How do you apply IP addresses to the systems so that they are all functional at all times? The major concern is the laptop users.

A. Use Static IP addresses for all the system, servers, desktop, and laptop users. This will allow you to better monitor the network because you will know where each IP address is assigned. As problems appear on the network, it will be much easier to track them down if each person is assigned his or her own IP address.

B. Use DHCP on all systems, servers, desktops, and laptops. This way, the laptops will work, no matter where they are plugged in. As users move from office to office and segment to segment, they will be able to work because they will each be assigned a new IP address.

C. Use a mixture of DHCP and Static IP addresses. Use Static IP addresses for the servers and desktop users, and use DHCP for the laptop users. This will allow the laptop users to plug into the network on any segment and access the servers.

D. Use a mixture of DHCP and Static IP addresses; use Static IP addresses for the servers and DHCP for everything else. This will allow the laptop users to access the network from anywhere.

**20.** You need an updated copy of a driver for your printer. You contacted the company and they said that the file you need is laser453.drv and it is contained in the zip file laserdrivers.zip located on their FTP server at Houston.printers.com. You downloaded the file after connecting to the site via FTP, but it does not work. WinZip states that this is not a valid zip file. You again call technical support and they tell you that you need to make sure you download it in a binary form, not ASCII. How do you do this?

A. Connect via FTP to the site. When you enter "anonymous" as your username, enter "binary" as the password and it will invoke the Binary transport protocol.

B. Open your FTP client. Click the Options menu and choose Type. Change the type from ASCII to Binary, and then click OK. Connect to the FTP site, log in, and download the file. It will download as a binary file.

C. Connect via FTP to the site. When you are logged in, issue the command get_bin, followed by a space and the filename. This will force the download to be done in binary.

D. Connect via FTP to the site. Once you are logged in, issue the command bin and press RETURN. You can now download your file in binary format.

**21.** You are completely new to the Internet and want to be able to easily browse the Web and have access to e-mail for keeping in touch with friends. You do not have a lot of room for a PC in your one-bedroom apartment. What would be a good option for someone like you who only wants browsing and e-mail and is not concerned with other options such as Web pages design and housing, Telnet, or FTP?

A. A laptop connected to an ISP. A laptop would not normally be connected to the Internet all the time, so housing a Web page is not feasible.

B. A handheld PC with Internet capabilities.

C. WebTV. You can hook it to your existing TV, so the only additional room needed is that for the WebTV box. This would allow you to browse and use e-mail.

D. A PC and a small 14" monitor. The PC and monitor can be placed on the kitchen table and not take up much room.

22. What is the collection of TCP/IP protocols and other required parts for TCP/IP to work, such as UDP called?

A. TCP/IP Tower

B. TCP/IP Stack

C. TCP/IP Utilities

D. TCP/IP PUT (Protocol Utility Tower)

23. When using a command-line FTP client such as those on UNIX systems or those that come with Windows, what is the command to transmit several files all beginning with "win" from your system to a remote system?

A. Get win*

B. Send win*

C. Put win*

D. Mput win*

24. You are running a system with UNIX as the operating system. You wish to browse the Internet. What browser options do you have?

A. Internet Explorer

B. Netscape Communicator

C. WebTV

D. UnixBrowse

25. When using Netscape Communicator, you enter http:\\www.hardhats.com to reach the Hardhats company Web page. If you needed to access their

secured server's Web page for ordering, what URL would you use if the page was located at the same site but the page name was orders.html?

A. http:\\www.hardhats.com\orders.html

B. http:\\orders.hardhats.com

C. https:\\www.hardhats.com

D. https:\\www.hardhats.com\orders.html

26. You are given the IP address of 134.44.88.192 for the local WINS server called WINS.BDC.SUPPLIES.COM via DHCP. This was working fine until a maintenance shutdown took place over the weekend. You are now unable to browse the network. When you ping 134.44.88.192, it shows that it's up and is responding 100%. You decide to check the server yourself, and upon some investigation you notice that the IP address that is assigned to it is 134.44.88.147. You ask the technicians that did the maintenance over the weekend and they confirm they did not change it. What happened?

A. Someone changed the IP address of the address of the WINS server information in the DHCP server, so it is now giving out bad IP addresses.

B. Your PC is not on the same segment anymore and therefore can't communicate with the WINS server.

C. The WINS server was configured to use DHCP and was assigned a new IP address after the maintenance shutdown.

D. Browsing has been turned off for the network.

27. You must connect to an FTP server at a customer site. This server is being brought online only for this connection so that you can transmit some new updates to their software. Your customer is not familiar with FTP servers and their network is behind a firewall. What port on the firewall must you have open to allow your FTP connection?

A. Port 80

B. Port 23

C. Port 21

D. Port 110

# i-Net+ Clients
# Answers

Q & A

# i-Net+ Clients

1. ☑ **D.** The IP address changes after a shutdown and boot up, especially after a weekend. It suggests that you have a DHCP server running on the network that assigns the IP address and other IP information at the time it is requested. This is common today where IP addresses are at a premium or PC users roam and are not always on the same network.

   ☒ **A** is wrong because, by running an NT system, any change to the IP address takes effect immediately. If someone did change the IP address, you would know it at the time it was done—it would not sit and await a reboot to become active. **B** is feasible, but not likely. DHCP is the best guess for this happening. **C** is incorrect because PCs do not randomly change their IP addresses. If this did happen, it would be a nightmare for administrators to manage a network if all the systems kept changing their IP addresses.

2. ☑ **C.** You need to Telnet to the UNIX system and log in using the assigned credentials for your user. Once you are logged in, you can access the directory via many options (menus, CLI). Once you are in the desired directory, you can run the program if you have the permissions set correctly so that your username has the rights to execute the file you wish to run.

   ☒ **A** is incorrect because FTPing to the system and downloading the executable to your local system to run will not help. Most executables for a UNIX system will not execute on a Windows system. There are generally many files associated with an executable that are both housed in the same directory and in the root directories on a UNIX system. Therefore, by copying just the executable you would not have a running program. **B** might work if there was an account called Anonymous, but this account would not be the same account created so that users can FTP to the system and log in via Anonymous. **D** is incorrect because you cannot execute a program on a system you are attached to via FTP, so even using the credentials assigned to you would not allow you to execute the program.

3. ☑ **B.** The correct answer would be to enter the open command to tell the FTP utility that you want to make an FTP connection, and then give it the system name.domain.

⊠ **A** and **D** are incorrect because FTP is an incorrect command. So, no matter what you enter after the FTP, the command is ignored and an error is returned. **C** is incorrect because open play.com would not work because you have not given it a system name to access at the play.com domain. The FTP client would attempt to find a system called play in the domain .com, but it would fail and return an error.

**4.** ☑ **C.** This would be an advertisement for WebTV. WebTV connects you to the Internet via your television. You can do many things, such as surf the Web, access e-mail, talk in chat rooms, and interact and play games. This choice would also allow you to monitor what your children are doing on the Web since it would be located primarily in the family room.

⊠ **A** and **D** are incorrect because a desktop system or laptop would allow you to do many of the things listed, but would not allow you to interact with TV shows. Using a laptop would make it more difficult to monitor what your children are doing on the Web as it could be used in their bedroom or any other areas of the home where a phone connection could be made. A desktop system placed in a family room would allow for better monitoring. **B** is incorrect because a handheld PC would not allow you to monitor your children very easily, and would not offer interactive TV shows.

**5.** ☑ **B.** E-mail would allow users to send you information in the form of an e-mail message, and by using your e-mail client you could retrieve that e-mail and respond to it. E-mail messages can contain both plain text and HTML messages if your e-mail client is HTML capable. The e-mail clients can use digital signatures and encryption to be sure of the sender's identity. Encryption can also be used to make sure that any e-mail message that is misdelivered is unreadable.

⊠ **A** is incorrect because FTP does not allow digital signatures, but does allow encryption. It would, however, require access to one of the systems so the message in the form of a file could be left or picked up. This is not the best choice for the problem at hand. **C** is incorrect because Telnet requires that either the other user has access to your system or that you have access to the other person's system. **D** is incorrect; with the advent of Web pages that allow users to leave messages, this might work for part of the problem, but the majority of the time those messages are taken off the Web page and e-mailed to someone who will read them. Sending a reply would not be feasible via a Web page because you would have to post it publicly, and that would not work with the need for confidentiality and encryption.

6. ☑ C. These are forms of e-mail clients, and are interactive with each other. They follow the X.500 specification for formatting, sending, and receiving e-mail messages, so no matter what client you use, you will be able to read the e-mails of others that are sent to you.
☒ A, B, and D are incorrect. These items have client names such as cute FTP, Internet Explorer, and KeaTerm.

7. ☑ A. The system name should come first, followed by at least one space, then by the IP address of the system, followed again by at least one space. Then any comment you wish to use to help you know where this system is should be proceeded by a pound sign.
☒ B and C are incorrect because anything following the pound sign is considered a comment. Therefore, in answer **B**, the IP address would be part of the comment and thus would not work because there would be no IP address associated with Sales_PC. **C** is incorrect because the entire line is considered a comment, so to the HOST file there is no entry for Sales_PC. **D** is incorrect because the system name must come first in a HOST file.

8. ☑ C. A browser would work here. The address was given and the filename ends in html, so this should trigger your knowledge of files and tell you that you need to use a browser and enter the URL http://accounts.ourcompany.com/accounts-receivable.html. Once the page comes up, you can print it.
☒ A is incorrect because FTP could be used to retrieve the file, but the question says it needs to be printed; it didn't say that you needed to retrieve the file. Once you retrieved the file with FTP, you would still need to use a browser to bring it up to print. **B** is incorrect because Telnet would allow you to gain access to the system if you had the proper rights and authorization, but you would still need some type of browser program to access the file to view and print it. **D** is incorrect because in order for e-mail to work, someone would have to send you the file via e-mail. You could not use e-mail to access a file on another system.

**9.** ☑ **D.** Most e-mail clients have a folder called Inbox that indicates that the e-mail in this box is unread or needs to be read.

☒ **A, B,** and **C** are all names of folders that you could create. Most e-mail clients allow you to create folders and store e-mail message in them to help organize your mail.

**10.** ☑ **B.** A NIC is a network connection that allows a system to communicate with other systems on the LAN/WAN or Internet. It is a piece of hardware that takes up one of the ISA / EISA or PCI slots on the motherboard. It has an external jack for connection to the network; connection types can be 10Base2, AUI, 10BaseT, FDDI, or Token Ring.

☒ **A, C,** and **D** are incorrect; they are other aspects of a computer but do not play a part in the communication of the system on the network.

**11.** ☑ **B.** The handheld PC would do everything he needs and more. You can acquire one with wireless Internet access. Programs can be installed for sales orders, e-mail, memos, and mail and contact lists.

☒ **A** is incorrect because even though the higher-speed chip would decrease the boot-up time, the laptop would still require substantially more time to boot then a handheld device. Laptops are still cumbersome and weigh about as much as the organizer. The only benefit would be the ability to keep all the salesperson's info in an electronic manner. **C** is not feasible. The salesperson needs to be able to retrieve information on-the-fly, and a voice recorder is mainly used for quick notes when you cannot write them down. **D** is not an option because some type of electronic device can make a person's life a little easier. In this case, the laptop or the handheld would be better than the organizer, but the handheld is the only one that gives the salesperson everything he needs.

**12.** ☑ **C.** A Web browser. To access the secured servers' pages, you would request the URLs of the suppliers' sites. The URLs should begin with https:\\, followed by the name of their Web sites. For example, if a site was www.gloves.com and the page was order.html, the URL would be https:\\www.gloves.com\order.html. If you enter http:\\, you would not be able to access the secured page. The https:\\ tells your browser to connect using secured protocols. If you are running IE, you will also notice a lock

icon at the bottom of your screen that will change from unlocked to locked.
☒ A would get you to a secured server, but it is not used much anymore; the ease of writing Web pages and the ability to display pictures such as a catalog online makes the Web a much better option. **B** is not the best option because if you were using FTP, you would have to fill out forms and copy them to the servers. This would require extra effort on both parties' parts. Again, with the advent of the Web and secured servers, Web browsers are the best option. **D** is incorrect. Gopher is a product that was used mainly in the past to allow a user to search documents on a site. Although it is still in use today, its use is minimal.

13. ☑ **B.** The size of the file would recommend that you FTP the file to the customer if they need it immediately. You would FTP to the customer's site, log in as either anonymous or with the credentials they provide, and then issue the send command to transmit the file from your system to theirs.
☒ A is an option, but FTP is much faster. Also, this answer is deemed wrong because there is no send command in Telnet. You can transmit a file via a transfer protocol if your Telnet client supports it. **C** is incorrect because the file is 25MB and most e-mail servers will not allow a file over 5MB to be transmitted attached to an e-mail message. **D** will not work because the customer said they needed the file immediately to get their system up and running; sending an overnight package is probably not an option.

14. ☑ **A.** The operating system is a major concern when purchasing software. Most software manufacturers write different variants for different operating systems. If you have a Windows 95 system, you cannot run programs for UNIX systems or programs especially written for Windows NT. You need to read the box and make sure it lists your operating system. Hardware such as memory size is also a concern, but if you don't have the correct OS to start with, you never get to the hardware.
☒ B is incorrect because the programs you purchase to run on your system have no concern with your ISP connection speed. **C** is incorrect because some companies will sell the same product in different levels (light, full) with different options. Although this is a concern, the OS is the first and most important issue you should address. **D** is less important. Again, see Answer A.

**15.** ☑ **B.** Purchase an Intel-based personal computer, because you work on a system that runs MS office products. MS runs on Intel platforms under the OS of Windows 95, 98, NT, and 2000. This is your best option, and will allow you to do the same work at home with the office products as you do at work. When purchasing, don't forget to buy a copy of MS Office; PCs do not usually come with Office preinstalled.

☒ **A.** Although an Apple MAC is a great system for both home and office use, you are already familiar with the Office products, which means you are familiar with the Windows operating systems. If you switch to MAC, you will have to learn a new operating system, and not all Windows programs run on a MAC. **C** is incorrect because an Alpha running UNIX is not the best idea for a home system. UNIX is not compatible with the Office software, so you would have to learn a new operating system. Alpha systems are not normally used in a home office, even when running Windows NT. The cost of the system makes it less than acceptable for the average home user. **D** is incorrect because WebTV does not offer the ability to use any of the Office products; it is mainly designed to browse the Web and send e-mail.

**16.** ☑ **A, B,** and **D** are correct. You need to know the IP address of the system and the subnet mask of your network. To reach servers on a remote segment, you will need to know the gateway address of the hardware that will get your packets off your segment and onto the other segment.

☒ **C** is incorrect because a DNS server is not required per the preceding statement. DNS is used to translate fully qualified domain names (FQDNs) to a TCP/IP address for access, usually over the Internet or over a large network that has many nodes. DNS is not a required field to be filled in.

**17.** ☑ **C.** You need to add the URL for your Proxy server into your browser in the configuration section.

☒ **A** will not work. Proxy settings are part of the program of the browser and require settings to be changed to utilize a Proxy server. **B** is also incorrect. Adding the Proxy address in front of the URL you wish to access would only make the browser think that the page you wish to view is located at proxy1.ourcompany.com/www.toy.com/cars.html. **D** is incorrect. Browsers have many files that are read each time a browser is opened, but proxy.html is not one of them. The Proxy settings must be configured from within the browser, and once configured will remain until they are changed.

18. ☑ D is one way to change the settings. Another is to access Control Panel via My Computer, or Start | Settings | Control Panel. Click the Display icon and then the Settings tab, and change the settings by using the slide bar for the desktop area.

☒ A is incorrect because there is no Desktop option under Administrative Tools. B won't work because there is no option choice for Desktop from the right-click. Also, the desktop area choice is a slide bar. C is incorrect because if you choose Console from the Control Panel, it will take you to a console prompt—some people still call it a DOS prompt.

19. ☑ D. By using Static IP addresses for the servers, you are guaranteeing that their IP addresses will always remain the same. This is very important if you are using Domain Name servers or WINS. A server should always have a Static IP address. Assigning all other IP addresses by DHCP is the best option. It allows for any PC to be moved to any connection on the network and be able to work. It also allows for easy configuration of the IP properties; as changes happen, they will take effect the next time the user renews his or her DHCP address or reboots.

☒ A, B, and C are incorrect. Using Static IP addresses for laptop users will not work. If they plug into a network segment other than the one to which they are assigned, they will not be able to access the network. Assigning DHCP addresses to servers is not a good option. If a server is taken offline for an extended period of time, another system might acquire its IP address. If that IP address was tied to programs or DNS entries for that server, information will not be routed correctly. DHCP is best used for roaming users and desktop users. It is easy to configure the system no matter where the users are. Also, there is no need for user intervention in making changes and no need for a technician to have to make changes on each system as the IP address of the gateway changes.

**20.** ☑ **D.** Issuing bin at the FTP> prompt on the remote site forces the download to be in a binary form. ASCII would force downloads to be done in ASCII format or text format. ASCII is the default on most FTP servers.

☒ **A** is incorrect. Entering "binary" as the password would only make an entry in the access log from user "anonymous" at e-mail address "binary." The password is nothing more than a log entry of your e-mail address used for tracking purposes. **B** is incorrect because there is no option in FTP client software that allows you to set your type before you connect to the remote host. **C** is incorrect because get_bin is an illegal command and would result in an error being returned.

**21.** ☑ **C.** WebTV is the best choice for the requested options you desire: Web browsing and e-mail. It also allows for interactive game playing with game shows, and provides an online TV listing. In addition, some VCRs can be programmed using the WebTV system.

☒ **A** is a good option since it is small and won't take up much room, but it is not the best option for this user. **B** is also an option because a handheld PC is very small and takes up almost no space. However, the e-mail clients on most handhelds truncate messages, so if the message is long you might not get all of it. Web browsing is also limited; Web pages are not displayed in their entirety, and many times, no graphics are displayed. **D** is incorrect because the requirements were for something that took up very little space. A PC, no matter how small the footprint, requires space, and space is at a minimum. Also, the cabling running from the system to the keyboard, the mouse and monitor, the phone jack, and the power cables would all have to be maneuvered around—not a good option in a limited space.

**22.** ☑ **B.** The collection of required items for TCP/IP to run on a system is called the TCP/IP stack. These are programs, drivers, and other bits of information that are loaded into the operating system and are necessary for TCP/IP to function properly.

☒ **A**, **C**, and **D** are all incorrect.

23. ☑ **D.** Mput is the command to transmit multiple files all starting with "win" from your system to a remote FTP server.
☒ **A** is incorrect because Get win* would return an error as "get" can only be used for a single file. MGET would allow you to get multiple files starting with "win" from the remote FTP server and download them to your local system. **B** would return an error, because "put" is not a recognized command. **C** is incorrect because "put," like "get," only allows a single filename, so wildcards are not allowed.

24. ☑ **A** and **B** are correct. Internet Explorer and Netscape Communicator offer versions for UNIX.
☒ **C** is incorrect. WebTV is a complete unit and has its own OS and specialty hardware. **D** is incorrect; UnixBrowse is a fictitious product.

25. ☑ **D.** You would enter the entire site name, a slash, and then the page name. You also need to make sure you use the https:\\ in front of the URL to indicate to the browser that you are attempting a secured connection.
☒ **A** would take you to a page if it weren't a secured server page. The secured server page requires the https:\\ to activate the additional security and encryption features of the browser. **B** would try to locate a page on a server called orders at the hardhats.com domain. **C** is incorrect. If the entire site was on the secured server this entry would work. However, with secured server URLs you either have to have a link from a page with the entire correct URL, or you must manually type the entire URL to browse the page.

26. ☑ **C.** This is most likely the cause of the problem. Upon investigation, it was determined that: 1) The IP address was changed; 2) No one working over the weekend changed the IP address; 3) Somewhere on the network that IP address is being used, which means it was reassigned to another system. Some suggestions to correct the problem include: find the system that has the 192 address and have it shut down or release the IP address; set the WINS server to be Static IP and enter that IP address in the IP properties; or remove that IP address from the DHCP scope on the DHCP server.

☒    **A** could have caused the problem, but if you confirmed that the IP address of the WINS server was .192 before, then DHCP is the best guess for the problem. This is easy enough to troubleshoot: Look at the Properties screen for the TCP/IP configuration; if it's set to DHCP, then that's the problem. **B** is incorrect. Unless you moved your PC, it should still be on the same segment. Its IP address is on the same network. If you moved it to another segment and didn't change the IP address, then nothing would work for you as you would not have a valid IP address. **D** is also an option, but you confirmed the IP address of the WINS server before and after the shutdown.

**27.** ☑    **C.** Port 21 is the standard TCP and UDP port for FTP.
☒    **A**, **B**, and **D** are incorrect. Port 80 is for HTTP traffic, Port 23 is for Telnet, and Port 110 is used for POP3.

# Client Security, Troubleshooting, and MIME Questions

$Q_{\&}A$

# Client Security, Troubleshooting, and MIME

**1.** MIME stands for _____?

   A. Making Internet Mail Electronic.

   B. Multi-Purpose Internet Mail Extensions.

   C. Manual Input Mail Extensions.

   D. MIME just means MIME; it is not an acronym.

**2.** You have been hired to design a Web page for a company. The owner wants the page to have something catchy right from the beginning. You decide to put in a RealPlayer video. What needs to be done to the Web page so that when the visitor arrives at the site, the correct application takes over and displays the RealPlayer video?

   A. You need to download RealPlayer to the client system before the video will be played.

   B. You need to encode the Web page with the MIME information for RealPlayer so that it will activate on the client's system when the video starts downloading.

   C. You need to ask the client in the form of a check box if he or she has RealPlayer installed.

   D. Nothing needs to be done, it will happen automatically.

**3.** What types of images are "Web ready," meaning that they can be viewed either on or offline without having to open an additional application?

   A. .GIF

   B. .TIF

   C. .BMP

   D. .JPG

**4.** What application would you use to connect from one system to another so you could access applications such as mail on the remote system without the need for a dial-up connection?

A. FTP

B. SLIP

C. PING

D. Telnet

**5.** News servers implement an encryption for "off color" posts. How does it work?

A. NNTP implements ROT23 encryption; it takes each line of the text and moves it down 23 lines.

B. NNTP implements ROT13 encryption; it takes each character and exchanges it with the character to its immediate right.

C. NNTP implements ROT13 encryption; it takes each character in the post and replaces it with the character 13 letters down the alphabet from it.

D. NNTP does not employ any type of encryption.

**6.** You joined a Web site discussion group less than a week ago, and up until today, you were able to just click on the link and enter the discussion group whenever you wanted to. Today when you click on the link, it asks for a username and password. Why?

A. The discussion group is no longer being offered.

B. The cookie that stored your information has somehow been modified or deleted.

C. Your password has expired on the site.

D. You have clicked on a wrong link.

**7.** What are some of the problems related to legacy programs?

    A. Slow response time

    B. Not compatible with newer versions

    C. Lack of support available

    D. Errors

**8.** You are setting up your company's security for its LAN, and several people need the ability to dial in to the company. Which of the following would be good security measures to implement?

    A. Clear text passwords

    B. Dial back

    C. Separate passwords for the dial-in server account and accounts on the LAN

    D. Use SLIP

**9.** When looking at ways to secure your desktop, you start looking at the browser as a major point of security. You access ActiveX, Java, JavaScript, and SSL connections from your browser. Which of these should be of the most concern when it comes to security?

    A. ActiveX

    B. Java

    C. JavaScript

    D. SSL

**10.** At what level of the OSI model does encryption for Web transmissions using SSL take place?

    A. Transport layer

    B. Application layer

    C. Network layer

    D. Session layer

**11.** E-mail applications offer different features, and some offer more than others, but a good e-mail client will offer _____?

    A. Spell checker

    B. Archiving

    C. S/MIME

    D. Multiple account definitions

**12.** A new install of a Web browser _____.

    A. Allows all cookies

    B. Denies all cookies

    C. Prompts before accepting a cookie

    D. Has no idea what a cookie is until you add a cookie extension

**13.** Other than through MIME and uuencode, how can you transmit a binary file via e-mail?

    A. Base16

    B. Base32

    C. Base64

    D. Base128

**14.** You are in charge of security on your company's LAN, and you have determined that many users are reusing the same passwords or a small number of passwords. What can you enable on the accounts server to stop this?

    A. Password history

    B. Password list

    C. Password memory

    D. Password length

CLIENT SECURITY
QUESTIONS

**15.** Strong encryption is considered anything using a key length of at least _____?

 A. 64 bits

 B. 128 bits

 C. 256 bits

 D. 512 bits

**16.** Secured Socket Layer (SSL) uses what form of encryption?

 A. SHA

 B. MDS

 C. PGP

 D. RSA

**17.** PGP works on what layer of the OSI model?

 A. Data Link layer

 B. Session layer

 C. Application layer

 D. Transport layer

**18.** You are running an e-mail application and notice that every time there are 31 days in a month, the e-mail messages are received with the day marker of 311. You decide that this is a bug; what do you do?

 A. Purchase a different e-mail application, because this one doesn't work correctly.

 B. Contact the company's tech support hotline and demand they send you your money back.

 C. Contact the company's Web site and look for a bug fix or new revision release of the product.

 D. Live with it and figure it's just a fact of life.

**19.** You are using NT 4.0 Workstation running Internet Explorer 5.0, and you need to locate the cookies stored on your system. Where would you find them?

A. C:\program files\cookies

B. C:\winnt\profiles\"username"\temporary Internet files

C. C:\windows\Temperary Internet files

D. C:\temp

**20.** You have determined through checking the revision level that you have a very old version of dial-up-networking. You decide to upgrade to the newest version. What benefits are you expecting to see?

A. Bugs fixed

B. Better quality connections

C. Speeds over 56 K

D. Better compression

**21.** RFCs 822, 1521, and 1522 define the use of MIME. MIME is used to deliver non-ASCII text to users via the Web or e-mail. Using MIME, which of the following can be delivered?

A. GIF images

B. QuickTime movies

C. A text file

D. Virtual Reality Modeling Language

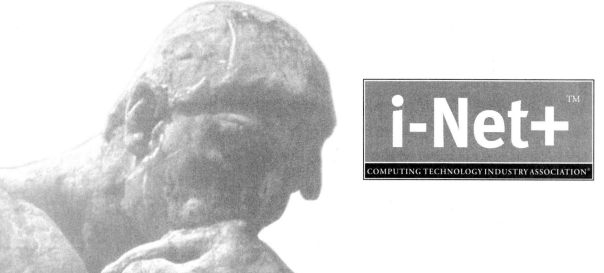

# Client Security, Troubleshooting, and MIME Answers

# Client Security, Troubleshooting, and MIME

1. ☑ **B.** MIME stands for Multi-Purpose Internet Mail Extensions. This is a method for sending nontext files in the form of an e-mail message.
   ☒ **A, C,** and **D** are all invalid terms.

2. ☑ **B.** When coding a Web page for special nontext processes, you need to have the MIME extensions encoded into the Web page. That way, when visitors arrive at the site and the page starts to download, their browser will know to activate the correct application to handle the information being downloaded.
   ☒ **A** is incorrect. You can and probably should have a link on your page so visitors can download RealPlayer if they need it; once the application is installed, it does not need to be entered again. **C** is incorrect. This is not needed. If clients do not have the RealPlayer application installed on their system, the page will still download, but they will not be able to view the video. **D** is also incorrect; you must encode the Web page with the correct extensions.

3. ☑ **A, D.** GIF and JPG, or JPEG, are considered Web ready and can be viewed from your browser.
   ☒ **B** and **C** are incorrect. TIF and BMP images cannot be viewed from your browser, and require an external application to view them.

4. ☑ **D.** Telnet allows a user to connect from one system to another and gain access via some form of authentication, usually a username and password. Once authenticated, a telnet session is the same as being physically connected to the host or remote station.
   ☒ **A** is incorrect. FTP allows a user to transfer files to and from a system, not access applications on the system. **C** is incorrect. PING is used to troubleshoot a network.

**5.** ☑ **C.** ROT13 is the encryption that is used on NNTP servers. A message that is encoded in ROT13 has each letter of the alphabet swapped with the 13th letter down from it; for example, As are Ns, Rs are Es, and so on.
☒ **A, B,** and **D** are all incorrect; these are not the correct forms of encryption for NNTP servers.

**6.** ☑ **B.** It is most likely that the cookie on your system has been modified, damaged, or deleted. Enter your information and allow a new cookie to be deposited on your system.
☒ **A** is incorrect. You would more than likely receive an error about the page not being found; you would not be asked for username and password. **C** is incorrect as passwords don't generally expire that fast. **D** is also incorrect. You are probably using a "favorites" or "hotlist" to reach this site, so this is not likely.

**7.** ☑ **A, B, C, D.** Older applications running on a system tend to have slower response times than newer versions. They are not compatible with newer versions; for example, Office 95 is unable to read Office 97 documents. It is very hard to get support for older applications; many times, the company does not exist or is no longer knowledgeable about the older version of code. Older software is more likely to have errors; bug fixes are a major reason for upgrades and revision changes.

**8.** ☑ **B, C.** Dial back would require users to either enter a number for the system to call them back at (this would be logged) or only call them back at a predetermined number such as a home office number. Having a separate password for the dial-in server and the accounts on the LAN adds an additional layer of security; if someone is able to break in to the dial-in server, that person would not have free rein on the network.
☒ **A** is incorrect. Using clear text is too easy to capture using network analyzers or other devices. **D** is incorrect as SLIP has very poor security. If security is needed, use PPP, which is a new protocol and offers higher security.

**9.** ☑ **A.** ActiveX has very little if no security built in. Ninety-nine percent of the ActiveX connections you make are not going to harm your system, but it is an easy way for hackers to gain entry into your system.
☒ **B** and **C** are incorrect. Java and JavaScript offer security measures to insure that your system cannot be probed or accessed. They are not 100% secure, but much more so than ActiveX. **D** is incorrect. SSL offers high security.

**10.** ☑ **D.** The SSL works at the Session layer.
☒ **A, B,** and **C** are all incorrect. They are layers of the OSI model, but are not responsible for the SSL.

**11.** ☑ **A, B, C, D.** A good e-mail application will offer all of the above. There are many other features that you may want or need; read about each application you are considering and choose the best one for your needs.

**12.** ☑ **A.** A new install of a Web browser has security set to low as a default, which allows for all cookies. This means that cookies can and will be placed on the system without the user's awareness.
☒ **B** and **C** are incorrect. These are settings you can have for cookies, but the default is to allow all cookies. **D** is also incorrect. All current browsers are aware of cookies and know how to handle them without additional software.

**13.** ☑ **C.** Base64 is another way to encode a binary file for transmit via e-mail or new server posting.
☒ **A, B,** and **D** are all incorrect; these are not actual encoding schemes.

**14.** ☑ **A.** Enabling password history on the users' accounts prevents them from reusing the same password. Usually the length of the history can be changed.
☒ **B** and **C** are incorrect; they are made-up answers. **D** is incorrect. The length of the password has nothing to do with users reusing it. A longer password requirement is a good security measure.

**15.** ☑ **B.** Strong encryption is considered 128 bits or more. Before sending encrypted data to other countries, be aware of the encryption laws of both the country you are sending from and the country you are sending to.
☒ **A** is incorrect. A 64-bit encryption is considered a medium-ranged key length. **C** and **D** are very strong, and are illegal in most countries.

**16.** ☑ **D.** SSL uses RSA encryption, which is a symmetric key algorithm.
☒ **A** and **B** are incorrect. SHA and MDS encryption is used for signing documents. **C** is also incorrect. PGP is a general file encryption, not a transport encryption.

**17.** ☑ **C.** PGP and MIME are Application layer encryption algorithms.
☒ **A, B,** and **D** are incorrect. The Data link PGP only works with applications. The encrypted packets will be passed down to each of the other layers per OSI specifications, but they have no bearing on PGP's operations.

**18.** ☑ **C.** First, look for a bug fix or a newer revision release of a product. Many times, products ship with bugs, and patches or revision releases are a company's way of fixing those bugs.
☒ **A** is incorrect. There is no reason to stop using a product because of a bug unless the bug is unfixable. **B** is incorrect. Tech support is there to help you troubleshoot your problem, and offer either a solution or refund your money. **D** is incorrect. You should never feel like you have to live with a bug. Contact the company by phone, mail, e-mail, or Web and see if there is a fix to your problem.

**19.** ☑ **B.** You will find the cookies stored in the temporary Internet files directory under your username. Other browsers store the cookies in other places.
☒ **A, C,** and **D** are all incorrect. You will not find the cookies stored here unless you have changed the system's configuration to something other than the original.

**20.** ☑ **A, D.** Upgrading to the newest revision will most likely fix bugs and offer better compression for data transmission.

☒ **B** is incorrect. The quality of the connection is generally based on the quality of the telephone line. **C** is incorrect, as you cannot achieve speed higher than 56 K on a standard telephone line.

**21.** ☑ **A, B,** and **D.** MIME can be used to deliver all of these to the user. Web designers need only to code in the correct MIME type, and the server will transmit the data with a special header in the first packet to instruct the end user's browser how to handle the data.

☒ **C** is incorrect. A text file is an ASCII file and does not need MIME encoding.

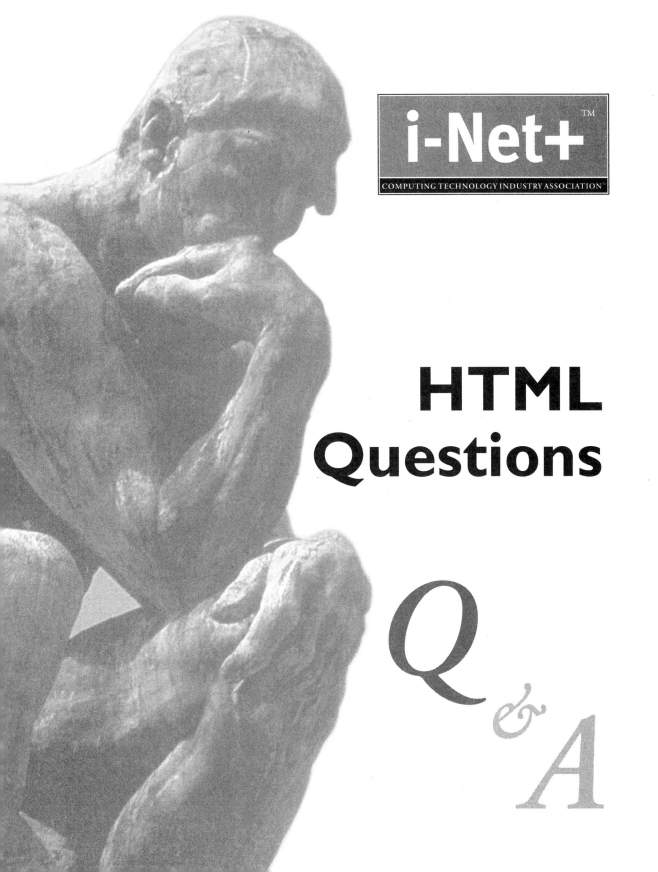

# HTML

1. You work in the Marketing department. There are five users all located on the same floor and they all use the same type of PC. The users need to exchange marketing documents that contain many pictures and have a very precise layout. All documents are now stored in PDF format in a desktop database (Microsoft Access). The users have a growing need to search for documents with simple criteria (predefined keywords, dates, etc.), and attach comments to documents when they enter new documents into the database. Taking into consideration cost and future needs, which solution can you suggest?

   A. Use e-mail to exchange these documents because we can attach documents to e-mail messages.
   B. Set up and develop an intranet application using HTML as the common format for document exchange. This application allows data entry and document searching.
   C. Buy third-party document management software.
   D. Enhance the database interface to allow data entry and document searching.

2. You work for a government agency maintaining public records. The agency has been receiving requests from the public through letters or telephone calls. An inhouse legacy application written in COBOL runs every night to produce the documents, and the document requested is then printed and mailed to the requester. The documents are in tabular format and contain only text information. The agency also has a static small Web site that provides some general information. You are asked to consider new solutions to improve the efficiency of this process because the agency has a limited budget and the need is still growing. Taking into consideration cost and time constraints, which solution can you suggest?

   A. Develop a telephony system that can print the documents requested. The documents then can be mailed to the requester.
   B. Enhance the legacy application so it can produce documents in HTML format, and put them in a special folder on the Web server. Enhance the Web site to offer a simple search page that can pull the requested document.

C. Buy a third-party document management software that offers the search capability needed.

D. Write a client application that the public can download from the Web site. This application can process the simple search criteria and pull the text documents from the legacy system over the Internet.

3. You work for a company that sells multimedia information (stock photos, sound tracks, video clips, and animations) through traditional channels such as mail order. Your company now wants to exploit the Internet as a new sales channel; the requirement from the Sales department is that the prospects should be able to try some samples before they buy. The media samples are stored in various formats. What HTML elements of choice can achieve this? (Choose all that apply.)

A. <IMG>

B. <APPLET> with JavaScript

C. <OBJECT>

D. Dynamic HTML

4. You are a Webmaster of your company's Web site. It is common practice to offer your users a means to send e-mail to the Webmaster. Your e-mail address is yourname@yourcompany.com. You want to show this address at the bottom of the welcome page (homepage) as a hyperlink to the user's e-mail client software. What HTML tag is appropriate?

A. `<A HREF="email: yourname@yourcompany.com>` `yourname@yourcompany.com</A>`

B. `<A HREF="mailto: yourname@yourcompany.com">` `yourname@yourcompany.com</A>`

C. `<A HREF="mailto:// yourname@yourcompany.com">` `yourname@yourcompany.com</A>`

D. None of the above

5. You are building a Web page to record payment of tuition from students for a State University. This is an intranet application and the university

workstations run Internet Explorer 4. There is a drop-down box that shows all payment types (cash, check, credit card). If the credit-card type is selected in the drop-down box, you want to show the Credit Card block that has three form controls: one drop-down box for the Credit Card type (Visa, MasterCard, etc.), one text box for the Credit Card number, and one text box for the Expiration Date. How would you do that?

A. Write script to handle the event ONCHANGE of the drop-down box (<SELECT> tag). Change the style attribute VISIBILITY of the Credit Card block to VISIBLE or HIDDEN depending on the payment type.

B. Write script to handle the event ONCLICK of the drop-down box (<SELECT> tag). Change the style attribute VISIBILITY of the Credit Card block to VISIBLE or HIDDEN depending on the payment type.

C. Write script to handle the event ONCHANGE of the drop-down box (<SELECT> tag). Change the style attribute SHOW of the Credit Card block to SHOW or HIDE depending on the payment type.

D. Write script to handle the event ONCLICK of the drop-down box (<SELECT> tag). Change the style attribute SHOW of the Credit Card block to VISIBLE or HIDDEN depending on the payment type.

**6.** You have a Web page that contains a drop-down box for the carrier (Fed-Ex, UPS, etc.). You want to show the price and the estimated delivery time when the user selects a carrier in the drop-down box. You use the ONCHANGE event of the <SELECT> tag to call a JavaScript function that calculates the price and the delivery time. It needs to get the value of the selected carrier code, which is defined as the Value of each option in the <SELECT> box. The HTML code for the drop-down box is as follows:

```
<FORM NAME=form1 ACTION = "\cgi-bin\projectdelivery.dll"
METHOD=POST>
...
<SELECT NAME=Carrier ONCHANGE="CarrierPriceTime()">
<OPTION VALUE="F">Federal Express</OPTION>
<OPTION VALUE="P">USPS</OPTION>
<OPTION VALUE="U">UPS</OPTION>
</SELECT>
...
</FORM>
```

What JavaScript snippet is appropriate for both Netscape 3 and Internet Explorer 3?

A. ```
Function CarrierPriceTime() {
...
var carrier = document.form1.Carrier.value
...
}
```

B. ```
Function CarrierPriceTime() {
...
var carrier = document.form1.Carrier.currentvalue
...
}
```

C. ```
Function CarrierPriceTime() {
...
var carrier = document.form1.Carrier.selectedIndex
...
}
```

D. ```
Function CarrierPriceTime() {
...
var carrier =
document.form1.Carrier.options[document.form1.selectedInd
ex].value
...
}
```

7. You are building a Web page that allows users to enter technical support requests. When the user submits the page, you examine the data entered such as Type of Computer, version of Operating System, version of the software, etc., and decide to load the page corresponding to the configuration entered. To dynamically load another page from this page, which JavaScript snippet is appropriate?

   A. location.load ("MACsupport.asp")
   B. window.href = "MACsupport.asp"
   C. location.href = "MACsupport.asp"
   D. window.load("MACsupport.asp")

8. Your company sells advertising space on its Web site. It also offers design of advertisement to advertisers in the form of a small "window" at the top of

some pages of the company's Web site. To get the attention of viewers, the advertisements usually have animation effects such as images or text flying around in that small "window," which is actually a frame. A <DIV> block can be used to contain the moving objects and its position dynamically changed to create the effect of moving. You use Dynamic HTML to build that frame and you know that the Web site must support Netscape 4 and later and Internet Explorer 4 and later. Therefore, some portions of JavaScript are written specifically for Netscape and some are written for Internet Explorer. To move a <DIV> block by a number of pixels to the left and to the top (to the upper-left corner) by *deltaX* and *deltaY* pixels, respectively (*deltaX* and *deltaY* are positive numbers), which methods or properties of the Document Object Model of Netscape and Internet Explorer can be used (the variable obj below represents the appropriate object in both browsers)?

A. `obj.MoveTo(deltaX, deltaY)` for Netscape; properties `obj.pixelLeft += deltaX` and `obj.pixelTop += deltaY` for Internet Explorer.

B. `obj.MoveBy(deltaX, deltaY)` for Netscape; properties `obj.pixelLeft -= deltaX` and `obj.pixelTop -= deltaY` for Internet Explorer.

C. `obj.MoveBy(deltaX, deltaY)` for Netscape; properties `obj.pixelLeft += deltaX` and `obj.pixelTop += deltaY` for Internet Explorer.

D. `obj.MoveTo(deltaX, deltaY)` for Netscape; properties `obj.pixelLeft -= deltaX` and `obj.pixelTop -= deltaY` for Internet Explorer.

**9.** You are building a Web page to welcome the customers of a multinational company. The Web page is rather simple and it shows the various languages that the site supports. The user can click on the flag corresponding to the language or the name of the language (written in its own language). You want to reflect the change of language on the page by rewriting the page in the language selected once the user selects a language. To optimize performance, you decide that you do this with JavaScript and rewrite the page without requesting another page from the server. What technique can be used?

A. Use the method window.reload() to rewrite the page.

B. Use the method document.write() to write the new content.

C. Use the property document.body.text to change the content.

D. Use the property document.URL to change the content.

**10.** You need to incorporate into your Web page the following paragraph:

I. HTML 4.0

    1. Internationalization

    2. Accessibility

II. Authoring Documents with HTML 4.0

    1. Separate structure and presentation

    2. Consider universal accessibility to the Web

This list is likely to change in the future, new items can be added at any level, and you would like to minimize the changes so you do not to have to renumber the list. What HTML elements can you use to achieve this?

A. Use the <NL> tag.

B. Use the <DL> tag.

C. Use the <UL> tag.

D. None of the above.

**11.** Your company manufactures printers and has a Web site to offer customer service and technical support. Your manager asks you to come up with a solution to streamline the technical support process by offering the printer manuals online for the customer to view. Printer operations are not very complicated and the manuals are not lengthy. If the customers can view the appropriate manual online before calling technical support, they will likely find the answer. This is usually the consequence of the customers misplacing the manual before they encounter problems. The manuals already exist in plain text documents and word-processor documents. How would you implement this solution?

A. Convert all word-processor documents into one HTML page and build a table of contents consisting of hyperlinks to each single-page manual.

B. Convert each word-processor document page of all manuals into one HTML page and on each page create a hyperlink to the next page and build a table of contents consisting of hyperlinks to the first page of each manual.

C. Use the text format documents as HTML pages and build a table of contents consisting of hyperlinks to the first page of each manual.

D. Build a table of contents consisting of hyperlinks to the word-processor documents; this allows the customers to download the manuals.

**12.** You are building a Web page entitled "Other Interesting Links" where you want to offer your users links to other useful Web sites that offer related information. You have identified a Web site and the URL is www.AcmeCorporation.com/welcome/index.html. You want to call the link "More information from Acme Corporation." How would you code this?

A. `<a link="http://www.AcmeCorporation.com/welcome/index.html">More information from Acme Corporation</a>`

B. `<link href="http://www.AcmeCorporation.com/welcome/index.html">More information from Acme Corporation</a>`

C. `<href a ="http://www.AcmeCorporation.com/welcome/index.html">More information from Acme Corporation</a>`.

D. `<a href="http://www.AcmeCorporation.com/welcome/index.html">More information from Acme Corporation</a>`

**13.** You are designing a Web page used for feedback. In addition to information such as category of feedback, satisfaction scores, etc., users can enter a comment about your Web site. You want to allow a long string of characters to be entered, and your database currently allows up to 255 characters for the comment field. You also want the users to be able to enter the comment in paragraphs just like a small document. What is the most appropriate HTML element?

A. `<input type=text size=255 maxlength=255>`

B. `<input type=text cols = 60 rows=5>`

C. `<textarea cols=60 rows=5></textarea>`

D. `<textarea paragraph="allowed">`

**14.** You are building a Web site for your company. This Web site has to display many reports that usually do not fit on one browser screen, which means the users have to scroll to read all the pages. All reports are in tabular format and have column headers. Since the users have to scroll and you want the column headers to always stay visible on the screen for readability, how can you achieve this design?

A. There is no way to do this. HTML does not allow parts of the document to be static.

B. Use JavaScript to bring up a second window that is on top of the report page and stays there until the report is closed or the user moves to another page.

C. Use frames in HTML; the header portion is in one frame while the data is in another frame.

D. None of the above.

**15.** You are reviewing the existing HTML documents for your company to prepare for new versions of browsers and other browsers that the customers may have when the Web site is open to the public. You found a lot of code similar to this sample:

```
<title>401(k) employee information</title>
<form action="Get401k.asp" method="post">Number of years
with company:
<input><br>Full-Time: <input type=checkbox>
```

What should you do? (Choose two answers.)

A. Add attribute ID to all HTML tags to program them.

B. Add missing tags such as <html>, <head>, <body>, </form>, etc.

C. Add paragraph tags <p> after the <title> section and where appropriate.

D. Put tags in order.

**16.** As a Webmaster, you are asked to design a series of HTML templates for your team members when they create new HTML pages. The templates must promote well-formed HTML pages and ensure the widest acceptance from multiple browsers. What HTML elements should you build into the template? (Choose all that apply.)

A. `<!DOCTYPE HTML PUBLIC "-//W3C//DTD HTML 4.0//EN"`
   `"http://www.w3.org/TR/REC-html40/strict.dtd">`
   `<HTML>`

B. `<HEAD>`
   `<TITLE>Put page title here</TITLE>`
   `</HEAD>`

C. `<BODY>`
   `<P>Start HTML body here`
   `</BODY>`
   `</HTML>`

D. `<FORM ACTION="<put script name here>". METHOD=POST>`
   `</FORM>`

**17.** You are part of a Web Development team and are asked to produce a Web page for the Sales By Region Report for your company's intranet. See the following illustration for the layout of the report. Which HTML code is most appropriate?

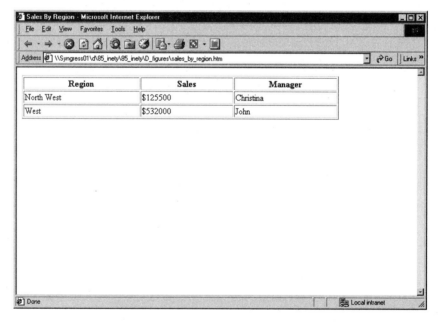

A. `<html>`
   `<head>`
   `<title>Sales By Region</title>`

```
</head>
<body>
<table border="1">
<tr>
<th>Region</th>
<th>Sales</th>
<th>Manager</th>
</tr>
<tr>
<td align="center">North West</td>
<td align="right">$125500</td>
<td align="center">Christina</td>
</tr>
<tr>
<td align="center">West</td>
<td align="right">$532000</td>
<td align="center">John</td>
</tr>
</table>
</body>
</html>
```

B.
```
<html>
<head>
<title>Sales By Region</title>
</head>
<body>
<table border="1" cellspacing="1" width="100%">
<tr>
<td align="center">Region</td>
<td>Sales</td>
<td>Manager</td>
</tr>
<tr>
<td align="center">North West</td>
<td align="right">$125,500</td>
<td align="center">Christina</td>
</tr>
<tr>
<td align="center">West</td>
<td align="right">$532,000</td>
<td align="center">John</td>
</tr>
</table>
</body>
</html>
```

C.
```
<html>
<head>
<title>Sales By Region</title>
</head>
<body>
<table border="1">
<tr>
<td><b>Region
<td><b>Sales
<td><b>Manager
<tr>
<td align="center">North West
<td align="right">$125,500
<td align="center">Christina
<tr>
<td align="center">West
<td align="right">$532,000
<td align="center">John
</table>
</body>
</html>
```

D.
```
<html>
<head>
<title>Sales By Region</title>
</head>
<body>
<table border="1">
<tr>
<th>Region</th>
<th>Sales</th>
<th>Manager</th>
</tr>
<tr>
<td valign="center">North West</td>
<td valign="right">$125,500</td>
<td valign="center">Christina</td>
</tr>
<tr>
<td valign="center">West</td>
<td valign="right">$532,000</td>
<td valign="center">John</td>
</tr>
</table>
</body>
</html>
```

**18.** You are part of a Web Development team and are asked to produce a Web page for the Sales By Region Report for your company's intranet. The code you wrote is:

```
<html>
<head>
<title>Sales By Region</title>
</head>
<body>
<table border="1" width="600">
<tr>
<th>Region</th>
<th>Sales</th>
<th>Manager</th>
</tr>
<tr>
<td align="center">North West</td>
<td align="right">$125500</td>
<td align="center">Christina</td>
</tr>
<tr>
<td align="center">West</td>
<td align="right">$532000</td>
<td align="center">John</td>
</tr>
</table>
</body>
</html>
```

You want the table to occupy the whole browser screen and have the proportion of each column width as in the illustration shown in Question 17. You notice that this works well with a screen resolution of 640 x 480 and the browser is maximized, but the table does not occupy the whole screen when the users switch to other resolutions or resize the browser. What is the problem?

A. There is no solution for this. You should ask the users to maximize the browser with the resolution of 640 x 480.

B. Change the <table> tag as follows:

```
<table border="1" width="600" resize="auto">
```

C. Change the <table> tag as follows:

```
<table border="1" width="100%">
```

D. Change each <td> tag as follows:

```
<td align="center" width="100%">North West</td>
```

**19.** You are part of a Web Development team and are asked to produce a Web page for the Sales By Region Search for your company's intranet. See the following illustration for the layout of the page. Which code is appropriate? (Choose all that apply.)

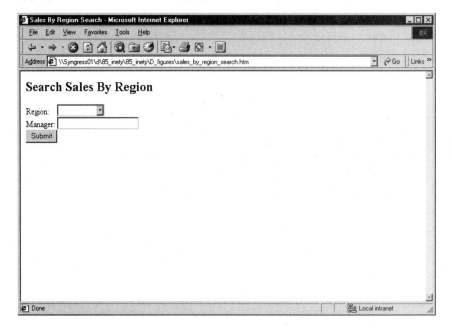

A.
```
<html>
<head>
<title>Sales By Region Search</title>
</head>
<body>
<h2>Search Sales By Region</h2>
<form name=form1 action="SalesByRegion.asp"
method="post">
```

```
        Region:   
        <select name="Region">
                    <option></option>
                    <option>North West</option>
                    <option>West</option>
        </select><br>
        Manager:
        <input type="text" name="Manager"><br>
        <input type="submit" value="Submit">
</form>
</body>
</html>
```

B.
```
<html>
<head>
<title>Sales By Region Search</title>
</head>
<body>
<h2>Search Sales By Region</h2>
<form name=form1 action="SalesByRegion.asp"
method="post">
        Region:   
        <select name="Region">
                    <option></option>
                    <option>North West</option>
                    <option>West</option>
        </select><br>
        Manager:
        <input name="Manager"><br>
        <input type="submit" value="Submit">
</form>
</body>
</html>
```

C.
```
<html>
<head>
<title>Sales By Region Search</title>
</head>
<body>
<h2>Search Sales By Region</h2>
<form name=form1 action="SalesByRegion.asp"
method="post">
        Region:   
        <select name="Region">
                    <option></option>
                    <option>North West</option>
                    <option>West</option>
        </select>
        Manager:
```

```
                    <input type="text" name="Manager"><br>
                    <input type="submit" value="Submit">
     </form>
     </body>
     </html>
D.   <html>
     <head>
     <title>Sales By Region Search</title>
     </head>
     <body>
     <h2>Search Sales By Region</h2>
     <form name=form1 action="SalesByRegion.asp"
     method="post">
            Region:   
            <select name="Region">
                      <option></option>
                      <option>North West</option>
                      <option>West</option>
            </select><br>
            Manager:
            <input type="text" name="Manager"><br>
     </form>
            <input type="submit" value="Submit">
     </body>
     </html>
```

**20.** Your company has a Web site that receives many visits, especially from customers. The customers use many different types of browsers, but the vast majority use Netscape 3 and later and Microsoft Internet Explorer 3 and later. You receive a new requirement from the Marketing department to add a new feature to the home page of your company. A short message is to be added that will be updated daily to let customers know about upcoming events that are of interest such as Special Promotion, etc. The Marketing department wants this message to be a "marquee" that runs across the page at the top. What HTML elements would you use? (Choose all that apply.)

A. Use Dynamic HTML and JavaScript to build the marquee. Use the <LAYER> tag with absolute positioning.

B. Use Dynamic HTML and JavaScript to build the marquee. Use the <LAYER> tag with relative positioning.

C. Use the <MARQUEE> tag.

D. None of the above.

**21.** You built a small Web site for a video store that allows members to request reservation of a movie for rent. The page has many text boxes for data entry (part number, movie name, expiration date, etc.) and they are empty for members to put in data (you use the <INPUT TYPE=TEXT...> element). You have built a database that captures the preferences in movie genre for members and want to preload the text boxes with suggestions. What HTML elements or techniques can you use?

A. Use the attributes DATASRC and DATAFLD of HTML <INPUT> element to bind data on the page.

B. Use the attributes SERVER, CONNECT, and SQL of HTML <INPUT> element to bind data on the page.

C. Use server-side script to create the HTML page from the database and load value using the VALUE attribute of the <INPUT> tag.

D. Use Dynamic HTML and JavaScript to fetch data and load it using the attribute VALUE of the <INPUT> tag.

**22.** You are building a Web page that allows the users to get medical information about arthritis. The selection page must get the body part as a selection criterion. To make your page easy to use, you decide to show the image of a human body, and the user can click on the various parts to get to the next selection page. What HTML technique would you consider and why?

A. Use JavaScript and Dynamic HTML to capture the coordinates of the mouse and load the next page. This is a perfect application of Dynamic HTML.

B. Use client-side image map because this is the appropriate use of client-side image map.

C. Use server-side image map because this is the appropriate use of server-side image map.

D. Use either client-side image map or server-side image map because both are appropriate.

**23.** Your company has an intranet Web site that works well and now wants to offer part of it to the customers. You are asked to verify the HTML code for cross-browser compatibility. You found this code:

```
<html>
<body>
Welcome to the Image Archive section of the ABC Group
</body>
<title>The Image Archive of ABC Group</title>
</html>
```

What would you decide to do? (Choose all that apply.)

A. The code is perfectly fine.

B. The <head> and </head> tags are missing.

C. The <title> and </title> tags must be inside the <head> section.

D. The <title> section must be placed before the <body> section.

# HTML

1. ☑ **D.** This is the simplest and most likely the least expensive solution that meets the needs. Since the database is already in place, we only need to develop or enhance the interface to allow for searching and data entry.
☒ **A** is incorrect because e-mail will not solve the problem of document searching. **B** is incorrect because one of the disadvantages of HTML is that it is simply a markup language that lacks precise positioning of elements. (It is possible to have HTML pages host Adobe Acrobat Reader documents in an intranet application, but this is still not a natural use of HTML, and there is the cost of setting up a new Web server environment.) Also, there is no need for deployment across heterogeneous machines. HTML is not appropriate in this case. **C** is incorrect because it is the most costly solution.

2. ☑ **B.** Enhancing the legacy application and the Web site is the simplest solution and is most likely the least expensive that meets the needs. Simple HTML tags can be added as output to the COBOL programs to produce HTML documents containing text in tabular format. A simple search page is also very easy to obtain through most popular Web authoring tools.
☒ **A** is incorrect because telephony will alleviate the burden of answering telephone requests; however, it will not solve the problem of mailing. **C** is incorrect because the solution involves high cost and will not solve the problem of mailing. **D** is incorrect because although it is a viable solution, it will encounter some resistance from the general public—most Internet users are reluctant to download code. Besides, we will have to cope with network setup issues on the client machines. Given the broad scope of the possible machine configurations, this is not a good solution.

3. ☑ **A, B,** and **C.** The <OBJECT> element allows you to control whether data should be rendered externally or by some program, specified by you, that renders the data within the browser. This mechanism ensures that all available supported media with rendering code can be hosted in the HTML page, thus

ensuring future expansion. The <IMG> element only renders graphics or optionally some specific types of animation, not other media such as video, sounds, etc. **B** is correct because <APPLET> allows you to run Java applets and is still valid for most browsers, but it is a deprecated element and is being replaced by <OBJECT>; therefore, it does not guarantee future expansion.
☒   **D** is incorrect because DHTML is mainly about programmatic control of the elements on the page, not about source and types of multimedia data as in this case.

**4.** ☑   **B.** The attribute HREF of the tag <A> is used to link to various services such as HTTP, gopher, file, newsgroups, Telnet, FTP, e-mail. The syntax in B is the correct syntax.
☒   **A** and **C** are incorrect because there the correct syntax for e-mail service is mailto:. **D** is incorrect because the attribute HREF of the tag <A> is used to link to various services such as HTTP, gopher, file, newsgroups, Telnet, FTP, e-mail. The syntax in B is the correct syntax.

**5.** ☑   **A, B.** The ONCHANGE event is raised when the user selects a choice in the drop-down box (<SELECT> box). To make an element visible or invisible, change the style attribute VISIBILITY to VISIBLE or HIDDEN, respectively. The event ONCLICK also can be used, but it is specific to Internet Explorer.
☒   **C** is incorrect. There is no style attribute SHOW. **D** is incorrect. There is no style attribute SHOW.

**6.** ☑   **D.** Function CarrierPriceTime… . To access the selected value of a <SELECT> box, we have to traverse the document object hierarchy starting with the *document* object, get to the *form* object, then to the select box, use the collection *options* to access a specific item in this collection, and use the index. The currently selected index is value of the property *selectedIndex* of the <SELECT> element.
☒   **A** is incorrect. The property *value* can be used but it is Internet Explorer specific. **B** is incorrect. There is no property called *currentvalue*.

C is incorrect. The property *selectedIndex* returns the index of the selected option in the select box, not the value.

7. ☑ **C.** Setting the property *href* of the object *location* to a new URL loads the document specified by the URL into the current window or frame.
   ☒ **A** is incorrect because there is no method *load* for the object *location*. **B** is incorrect because there is no property *href* for the object *window*. The correct object to use is *location*. **D** is incorrect because there is no method *load* for the object *window*. The correct object to use is *location*.

8. ☑ **B.** In Netscape, to move an object by a certain number of pixels, use the method *moveBy*. In Internet Explorer, to move an object to the left and to the top by a certain number of pixels, decrement the properties *pixelLeft* and *pixelTop*.
   ☒ **A** and **C** are incorrect because in Netscape, the *moveTo* method moves the object to the specific position determined by the coordinates. In this situation, we have a number of pixels to move, not the position, so the easiest way is to use *moveBy*. **C** is incorrect because in Internet Explorer, to move an object to the left and to the top, we have to decrement the *pixelLeft* and *pixelTop* values, not increment them.

9. ☑ **B.** When invoked as the page loads, the method document.write (or writeln) dynamically adds content to the page. When invoked after the page has loaded, a single method invocation clears the current document, opens a new output stream, and writes the content to the window or frame. In this case, knowing the language, the JavaScript code just clears the current content and loads the new "welcome" page in the language of choice without making a request to the server for a new document.
   ☒ **A** is incorrect because the window object has no method reload. **C** is incorrect because in Internet Explorer, the property text represents the color of text for the entire document body, not the content of the document. Therefore, document.body.text is syntactically correct but refers to a wrong property. **D** is incorrect because the property URL of the document object represents the URL of the document, so changing it is

equivalent to loading a new document. This will achieve the expected result, which is to load a new content, but requires a request to the server and thus is not efficient.

**10.** ☑   **D.** The correct tag to use is <OL>. This tag allows us to build an ordered (numbered) list. The attribute TYPE can be used to specify the type of number used (Roman numeral, number, etc.).
☒   **A** is incorrect because there is no tag <NL>. **B** is incorrect because the <DL> tag is for creating a Directory List and does not achieve the presentation required. **C** is incorrect because the <UL> tag is for creating an unordered (unnumbered) list.

**11.** ☑   **B.** Linking the pages like this allows the users to browse through the manual, the word-processor pages are short enough to offer reading comfort, and the links allow the users to continue or go back to the table of contents. This is a good use of hyperlinks for site navigation.
☒   **A** is incorrect because even though the manuals are not very long, putting all the word-processor pages on one HTML page can make this page very long, and scrolling through a lengthy page like this is not comfortable. **C** is incorrect because plain text documents do not have formatting features; therefore, the converted HTML pages will not be aesthetically acceptable. Text formatting in HTML or in Word makes the documents easy to read. **D** is incorrect because the users have to download the manual and open it in the corresponding word processor. There are many problems associated with this solution: the users must have at least word-processor viewer, and the document may be outdated in the future.

**12.** ☑   **D.** This is the right syntax of the anchor tag. The attribute HREF contains the URL of the link. The start tag <a href…> and end tag </a> surround the element that constitutes the hyperlink.

⊠  **A** is incorrect because the attribute name is HREF, not LINK. **B** is incorrect because the tag for hyperlink is <a ...>, not <link...>. **C** is incorrect because the tag for hyperlink is <a ...>, not <href...>, and the attribute name is <href>, not <a>.

13.  ☑  **C.** This is the HTML tag to use to present a data entry text box that has multiple lines. The number of lines is specified with the attribute ROWS, and the number of characters per line is specified with the attribute COLS. During data entry, the user can simply press ENTER to go to the next line.
⊠  **A** is incorrect because the attribute SIZE specifies the length in characters of the text box on the form. If SIZE is set to 255, the text box is 255 characters long and will certainly exceed the normal width of the browser screen (or the container frame), and the user has to scroll left and right to see all the text. Besides, it is not possible to break the comment text into small paragraphs. **B** is incorrect because there are no such attributes as COLS and ROWS for the tag <input>. **D** is incorrect because there is no attribute PARAGRAPH for the tag <textarea>.

14.  ☑  **C.** Frames are like subwindows inside the browser window. This means that each frame can host a specific HTML document so that the user can scroll the document in one frame without changing the documents in other frames.
⊠  **A** is incorrect. We can use frame in HTML to achieve this design. **B** is incorrect because this is not a realistic approach. A new window has its own title bar on top and it will require considerable programming effort to synchronize the two windows, especially to keep the new window on top of the report page. **D** is incorrect. We can use frames in HTML to achieve this design.

15.  ☑  **B, D.** The structure of an HTML document is important for maintainability and cross-browser compatibility. Some browsers are more forgiving than others in regard to document structure. So, we should add all missing tags such as <html>, <header>, <body> and corresponding end tags even if they are not required and put them in order (<HTML>, <HEAD>, <BODY>,<FORM>).

☒ **A** is incorrect. Not all HTML elements need ID for programmatic access and there is no requirement at this point for this. **C** is incorrect because although paragraph tags should also be used where appropriate, it is not required here after the <title> section.

16. ☑ **A, B, C.** An HTML 4.0 document is composed of three parts: A line containing HTML version information; a declarative header section (delimited by the HEAD element); a body, which contains the document's actual content. The body may be implemented by the BODY element or the FRAMESET element. In addition, it is also good practice to include the <HTML> tag (and corresponding </HTML> end tag) to delimit the document.
☒ **D** is incorrect. Not all HTML pages are data entry forms and therefore do not need the <FORM> tag.

17. ☑ **C.** This code is well structured (notice the start-tag, end-tag pairs) and produces the expected result.
☒ **A** is incorrect because the correct value of the attribute ALIGN of the tag <H1>, <H2> is "center," not "middle." **B** is incorrect because the order of the header tags <H1>, <H2>, <H3> is wrong. **D** is incorrect because the "line break" tag <br> will cause an additional line break. The end tag </h3> already signals the start of a new paragraph, so in this case we have an extra blank line between the header "4$^{th}$ Quarter 1999" and the last line.

18. ☑ **C.** The attribute WIDTH with a value "100%" will make the table adjust automatically to the container width; in this case, the browser screen.
☒ **A** is incorrect. We can use the attribute WIDTH of the tag <table> as described above. **B** is incorrect. There is no such attribute (resize). **D** is incorrect because the attribute WIDTH with a value of "100%" will make the cell adjust to its content. What we want here is the table to adjust to the width of the browser screen.

19. ☑ **A, B.** The type TEXT is the default value for the attribute TYPE in the <input> tag, so the two code samples give the same expected result.
☒ **C** is incorrect. The end tag </select> as well as the line break <br> is missing; this will give unexpected results depending on the browser. **D** is incorrect. The tag <input type="submit"…> must be inside a <form> and </form> section.

20. ☑ **D.** We are having a cross-browser compatibility issue. The <MARQUEE> tag is specific to Internet Explorer 3, whereas the <LAYER> tag is specific to Netscape 3. A, B and C can be implemented, so the solution would be to have two versions: one for Netscape 3 and later using <LAYER>, and one for Internet Explorer 3 and later using <MARQUEE>. The <MARQUEE> tag represents the simplest implementation since it does not involve any scripting with Dynamic HTML. Note that users who do not use Netscape or Internet Explorer will be left out, but it seems that the company wants to exploit advanced features of new browsers and offer the customers a more visually pleasing Web site, so these users should be invited to upgrade.
☒ **A and B** are incorrect because they use the <LAYER> tag, which is Netscape 3 specific. Users with Internet Explorer will not see the marquee correctly. **C** is incorrect because it uses the <MARQUEE> tag, which is Internet Explorer 3 specific. Users with Netscape will not see the marquee correctly.

21. ☑ **C.** Among all the techniques proposed, this is the only one that is correct. Server-side scripting like Active Server Pages, Common Gateway Interface (CGI), etc., can get data from a database and build the HTML page before returning it to the browser for display.
☒ **A** is incorrect because although the attributes DATASRC and DATAFLD are used to bind data to a data source, this technique requires Internet Explorer 4.0 or later and will cause problems with other browsers. **B** is incorrect because there are no such attributes. **D** is incorrect because Dynamic HTML and JavaScript can only affect the page; they cannot get the data from the server. (Remote Scripting technologies exist but they are not cross-browser compatible and they are not mentioned here.)

**22.** ☑ **D.** Both client-side image map and server-side image map give the same results. The main difference is that with server-side image map, the coordinates are transmitted to the server and processed based on an image map stored on the server.

☒ **A** is incorrect. Although this can work, it is more complicated than necessary. Most browsers support client-side image map, and server-side image map also is simple and gives the expected result. **B** and **C** are incorrect because either one can be used.

**23.** ☑ **B, C, D.** The page as it is coded may work well with some browsers, but for compatibility purposes, we should adhere to the HTML standard for well-formed document. The <title> section must be inside the <head> section, and the <head> section must be placed before the <body> section in the flow of the HTML document.

☒ **A** is incorrect. Although the page may work with some browsers, we should adhere to the HTML standard for well-formed document.

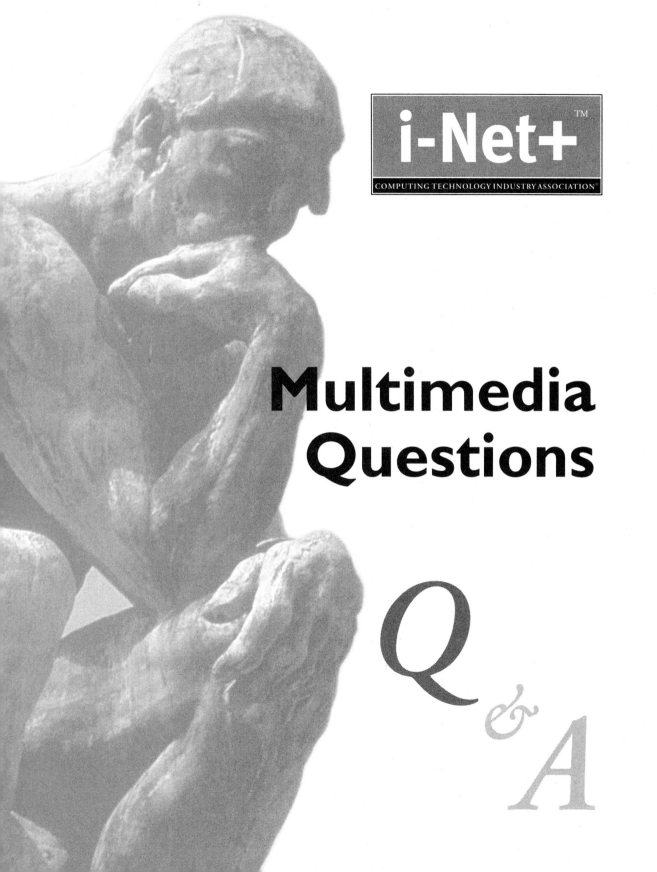

# i-Net+™

COMPUTING TECHNOLOGY INDUSTRY ASSOCIATION®

# Multimedia Questions

Q & A

# Multimedia

1. You have just found a Web site with an icon for an executable file. When you double-click on the icon, an animation runs in a separate window. What type of browser software is being used?

   A. Plug-in
   B. Helper
   C. Extension
   D. There is not enough information to answer.

2. A real estate agency has asked for your help in designing their Web site. They would like users to be able to download files of the houses for sale. When users execute these files, they will see a three-dimensional (3D) graphical representation of the house, and by clicking the proper buttons, they will be able to "walk" through the house and view the rooms from different angles. Which program can you use to create these files?

   A. QTVR
   B. Flash
   C. RealPlayer
   D. Windows Media Player

3. You have decided to create vector graphics on a Web page. Which of the following file formats can you use?

   A. GIF
   B. Flash
   C. JPEG
   D. PDF

4. A friend has told you about an interactive game he has been playing on an Internet Web site. You plan to visit the Web site and see the game for yourself. Of the following, which plug-in will your browser most likely need?

    A. QuickTime

    B. Flash

    C. Shockwave

    D. RealPlayer

**5.** Employees in your company want to be able to get news, sports, and entertainment information over the Internet. They also want to be able to view televised conferences with a branch in another area. Which program should you recommend?

    A. Flash

    B. Shockwave

    C. RealPlayer

    D. MP3

**6.** You are using HTML to create your own Web page. You have just downloaded a .gif file to use in the page. What can you tell about this file before you even open it?

    A. Users visiting your Web site will need to use the Shockwave plug-in to view it.

    B. The file will run streaming animation.

    C. The file contains a bitmapped graphic.

    D. You will need to download a Flash plug-in to incorporate the .gif file into your Web page.

**7.** You are planning to send some graphics to a colleague as an e-mail attachment. Your first priority is the clarity of the image, but you would also like to compress the image. Which file type should you use?

    A. GIF

    B. TIFF

    C. BMP

    D. MPEG

**8.** When you visit a particular Web site, you see an animated graphic of a pair of feet tap dancing. The animation file is named dancefeet.gif. Which plug-in is your browser most likely using to run the animation?

A. Shockwave

B. Flash

C. GIF

D. None of the above

**9.** A streaming animation on a Web site uses bitmapped graphics and appears to fade into view when the Web page first loads. Which of the following file types is this animation?

A. BMP

B. GIF

C. JPEG

D. PNG

**10.** You are considering the use of JPEG graphics in your Web page. Which of the following will these files not be capable of?

A. Slowly fading into view rather than loading from the top down

B. Supporting 32-bit color

C. Animation

D. Compression

**11.** When you visit a particular Internet Web site, you see a picture slowly fade into view. The image is gradually improved until it is fully defined. The filename of the picture is picture.jpg. What do you know about this file?

A. It is a vector graphic.

B. It is a form of streaming media.

C. It is an interlaced JPEG.

D. It can support lossy compression.

**12.** You are creating a Web page that will have interlaced animations. You want to use raster graphics that use lossless compression and allow you to control their opacity. A colleague tells you to avoid using PNG files. Why?

A. PNG images cannot be interlaced.

B. PNG images cannot be animated.

C. PNG files use lossy compression.

D. You cannot control the opacity of a PNG image.

**13.** A client has asked you to design a Web site that will contain many pictures of the items they sell. Assuming that each file type is supported by the Web browser, should you consider using BMP or GIF files?

A. Use BMPs because GIFs are not supported by older browsers.

B. Use GIFs because BMPs can cause the Web site to load slowly.

C. Use BMPs because GIFs require a browser plug-in.

D. Use BMPs because GIFs can lose data during compression.

**14.** A large international company uses the Internet to distribute documents to its many branches. However, the branches do not all use the same word processor. The company is concerned that some files may be altered when users are viewing them in a program other than the one in which the file was created. Which file type should you suggest they use?

A. PostScript

B. PDF

C. RTF

D. None of the above

**15.** You are using a particular word processor to create an important document. However, the person you are e-mailing the document to uses a word processor that is not compatible with yours. What should you do to ensure the recipient can open and read the content of the document in his word processor?

A. Nothing—the recipient's e-mail program will convert the document.
B. Save the document as a PDF file.
C. Nothing—the recipient's Web browser will convert the document.
D. Save the document as an RTF file.

**16.** A particular printer uses a language that treats images and fonts as geometrical objects. Before a document is printed, the printer's interpreter translates it into this special language, which is now the standard for desktop publishing. What is this language called?

A. PDF
B. RTF
C. PostScript
D. BinHex

**17.** Documents can be translated into the PostScript language for improved resolution. Which of the following uses PostScript?

A. Word processors
B. Printers
C. E-mail programs
D. Internet browsers

**18.** The PostScript language contains commands that will print a document with high resolution and object-oriented graphics and fonts. How can you see what the document will look like once it has been converted to PostScript?

A. Open the PostScript file by double-clicking on it.
B. Open the associated EPS file.
C. Open the PostScript file in a word processor.
D. None of the above.

**19.** You are using a Windows 98 computer to access the Internet. You find a Web site with the file movie.mov, which displays a video clip that runs once. Your browser has no additional plug-ins. Of the following, which application is running the movie?

A. Windows 98 media player

B. QuickTime movie player

C. The browser

D. None of the above

**20.** A colleague has just created an animation for your company's Web site. The animation has been compressed so that only the "moving" parts are saved. Which of the following types of files could this animation be?

A. GIF89a

B. PNG

C. MPEG-1

D. JPEG

**21.** You have just installed Windows 95 on a computer. Which of the following file types will you be able to run without installing additional software?

A. MPEG

B. MP3

C. AVI

D. MOV

**22.** A computer uses BinHex to convert messages between computers using different operating systems. Which file formats are being encoded and decoded by BinHex?

A. MOV and AVI

B. RTF and ASCII

C. ASCII and binary

D. PDF and RTF

**23.** When you visit a Web site, a video clip automatically loads and begins to play. What is the name for this type of media?

A. Active

B. Streaming

C. MOV

D. Looping

**24.** You find a Web site that contains a nonstreaming video file. What advantage does this file have over a streaming file?

A. It can be downloaded.

B. It will play only once, so it won't slow the loading of the Web page.

C. It will fade in gradually, allowing you to see the image before it has finished loading.

D. It is capable of greater compression than streaming media.

**25.** You want to include a video in your Web page. However, instead of the video playing by itself, you want users to be able to play and stop the video within the browser. Which HTML tag should you use?

A. IMG DYNSRC

B. EMBED

C. Either of the above

D. None of the above

**26.** You are helping a friend build a Web page in HTML. He is unable to make an animation run on the page, even though it will run in a separate program. He shows you the following code. Assume the browser has the proper plug-ins and that all files are in the proper location. What is wrong?

```
<HTML>
<BODY BACKGROUND="BACKGROUND.GIF">
<IMG SRC="MOVIE.MOV">
</BODY>
```

A. The background code is in the wrong place, causing the rest of the code to be ignored.

B. HTML files cannot support MOV files.

C. The wrong tag is being used with the MOV file.

D. The filename MOVIE.MOV shouldn't have quotes around it.

**27.** A Web page has the following HTML source code. Which of the following will this Web page include?

```
<HTML>
<BODY>
<img src="picture.gif">
<img dynsrc="movie.mov">
<background="background.gif">
</BODY>
```

A. The page will show the picture and the movie, but not the background.

B. The page will show the background and the movie, but not the picture.

C. The page will show the picture and background, but not the movie.

D. The page will show the picture, background, and movie.

**28.** You have just created a Web site for a company that sells products online. Which of the following should you do before you post the Web site to the Internet?

A. Perform load testing on the site to ensure the database is properly maintaining customer records.

B. Perform testing at different speeds to ensure the hot links work properly.

C. Perform testing on different browsers to ensure the Web page maintains its original look.

D. All of the above.

**29.** A Web site includes a hyperlink to the URL  http://www.site.com. However, the URL has now changed to  http://www.newsite.com. What will happen when a user clicks on the hyperlink?

A. The browser will open www.site.com and display a blank page.

B. The browser will report a URL error.

C. The browser will automatically search for the new URL and open it.

D. The new URL's server will intercept the request and redirect the browser.

**30.** You have just created a Web site in HTML and checked to make sure the links work within your browser. Why should you also test the Web site on other browsers?

A. Because different browsers can interpret HTML commands differently.

B. You don't need to—HTML is universally understood by browsers.

C. Because most browsers do not use HTML.

D. You don't need to—the browser's plug-ins will ensure the links work properly.

**31.** You have just created an e-commerce site, through which you plan to offer online shopping to your customers. You have already ensured the Web site works with several types of browsers, and you have checked the hot links and done load testing. Which of the following should you do next?

A. Test the site's e-mail accounts to ensure they work properly.

B. Enter mock orders to ensure they are processed properly.

C. Use software that determines the site's ability to handle multiple concurrent users.

D. All of the above.

**32.** You have just finished creating a Web site, and before posting it to the Internet, you decide to perform some load testing to ensure the site can handle multiple concurrent users. Which of the following is the best method for load testing?

A. Use load testing software.

B. Test the site yourself before you post the Web site to the Internet.

C. Have two people simultaneously access the site and measure the performance of the site.

D. There is no such thing as "load testing."

**33.** You have just created a Web site, but you're not sure all users will be able to view all of the site's components. Which of the following can you do to ensure these users can still benefit from your Web site?

A. Create two versions of the Web site: one for newer browsers and one for older browsers.

B. Ensure all links are entered in the same case (upper or lower) as the destination address.

C. Use the ALT= command in your HTML document.

D. All of the above.

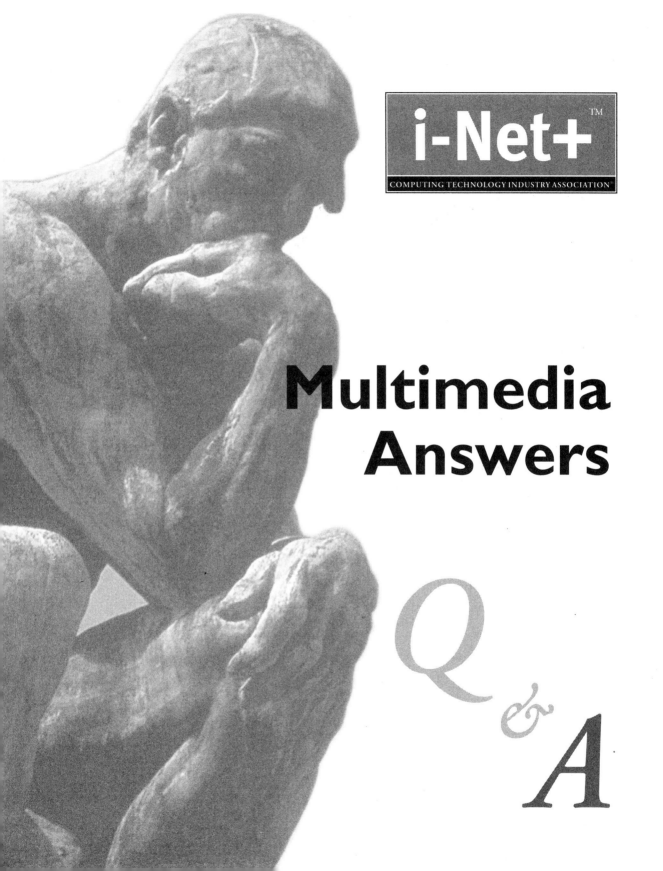

# Multimedia

1. ☑  **B. Helper.** Helper programs work outside of the browser to run executable files. They are an older type of software, but are still used today.
☒  **A** and **C** are incorrect because these are both terms for the same thing. Plug-in, or extension software, allows an executable file to be run in the browser window itself. These programs are integrated into the browser, so they do not run separately. **D** is incorrect because it states there is not enough information to answer the question. This is untrue since "Helper" and only helper fits the description given.

2. ☑  **A. QTVR.** The QuickTime Virtual Reality program compiles different angles of the same object into a 3D image. Users can view the object from different angles, and get the impression that they are moving around or through the object.
☒  **B** is incorrect because this is a plug-in used to run files with animation, video, and audio, but does not support 3D rendering. **C** and **D** are both incorrect because these plug-ins support live or stored video and audio, but will not render multiple images into a single 3D image.

3. ☑  **B. Flash.** Flash files contain vector graphics, which are images created using a series of lines rather than dots. Vector graphics can be resized without a loss of resolution, and they support better overall resolution than their bitmapped counterparts.
☒  **A** and **C** are incorrect because these are both types of bitmapped image formats. Bitmapped images are made up of a series of independent dots on the screen. They are generally unaffected by increased monitor resolution, and appear grainy when enlarged. **D** is incorrect because this is a text file format, not a graphic file format.

4. ☑  **C. Shockwave.** This plug-in allows users to view a Web site and interact with games or other Internet files. Users actually play the game directly on the Web site, but must have the Shockwave plug-in to access the game.

☒  **A** is incorrect. This plug-in allows users to run stand-alone animations, video, and audio, but does not support online user interaction. **B** is also incorrect because although it does support some forms of user interaction, it is not the most likely choice. Shockwave is better able to process complex user input, such as in an interactive game. **D** is incorrect because this file type supports live audio and video, such as teleconferencing, but is not interactive.

5. ☑  **C. RealPlayer.** This media format is designed to deliver streaming, real-time audio and video over the Internet. It is ideal for viewing live or previous television broadcasts. RealPlayer also provides users with "channels" for up-to-date news, sports, and entertainment information.
☒  **A** and **B** are incorrect because these programs are designed to display still or animated graphics. They do not offer channels for news or other media broadcasts. **D** is incorrect because this is an audio file format. MP3 files do not support video content of any type.

6. ☑  **C. The file contains a bitmapped graphic.** GIF files (GIF87a and GIF89a) use a method of displaying images as a series of dots. A disadvantage of bitmapped images is that they can appear grainy when enlarged. An advantage to these images is that they are very popular, and are supported by almost every Web browser.
☒  **A** is incorrect because it states that users will have to have the Shockwave plug-in in order to view the .gif file on your Web page. Although Shockwave will display GIF files, it is not necessary, since the browser itself will display the GIF file. The Shockwave plug-in is used for viewing special interactive graphic animations. **B** is incorrect because there is not enough information to say this for sure. GIF89a files are capable of displaying streaming animation, but do not always. GIF87a files cannot display animations at all. Both types of files have the .gif extension. **D** is incorrect. Again, the browser itself will display the GIF file, so there is no need to use a separate plug-in.

7. ☑  **A. You should use GIF files.** GIF files use lossless compression, meaning that the image's quality is not sacrificed in order to compress

the file. Although GIFs do not offer the greatest compression ratio, the first priority here is image quality.

☒   B and C are incorrect because they do not use compression. Although the quality of BMP images is equal to that of GIF files, they do not satisfy the compression requirement. The quality of TIFF files is not as good as that offered by GIF files. D is incorrect because this type of file uses lossy compression, in which redundant parts of the image are sacrificed in order to compress the file. This can result in a loss of image clarity. MPEG files are capable of a much greater compression ratio than GIF files, but the image quality is not as good as GIFs after compression. The first priority is quality, and the second priority is compression.

8. ☑   D. None of the above. It is most likely that the browser itself is running the animation. Almost all Web browsers support the GIF file format, so no additional plug-in is required.

☒   A and B are incorrect because although they both support animation, they are not required in this case. C is incorrect because GIF files do not require a special GIF plug-in. Again, the browser itself is able to display GIF animations, and there is no program called a GIF plug-in.

9. ☑   B. GIF. This is the only file type listed that has all of the characteristics mentioned. GIF files can be used for stationary or animated bitmapped graphics. GIF files support streaming, which means the animation will run directly on the Web site. This means that users don't have to download the file in order to run it—it loads and runs automatically within the Web page. GIF files can also be interlaced, meaning they appear gradually, sharpening in image as they load. This is the opposite of noninterlaced GIFs, which are loaded from the top down.

☒   A is incorrect because although BMP files are bitmapped, they cannot be animated (so they cannot support streaming). BMP files are always noninterlaced, so the image appears in full clarity from the top down, not gradually throughout the entire image like interlaced images do. C is incorrect because although these are bitmapped images, JPEG does not support animation or streaming. However, JPEG files can be configured to gradually fade in (progressive JPEG). **D** is incorrect because although this file type is bitmapped and supports interlacing, it does not support animation or streaming.

**10.** ☑ **C.** JPEG graphics are not capable of animation. JPEGs offer photo-like images. Each file holds only one image, so you cannot create the illusion of animation by running a series of slightly different images, like you can with GIF89a files.

☒ **A** is incorrect because it states that the JPEG files will not be able to slowly fade into view. This is untrue because that is exactly what progressive JPEG files do. Rather than load with full clarity one line at a time, progressive JPEGs load colors over the whole area of the object. With each pass, the object becomes clearer and more defined until full clarity is achieved. This is similar to the action of interlaced GIFs. **B** is incorrect because this is a characteristic of JPEG files. They support many more colors than GIFs, and this is what makes them ideal for displaying digital or scanned photos. **D** is incorrect because JPEG files are capable of compression. They use lossy compression, meaning that redundant parts of the image are removed. Although this can lead to grainy images at very high compression, it makes JPEG files easy to download because of their reduced size.

**11.** ☑ **D.** It can support lossy compression. The .jpg extension identifies this file as a JPEG, and this is the only answer given that represents a characteristic of JPEG files. Lossy compression is a method of saving only the necessary parts of an image, and removing the redundant parts. An advantage to this is that JPEG files can be made very small for quick downloading. However, the more a JPEG file is compressed, the more parts of the image are left out, which can result in a grainy, less-defined picture.

☒ **A** is incorrect. Remember, .jpg indicates a JPEG file. All JPEG files are raster, or bitmapped images, not vector images. Bitmapped images use pixel color alterations to create an image. Vector images use lines and geometrical formulas to create images. **B** is incorrect. Streaming media refers to video, animation, or sound clips that can be run directly from the Web site on which they are located; there is no need to download first. JPEG files include still photos and graphics only. They are not capable of animation, or any other type of executable media; therefore, they do not support streaming. **C** is incorrect. Although the fading-in action of this JPEG is similar to the action of an interlaced GIF, it is known as a *progressive* JPEG, not an interlaced JPEG.

12. ☑   **B.** You cannot use PNG files because PNG images cannot be animated. Unlike GIF files, which can contain several images, PNG files can contain only one image. This precludes the rapid display of slightly different images to create the illusion of movement.
    ☒   **A** is incorrect because PNG files do support interlacing. **C** is incorrect because they use lossless compression. This means that they cannot be compressed as much as lossy files can, but it also means you won't sacrifice image quality when the image is compressed. **D** is incorrect because opacity control is a feature of PNG files. Opacity is the transparency of an image. You can choose to make a color on the PNG image completely transparent, or you can configure it to different degrees of transparency or opacity.

13. ☑   **B.** Use GIFs because BMPs can cause the Web site to load slowly. GIF files are capable of compression, but BMP files are not. Therefore, the same image can be twice as large as a BMP as it would be as a GIF. Larger images load into the browser more slowly, and take longer to download.
    ☒   **A** is incorrect because it suggests that GIF files are not supported by older browsers. In fact, GIF is a very common image format that is supported by almost all browsers and graphics programs. **C** is incorrect because it suggests that GIFs require a browser plug-in. This is untrue because almost all browsers support the GIF format, so no external plug-in is required. **D** is incorrect because it states that GIF files can lose data during compression. GIF files use lossless compression, meaning no parts of the image are removed (as in lossy compression). A GIF image looks the same with or without compression.

14. ☑   **B.** PDF. The problem here is that a document created on one computer looks different when opened on another computer. This can

occur when someone tries to read a document on a computer that does not support that document's fonts or graphics. In this case, the computer will substitute its own fonts and image formats for the proper one. A PDF file is a graphic image of a document. Because the document is now an image, it is unaffected by the fonts in the reader's computer, and will look the same on any computer that opens it. PDF files must be created and opened using Adobe Acrobat software.

☒    **A** is incorrect because this is a formatting language used to translate screen images into printed images. PostScript uses scalable fonts and vector graphics to create printouts. **C** is incorrect because this is a plain text file format that can be interpreted by many different programs, including word processors and HTML editors. The look of an RTF file depends on the program being used to view it. This is exactly the situation the company in this scenario is trying to avoid—they want everyone to view files in exactly the same way. **D** is incorrect because it states that no answer given is correct.

**15.** ☑    **D.** Save the document as an RTF file. RTF files contain commands about the layout and fonts used in a document. The commands appear in such a way that they are interpreted by whichever program is being used to open the document. This allows files to be opened and formatted by programs that are incompatible with the program used to create the document. However, the document may have a slightly different layout and use different fonts than the original.

☒    **A** and **C** are both incorrect because they suggest you should do nothing because the e-mail or browser program will automatically convert the document. This is incorrect because although they are capable of downloading different file types, neither of these programs can convert or alter the contents of a document. **B** is incorrect because it suggests sending a PDF file. Although this will allow the reader to view your document in its original formatting and layout, it will not allow the reader to open the document in his word processing program. PDF files are opened using a separate reader program. One requirement in this scenario is that the reader will open the file in his word processor (perhaps to do some editing of the document).

**16.** ☑ **C.** PostScript. PostScript is a Page Description Language, developed by Adobe. PostScript translates documents into a series of commands that use geometric images and fonts instead of bitmaps. PostScript is typically used on laser printers to increase a document's resolution, and includes scalable, object-oriented fonts.

☒ **A** is incorrect because this is a file format, also created by Adobe, that converts a document into an image so that it will appear the same to every user who opens it, even on computers that don't support that document's fonts. The Adobe Acrobat reader is used to open PDF files. PDF is a file format used strictly for viewing documents, and is unrelated to the language used by the printer. **B** is incorrect because this is a file format that contains ASCII commands. RTF files allow for file transfer between incompatible applications or operating systems. **D** is incorrect because this is a translation method that converts ASCII to binary and back. It is used when transferring files between different platforms, but does not control the way the file is printed.

**17.** ☑ **B.** Printers use the PostScript language. Documents being sent to PostScript printers are first interpreted into the PostScript language, which applies higher resolution and object-oriented graphics and fonts to the document.

☒ **A** is incorrect because although these documents may eventually be translated into PostScript, the word processor itself does not use this language. It is not until the document is sent to the printer that PostScript is used. **C** and **D** are both incorrect because any documents coming from these sources are not translated into PostScript until they reach the printer.

**18.** ☑ **B.** Open the associated EPS file. The PostScript file itself contains only commands for printing a document. If you viewed a PostScript file, you would see line after line of commands, not the actual image to be printed. Because of this, EPS (Encapsulated PostScript) files are created that display how the printer will interpret the PostScript commands. In essence, EPS provides a sort of "print preview" of the PostScripted document.

☒ **A** and **C** are both incorrect because they suggest opening the PostScript file itself to see how the printout will look. However, the PostScript file itself contains only commands, not a representation of the actual document. **D** is incorrect because it is possible to view PostScript documents using EPS.

19. ☑ **A. Windows 98 Media Player.** The Windows 98 Media Player comes with Windows 98 and supports .mov, .avi, midi, and .wav files. *Note: The Windows 98 ActiveMovie application will also run these files.*

☒ **B** is incorrect because although this program will run .mov files, it is a separate plug-in program. In this scenario, there are no additional browser plug-ins. **C** is incorrect because the browser itself cannot interpret .mov files; it requires the aid of an external plug-in or application, such as Windows Media Player or QuickTime. **D** is incorrect because it states that no answer given is correct.

20. ☑ **C. MPEG-1.** MPEG files are capable of supporting video, audio, and graphic animation. However, MPEGs use lossy compression, so redundant parts of the file are omitted. Any part of the animation that does not change from one image to the next is not saved with the rest of the file.

☒ **A** is incorrect because although this file type supports animation, it uses lossless compression, meaning that no parts of the file are left out when it is compressed. **B** is incorrect because this file type does not support animation or lossy compression. **D** is incorrect because although this file type supports lossy compression, it is not capable of displaying animation.

21. ☑ **C. AVI.** The AVI format is supported by Windows 95 itself, so there is no need to install additional software. AVI videos can be run through Windows Media Player or ActiveMovie.

☒ **A** and **B** are both incorrect because these files require external plug-ins or applications to run on the computer. Both of these file types are part of the MPEG family, which is not supported intrinsically by Windows. **D** is incorrect because a Windows 95 machine requires a separate application to support this file type (typically QuickTime). However, Windows 98 and Windows 2000 support MOV files through the Windows Media Player.

22. ☑ **C.** ASCII and binary. BinHex is an encoding and decoding method that enables computers using different software to access the same data. Different programs (e-mail, applications, operating systems) use dissimilar binary coding. However, most programs recognize ASCII coding. When BinHex is used, the binary code of a file is converted to ASCII. The computer receiving the file uses BinHex to convert ASCII into the appropriate binary code for the host application.
    ☒ **A, B,** and **C** are incorrect because BinHex works strictly at the ASCII and binary coding level. Although the file being encoded may be an image or a video or audio clip, BinHex is not sophisticated enough to translate between the file types in these three answers.

23. ☑ **B.** Streaming. Streaming media includes movies, audio files, or animations that run within the browser while the Web page is loaded. There are many different file formats that can be streamed, including GIF animations, MOV, AVI, and Shockwave.
    ☒ **A** is incorrect because this is not a valid file type name. **C** is incorrect because although MOV files can be streaming, not all streaming files are MOV files. **D** is incorrect. When a file is set to loop, it is set to play over a specified (or infinite) number of times. However, not all streaming media is looped, and the term "looping" is not a valid file type; rather, it is a file attribute.

24. ☑ **A.** The streaming file can be downloaded. Nonstreaming media does not run within the browser when you are online. In order to run the file you must download it, then run it within a separate application. The advantage to this is that you can use the file within other applications, and you can run it whenever you want to, without having to go online to do so. Streaming files run directly from the Web site, so they cannot be downloaded.
    ☒ **B** is incorrect because nonstreaming media does not run within the browser when you are online. Only streaming media is capable of this. The number of times a video clip is repeated online is a characteristic of streaming media called "looping." **C** is incorrect because this is a method of image loading called "interlacing" (called "progressive" in JPEG files). The term "streaming" refers to the ability of a file to run while you are visiting that particular Web

site. It is unrelated to whether an image gradually fades in or loads one line at a time. **D** is incorrect because it refers to the amount of compression of nonstreaming media. Streaming files are simply files that have the "streaming" option enabled. Their degree of compression depends on the file type itself (e.g., MOV, AVI, GIF), rather than the presence or absence of the streaming attribute.

**25.** ☑  **C.** Either of the above. You can choose to run a video by itself, or you can include VCR-like controls that allow the user to start and stop the video. When you use the embed tag, the controls appear automatically (the embed tag can only be used by Internet Explorer). When the IMG DYNSRC tag is used, the video will run by itself by default. However, by adding the code "CONTROLS" to the tag, you can add the same type of start and stop functions as in the embed tag.

☒  **A** and **B** are incorrect because the most appropriate answer is C, which includes A and B. **D** is incorrect because it states that no answer given is correct.

**26.** ☑  **C.** The wrong tag is being used with the MOV file. The <IMG SRC=> tag can only be used to display still images and GIF animations. Movies, videos, and audio clips must be associated with the <IMG DYNSRC=> tag.

☒  **A** is incorrect because it states that a problem with the background code is causing the problem with the movie. Although one line of code can interfere with the function of the code following it, this isn't true in this case. The background tag is in the proper syntax and location, so it cannot be at fault. **B** is incorrect. HTML can be used to incorporate all of the files mentioned in this section in your Web page, including GIF, JPEG, PNG, BMP, MOV, AVI, MP3, QuickTime, RealPlayer, and many more. **D** is incorrect because it suggests the syntax of the movie code is incorrect because the quotes shouldn't be there. This is untrue because the quotes are required, but the type of tag itself, <IMG SRC>, is incorrect.

**27.** ☑  **A.** The page will show the picture and the movie, but not the background. The background code must appear within the <BODY> tag at the top of the file. The syntax for the picture and movie files is correct and they will be displayed.

☒    **B** is incorrect because it states the background will be displayed. The background code must appear within the BODY tag to work. It cannot be used as a separate tag. This answer is also incorrect because it states the picture will not be displayed. There is nothing wrong with the code for the picture, so it will be displayed. **C** is incorrect because it states the movie will not be displayed. This is incorrect since the movie code is correct. **D** is incorrect because it suggests all three elements will appear in the Web page. However, because of the incorrect coding of the background element, it will not appear on the page.

28.  ☑    **C.** Perform testing on different browsers to ensure the Web page maintains its original look. Different browsers can interpret HTML code differently, resulting in layouts, colors, images, or fonts that do not appear as intended. Test the site through the most commonly used browsers to ensure a majority of people will see the Web site properly.

☒    **A** is incorrect. Load testing is performed to ensure the Web site can handle multiple simultaneous users. It is unrelated to the server's ability to properly save customer order information. **B** is also incorrect. When you test the hot links, you ensure that the URLs your links refer to actually exist, and have not been moved. If a link points to the proper URL, the link will work, regardless of the connection speed. Conversely, a link that points to the wrong URL will not work properly at any speed. **D** is incorrect because **C** is the only correct answer here.

29.  ☑    **B.** The browser will report a URL error. Anytime a browser is instructed to open a Web page that doesn't exist, it will report this type of error, regardless of whether the URL has been mistyped, has moved, or never existed.

☒    **A** is incorrect. The browser cannot open a page that doesn't exist anymore. In fact, the browser cannot distinguish between pages that have moved and pages that never existed. **C** is incorrect. Some people will leave an old URL on the Internet with a link that points to the new address. In this case, you simply click on the link to visit the new URL. However, if a URL is taken off the Internet entirely, the browser has no resources to find where it moved. There is no tracing feature on the Internet that automatically points browsers in the right direction. **D** is also incorrect because it states that the server for the new URL will intercept the request. This would be an impossible task, since the server would have to poll every one of the thousands or millions of people online, just waiting for someone to try to visit the old URL.

**30.** ☑ **A.** Because different browsers can interpret HTML commands differently. HTML is a series of commands that are run by the browser when a Web page is viewed. Browsers can differ in their interpretation of these commands so that text and links that should appear one way actually show up or behave in a different way. You should test your Web page on two or three of the most commonly used browsers to ensure that a majority of people can view and use the page properly.

☒ **B** is incorrect because it states that you don't need to test the Web page. This is incorrect because HTML is not universally understood by browsers. Although most browsers can read HTML, they do not all translate its commands in the same way. **C** is incorrect because it states that most browsers do not use HTML. This is incorrect because although they may interpret its commands differently, almost all browsers can read HTML. **D** is incorrect because it suggests you don't need to continue testing the browser. The browser itself is responsible for interpreting HTML commands. There are no plug-ins that help the browser read HTML and ensure links work properly.

**31.** ☑ **B.** Enter mock orders to ensure they are processed properly. This will allow you to see if the site's database is properly maintaining and processing records. It will also allow you to ensure that payments are properly processed and received.

☒ **A** is incorrect. A Web site does not have e-mail accounts. Although the site may contain links to e-mail addresses, e-mail runs in a separate e-mail program, not within the Web site itself. **C** is incorrect. This is known as "load testing," which, as indicated in this scenario, has already been done. D is incorrect because it states that all of the answers given are correct.

**32.** ☑ **A.** Use load testing software. This can usually provide you with information about the probable problems with the Web site, how fast your pages will load, and can track the number and time of accesses to your site. Some load testing software will simulate multiple user accesses and report the results to you.

☒ **B** is incorrect because load testing deals with the ability of the server's hardware to handle multiple requests at once. By using the site yourself before you post it to the Internet, you will not be able to determine its ability to handle requests from more than one user. **C** is also incorrect because two simultaneous accesses are not a realistic measure of real online activity. When performing load testing, you should be aware of how your Web site performs with 20, 30, or even 100 simultaneous accesses. **D** is incorrect because it states that there is no such thing as "load testing." This is untrue, and load testing is actually a very important part of testing Web sites that you expect to generate lots of traffic.

**33.** ☑ **D.** All of the above. There are many reasons why some users may not be able to properly view your Web site. Your site may contain graphics or streaming media that causes the site to load very slowly (or not at all) on older browsers. You can avoid this by creating a plain index page that gives users a choice between a low-end main page (without all the bells and whistles) or the high-end version of the main page (with the works). You should also make sure all links are in the same case as the destination. UNIX servers are case sensitive when it comes to linking URLs, so users connecting through a UNIX server may run into links that don't work if you're not careful. Finally, users in high-traffic areas, or those with slow connections, may have to wait a very long time for the graphics on your page to load. If you use the ALT= command in your page, you can make some descriptive text appear in place of the graphic until the image fully loads. This way, users can tell from the description whether to move on or wait until the page is completely loaded.

☒   **A, B,** and **C** are incorrect because although these are important steps, the best answer is **D,** which includes all of the steps listed.

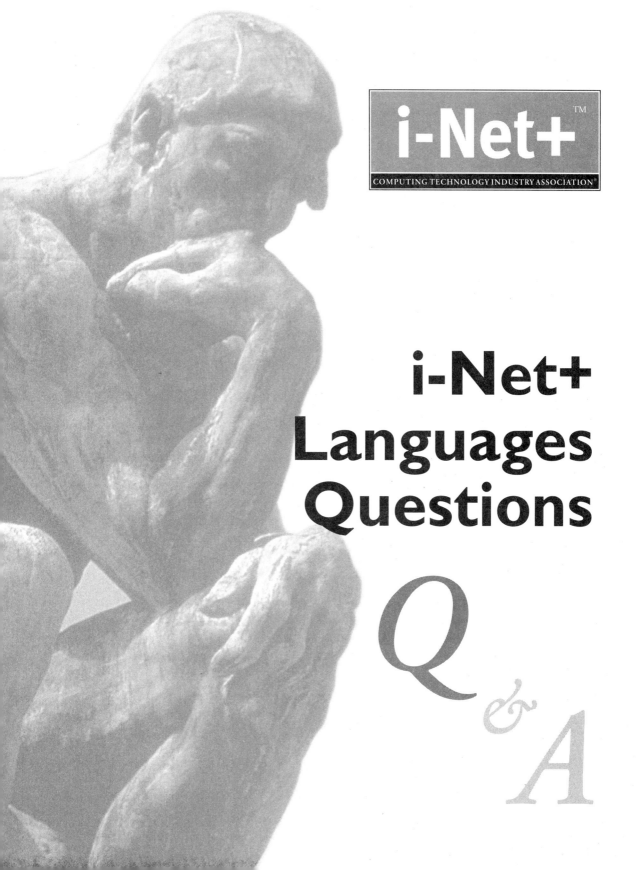

# i-Net+

**COMPUTING TECHNOLOGY INDUSTRY ASSOCIATION**

# i-Net+
# Languages
# Questions

*Q & A*

# i-Net+ Languages

1. What are some of the advantages of using API?

   A. Standardization of commands

   B. Reduces hardware requirements

   C. Eases the usability of your applications

   D. Uses propitiatory commands

2. You are updating a Web site with newer information, and bringing the software and page "up to date." What language can be replaced with DHTML to allow for easier coding?

   A. CGI

   B. Perl

   C. JavaScript

   D. ISAPI

3. What driver is needed to link an NT Web server to an Oracle database running on a UNIX system?

   A. ODBC

   B. JDBC

   C. External NT DB Connector

   D. None needed

4. Which programming language is object-oriented?

   A. Perl

   B. Java

   C. C++

   D. Visual Basic

5. Web sites such as www.snap.com or www.msn.com, that allow you to customize how you wish to view the Web page, use what type of language to code this ability?

A. CGI

B. VRML

C. Perl

D. ASP

**6.** A database that consists of two or more tables used in conjunction with each other would be a _____ .

A. Multitiered application

B. Relational database

C. Nonrelational database

D. Database server

**7.** Java is based on _____ and was created by _____?

A. Visual Basic

B. Microsoft

C. Sun Microsystems

D. C++

**8.** Long before Macromedia's Shockwave, what language could be used to create 3D images?

A. Java

B. C++

C. VRML

D. XML

**9.** You are studying languages to decide what to use for the base coding of a Web page. You come across _____, which states that each object has its own properties and events. Which programming language is this?

A. DHTML

B. Java

C. C++

D. Perl

**10.** The C programming language was developed after and modeled on the B language. What was the main reason for its development?

A. B lacked a compiler.

B. B could not be used on a UNIX system.

C. B didn't offer type checking.

D. B did not allow for looping in the program.

**11.** ECMAScript standards were developed by Microsoft and Netscape and applied to _____?

A. Java

B. Visual Basic

C. JScript

D. XML

**12.** Who is responsible for creating the code standards for the new XML language?

A. IEEE

B. Microsoft

C. World Wide Web Consortium

D. There are no standards; each programmer uses it how he or she wishes.

**13.** You have been hired to redesign a company's Web site. The company uses NT 4.0 and requires its users to use Netscape as their browser. You use VBScript to code your new Web page. After testing the pages at your local office, you load them on the company's Web server. The next day you receive 50+ calls stating that much of the Web page is not viewable. Why?

A. The revision of the server operating system is not compatible with the version of VBScript you used.

B. Users still have the old page in cache. They need to clear their cache to see the new pages correctly.

C. VBScript is not compatible with Netscape.

D. The users need to reboot to get the new pages to come up correctly.

**14.** SELECT * FROM DATABASE_B WHERE NAME = 'JOHNSON' is an example from what language?

A. Java

B. Perl

C. C++

D. SQL

**15.** You have recently taken over the responsibilities of administrating the network. You begin to look around to see what each of the servers hold, so you can better do your job. You come across a database server and find that all the data is stored in separate files according to their database, but within each of the files all the data is lumped together instead of being spread out in tables. What types of databases are these?

A. Relational databases

B. Nonrelational databases

C. Not enough data to determine the type

D. These are not databases

**16.** You are experiencing a problem on your system. You notice that you can run a program for a long time and never run out of memory. However, when you open a document and print it, close that document, open another and print it, and repeat this process several times, you start to run out of memory. You determine that the printing process is eating up the memory, because it is not being released correctly when called. Programs that are called from within another program, loaded into memory, run and then released from memory, are what type of libraries?

A. Static Linking Libraries

B. Procedure Linking Libraries

C. Driver Linking Libraries

D. Dynamic-Link Libraries

**17.** You are developing a Web page and wish to add a scrolling text along the bottom that gives weekly "deals and steals" for your company's products. What language can you write the scrolling text in?

A. Java
B. SQL
C. XML
D. API

**18.** You are programming for many companies. Several of these companies store the customer information and other information in the same manner. Instead of rewriting the same code each time you write a program, you decide to write a module and then call that module inside your code. What language will allow you to do this?

A. JScript
B. HTML
C. XML
D. C++

**19.** While programming in Visual Basic, you cannot access the hardware of the system using just VB code. Within the VB program, you can call _____ to access the systems hardware.

A. CGI
B. DLL
C. API
D. SQL

**20.** Each time _____ is called, it must run a new process. After it finishes its request, it will unload itself from memory.

A. CGI
B. ISAPI
C. VRML
D. Perl

**21.** You are writing a Web page for a new company. Their main requirement is that the page must have a quick response to the user. With a slow response of more than a few seconds, they run the risk of the user leaving their site for another site offering the same products. You decide on a coding using a program that is loaded when the Web server is booted and will remain in memory. Which would you choose?

A. CGI

B. ISAPI

C. C++

D. Java

**22.** What is the one big difference between Java and JavaScript?

A. Java is interpreted.

B. JavaScript is interpreted.

C. JavaScript is compiled.

D. Java is older and slower.

**23.** What programming language can be used on Web pages to greatly increase search programs and allow for more accurate responses to search inquiries?

A. JScript

B. Perl

C. XML

D. VRML

**24.** Which of the following are interpreted languages?

A. Java

B. Perl

C. C++

D. JavaScript

**25.** You want to write a small applet that will be able to run quickly. What would be a good language to write it in?

 A. Java
 B. Visual Basic
 C. C++
 D. JavaScript

**26.** Which languages are considered client-side programming languages?

 A. VBScript
 B. CGI
 C. Java
 D. ASP

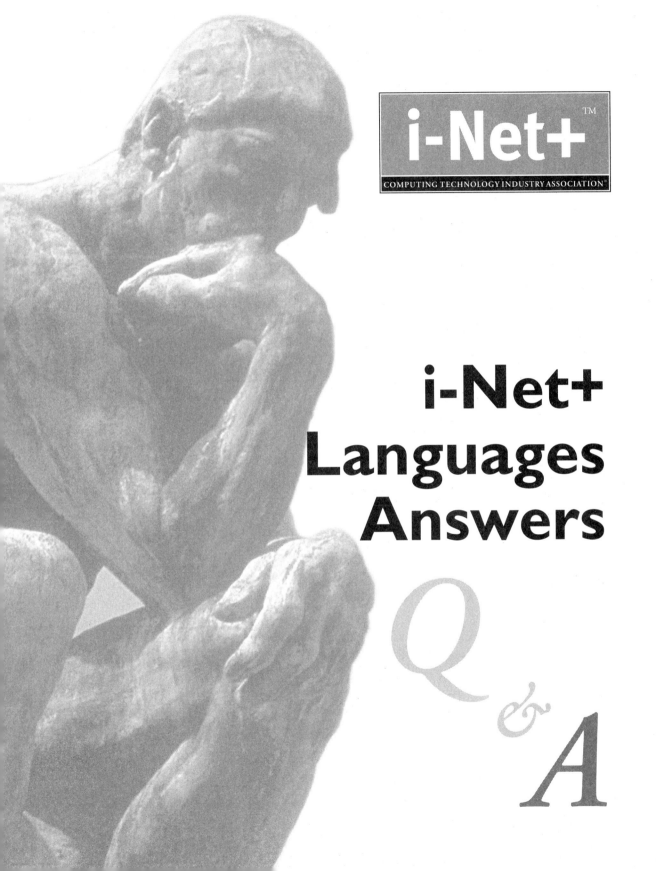

i-Net+
Languages
Answers

*Q & A*

# i-Net+ Languages

1. ☑ **A** and **B**. API offers to the user the standardization of commands; no matter what version or brand of the program language you purchase, the commands are all the same. It has been tested and redesigned numerous times, and a set of standards have been developed for API insuring users that the correct response will be returned to their calls. API has little resource requirements on the system. It uses existing functions imbedded in the operating system so that additional demand on the CPU is not required. Requiring less hardware also means it uses less memory, leaving more memory for other applications to run on.

   ☒ **C** is incorrect. API actually eases the usability of your applications by extending the functionality of existing applications. **D** is incorrect as API uses functions and commands already imbedded in the operating system.

2. ☑ **C**. DHTML has replaced the need for JavaScript. Dynamic HTML has all the functionality of Java and JavaScript, but allows for much easier coding. DHTML can be used to create the scrolling text boxes on a Web page and other "Java only" effects. DHTML does not offer the security that Java does by hiding the code from the end user; DHTML is completely visible just as normal HTML code is.

   ☒ **A**, **B**, and **D** are all incorrect. DHTML is only comparable to Java and JavaScript languages.

3. ☑ **A**. You will need an ODBC (Open DataBase Connectivity layer) driver to link a database on a UNIX system to an NT Web server. ODBC is loaded with the install of NT or any other MS operating system, so in reality nothing needs to be done. When you install the database software, it will add the correct linking information to your ODBC database.

   ☒ **B** is incorrect. JDBC offers developers access to a database. To use JDBC, you must have the Java Developers Kit installed on your system. **C** and **D** are incorrect. There is no such thing as an External NT DB Connector other than ODBC.

**4.** ☑ **B** and **C**. Java and C++ are object-oriented programming languages. They allow programmers to write in a style similar to normal life where each object can interact with another object.

☒ **A** and **D** are incorrect; they are not object-oriented programming languages.

**5.** ☑ **D**. ASP is used to retrieve information from the user and then configure the Web page by data stored in a database for the user. Once users set up a design or view preference, each time they return to the site they will get their personally designed Web page. ASP is similar to CGI, as it runs on the server side, not the client side.

☒ **A** is incorrect as CGI cannot manipulate a page layout per a user's response. **B** is incorrect as VRML is used to display 3D images in a client's browser. **C** is incorrect as Perl is used to search for data in a text document and return information to the user.

**6.** ☑ **B**. This would be a relational database, meaning the data in each table have a relational connection to the data in every other table. This would be a main table with Name, Address, City, and State listed out with another table with just Names, and another with just the Addresses. The other tables have no meaning to each other without the main table tying them together making the relational database.

☒ **A** is incorrect. A multitiered application is one where the user on one system is accessing data on another system such as a database on a database server. **C** is incorrect. A nonrelational database is a database where the data is contained in one large file or database. **D** is also incorrect. A database server is a server usually dedicated solely to housing databases.

**7.** ☑ **C** and **D**. In 1995, Sun Microsystems developed Java based on the C++ programming language.

☒ **A** and **B** are incorrect. Microsoft developed Visual Basic, and neither had anything to do with the development of Java; Microsoft has since developed a Microsoft answer to Java called JScript.

8. ☑ C. VRML was the precursor to Shockwave, and allowed programmers to load a sequence of images into a Web page, and allowed visitors to manipulate the image by rotating, flipping, and zooming the image being displayed. VRML required a VRML plug-in to be installed on the browser at the end-user side of the connection.

   ☒ A, B, and D are incorrect. These are languages used for many great things, but not 3D imaging.

9. ☑ C and D. C++ and Java objects offer their own properties, characteristics, and methods of operation. This is a very welcome idea in that it allows programmers to write better working programs with fewer requirements.

   ☒ A and B are incorrect. They are programming languages but do not offer the features listed above.

10. ☑ C. One of the major problems with B was that it did no type checking, meaning that it did not verify the type of data stored in a variable. You could store the letters A I in an integer variable and the program would crash as the integer is supposed to be a number. C fixed this and many other problems experienced with B.

    ☒ A is incorrect, as B was compiled. B is incorrect as it was originally designed on UNIX. D is incorrect as all programming languages allow for program looping.

11. ☑ C. Netscape and Microsoft jointly developed the standards to which JScript adheres.

    ☒ A is incorrect. Java was written by Sun Microsystems. B is incorrect. Visual Basic was a sole venture by Microsoft. D is incorrect. XML is believed to have been written by Sun Microsystems.

12. ☑ C. The W3C is responsible for creating the standards for XML. These standards will be used so that when a tag is placed in an XML program, it will mean the same in every XML program created—much like HTML tags are today.

☒ **A** is incorrect. IEEE is responsible for creating the standards for cabling and protocols such as IEEE 802.3 Ethernet. **B** is incorrect. Microsoft is a developer, not a standards commission. **D** is incorrect because each language has standards that must be followed to allow for interoperability.

13. ☑ **C.** VBScript was developed by Microsoft in response to Java, and was created for sole use on the Internet Explorer platform. If you as a programmer choose to use it, you need to be aware that Netscape users will be unable to access the information that the VBScript will create.

☒ **A** in incorrect. The revision of server operating system would have no bearing on the Web page language. **B** is incorrect. The calls said that much of the Web page is not viewable; if it was a cache problem, then none of the page would be viewable, or the old page would be displayed. **D** is incorrect. Rebooting would not fix a Web page display problem.

14. ☑ **D.** This example is from a SQL request. The "*" tells the database to select all from database_B when the name identifier is equal to "Johnson." If there were 30 people in the database with the name Johnson, it would return 30 responses.

☒ **A, B,** and **C** are all incorrect. This example would not work under these languages. Each of the above languages has its own coding sequence and call format, but this only matches a SQL request.

15. ☑ **B.** A nonrelational database is where the data is maintained in a large file.

☒ **A** is incorrect. A relational database is where data is separated into tables, with one table making the relationship between the others. **C** is incorrect. The statement was conclusive in determining what type of database this is. **D** is incorrect, as these are databases.

16. ☑ **D.** A DLL, or dynamic-link library, is a library or set of programs that can be called from within another program. Once they are finished, they are released from memory.

☒   **A** is incorrect. Static Linking Libraries are loaded once and remain in memory. **B** and **C** are incorrect, as they are not libraries.

17. ☑   **A.** Java is used to create the applets that would make scrolling text on a Web page easier.
☒   **B** is incorrect. SQL is used as a communication connector between databases. **C** is incorrect, as XML is a new idea for creating a standard tagging to describe data on a Web page for better searching. **D** is also incorrect. APIs are used to carry out low-level services on a system.

18. ☑   **D.** C++ allows a programmer to write or use prewritten modules of code. These modules are lines of codes that are reused many times either in the same program or in different programs. Modules allow the programmer to write the code once, store it in a module, and then call that module to manipulate the code as needed.
☒   **A**, **B**, and **C** are incorrect as they do not allow for modules.

19. ☑   **C.** You can call an API application from within a VB program to access the hardware. This is a common process used in several programming languages that do not have the ability to touch or access a system's hardware.
☒   **A** is incorrect. CGI is a script that runs on a Web server. **B** is incorrect. DLLs are sets of programs that are required for a program to perform a function such as print or scan. **D** is incorrect, as SQL is the connector between databases.

20. ☑   **A.** CGI applications load into memory each time they are called. This can cause a resource problem and become a bottleneck for a Web server if many CGI calls are made.
☒   **B** is incorrect. ISAPI is loaded once and stored in memory. **C** is incorrect, as it is called the first time and stored in memory until the system is rebooted. **D** is also incorrect, as it can be loaded into memory and remain there for future requests. Perl is a good replacement for CGI because it can be loaded permanently in memory so that it does not require the additional time to load the program into memory to return the requested information.

**21.** ☑ **B.** ISAPI applications run very fast, and are a great replacement for CGI applications that must be loaded into memory each time they are run. ISAPI applications are loaded when the Web server software is loaded and can run as part of the HTP application's processes and address space.

☒ **A** is incorrect. CGI is much slower because it requires the application to be loaded each time the program is run. **C** is incorrect. C++ cannot be loaded into memory. **D** is incorrect, as Java is not loaded into permanent memory either.

**22.** ☑ **B.** JavaScript is interpreted where Java is compiled. Being interpreted, it is slower to execute than Java because it has to be interpreted each time it is run.

☒ **A** is incorrect. Java is compiled, not interpreted. **C** is incorrect. JavaScript is interpreted, not compiled. **D** is also incorrect. Java is old, but it is faster than JavaScript.

**23.** ☑ **C.** XML is the eXtended Markup Language. It is a newer programming language that is great because as more and more designers start using it, it will make for a better Web. Data coded in XML can be compared to similar data on other pages coded in XML. For example, when a search is done on the word "Car," the pages that are coded in XML are more accurate when it comes to hits than other pages. Any page with the word "Car" in it will be returned, but you can use XML to describe the data in a page so that it will not be returned via a search unless it is a perfect match. The W3C is developing standards to be used with XML, so that whenever a programmer uses the word "<ISBN>," for example, it would always mean the information following is an book's ISBN number.

☒ **A, B,** and **D** are incorrect. They are used greatly in Web design, but have no way to increase the correct return of data via a search.

**24.** ☑ **B** and **D.** Both Perl and JavaScript are interpreted languages, meaning they are compiled just before execution.

☒ **A** and **C** are incorrect. Both Java and C++ are compiled programs, meaning they are written and compiled, and then executed as an executable program.

**25.** ☑   A. Java is great for writing small applets; it is easy to use, and runs quickly as it is a compiled program.
☒   B is incorrect, as it does not allow for writing applets. It is also an interpreted language, meaning it must be compiled just before execution, thus making it a slower program. C is a great option and runs quickly, but not for applets. D is incorrect. JavaScript runs much slower than Java, as it is an interrupted language like Visual Basic.

**26.** ☑   A and C. Both VBScript and Java are client-side languages, meaning they run on the client side. They require either a plug-in or an add-on to the browser to work correctly.
☒   B and D are incorrect. CGI and ASP are server-side languages, meaning they run on the Web server and have no requirements for the browser.

# Networking and Infrastructure Questions

# Networking and Infrastructure

**1.** You are attempting to reach your company's Web page, www.mycompany.com, and you receive an error stating that the page cannot be found. You attempt to access the Web page again, give it its IP address of 135.33.18.192, and are successful in retrieving the page. You double-check your spelling, attempt the page again, and find that you cannot get to it. What would be your first step in troubleshooting this problem?

  A. Ping the site using PING.
  B. Check the DNS entries to make sure there is an entry for www.mycompany.com and that its IP address is correct.
  C. Assume that the Proxy server is rebooting and check back later.
  D. Telnet to the Web server and reboot it.

**2.** The ISP you are working for needs to apply for a Domain Name before offering services. You fill out the paperwork for your company. What do you enter for the Domain name?

  A. www.myISP.isp
  B. www.myISP.org
  C. www.myISP.net
  D. www.myISP.gov

**3.** You are browsing the Web and click on a link from a Web page and notice that the URL you went to is http://uk.bigsales.com You also noticed that you can just type http://bigsales.com and get to the site; however, the page presented is not the same page. Why is this?

  A. The uk in front of the URL tells the site what type of browser you are running so it can configure the page for best viewing.
  B. The uk in front of the URL means unknown, meaning it can't read your browser type so it is giving you a default page.
  C. The uk in front of the URL indicates that this is the Web page for bigsales.com's United Kingdom's division.
  D. The uk in front of the URL indicates you are at a secured site.

**4.** Top-level domain names such as .com and .org are maintained by 13 systems that are constantly exchanging information to make sure all the data is kept up to date. What are these servers also known as?

A. Root UNIX Systems

B. Root Domain Servers

C. Root WINS Servers

D. Primary Domain Servers

**5.** www.salesdepartment.com represents the address of what?

A. Mail server

B. Web site

C. DNS Server

D. None of the above

**6.** You are studying for a network certification and you come across the following question on the sample test. Of the following, which are considered top-level domains?

A. Store

B. Education

C. Internet Service Provider

D. Military

**7.** We currently know that there are 13 Root DNS servers. Each second-level DNS server is responsible for data for only one domain type. How many different domain types do the second-level DNS servers keep track of?

A. 4

B. 6

C. 8

D. 10

**8.** Each connection in the Internet is considered a hop. What makes up these hops?

A. ATM Switches

B. Routers

C. Repeaters

D. FDDI cabling

9. Connections to the Internet can be made at many different speeds. The speeds can range from 14.4baud (this is about the lowest today) to OC12 levels, and just about anything in between. Connections can be digital or analog. A low-end digital signal would consist of an ISDN B channel and an ISDN D channel. At what speed would you be connecting to the Internet?

A. 56K

B. 64K

C. 128K

D. 1.544Mb

10. A collection of information spanning multiple pages or links made available via HTTP is know as?

A. An FTP Server

B. An Archie Server

C. A Web site

D. A Web page

11. You have been brought in to help clean up a network from top to bottom. This includes removing unneeded wiring, removing users from systems who are no long employed at the company, and cleaning up the DNS and WINS servers. You first decide to tackle the DNS server. You have a list of all the nodes on the network that need to have DNS entries in them. You start looking at the DNS database and come across an MX record for the company you are working for. What is a type MX record?

A. It is a reverse lookup record and points to the IP address of the host.

B. It is used by other name servers on the network to locate it as a name server.

C. It is the mail record for the domain.

D. It is the primary host record for the domain.

12. You are the Web page designer for your company. You created a very detailed Web page with lots of graphics that are both high res and moving. You also have designed the page to play music while the user browses your site. You installed your Web page on a 75mhz Pentium with 32MB of memory; the Pentium is also acting as a backup domain controller (BDC) for your network. Many users have complained that when they connect to your site, some of the pictures are not displayed. You do some checking and determine that the cause of the problem is what?

A. The users are using old browsers and can't display the high-res graphics.

B. The server you are running the Web page on is a slow server and is timing out when it downloads the page to the user's system.

C. The firewall between the system housing the Web page and the user is blocking the pictures.

D. The user's dial-up connection is too slow.

13. When configuring a DNS server for a new domain, what record type should you enter for the primary domain name?

A. A

B. MX

C. PTR

D. CNAME

**14.** You enter the URL http:www.shoestore.com. What is the process that gets the page you requested?

A. The FQDN is sent to the local DNS server. If the local DNS server doesn't know where the shoestore.com domain resides, it will contact the root domain server for location of the .com domain DNS server. The .com domain DNS server will in turn contact the domain server that maintains the shoestore.com domain. That DNS server will return the IP address of www.shoeshoestore.com back up the chain until it reaches your DNS server, which will transmit it to your PC. Then the Web browser will contact the Web site via the TCP/IP address and display the page.

B. The Fully Qualified Domain Name (FQDN) is transmitted on the Web, and the Web site that owns the name will respond with the Web page.

C. The FQDN will be transmitted to your DNS server where it will be translated into the TCP/IP address and then forwarded back to your PC. Your Web browser will then contact the site and display the page.

D. Your PC is aware of the location of the Web page because of a log file being downloaded to your PC each time you connect to your ISP. The browser will look up the FQDN in the log file and contact the Web page.

**15.** The Internet is made of up several different components. What are the components of the Internet?

A. TCP/IP

B. Physical cabling

C. Routers

D. All of the above

**16.** When looking at the infrastructure of the Internet, you notice that the majority of the connections between routers are very high-speed connections. You start reading the specifications of the connection between your company and the Internet and determine that you have an OC12 connection. At what speed are you communicating to the Internet?

A. 1.5MB/second

B. 155MB/second

C. 622MB/second

D. 4.632MB/second

**17.** You notice that after some upgrades to the DNS server over the past weekend, you have not received any e-mail on your e-mail server. This is very unlikely since this server supports over 500 users, and the likelihood of no one receiving e-mail is almost zero. What steps should you take to troubleshoot this?

A. Check the settings on the mail server. It is quite possible that since the DNS server was offline for upgrades, the mail server took itself offline also.

B. There is nothing wrong. Since the upgrade was done over a weekend, most users would not receive e-mail.

C. Check the DNS server to make sure it is up and running. Also, check the entries to make sure there is a PTR record for your site.

D. Check the DNS server to make sure it is up and running. Also, check the entries to make sure there is an MX record for your site.

**18.** You are searching through a log file on your proxy server to find out where your users are browsing, and you notice that several of the requested pages have returned in error. You look closer and determine that the user requesting the pages was not using the correct format or name for the site. Which of the following are correct FQDNs?

A. 123.45.33.23

B. www.ourplace.org

C. mail

D. www.salesdepartment

**19.** You enter www.desktopicons.com in your browser and your system does not find that location. You then ping www.desktopicons.com and, again, nothing. You attempt other sites that you have attached to in the past and are unable to view or ping them. You are able to reach the page you requested when you enter  http://123.45.68.99 in your browser. What is likely the problem?

A. Your WINS server is down.

B. Your connection to the Internet is down.

C. Your PC is not set up with a DNS server address.

D. Your gateway is not functioning.

**20.** When configuring a DNS server for a reverse lookup for your company's payroll system named payroll.carsales.com with an IP address of 226.99.32.58, how would you enter the information?

   A. 226.99.32.58
   B. 32.99.226.payroll
   C. payroll.32.99.226
   D. 32.99.226

# Networking and Infrastructure
# Answers

$Q$ & $A$

# Networking and Infrastructure

1. ☑ **B.** Check the DNS entries to make sure there is an entry for www.mycompany.com and that its IP address is correct by entering www.mycompany.com on the URL line of your browser. The browser sends a request to the DNS server for the IP address associated with www.mycompany.com. If the entry is found, the IP address is sent back and the browser then connects to the page via the IP address. If no IP address is found, you will receive an error when attempting to connect to the page.
   ☒ **A** is incorrect because we have already proven that the site is up and running via PING and that we cannot reach it using the DNS name. PING would either use the DNS server to translate the name if you use the FQDN, or would use the IP address you give it. **C** is incorrect because you are able to reach the site via the IP address, so we know this is not a Proxy server problem. **D** is incorrect because, again, there is no reason to reboot the server because we are able to reach it via the IP address. Therefore, the problem must lie with the DNS server.

2. ☑ **C.** 99% of all ISPs are a .net or network domain.
   ☒ **A** is incorrect because there is no .ISP domain. **B** is for not-for-profit organizations only. **D** is for government facilities only and is not for private or public use.

3. ☑ **C.** The uk in front of the URL indicates that you are attached to a Web page in the United Kingdom. Other country codes include dk for Denmark, ca for Canada, and au for Australia.
   ☒ **A** is incorrect because there is no standard coding for displaying what type of browser you are running. Some sites do not check for the browser type. Others do; however, they do not indicate anything other than you will notice that the page looks different from browser to browser. Some might add a code like IE4 to their URL to indicate Internet Explorer 4.0. **B** is incorrect because, again, most companies don't check, and the ones that do would not code for an unknown browser type; they would take you to a default type unless they can determine your browser. **D** is incorrect because to be at a secured site, you would have an https:// instead of the normal http:// *before* the URL, not as part of the URL.

**4.** ☑  **B.** These systems are called the Root Domain Servers. They maintain all the information for the top-level domains. They propagate the information down to the second-level domain servers, which in turn propagate the information down the branches.

☒  **A, C,** and **D** are invalid choices.

**5.** ☑  **B.** www.salesdepartment.com is the URL for a Web site. The www represents the World Wide Web and indicates that it's a Web site address.

☒  **A** is incorrect because a mail server would not have the prefix www. It would most likely have the system's name as the prefix such as mail1.salesdepartment.com or some other system name to direct packets to the correct location. **C** is incorrect because a DNS server would also not have an Alpha address; DNS servers are generally referred to by their TCP/IP address. You cannot send a DNS server the FQDN of a server unless you have the location of a DNS server to translate it. Therefore, you could not send dns.salesdepartment.com to locate the DNS server because you do not have the location of a DNS server to translate the FQDN to an IP address.

**6.** ☑  **B** and **D.** Both Education and Military are considered top-level domains and are represented by .edu and .mil, respectively.

☒  **A** and **C** are still in debate, but should be available to the public for use soon. They will be represented by .STO and .ISP, respectively. They will be considered second-level domains registered under a .com domain.

**7.** ☑  **B.** There are six second-level DNS domain types: .edu, .com, .mil, .net, .gov, and .org. Each of these domains is controlled by one or more second-level domain servers. Each second-level domain server is responsible for only one type of domain. Under each second-level domain server are hundreds of DNS servers that maintain the information for each of the domains they represent. They might maintain information on one or more domain types.

☒  **A, C,** and **D** are incorrect.

8. ☑ **B.** A router is considered a hop on the Internet. Each connection begins and ends at a router. These routers have multiple connections on them branching off like a tree. As a packet enters the router on a port, it is checked and a determination is made on which port the packet is to be sent out based on several criteria, including destination address, protocol, filters, and such. Routers operate on the third layer of the OSI model.

   ☒ **A** is incorrect because ATM switches operate on layer 2 of the OSI model and are not considered a hop on the Internet. They are very fast at what they do and can switch packets much quicker then many routers, but since they operate only on layer 2 of the OSI model, they cannot make routing decisions. **C** is incorrect because repeaters are used on a network to extend the cable and clean up the signal. Packets take no notice of a repeater. **D** is incorrect because FDDI is a type of physical cabling that is used between network devices. It could be and many times is used to connect routers, but it is a layer 1 product.

9. ☑ **B.** An ISDN connection consisting of one B channel is a 64K digital/dedicated connection. This means you will have 64K throughput to the remote end at all times.

   ☒ **A** is incorrect. 56K is the basis for the highest-end analog modems. The modems do not truly communicate at 56K due to limitations and restrictions placed on them. Many times the lines from your telephone connection to the central office are old and at best carry a 36K signal. The best you can get out of a 56K modem is roughly 53K. **C** is incorrect. 128K is the standard for a full ISDN. This consists of two B channels and one D channel. Each B channel is 64K, and the D channel is purely for administration and overhead. No data destined for the Internet or other station is transmitted over the D channel. **D** is incorrect because 1.544Mb is the specification of a T1 connection.

10. ☑ **C.** This would be a Web site. A Web site is a collection of related information maintained on a server for access by HTTP browsers. This information can be public or private. It has the ability of being held behind a firewall or other security so authentication is required to access it.

☒   **A** is incorrect because an FTP server maintains files for download. **B** is incorrect because an Archie server is used to search a database of FTP sites for a file that is needed or requested. **D** is incorrect because a Web site consists of Web pages; a Web site requires more than one page to be considered a site.

11.  ☑   **C.** An MX record is a mail record. It directs incoming mail to the correct mail server. You can have multiple MX records for a given domain. The DNS will try them in order until it finds a working mail server.
☒   **A** is a PTR record. PTR records are used for reverse lookup, meaning you give it an IP address and it gives you the domain name. **B** is an NS record. NS records are used by name servers to locate other name servers on a network. **D** is incorrect because the A record is the primary record type entry for a domain.

12.  ☑   **B.** If you are going to install your Web site on a slow system, you need to make sure that it is only running the Web page server process. A BDC is a processor-intensive activity and should be housed on a system that is not used for any other activity.
☒   **A** is incorrect. While the version of the browser can limit the amount/type/quality of data it processes, with the given information this would not be the first fix to try. **C** is also incorrect. If the firewall were blocking the images, none of the images would be displayed on the system. **D** is incorrect. You should write your Web pages so users can browse your site, no matter what speed they are connecting at.

13.  ☑   **A.** The type of record you would enter for the primary domain name of a site is a type A record.
☒   **B** is incorrect. An MX record type is a mail record. An MX entry points to a mail server on your network. **C** is incorrect. PTR records are for reverse lookup on your domain's name and IP address, where a user could enter an IP address and be returned the FQDN of the domain and system. **D** is also incorrect. CNAME records are the canonical name records. This is where you would enter your www.company.com name or ftp.company.com.

14. ☑ **A.** Each DNS server on the Internet only knows about a small portion of the Internet plus its next higher DNS server. The root domain servers know each domain (.com, .edu, .org, .gov, etc.). They in turn can direct you to the correct domain server that maintains the tables for the domain you are contacting.
    ☒ **B** is incorrect. Before a Web page can be displayed, a translation of FQDN to TCP/IP address must be made; only a numeric address can be transmitted over the Internet in a packet. **C** is incorrect—see Answer A. **D** is incorrect because a log file containing all the FQDNs would be too large to house on a single PC, not counting the time it would take to download this log file and search it.

15. ☑ **D.** All of the above are parts of the current Internet infrastructure. TCP/IP is the protocol of the Internet. The physical cabling is what carries the signal from router to router and from one station to the next. Types of cabling are 10BaseT, 100BaseT, and FDDI. The router is the point in the network where data leaves the network destined for another network. Routers operate on the layer 3 of the OSI model and transmit packets out the proper interface based on the destination address or protocol being used.

16. ☑ **C.** An OC12 connection runs at 622mb/second. This is the fastest Internet connection standard at this time. OC3 and OC12 are both standards used. OC3 transmits at 155mb/second.
    ☒ **A** is incorrect. 1.5mb/second is what BASEband cable runs at; for example, cable modems and such. **B** is also incorrect. 155mb/second is the OC3 specification. **D** is incorrect. 4.632MB per second is the specification of a T3 link.

17. ☑ **D.** Each site must contain at least one MX record for e-mail to be directed to the correct server. More than one MX record can be in place for a site as a backup to make sure e-mail is delivered and not returned as unknown recipient.

☒ **A** is incorrect. The mail server would have no way of knowing that the DNS server was taken offline. There is no communication between the server and the DNS server. **B** is incorrect, because although it was over a weekend, it is highly unlikely that there would be no e-mail arriving to your mail server. There are numerous e-mail lists available on the Internet, and an e-mail might have been sent from another time zone where it was possibly still working hours. **C** is incorrect. The PTR record on the DNS server is for reverse lookup, where you give the DNS server the number address of a site and it returns the FQDN of the site.

18. ☑ **B.** www.ourplace.org is a fully qualified domain name.
    ☒ **A** is incorrect. Although it might work, this is the IP address of a site, not the FQDN. **C** is also incorrect. Mail is not a site name. It might be the name of a system and you might have a localhost file setup that knows where this system is located, but a DNS server would not be able to determine its location. **D** is incorrect. The name is missing a domain suffix; .com, .org, or some other domain type is needed to determine the TCP/IP address of the site.

19. ☑ **C.** The PC is not set up with a working DNS address. A TCP/IP address for a DNS server must be entered in the TCP/IP properties of your system before you can use FQDNs to browse the Internet.
    ☒ **A** is incorrect. WINS is used for NetBEUI names, such as getting to system payroll by typing \\payroll. Payroll is the NetBEUI name of the system, and when you enter it, a WINS server translates it to the MAC address of the remote system. **B** is incorrect. If your connection to the Internet was down, you would not be able to reach the site using the IP address. **D** is also incorrect. If your gateway was not functioning, you would not be able to access anything on the Internet. You could, however, access systems on your local network.

20. ☑ B. You would enter the IP address in reverse order without the host portion. When a person sends a request to find out what 226.99.32.58 belongs to, the DNS server will send the following information to the DNS server at your site 58.32.99.226 because it knows where the 226.99.32 domain is located via its DNS server. Once it reaches your domain server, all it needs to ask is what is the FQDN of host #58. Your DNS server would return payroll.carsales.com, and that would be returned to you.

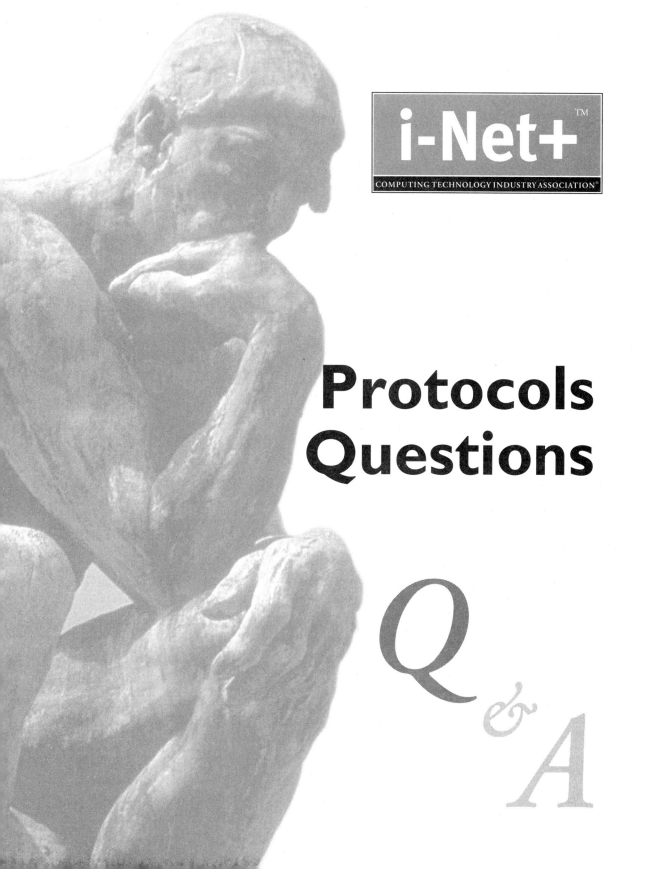

# Protocols
# Questions

$Q$ & $A$

# Protocols

**1.** A friend gives you an address to a great new site she uses at work to look up RFCs (Request for Comments). The URL is http://192.168.100.1. When you attempt to connect to that URL from home, you receive an error. What is most likely the problem?

    A. The URL is wrong and should be 192.168.100.100.

    B. It is a securing link so you need to use HTTPS://.

    C. It is an internal site only for the company where your friend is employed.

    D. There is a firewall blocking your access to the site.

**2.** You have decided to set up a small network at home to study different protocols. You will have one PC that is connected to the Internet via a dial-up connection. This PC will be running Windows NT 4.0 with routing turned on, TCP/IP, IPX, and DECnet. You will have one PC that runs IPX, one that runs only IP, and another that will run only DECnet. You do not wish to purchase an additional IP address from your ISP for the second PC that will have IP on it since it will not be connected to the Internet. You will be running a proxy/firewall application on the PC that is connected so that all systems will be able to access the Internet. What IP scheme could you use to accomplish this?

    A. Give the PC that is running IP that is connected to the Internet the IP address your ISP assigned you, and assign 43.17.94.6.31 as a private address for the system running IP on your local system.

    B. Give the PC that is running IP that is connected to the Internet 192.168.101.1. The local system won't need an IP because you told the system that is connected to your ISP that this is a private network.

    C. Give the PC that is on your local network any IP address, and then assign the ISP's IP to the system that is on the network.

    D. Give the PC that is connected to the Internet the assigned IP address, and then assign a private address such as 192.168.101.1 to the other IP system on your network.

**3.** You are thinking of buying a PC, but you want to get information from others who have purchased this brand of system. You are aware of a collection of information that is maintained by individuals and is propagated throughout the Internet on several servers. To what type of server do you need to connect to find the information you are looking for?

A. Archie Server

B. Directory Server

C. News Server

D. Gopher Server

**4.** You need to configure a dial-up connection to your company's LAN. You will only use IPX on this connection. What type of dial-up connection should you implement?

A. SLIP

B. PPP

C. HTTP

D. LDAP

**5.** Your company is assigned a Class B network address of 132.16.0.0. You need additional IP addresses. You decide to subnet your network to a Class C subnet to gain the additional IP addresses you need. What should the subnet mask be for your network?

A. 255.0.0.0

B. 255.255.0.0

C. 255.255.255.0

D. 255.252.255.255

**6.** A protocol used for the uploading and downloading of files to and from a server by way of anonymous access is a definition of what?

A. FTP

B. Telnet

C. POP3

D. HTTP

**7.** A user calls and says that he cannot ping the gateway or any other station on the network. His IP address is 145.99.32.18. You look it up and it's the correct IP address. The user informs you that other people on the network are able to access systems and ping the gateway. You do some additional research and determine that the problem started after a hard drive was replaced the day before. The user says that the cable is plugged into the wall. You are not running DHCP on this network. What is likely the problem?

    A. The IP was assigned to this user when he was in a different location. He gave the technician the wrong IP to put on the PC when it was rebuilt; therefore, he is unable to access the network.

    B. The gateway has a filter installed to block data from this PC.

    C. The DHCP server is down.

    D. The subnet mask is probably wrong. The helpdesk person did not check this. It is likely that they are using a nonstandard subnet mask, and the technician put a standard Class B subnet mask on the system when it was rebuilt.

**8.** Before the World Wide Web, what was the primary way to locate information on the Internet?

    A. Archie

    B. Gopher

    C. FTP

    D. Telnet

**9.** Your company has asked you to add additional security to the network. Your primary focus is to be the work from home employees. What protocol would you suggest for the users to use to access the corporate LAN?

    A. SLIP

    B. PPP

    C. PPTP

    D. Point-to-Multipoint

**10.** You are setting up several new systems, and Mail is one application you are required to install and configure. What needs to be configured to send and receive mail?

A. SMTP

B. SNMP

C. POP3

D. PPTP

**11.** You are logged on to a UNIX node called Development. You need to run a program on the node Production. How would you best access and run the program?

A. FTP to Production, log in as anonymous and run the program from the command line.

B. Telnet to Production, log in as Guest and run the program from the command line.

C. Telnet to Production, log in using your assigned username and password, and run the program from the command line.

D. Use your browser to access HTTP://Production, log in using your assigned username, and run the program from the browser window.

**12.** When accessing a system via FTP, you want to download a large ZIP file. What file type is needed to make sure the file is downloaded in a manner that will allow you to unzip it and run the program inside?

A. IEEE

B. ASCII

C. TEXT

D. BINARY

**13.** Your company's network is experiencing a large number of collisions. You have been assigned the task of figuring out why the network is so congested with collisions and where they are coming from. You have a feeling the problem is being caused by a bad NIC card on the network. What would be your best procedure to troubleshoot and locate the problem?

A. Use a Network Analyzer

B. Use a Protocol Analyzer

C. Use TDR

D. Use the Trace Route Utility

**14.** The following is an example of what?

```
1    20 ms    10 ms     7 ms     120.141.42.111
2    10 ms    10 ms    10 ms     r1-fe0-0-100bt.mycompany.com [124.34.163.1]
3    70 ms    50 ms    30 ms     210.0.16.161
4    30 ms    20 ms    30 ms     124.2.1.1
5    20 ms    40 ms    20 ms     c1-pos9-0.mycompany.com [124.74.172.173]
6    30 ms    30 ms    50 ms     c1-pos3-0.mycompany.com [124.74.164.74]
7    40 ms    50 ms    50 ms     c1-pos5-3..mycompany.com [124.74.167.58]
8    41 ms    40 ms    50 ms     bb1-pos1-0-0.bibsy.net [124.74.172.114]
9    50 ms    60 ms    60 ms     p219.t3.anq.org [192.157.69.13]
10   60 ms    70 ms    60 ms     185.23.161.229
11   50 ms    70 ms    60 ms     f4-1-0.t200-4.Reston.t3.anq.org [120.243.160.219]
```

A. PING table

B. ARP table

C. NETSTAT table

D. Traceroute table

**15.** You receive your approved request for a TCP/IP address block and notice you were assigned 193.47.44.0 to 193.47.49.255. What class of IP address did you receive?

A. Class A

B. Class B

C. Class C

D. Class D

**16.** You are hired by a company to stage 1500 PCs for use on their LAN. What is the minimum information you require for setting up the IP information on the PCs if they are not using DHCP?

A. IP address

B. Gateway

C. DNS server

D. Subnet mask

**17.** You receive the following from a ping of sales.ourcompany.com. What do you make of it?

```
C:\ping sales.ourcompany.com -t
Pinging sales.ourcompany.com [107.246.81.48] with 32
bytes of data:
Request timed out.
Reply from 107.246.81.48: bytes=32 time=130ms TTL=240
Request timed out.
Request timed out.
Reply from 107.246.81.48: bytes=32 time=210ms TTL=240
Request timed out.
Request timed out.
Request timed out.
Reply from 107.246.81.48: bytes=32 time=180ms TTL=240
```

A. The network is extremely busy or possibly congested.

B. The sales node keeps being rebooted.

C. You have a poor connection to the network from your station.

D. The router between you and the end system is rebooting.

**18.** You are consulting as a technician for an ISP. While looking at the list of problem calls that came in overnight, you notice one that reads, "unable to do anything." You decided to take the challenge and give the user a call. You ask the user if she is still unable to ping, send mail, browse the Web, or do anything. She says yes. You determine that she is running a Pentium III 350mhz system with Windows 95 OS. She has a 1.2GB hard drive with 60% free space, 128MB of memory, and uses IE 5.0 as her browser. You need to check out her IP address to confirm there isn't a problem with the mask. How do you go about doing this?

A. Type IPCONFIG from the DOS prompt.

B. Ping her station from your client.

C. Click on the TCP/IP icon in the Control Panel.

D. Type WINIPCFG from the DOS prompt.

**19.** You have been hired to design the TCP/IP address scheme for a new company that is being spun off from its parent company. It will remain a subsidiary of the parent company so it will utilize the TCP/IP address range assigned to the main network. The company was assigned a Class A address range of 113.0.0.0 many years ago, but has never even come close to using them all. You have been assigned 113.45.0.0 network to use. To give yourself plenty of room to grow segments, you are going to use VLSM to make this a Class C address. You have very few users in each of your offices, but have many offices, so you'll need a larger number of networks that will support a smaller number of users on each. What is the correct subnet mask to use?

A. 255.0.0.0

B. 255.255.0.0

C. 255.255.255.0

D. 255.252.0.0

**20.** You are away on business and need to read your mail that is housed on your UNIX system back in the office. All you have is a dial-in connection to a dial-in server that will allow you to work on your company's network, but does not offer Web services. You also do not have an e-mail client installed on your laptop. The node that houses the e-mail is SALES, and the node you are dialing in to is DIAL. How will you gain access to your mail?

A. Run POP3 on DIAL and read your mail there.

B. Run SMTP on DIAL and read your mail there.

C. Use TFTP to pull down your mail from SALES to DIAL.

D. Use Telnet to connect to SALES to read your mail.

**21.** You need to connect to a Web page for another company to purchase some equipment. You know they use a secured server for this purpose. You are given the URL of www.bigdiscounts.com\purchase\login.cgi. What do you need to put in front of the URL so that the Web browser will know it is making a securing connection?

A. HTTP://

B. HTTS://

C. HTTPS://

D. HTSP://

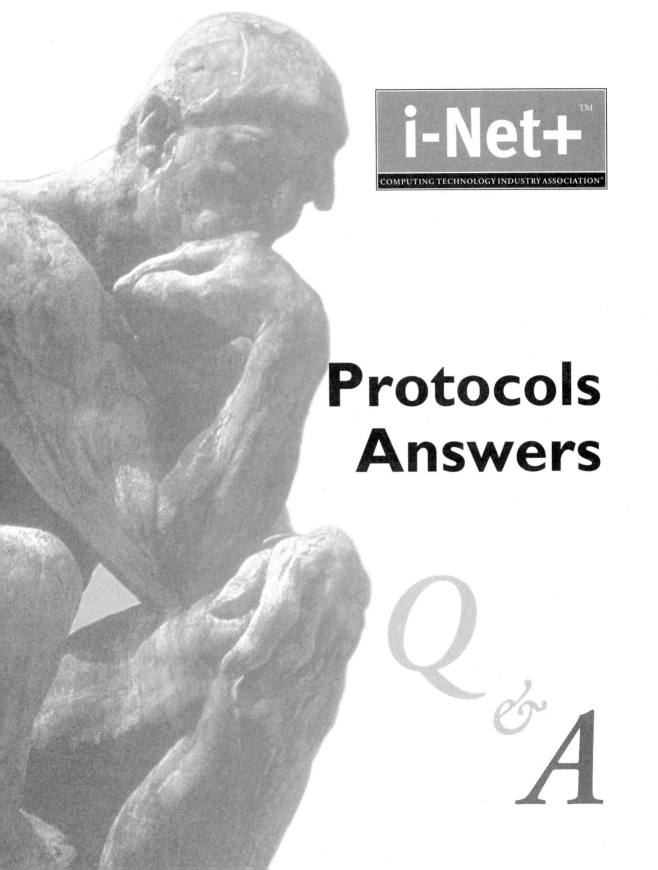

i-Net+ ™
COMPUTING TECHNOLOGY INDUSTRY ASSOCIATION®

# Protocols
# Answers

$Q$ & $A$

# Protocols

1. ☑  C. The URL is a private IP address. Companies and individuals have
   the right to use the 192.168.0.0 network for any station on their network,
   but the routers will recognize this as a private address space and block
   access to it.
   ☒  A is wrong because the URL is not wrong; it's just part of the private
   access space and cannot be reached from the Internet. B is incorrect because
   it could be a securing link, but again, it's a private address so you will not be
   able to retrieve it. D is incorrect because a firewall would have no barring on
   this IP address. In general, a firewall would block your access to internal
   Web servers for security reasons.

2. ☑  D. The PC that is connected to the Internet must have a valid IP
   address. Since it will act as the proxy/firewall for the network, any system
   behind it could use a private address. This system will strip off the IP of the
   local system and attach its IP to any packets being sent to the Internet.
   ☒  A is wrong because a valid IP has only four octets. B is wrong because if
   you put the 192 address on the system that is connected to the Internet,
   your packets will never be sent. C is incorrect because you should never
   assign a random IP address that is not a "private address" to a system that
   will be sending or receiving information from the Internet.

3. ☑  C. The News Server is where you would find the discussion groups on
   thousands of subjects. The newsgroups are maintained by companies, ISPs,
   and individuals. They are stored and updated from hundreds of points
   around the world. Most ISPs maintain an ISP and a select number of
   groups. If there is a group you would like to read that your ISP doesn't
   carry, contact your ISP and ask for it; most will comply if space is available.
   See RFC 977 for additional information concerning News Servers.

☒ **A** is wrong because the Archie servers are used, or were used, to search FTP sites for files to download. **B** is wrong because a Directory server is the server side of the LDAP protocol where the information is housed. This information can contain as little as you want it to (e.g., only the person's name and e-mail address), or as much as you want (e.g., pictures, performance figures, and just about anything else). Each entry will have a Distinguished Name (DN) plus one or more types; these can be common name (cn), mail, or e-mail address. **D** is another type of search engine that was the predecessor to the great ones we have today.

4. ☑ **B.** PPP will support IP and IPX. This would be the only option for your connection to the local LAN of your company. PPP provides a serial connection over both Asynchronous and Synchronous circuits. PPP can handle non-TCP/IP packets such as IPX, and can also handle authentication.
☒ **A** is incorrect because SLIP supports only TCP/IP, so this option would not work for an IPX-only network or connection. **C** and **D** are not dial-up options.

5. ☑ **C.** 255.255.255.0 is the correct subnet mask for a Class C network.
☒ **A** is a Class A subnet mask, **B** is a Class B subnet mask, and **D** is a bad or invalid subnet mask.

6. ☑ **A.** FTP is used to download and upload files to and from a server. FTP servers can be configured to allow anonymous access where a user types anonymous for the username and generally his or her e-mail address for the password. The e-mail address is for tracking access to the system. The password is not checked against any database used only for logging. FTP can also be configured with usernames and passwords for secured access.
☒ **B** is incorrect because Telnet is used to access the CLI on a remote system, such as connecting to a UNIX box to compile a C+ program or read mail. **C** is incorrect because POP3 is used to retrieve e-mail from a server to an e-mail client. **D** is incorrect because HTTP is used to access Web pages via a browser.

**PROTOCOLS
ANSWERS**

7. ☑ **D.** The user said the system was rebuilt, which means that the data had to be reentered or restored. Since DHCP is not being used, TCP/IP info would have to be entered manually. Errors on the IP, subnet mask, and gateway are likely when information is entered manually.

☒ **A** is incorrect as documentation should have been updated if the user moved. The technician should have also contacted the helpdesk to acquire the TCP/IP information instead of relying on the end user for it. **B** is unlikely, unless someone has entered the info by mistake. We know that the hard drive was replaced, so this leads us to an incorrect setup as the likely problem. **C** is incorrect because it was stated in the problem that there was no DHCP server on the network.

8. ☑ **B.** Gopher was the primary tool for searching for information on the Internet. It was a text-only program that ran in a window much like our browsers do today. You would attach to a Gopher server and perform your search by category.

☒ **A** is incorrect because Archie was used to search for files for FTP. **C** is incorrect because FTP is used to retrieve and send files over the Internet. **D** is incorrect because Telnet is used to attach to a remote system to gain access to the CLI of that system.

9. ☑ **C.** PPTP is the Point to Point Tunneling Protocol. This allows for additional security when communicating to a private network via the Internet. PPTP encapsulates other protocols for transmission over an IP network. You could use it for transmitting DECnet or IPX over the Internet from a local system to a remote network. PPTP is also considered a secured packet because it encrypts all data in the packet for transmission.

☒ **A** and **B** are connection protocols that you would use to connect to the Internet, not to your corporate network via the Internet. **D** is what you are doing when you connect a system to a repeater or concentrator. Your PC is the point, and multipoint means you are connecting to a device that will broadcast your packets out all interfaces.

**10.** ☑ **A** and **C.** SMTP and POP3 are required to send and receive mail. SMTP is used for outgoing mail, and POP3 is used to receive mail. Many times, these are the same server, but not necessarily.

☒ **B** is incorrect because SNMP is the protocol used to talk to and configure network equipment such as routers, switches, and bridges. **D** is incorrect because PPTP is a protocol used to transmit packets into a private network via the Internet.

**11.** ☑ **C.** You should Telnet from the system you are on to the system you need access to, and then log in using your assigned username and password. At this point, you should be able to run the needed program if you have the permission set to do so. Root on a UNIX box will have permission to run any program.

☒ **A** is incorrect because by FTPing to the end system, you would not be able to execute a program, only retrieve or send programs. **B** is incorrect because although Telneting would be the best option, my systems either have the Guest account disabled or at least have the permissions set so low that you would not be able to run the program needed. **D** is incorrect because although HTTP could be used, most systems' Web pages do not give you access to execute a program. Most times they will display requested data or accept data from the user to be placed into a file.

**12.** ☑ **D.** BINARY is used to download files that are considered programs or nontext files.

☒ **A** is incorrect because IEEE is a standard such as IEE 802.3; it is not an FTP type. **B** and **C** are used to download text files from FTP servers.

**13.** ☑ **A.** You would use a network analyzer to determine if the problem is being caused by one particular system. If it is, you could chase the NIC down via your network's documentation that is on file. The analyzer would show storms and a chatty NIC that could be causing the problem. If you are seeing storms on one particular segment, you could disconnect that segment from the rest of the network to allow better troubleshooting.

☒ **B** is incorrect because a protocol analyzer is used to analyze protocols on a network, not for troubleshooting a network problem. **C** is incorrect because a TDR is used to measure the length of a cable and to do additional physical tests to make sure the cable is good with no breaks. **D** is incorrect because the Trace Route Utility is used to determine the time and route that a packet takes to another system.

14. ☑ **D.** This is a printout of a traceroute. Notice the timing information in the display for each hop. This information can be vital when troubleshooting a poor or slow connection. You can follow your packet from your local system to the end system and determine by times where the slowdown is. If the slowdown is between you and the exit port of your ISP, you can contact your ISP and provide a copy of your traceroute to assist them in troubleshooting the problem. If the problem is between your ISP and your remote system, you can ask for your ISP's assistance in determining where the slowdown is and how to go about correcting the problem.

   ☒ **A** is incorrect because a PING table would show response from the end system only, not each system between the local system and end system. **B** is incorrect because an ARP table would show information concerning MAC addresses of stations that the local station has exchanged data with. **C** is incorrect because NETSTAT would show active connections from the local station.

15. ☑ **C.** Class C's address space is 192.1.1.1 to 254.255.255.255.

   ☒ **A**'s address range is from 1.1.1.1 to 126.255.255.255. **B**'s address range is from 128.1.1.1 to 191.255.255.255. **D** is a multicast address space.

16. ☑ **A** and **D.** You require the IP address and subnet mask for the network that the PC will be transmitting on. It would be helpful to know the DNS and gateway also, but that information is not required.

   ☒ **B** and **C** are helpful to know when staging a PC, but are not required. If the PC will communicate only on a local network (not leaving its segment), there will be no need for a gateway. If all the systems are using NetBEUI or TCP/IP address for connection, a DNS server is also not required.

**17.** ☑ **A.** From the looks of the printout and the idea that it's on your local network, it would be best determined that the network is extremely congested based on the request timed outs and the time being extremely high.

☒ **B** is incorrect because if the sales node were being rebooted, you would see many more request timed outs. A system cannot reboot in the time it takes for three packets to be transmitted. **C** is incorrect because if your system had a poor connection, you would not get info. Request timed out means that the end station did not respond. **D** is incorrect because a router cannot reboot in the time it takes for three ping packets to be transmitted. If you were getting no responses and knew the system was up, you could try pinging the router.

**18.** ☑ **D.** Type WINIPCFG from the DOS prompt. On a Windows 95 system, the correct command to look up the IP information is WINIPCFG from the DOS prompt. This will give you your IP address, subnet mask, gateway address, DNS server, and possibly WINS server if you have one configured.

☒ **A** is incorrect because IPCONFIG is the command to acquire this info from a Windows NT workstation/server. **B** is incorrect because until you know what her IP address is you cannot PING her. Even though you might have it listed in your database, it is best to confirm the info via WINIPCONFIG to make sure it has not been incorrectly entered in the database. **C** is incorrect because there is no TCP/IP icon in the Control Panel. There is a network icon and you can acquire this info there.

**19.** ☑ **C.** The correct Class C subnet mask is 255.255.255.0. This would allow for a larger number of networks. If you kept the Class A address and a Class A subnet, you would be limited to one network.

☒ **A** is a normal Class A subnet mask. **B** is a standard Class B subnet mask. **D** is a Class B VLSM, not a Class C.

**20.** ☑ **D.** You would use Telnet to connect from DIAL to SALES where you would log in using your assigned credentials and access your e-mail on a character-based system.

&#x2612;  A and B are used only when you are running an e-mail client on a system that will fetch your e-mail from a server and send your e-mail from your system to a server to be processed. C is used to download files, not e-mail. TFTP is mainly used to install or upgrade software on equipment such as a router or switch.

21. &#x2611;  C. You would use HTTPS:// for a securing connection to a server.
&#x2612;  A is used for normal unsecured connections to Web pages. B and D are invalid choices.

# Hardware and Software Questions

*Q & A*

# Hardware and Software

1. A customer is inquiring about analog modems and wants to know the available speeds. Which of the following is *not* a typical analog modem speed?

   A. 14.4 Kbps
   B. 28.8 Kbps
   C. 56.6 Kbps
   D. 64.4 Kbps

2. A client is complaining that he cannot use the Internet and the telephone at the same time. What type of modem is he using?

   A. Analog
   B. ISDN
   C. DSL
   D. There is not enough information to determine this.

3. What is the maximum speed of an Internet connection on a Basic Rate Interface (BRI) ISDN line if the telephone is in use at the same time?

   A. 56.6 Kbps
   B. 64 Kbps
   C. 128 Kbps
   D. 3 Mbps

4. Modem is an acronym for MOdulate/DEModulate. Which type of Internet connection technology uses a true modem?

   A. BRI ISDN
   B. PRI ISDN
   C. DSL
   D. Cable

**5.** A client has recently purchased an external ISDN modem, and is shocked to find out that it does not deliver 128 Kbps. What is the problem?

A. ISDN is not capable of communicating at 128 Kbps.

B. External ISDN modems cannot support 128 Kbps.

C. The ISDN bandwidth is being shared by other users in the neighborhood.

D. There is no Ethernet NIC connection.

**6.** What do you recommend to someone who wants Internet access that is purely digital and uses a regular telephone line, but will not interfere with use of the telephone?

A. Analog

B. ISDN

C. DSL

D. Cable

**7.** Which type of DSL service should you recommend to users who plan to visit many Web sites and download files from the Internet?

A. ADSL—there is more downstream than upstream bandwidth.

B. SDSL—it is faster in both directions than ADSL.

C. SDSL—ADSL is only available in Europe.

D. There is no performance difference between the two for these types of Internet activities.

**8.** In setting up DSL Internet access, you have purchased the DSL adapter, Ethernet network card, and the proper cables for attaching them to your computer and the wall outlet. What additional equipment must be installed?

A. A special DSL digital line must be installed between your building and the telephone company's switching station.

B. A bridge must be installed between the adapter and the wall outlet.

C. A modem.

D. A line splitter.

**9.** A customer wants a high-speed, high-security, direct Internet connection. The customer is located four miles from the Internet Service Provider (ISP). Should you recommend cable?

A. Yes, cable fulfills all of the customer's requirements.

B. No, the customer is located too far away from the ISP.

C. No, cable uses a dial-up connection.

D. No, cable does not provide high security.

**10.** Which type of Internet access method is most susceptible to and most likely to have noise on the line?

A. Analog

B. ISDN

C. DSL

D. Cable

**11.** What modem command should you use when you want to dial up another computer at the number 555-1234 using tone dialing?

A. AT5551234DP

B. ADTD5551234

C. ATDT5551234

D. ATDP5551234

**12.** You have just suggested the purchase of a network card to a home computer user who wants Internet access. Which type of card do you recommend, and why?

A. You suggest a Token Ring NIC to connect her cable modem to the computer.

B. You suggest an Ethernet NIC to connect her DSL adapter to the computer.

C. You suggest a Token Ring NIC to connect her ISDN modem to the network.

D. You suggest an Ethernet NIC to provide firewall protection.

**13.** What method does a hub use to ensure that data from one computer is received by another computer on a star network?

A. Broadcasting.

B. MAC addressing.

C. IP addressing.

D. The hub retains all data packets. All computers periodically poll the hub and pick up only the data packets addressed to it.

**14.** Which of the following network connection devices uses broadcasting to send data between segments on the network?

A. Router

B. Hub

C. Switch

D. Bridge

**15.** What does a bridge use to identify the computers on different segments of a network in the bridge routing table?

A. IP addresses

B. Physical location

C. MAC addresses

D. Usernames

**16.** Which statement most accurately describes the method by which a bridge sends data between two segments of a network?

A. The bridge uses the computer's MAC address to direct data to the destination computer.

B. The bridge uses the computer's IP address to direct data to the destination computer.

C. The bridge uses the computer's MAC address to filter out data that does not need to cross the bridge and sends everything else to all other segments.

D. The bridge holds all data. Each network segment periodically polls the bridge and picks up data for computers within that segment.

**17.** A business is planning the installation of a large multisegment network. They want to minimize network traffic and have some network fault tolerance. Which device should you recommend for connecting the segments of the network?

A. Bridge

B. Switch

C. Router

D. Gateway

Note: The next three questions are based on the following Illustration.

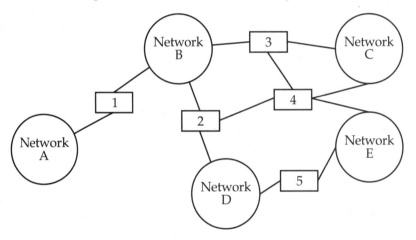

**18.** Refer to the preceding illustration and assume the numbered positions represent routers. What would be the result of a failure of the router at position 2?

A. Networks B and D would lose connectivity with each other.

B. Networks B and D would lose connectivity to all other networks.

C. The entire network would fail.

D. None of the above.

**19.** Refer to preceding illustration. The numbered positions mark the locations of connection devices. Which device is most suitable to place at position 4?

A. Router

B. Bridge

C. Switch

D. Any of the above

**20.** Refer to preceding illustration and assume the numbered positions indicate network connection devices. Which is the *best* place for a switch?

A. 1

B. 2

C. 3

D. 4

**21.** Which network operating system software is the best for providing users with access to some network resources, while maintaining security and applying restrictions to other network resources?

A. Peer-to-peer

B. Client

C. Server

D. None of the above

**22.** A two-segment network has DSL access to the Internet. The network has a screened host firewall, and uses the TCP/IP network protocol. Where is the best place to put an Internet-in-a-box on this network?

A. Outside the firewall.

B. Installed on the server.

C. Inside the firewall.

D. An Internet-in-a-box will not work on this network.

**23.** You are helping a company set up their network and establish Internet access. You recommend an application-level firewall. How will this firewall provide security for the network?

   A. The firewall's proxy server examines all incoming data and screens out unwanted packets based on their content and/or application type.

   B. The firewall screens out all requests from unrecognized external IP addresses.

   C. The firewall examines all incoming data and removes viruses and restricted content from it before sending it to the internal network.

   D. Both A and B.

**24.** Under what circumstances would you recommend a packet-level firewall instead of an application-level firewall?

   A. When the network requires the highest security possible

   B. When the network requires the highest speed possible

   C. When ease of configuration is an issue

   D. When the maintenance of a detailed account of Internet access is required

**25.** You are planning to set up a screened host firewall on a network with Internet access. Which of the following best describes the proper devices and their locations?

   A. Place a packet screening router between the network and the Internet.

   B. Place a proxy server outside of the network, and a packet screening router between the proxy server and the Internet.

   C. Place a proxy server inside the network and a packet screening router outside the network.

   D. Place a packet screening router outside the network, and a proxy server between the router and the Internet.

**26.** An organization's Web site has the domain name www.blitz.org. What does this domain name reveal about the organization?

A. It is located in the United States.

B. It is a nonprofit organization.

C. It is a networking organization.

D. It is located outside of the United States.

# Hardware and Software Answers

## Q & A

# Hardware and Software

1. ☑   **D.** 64.4 Kbps is not a typical analog modem speed. In fact, 56.6 Kbps is the highest speed that analog modems can attain, due to limitations with analog telephone communications.
   ☒   **A, B,** and **C** are all incorrect because they are valid (and common) speeds for analog modems. As you would probably guess, the slower speeds are typically found in older modems. The most common speed of analog modems today is 56.6 Kbps.

2. ☑   **A.** Analog. Analog modems are the only modems that interfere with the function of the telephone.
   ☒   **B** is incorrect because this technology allows for concurrent use of the telephone and Internet. ISDN lines have two channels, so while you are accessing the Internet on one channel, the telephone can be used on the other. **C** is also incorrect because it allows you to use the telephone and Internet at the same time. DSL technology uses a line splitter to divide the telephone line into two channels, one for voice and fax communications, and one for digital Internet communications. **D** is incorrect because it states that there is not enough information to determine the answer.

3. ☑   **B.** 64Kbps. A BRI ISDN line is made up of two "B" channels (data-carrying channels). Each B channel can transmit at 64 Kbps, making a total of 128 Kbps. However, if one of the channels is unavailable, in this case due to telephone use, only one channel can be used to access the Internet. The maximum speed of that one channel remains 64 Kbps.
   ☒   **A** is incorrect because this is the maximum speed for analog modems. ISDN channels each transmit at 64 Kbps, so the total speed must be a multiple of 64. **C** is incorrect because this is the maximum ISDN speed if both lines can access the Internet. In this case, only one line can be used for Internet access, so the maximum speed is cut in half. **D** is incorrect because this speed is unattainable by BRI ISDN. However, PRI ISDN, cable, and DSL modems can support speeds up to and above 3 Mbps.

4. ☑ **D.** Cable technology uses a true modem. Cable lines use radio frequencies, which are analog. Therefore, part of the job of the modem is to convert the computer's signals from digital to analog for outgoing traffic, and from analog back to digital for incoming traffic.

☒ **A** and **B** are both incorrect because these are special digital lines installed at the user's location to make a complete end-to-end digital path. Because the computer's signal never needs to be converted to analog, it does not modulate or demodulate. Thus, an ISDN modem is not *technically* a modem and, in fact, is usually referred to as an ISDN adapter. **C** is also incorrect. DSL technology splits a regular telephone line into an analog channel for telephone use and a digital channel for Internet access. The computer's digital signal doesn't need to be converted to analog, so a DSL adapter is not technically a modem

5. ☑ **D.** There is no Ethernet NIC connection. When an external ISDN modem is connected to the computer via a serial port, there can be data bottlenecks. The serial port cannot transfer information to the computer as fast as it is received by the modem. However, if the external modem is connected to the computer through an internal Ethernet NIC, there are no bottlenecks (Ethernet cards can support speeds of 10–100 Mbps, far greater than the 128 Kbps coming in through the ISDN line!).

☒ **A** is incorrect. ISDN does, in fact, support speeds of 128 Kbps. **B** is incorrect because it suggests that external ISDN modems cannot support 128 Kbps. They can if they're attached to the computer's Ethernet NIC rather than its serial port. Furthermore, this method entails no more configuration than installing an internal modem. **C** is incorrect because it suggests that the customer's bandwidth is being shared by other users. ISDN is a dedicated line that is not shared by users at other sites. Bandwidth sharing is a characteristic of cable, not ISDN.

6. ☑ **C.** DSL. In DSL technology, a splitter is placed on a regular telephone line to divide it into two channels: one analog channel for telephone communications and a digital channel for Internet access. The Internet connection is end-to-end digital, uses a regular telephone line, and because the line is split into two channels, the telephone and Internet can be used concurrently.

☒    **A** is incorrect because this technology uses a regular phone line, but is not digital, and does not allow concurrent use of the Internet and phone. **B** is incorrect because although it provides a pure digital connection and concurrent phone/Internet use, a special ISDN line must be installed to bypass the regular (analog) telephone line. **D** is incorrect because it uses cable rather than telephone lines and is analog, not digital.

**7.** ☑    **A.** ADSL—there is more downstream than upstream bandwidth. In ADSL, the downstream (incoming) bandwidth is much wider than the upstream (outgoing). During Internet access, users spend most of their time pulling data downstream into their computers, and very little time sending e-mail or other requests upstream to other computers.

☒    **B** is incorrect. SDSL allocates equal bandwidth to upstream and downstream data. Because more Internet time is spent downloading information, users can benefit from having a large downstream bandwidth and small upstream bandwidth. Furthermore, the maximum speed of SDSL is about 3 Mbps, which is slower than the 10 Mbps maximum speed for downstream ADSL. **C** is incorrect because it states you should recommend SDSL because ADSL is only available in Europe. ADSL is much more popular in North America than SDSL. SDSL is more popular in Europe than ADSL. **D** is incorrect because it states there is no performance difference between ADSL and SDSL.

**8.** ☑    **D.** A line splitter. DSL technology makes use of existing telephone lines by splitting the line into two channels: an analog channel for telephone use, and a digital channel for Internet access.

☒    **A** is incorrect because DSL takes advantage of existing telephone lines. ISDN technology requires a special digital line between your building and the switching station. **B** is incorrect. Bridges are used to connect networks, and while a bridge may be used in a network that uses DSL Internet access, it is not necessary for the DSL access itself. When a bridge is used on a network with DSL, it is placed somewhere central to the two (or more) networks, not between the DSL adapter and the wall outlet. **C** is incorrect. In this scenario, you already have a DSL adapter. The term *DSL adapter* is often used instead of the term *DSL modem*, because there is no need for data to be modulated or demodulated.

**9.** ☑ **D.** No, cable does not provide high security. The cable system is laid out in a large bus network. This means that users in a neighborhood share the main cable backbone to the cable company. Data from one user shares the same line as data from other users, so it is possible for the wrong person to intercept data packets.

☒ **A** is incorrect because it states that you should recommend cable to the customer. Because of the security issues discussed, you should not recommend cable. **B** is incorrect because cable Internet access is not limited by distance. If cable lines exist in an area, they may be used for Internet access just as easily as for cable TV. However, this customer shouldn't use DSL, because it has a limit of three miles from the ISP. **C** is incorrect because cable access is direct. The modem is connected to the ISP as soon as the proper channel is found (on the first installation), and the connection is never dropped. It works just like your TV. As soon as you turn the TV on, the channels are there; you don't have to dial up to find them each time you turn the TV on.

**10.** ☑ **D.** Cable. The cable upstream bandwidth uses the frequency range 5–40MHz. This range is quite susceptible to interference from household appliances and radios. Furthermore, because the cable is shared among many users, the interference generated at each location is added to and compounded on the line.

☒ **A**, **B**, and **C** are all incorrect. Although these modems are susceptible to line noise, they all connect to the ISP via an independent telephone line. Each user has his own line to the ISP, so interference generated by one user does not affect the line of another user.

**11.** ☑ **C.** ATDT5551234. Most AT commands must start with the letters AT, and are directly followed by the command itself. In this case, the command is DT, for Dial using Tones. When dialing, the telephone number itself is entered immediately following the dial command.

☒ **A** is incorrect because the command to dial (D) must come before the number to be dialed. Furthermore, DP indicates pulse, not tone, dialing. **B** is improper syntax for the AT dial-up command. In this case, the Ds have been transposed with the Ts. **D** is incorrect because although this is a legitimate command, it will result in pulse dialing, not tone dialing.

**12.** ☑ **B.** You suggest an Ethernet NIC to connect her DSL adapter to the computer. While it's true that there may be many reasons for using a network card in Internet access, this is the only correct answer listed here. DSL adapters (and cable modems) typically connect to the computer through an internal Ethernet card because it is the only port on the computer capable of keeping up with the high speeds of the modem or adapter itself.

☒ **A** is incorrect because it states that you would suggest a Token Ring card. While a Token Ring card could be used to attach a cable modem to the computer, it is not capable of the same speeds as an Ethernet card, so you would not recommend it over an Ethernet card. **C** is incorrect because it states that you would suggest a Token Ring card to attach an ISDN modem to a network. Again, you normally wouldn't suggest Token Ring over Ethernet, and a home user is not likely to want to use ISDN in a home network for Internet access. However, if this was the case, you should recommend an *internal* ISDN modem, so that there is no data bottleneck at all. **D** is incorrect because it states that an Ethernet card could be used to provide firewall protection. Firewall protection is provided to home users by their ISP. Firewalls are typically used to keep outside Internet users from accessing information on an internal network. In any case, a network server or dedicated firmware is required to create a firewall, not a network card.

**13.** ☑ **A.** Broadcasting. All computers on a star network attach to a separate port on the hub. When the hub receives data from a computer, it resends the data to every other port. This is called *broadcasting*. All computers receive the packet, but only the destination computer opens it.

☒ **B** is incorrect. Networked computers have a MAC address based on their network card. While this addressing method is used in bridge routing tables to identify computers from different network segments, hubs do not use it. Hubs simply copy and send all data from one port to all other ports. **C** is also incorrect. This is a more sophisticated addressing method, based on the configuration of each computer, and is used by routers to determine where specifically to send data. **D** is incorrect because it describes the hub as being totally passive. The hub is not just a holding container for data; rather, it is responsible for passing data back and forth.

**14.** ☑ **D.** Bridge. When the bridge receives data, it checks its routing table for that segment. If the sending and receiving computer reside in the same segment, the packet is filtered out. If the two computers are in different segments, the bridge broadcasts the packet to all other segments, since it is incapable of addressing the packet directly to the destination computer.
☒ **A** is incorrect because routers are capable of maintaining large and sophisticated routing tables. They can send a packet directly to the destination computer only, and are capable of determining the best route for the data to take through the network. **B** is incorrect because although it uses broadcasting, it is unable to send data between segments on the network. It is capable only of sending data between computers on the same segment. **C** is incorrect because it is also capable of direct addressing. However, the switch is not capable of addressing packets to destinations more than a few hops away.

**15.** ☑ **C.** The bridge uses the computer's MAC (Media Access Control) address to identify it in the routing table. The MAC address is based on the network card installed in each computer. This can cause problems when the network card must be replaced in a computer, because the routing table must be updated.
☒ **A** is incorrect because this is a more sophisticated addressing method used by switching hubs and routers, but not bridges. **B** is incorrect. A network may actually be laid out so that two nearby computers are not on the same network segment. The bridge has no knowledge of a computer's location or proximity to other resources on the network. **D** is also incorrect. The username is used by the Network Operating System (NOS) to identify users, but not by bridges. This is beneficial, because it allows users to log in and use the network from any workstation.

**16.** ☑ **C.** The bridge uses the computer's MAC address to filter out data that does not need to cross the bridge and sends everything else to all other segments. This is a broadcasting method. When a computer sends data, the bridge looks up the routing table for that computer's segment. If the destination computer is also listed in that segment's routing table, then the two computers must be in the same segment, so there is no need to send it to the other segments. The bridge is not sophisticated enough to do direct addressing, so data traveling between segments is sent to all parts of the network to ensure it gets to the destination computer.

☒   **A** and **B** are incorrect because they state that the bridge uses either MAC or IP addresses to direct data to the destination computer. Although a bridge does use MAC addresses, it cannot direct data to the destination computer. The bridge is not sophisticated enough to send data only to the destination computer, so it sends data to *all* computers. Only the destination computer will open and read the packet. **D** is incorrect because it suggests that the bridge is a holding place for data until the destination segment picks up its own messages. The bridge is not a buffer and cannot hold data.

17. ☑   **C.** You should recommend routers to connect the segments of the network. Routers are capable of sophisticated direct addressing, so they do not cause unnecessary traffic or broadcast storms like bridges can. Also, routers are able to monitor the condition of network cables and devices, so they can select an alternate route for data if there is a problem in one area of the network. Routers can provide fault tolerance, meaning that if a network device, or even another router, fails, the other routers will work around the problem.

☒   **A** is incorrect. Although bridges can be used to connect multisegment networks, their method of broadcasting creates unnecessary traffic. Multiply each data packet by the number of segments in the network, and the excess traffic would become crippling. Bridges are not capable of fault tolerance because they are not able to determine which route is the best for data to reach its destination. **B** is also incorrect because switches don't provide fault tolerance. Switches are able to directly address a packet to its destination, but only if the destination is only one or two hops away. Switches are unable to keep track of the layout of an entire large network, so they are unable to look ahead and determine the best route for a packet. **D** is incorrect because this is a translation device, not a connection device. A gateway can be software that runs on a server or a dedicated firmware device that translates data between segments using different protocols. The connection between segments must already be established for a gateway to work—it cannot provide the connection itself.

18. ☑ **D.** None of the above. Routers provide fault tolerance, meaning that if one router fails, the others will work around it and find alternate routes between sending and receiving computers. In this network, there is an alternate path between all networks in the event of a failure of router 2.

☒ **A, B,** and **C** are all incorrect because they suggest the loss of connectivity between two or more networks. In the scenario given here, router 2 provides the best, but not the only, pathway between networks. The only router failure that will result in a lost connection is router 1. If this router fails, network A will lose connectivity because it has no alternate route to the other networks.

19. ☑ **A.** A router is the most suitable device to have at position 4. The device at this position must be capable of sophisticated addressing because it is connected to so many networks and other connection devices. Data passing through this position is likely to be at least two hops away from its destination. Of the choices given, the router is the most sophisticated device, and is certainly capable of handling the tasks required at this position.

☒ **B** is incorrect. Because of the number of segments connected, a bridge should not be used on this network at all. Remember, bridges broadcast data to all segments, so every message reaching the bridge from any of the five networks would be broadcast to each of the remaining four networks. This would cause the network to be so slow as to be nearly ineffective. C is incorrect because switches must be located close to destination or source segments. Although they are capable of direct addressing, they do not have very sophisticated routing tables and are unable to direct packets to destinations that are more than a few hops away. D is incorrect because it suggests that all of the devices listed could do the job equally.

20. ☑ **A.** 1 is the best position for a switch on this network. Because the switch has limited routing abilities, it is ineffective at more than a few hops from the source or destination computer. Switches are unable to determine long routes for data the way routers can. A switch in position 1 needs only a small routing table and does not need to make complex decisions about how to get a packet to its destination.

☒ **B, C,** and **D** are all incorrect because they are not the *best* place to put a switch. Although a switch may be made to work in one or more of these positions, they really involve more addressing than a switch is designed to handle. Positions 2 and 3 are both connected to two network segments and another connection device, and position 4 is connected to two segments and two connection devices. These positions require more complex routing abilities than the switch has.

21. ☑ **C.** Server software. This type of NOS is installed on the network's server(s), and is responsible for applying administrator-defined rules about which users can access which resources on a network. Restricted resources cannot even be viewed, let alone accessed, by users who do not have permission to use them.
☒ **A** is incorrect because this type of NOS simply allows all users to access all resources. The only restrictions on this type of network are device passwords. If you don't know the password of a particular printer, for example, you cannot use it. Server-based software is more secure because you cannot even see a restricted printer, so there is no chance of you guessing its password and gaining access to it. **B** is incorrect. This type of NOS is installed on the workstations in a server-based network. It allows users to log on to the network, but does not manage user profiles and enforce security restrictions. **D** is also incorrect.

22. ☑ **C.** You should place the Internet-in-a-box anywhere on the network as long as it is inside the firewall. The Ibox is a physical device that can plug into the network to provide it with DHCP, Web caching, and security features. It also may provide e-mail and Web browser programs for Internet access. Network traffic can significantly decrease if requests must leave the internal network, go through the firewall, and then reenter the network.
☒ **A** is incorrect because the network computers must have easy access to the Ibox. The Ibox is a part of the internal network itself. **B** is incorrect because Internet-in-a-box is not software, rather it is a firmware device (hardware with software hardwired into it). **D** is incorrect because it states that an Ibox will not work on the network in this scenario. The network has no apparent characteristics that would prevent the use of an Ibox. However, some Iboxes cannot be used on multiprotocol networks.

**23.** ☑   **A.** The firewall's proxy server examines all incoming data and screens out unwanted packets based on their content and/or application type. The proxy is typically installed on a server located between the internal network and the Internet. This type of firewall provides more security than other types because it does not rely simply on IP addresses to make screening decisions, and is not susceptible to IP spoofing.

☒   **B** is incorrect because this is a description of how a *packet*-level firewall works. A packet-level firewall examines the source IP address of all incoming data and screens out all data from unrecognized or restricted IP addresses. **C** is incorrect because it states that the firewall examines the contents of incoming data and removes viruses and restricted content from it. Firewalls are not sophisticated enough to read and rewrite the content of a data packet. **D** is incorrect because A is the only correct answer here.

**24.** ☑   **B.** When the network requires the highest speed possible. Packet-level firewalls screen information based on the sender's IP address. The packet is not opened or altered, so this is the fastest type of firewall. Application-level firewalls perform a more thorough examination of incoming data, which can cause Internet access to slow down.

☒   **A** is incorrect because packet-level firewalls provide the *lowest* security. They make screening decisions based on IP address alone, and are susceptible to being fooled by IP spoofing. **C** is incorrect because packet-level firewalls can be very difficult to configure. This type of firewall is configured with rules about which IP addresses to accept or reject information from. The more rules you add, the more likely it is to inadvertently allow wide-open access to your network, or create conflicting rules that create unwanted results. **D** is incorrect because it suggests that packet-level firewalls provide a detailed account of Internet access activity. In fact, packet-level firewalls provide very poor activity accounts, and application-level firewalls provide detailed accounts.

**25.** ☑   **B.** Place a proxy server outside the network, and a packet screening router between the proxy server and Internet. A screened host firewall is an application-level firewall that is first screened by IP address. Incoming data first passes through the packet screening router, and then data from valid IP addresses is screened at the proxy server before being passed on to the network.

☒  A is incorrect because it only includes a packet screening router. This will provide packet-level screening only, but a screened host firewall includes both packet-level and application-level screening. **C** is incorrect. The proxy server should be placed *outside* the network so it can be screened before it has a chance to enter the network. **D** is incorrect because it has the router and proxy server positions switched. In a screened host firewall, the host (proxy server) is screened first by the router.

26. ☑  **B.** This is a nonprofit organization. There are many domain name extensions, and .org can be used only by nonprofit organizations.

    ☒  A and **D** are incorrect. Although this may be an American Web site, you cannot determine this for sure, since other countries may use the .org extension as well. **C** is incorrect because this type of organization typically uses the .net extension. Although they may choose the more popular .com extension instead, the .org extension is unavailable to them unless it is also a nonprofit organization.

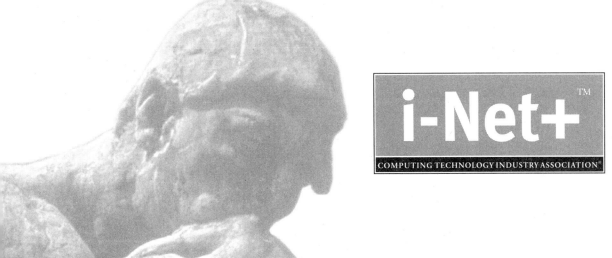

# Servers and Bandwidth Technologies Questions

Q & A

# Servers and Bandwidth Technologies

1. An ISP offers a 1.5Mbps line with 24 channels. Users can lease a portion of the line for their Internet connection. What type of line is this?

   A. DSL

   B. T3

   C. Fractional T1

   D. Frame Relay

2. Much of the Internet's backbone is comprised of a line that will transmit at about 43 Mbps. What type of line is this?

   A. DSL

   B. T1

   C. T3

   D. E1

3. You work for a company that creates and maintains internal networks for small businesses. A colleague mentions that he has never worked with T3 line. What is the most likely reason for this?

   A. T3 line is typically used to connect businesses to their ISP.

   B. T3 line is typically used in the backbone of the Internet.

   C. T3 line is typically used to create internal networks for large businesses (over 500 users).

   D. T3 line is not used in North America.

4. A company has a wide area network, with intermittent traffic between the two farthest endpoints. The company doesn't need a dedicated T1 line, but wants to occasionally use their ISP's existing T1 Internet lines to send data between the two farthest endpoints. What type of service will provide this occasional, but not dedicated, T1 line access?

   A. Frame Relay

   B. Fractional T1

   C. T2

   D. There is no such service.

**5.** A company is planning to use a Frame Relay service to save money, while enjoying the benefits of T1 line transmission. The company plans to send video transmissions from point A to point B on its WAN, and wants the servers at each end to perform error checking on the data. What should you tell this company?

   A. Frame Relay will not help save money.

   B. Frame Relay does not use T1 lines.

   C. Frame Relay is not suited for video transmission.

   D. Frame Relay performs its own error checking.

**6.** A company currently uses regular telephone lines in their WAN, and they are looking to speed up data transmissions. They want a service that provides thorough error correction, and for which they are only billed for the time they use the service. What advice should you give them?

   A. Use Frame Relay because customers are billed for the X.25 line regardless of usage.

   B. Use X.25 because Frame Relay does not provide error correction.

   C. Use Frame Relay because X.25 is no faster than regular telephone line service.

   D. Use X.25 because Frame Relay offers identical service, but is not widely available.

**7.** You are considering using an ISP-provided ATM service to connect your network to the Internet. Which type of ATM service should you get if your data must always be sent and received in a steady stream?

   A. Variable Bit Rate

   B. Constant Bit Rate

   C. Unspecified Bit Rate

   D. Available Bit Rate

**8.** A particular fast-packet technology transmits fixed-length cells with a payload of 48 bytes. Which type of service is this?

A. Frame Relay

B. X.25

C. ATM

D. DSL

**9.** An ISP offers an Internet service that makes use of existing telephone lines and supports speeds up to 10 Mbps. What type of service is this?

A. Frame Relay

B. X.25

C. ATM

D. DSL

**10.** You work for an ISP that offers many Internet access methods. A client wants a fast, dedicated Internet connection for their Ethernet network, but does not want to install special cabling at their location. What should you recommend?

A. Frame Relay

B. X.25

C. ATM

D. DSL

**11.** You are planning to set up a network that provides proxy, caching, and firewall services to internal users. What is the minimum number of computers you can use to provide these services?

A. Three—a proxy server, a cache server, and a firewall server

B. Two—the proxy and cache services on one server, and the firewall services on another

C. Two—the proxy and firewall services on one server, and the cache services on another

D. One—the proxy, cache, and firewall services all on one server

**12.** Your company is planning to create two networks: one to host a Web site, and a separate network to provide employees with Internet access. Which of the two is most likely to be used on the employee network, but not on the network hosting the Web site?

A. Certificate server

B. Cache server

C. Web server

D. FTP server

**13.** A network server has the ability to make Internet requests on behalf of the network's users. What type of server is this?

A. Cache server

B. Proxy server

C. Web server

D. FTP server

**14.** A network computer has been set up to retrieve POP3 account messages, and then sort and forward the messages to the proper users on the network. What type of computer is this?

A. Proxy server

B. Cache server

C. List server

D. Mail server

**15.** Access to the Internet is a vital part of your business. What can you do to help ensure Internet connectivity for your network in the event of a server failure?

A. Install cache software on the server

B. Set up a mirrored server on the network

C. Set up a UPS for the server to maintain uninterrupted power

D. Limit the number of concurrent Internet connections to four

**16.** A network has been set up with a primary server and a secondary server. The secondary server is mirrored, and is configured to take over the function of the primary server only in the event of a failure. What does this setup provide for the network?

A. Load balancing

B. Fault tolerance

C. Faster Internet access

D. Request filtering

**17.** A network computer has been set up as a cache server. What is the primary purpose of this computer?

A. To protect internal networks from access by external Internet users

B. To prevent network users from accessing particular Web sites

C. To maintain transaction records in the event of a server failure

D. To speed up Internet access to previously viewed sites

**18.** A client is setting up a network that will have Internet access, and cannot decide whether to use a proxy server or a cache server. Internet speed is the first priority, and fault tolerance is the second priority. What is your advice?

A. Use a proxy server—it acts as a proxy and also does the job of a cache server.

B. Use a cache server—it is a more robust version of a proxy server.

C. Use proxy software on the primary server and cache software on the backup (mirrored) server.

D. Install proxy and cache software on the network server.

**19.** A company has asked for your help in setting up a network that has Internet access. You have decided to use one of the network's machines as a list server. Why?

A. To sort and forward e-mail messages to the proper users

B. To provide fault tolerance

C. To maintain mailing lists and distribute messages to groups of users

D. To speed up access to previously viewed Web sites

**20.** The company Blitz, Inc has asked for your help in implementing their new Web site. Users who download software from this site will receive the following follow-up letter:

*"Thank you for visiting blitz.com. You are now among the 20,000 users who have discovered the benefits of using our online downloads. You will now receive automatic updates for your new software. If you wish to unsubscribe, please e-mail us at unsubscribe@blitz.com."*

From the information given, which is the most important thing you can recommend to help Blitz maintain their Web site?

A. A list server

B. An FTP server

C. A mirror site

D. A cache server

**21.** Your company's network hosts a Web site and provides Internet access to internal users. How many servers should you have on the network if you want to prevent access to the internal network from external users?

A. One—a single server can act as a Web server, proxy server, cache server, and firewall server.

B. At least two—the Web server should be placed closest to the Internet, and the firewall/proxy server should be placed between the Web server and the network.

C. At least two—the firewall server should be located closest to the Internet, and the Web server should be located inside the firewall.

D. One—the Web server will automatically provide cache, proxy, and firewall services to the network.

**22.** You have just subscribed to a newsgroup on USENET. What type of protocol does this news system use?

A. NNTP

B. SMTP

C. FTP

D. HTTP

**23.** A company hosts a Web site where users can view their investment account information. A security feature has been implemented so that only authorized users can enter the Web site, and each user can only view his or her own account information. What type of server is responsible for maintaining the confidentiality and security of this Web site?

A. Certificate server

B. Authentication server

C. Authorization server

D. Web server

**24.** You are planning to make an online purchase at blitz.com using your credit card. Who is most likely hosting the certificate authentication?

A. Your ISP

B. Blitz

C. The credit card company

D. Your computer

**25.** A large network uses LDAP directory services. What is the function of LDAP on this network?

A. To organize e-mail addresses into groups of related users

B. To enable users to locate resources on the network

C. To enforce user access/restriction rules for specified network resources

D. To prohibit external access to the internal network

**26.** A company has several employees who typically log on to the company network from their offices, but occasionally use the Internet to access the network from home. Of the following, which type of server can provide this remote access?

A. Web server

B. FTP server

C. Telnet server

D. Remote server

# Servers and
# Bandwidth
# Technologies
# Answers

*Q & A*

# Servers and Bandwidth Technologies

1. ☑ **C.** This is a fractional T1 line. T1 lines have 24 channels, and the entire line is capable of supporting speeds of up to 1.5 Mbps. Although some users may lease an entire T1 line, it is typically faster and provides more bandwidth than is needed by many users. Therefore, the ISP may decide to divide the channels of the T1 line, and lease out only a portion of them to individual users. When this is the case, it is called a *fractional T1 line.*
   ☒ **A** is incorrect because although this line type can transmit at 1.5 Mbps, it consists of only two channels, both of which are required for Internet connections. The channels cannot be divided and leased to different parties. **B** is incorrect because this type of line consists of 672 channels, and can transmit at 43 Mbps. **D** is incorrect because this is a type of service, not a type of line. Frame Relay is a service offered by Internet Service Providers (ISPs) that allows users to temporarily use T1 or T3 lines without having to lease the line.

2. ☑ **C.** T3. T3 is comprised of 672 channels, and combined, they can transmit at 43 Mbps. The most common implementation of T3 line is within the Internet backbone, and in connecting ISPs to the backbone.
   ☒ **A** and **B** are both incorrect. Both of these line types are restricted to transmission speeds of about 1.5 Mbps, so they are not capable of meeting the high-speed demands of the Internet backbone. **D** is incorrect because this is the European version of T1, and it is restricted to 2 Mbps. Again, this is not sufficient to handle the transmission requirements of the Internet backbone.

3. ☑ **B.** T3 line is typically used in the backbone of the Internet. T3 line consists of 672 channels, and can transmit at 43 Mbps. It is used to connect mainframes, which make up the Internet backbone, and to connect ISPs to the backbone. Because of this usage, it is very unlikely that someone working only on small internal networks would need to use T3 line.

☒   **A** is incorrect because it states that T3 line is typically used to connect businesses to their ISP. Although T3 can be used for this purpose, it offers much more bandwidth and speed than is required by most clients. T1, DSL, or ISDN are much more appropriate choices for connecting businesses to their ISP. **C** is incorrect because it suggests that T3 is most often used in creating large internal networks. T3 is a telephone line technology that must be accessed by the computer using a modem. Internal networks most often use network cables and network cards, not telephone lines and modems. **D** is incorrect. T3 line is used predominantly in North America, and E3 line is used in Europe.

**4.**   ☑   **A.** Frame Relay. This is a service provided by some ISPs to allow users occasional access to T1 lines without having to lease their own T1 line. Data is sent normally across the network, and customers are billed only for the time that data is relayed through the T1 line.

☒   **B** is incorrect because this is a method of dividing the 24 channels in a T1 line and leasing them to different parties. In the case of a fractional T1, each customer has a dedicated portion of the line. **C** is incorrect because there is no service or line called a "T2." **D** is incorrect because it states that there is no service that allows for occasional use of the Internet's existing T1 lines.

**5.**   ☑   **C.** Frame Relay is not suited for video transmission. Frame Relay is the use of ISP-owned T1 or T3 lines. The ISP can relay information from users across these lines, and bill them according to usage. Because the line is not dedicated to one company or user, the line is "shared," so data from point A to point B may not be transmitted in a steady flow. If a video file is not received in a steady flow, it will appear choppy, and the sound may not coincide with the video.

☒   **A** and **B** are incorrect. Frame Relay will not help save money, and it does not use T1 lines. Frame Relay allows users to occasionally access T1 lines without having to lease their own dedicated line. This means that users get the benefits of the T1 line, but only pay for the time they use it. This solution is much cheaper than leasing a dedicated T1 line. **D** is incorrect because this service is responsible only for relaying frames of data. The sending and receiving computers are responsible for checking the data for errors and retransmitting if necessary.

6. ☑ **B.** You should advise this company to use X.25 because Frame Relay does not provide error correction. X.25 is much slower than Frame Relay (64 Kbps vs. 1.5 Mbps) but is more thorough and is responsible for providing error correction and retransmitting data when necessary.
☒ **A** is incorrect because it states that customers are billed for the X.25 service regardless of usage. This is untrue because in both X.25 and Frame Relay, customers are only billed for the time they use the line. Conversely, with a dedicated T1 line, users are billed for the line, whether they actually send information over it or not. **C** is incorrect because it states that X.25 is no faster than regular telephone lines. While phone lines offer a maximum of 56 Kbps, X.25 is able to deliver data at 64 Kbps. **D** is incorrect because it suggests that X.25 and Frame Relay are the same service, with Frame Relay being less available than X.25. X.25 and Frame Relay are equally available in most areas, and the two technologies are not equal. X.25 is slower, but "smarter," because it provides error correction. Frame Relay can be much faster, but simply relays packets, without checking for errors or requesting retransmissions.

7. ☑ **B.** Constant Bit Rate. This type of ATM service sends data in a continuous, steady stream, so for the time the line is being used, it is dedicated only to that particular transmission.
☒ **A** is incorrect because this type of ATM service can maintain a high speed, but data cells may be sent sporadically during data transmissions. **C** is incorrect because, like Variable Bit Rate service, UBR does not send data in a steady stream. The difference between VBR and UBR is that VBR guarantees a minimum transmission rate, while UBR does not. **D** is incorrect because data is not sent in a steady stream. ABR is similar to VBR in that they both guarantee a minimum data transfer speed, but ABR supports speed bursting when the line is free.

8. ☑ **C.** ATM. This type of Internet service transmits data in cells that are each 53 bytes in size. The first 5 bytes constitute the header of the data, which contains addressing information, and the remaining 48 bytes are the actual data being transmitted (called the "payload"). The fact that each cell is a fixed size means that data is sent in a relatively even stream, and the small size of each cell reduces the amount of data that must be retransmitted in the case of a cell error.

☒   **A** and **B** are both incorrect because although they are forms of fast-packet technology, they do not transmit fixed-length cells. The size of each packet can vary greatly from transmission to transmission in these two technologies. **D** is incorrect because this is a type of dedicated line, while Frame Relay, X.25, and ATM are types of relaying services. When you use a DSL service, a line splitter is installed on your telephone line, and it becomes a dedicated circuit between you and the Internet.

9. ☑   **D. DSL.** This type of service makes use of regular telephone lines by using a splitter that divides the line into two "channels": one for voice (telephone) communications, and one for digital (Internet) communications. Asynchronous DSL supports up to 10 Mbps downstream, and does not interfere with the use of the telephone.
   ☒   **A** is incorrect because this is a service that uses either T1 or T3 lines, and is limited to 1.5 Mbps (T1) or 43 Mbps (T3). **B** is incorrect because it supports speeds up to 64 Kbps, which is only slightly faster than regular analog telephone communications. **C** is incorrect because this requires a special ATM connection, and supports speeds up to 155 Mbps.

10. ☑   **D.** You should recommend DSL. This technology makes use of existing telephone lines, so no additional cables need to be installed at the customer's location. DSL is much faster than analog communications, as it typically supports up to 10 Mbps. Finally, since DSL uses the customer's existing phone line, the Internet connection is dedicated to that user or network.
    ☒   **A** is incorrect because this service provides fast communications; it does not provide customers with a dedicated line. A Frame Relay service allows customers to make temporary use of their ISP's T1 or T3 lines. Customers are billed only for the data that was relayed, and the line is not dedicated to any single customer. **B** is incorrect because this is also a type of relaying service. No additional cabling is required, but the connection is not dedicated, and it supports speeds of only 64 Kbps. **C** is incorrect because although this technology provides a very fast connection (up to 155 Mbps), it is designed to work with a special ATM network. The client in this scenario has an Ethernet network, so a great deal of hardware and cable installation would be required to convert the network from Ethernet to ATM.

11. ☑ **D.** The minimum number of machines in this case is one; the proxy, firewall, and cache services can all be provided by one server. These services can be installed on a single machine. In fact, using one server for these three services is a very common and practical configuration.

☒ **A** is incorrect because it suggests you need a minimum of three servers. Although this configuration would work, it is not the minimum number of machines required. In cases where the networking budget is small, this solution is not practical, since there is no need to separate proxy, firewall, and caching services. **B** and **C** are both incorrect because although they each represent valid server configurations, they do not represent the minimum number of machines required. Although it is common to separate the firewall from the proxy/cache server, it is not necessary, so there is no need to have two servers on the network.

12. ☑ **B.** A cache server is likely to be used on the employee network, but not on the network hosting the Web site. Cache servers are used to help speed up Internet access for users who frequent the same Web pages as other users. When a user accesses a particular Web page, the cache retains a copy of that page. When the same page is requested at a later time, the cache server delivers its own copy of the page, rather than accessing it again from the Internet. A network whose only function is to host a Web site does not support access to the Internet for the company's employees, so there is no need to install a cache server.

☒ **A** is incorrect because this type of server is used only on networks or computers that host Web or FTP sites. The certificate server is responsible for filtering out requests so that only authorized Internet users can access all or part of the site. **C** and **D** are both incorrect because the function of these types of servers is to host Internet sites, not to provide Internet access to groups of users on a network.

13. ☑ **B.** This is a proxy server. The function of a proxy server is to intercept users' requests to the Internet and make the request on the Internet on behalf of the user. The proxy server can help enforce network security by filtering requests from users, as well as masking the user's ID by imposing its own IP address on the request.

☒ **A** is incorrect. Although a proxy server may include caching functions, a cache server is used to "remember" previously accessed Web sites, so that they can be quickly recalled later. A cache server by itself cannot make Internet requests on behalf of network users. **C** is incorrect because the function of this type of server is to deliver Web pages from the Internet to the user, either directly or via a proxy server. Web servers are used to host Web pages, and each Web server has a URL. For example, when you visit the site www.syngress.com, the Web server at that address is responsible for delivering the Web page to you. **D** is incorrect because this is another type of delivery server. While Web servers deliver Web pages using HTTP, FTP servers deliver files to users. *HTTP (Hypertext Transfer Protocol) is used on the Internet to download Web pages. FTP (File Transfer Protocol) is used in downloading files (without the fancy Web pages).*

14. ☑ **D.** This computer is a mail server. A POP3 (Post Office Protocol) account is simply a large mailbox that stores mail for all users at a particular location. For example, the POP3 account at business.com may be mail@business.com. The job of the mail server is to intercept these messages, sort them, and forward them to the proper users. For example, messages in the POP3 account may be individually addressed to mary@business.com or fred@business.com.

☒ **A** is incorrect because this type of computer is used to make Internet requests on behalf of network users, such as opening a particular Web page, or downloading files. **B** is incorrect because the function of this type of server is to "remember" previously viewed Web pages so that they can be delivered faster in the future. **C** is incorrect because this type of computer is used to maintain mailing lists of individuals or groups. Although a list server may be used in addressing mail messages, it is the responsibility of the mail server to actually distribute and send mail.

15. ☑ **B.** Set up a mirrored server on the network. A mirrored server is a separate computer on the network that maintains a backup of all transactions carried out by the primary server. In the event of a primary server failure, the mirrored server takes over its functions, picking up where the primary server left off.

☒   **A** is incorrect. The function of a cache is to remember previously viewed Web pages in order to deliver them faster the next time they are requested. This may give the appearance of connectivity even if the Internet connection is lost, but only for users accessing pages already stored in the cache. All other Web pages will be inaccessible. Furthermore, if the server fails, it is likely that all of its functions will fail, including its caching function. **C** is incorrect because this will only maintain the server's function in the event of a power loss or surge. There are many other reasons for a server to fail, including corrupt software, or hardware problems. A UPS will not maintain the function of the server in these cases. **D** is incorrect. Although limiting the number of Internet connections may help to avoid a server failure, it will do nothing to maintain Internet connectivity if the server has already failed.

16. ☑   **B.** The mirrored server provides fault tolerance to the network. Fault tolerance is the ability of a computer or network to maintain its function in the event of a failure of any one of its components. In this case, the mirrored server contains a duplicate copy of the primary server's information, and will maintain the network's function if the primary server fails.
☒   **A** is incorrect. Load balancing typically refers to the division of tasks between servers in order to speed up network activity and reduce the processes carried out by any one server. Although some secondary servers can provide load balancing, this scenario states that the mirrored server will only be used if the primary server fails. **C** is also incorrect. Mirrored servers can speed up Internet access if they are closer to the user than the original server, but in this scenario, the mirrored server is only to be used if the primary server fails. **D** is incorrect because this is the function of a proxy server. Although both the primary and mirrored servers may have proxy software installed on them, the mirrored server will only perform this function if the primary server fails.

17. ☑   **D.** The main purpose of a cache server is to speed up Internet access to previously viewed sites. A server with cache software installed on it is able to remember recently viewed Web sites. The first time a page is requested, it is delivered from the Internet, and the server retains a copy of the page in its cache. The next time the page is requested, the server delivers its cached copy, which is much faster than accessing the Internet again.

☒ **A** is incorrect because this is the function of a firewall server. A cache server is unable to mask or filter requests to and from the Internet. Its only function is to retain previously viewed Web sites for faster future recall. **B** is incorrect because this is a function of a firewall or proxy server. Every Internet request from a network goes through the proxy server. The proxy filters messages based on predefined access rules, and delivers only requests that are not prohibited by these rules. **C** is incorrect. This is the function of a mirrored server. A mirrored server contains an exact duplicate of the primary server's transactions so that it may take over if the primary network fails. A cache server also retains information, but only about viewed Web sites. It cannot maintain a network with an Internet connection.

18. ☑ **D.** Install proxy and cache software on the network server. Although proxy and cache software perform two different functions, they can coexist on one machine, and are often designed to work with one another. Cache software allows the server to retain copies of previously viewed Web sites, and proxy software makes Internet requests on behalf of the network's users. When a user makes an Internet request, it is first intercepted by the server. If the requested page exists in the cache, the server delivers it to the user. If not, the proxy software filters the request using predefined access rules. If the request is valid, the proxy sends the request out to the Internet on behalf of the user.

☒ **A** and **B** are both incorrect because they suggest that proxy and cache software are essentially different versions of the same thing. A proxy server does not have the same functions as a cache server, and a cache server is not a robust version of a proxy. Remember, both types of software perform complimentary, but different roles. **C** is incorrect because it suggests using proxy software on the primary server, and cache software on the mirrored server. There is no need to separate proxy and cache functions across machines. Furthermore, if a machine is to act as a mirrored server, it must be identical to the primary server. This means that it must include the same functionality as the primary server so that it can take over the role of network server in the event of a failure. If the primary server includes proxy and/or cache software, the mirrored server must include the same configuration.

19. ☑ **C.** You may use a list server to maintain mailing lists and distribute messages to groups of users. The function of a list server is to maintain users' addresses, and to organize them into groups. The list server can then be used to mail out messages, newsletters, updates, etc., to different users on a prescheduled basis, depending on the criteria you define. For example, if you work with a retail store, you can use a list server to automatically mail out discount information to all clients who typically buy a particular product.

☒ **A** is incorrect because this is the function of a mail server. Although a list server can aid in the addressing and automation of sending e-mail (or other types of messages), list servers are not responsible for actually transferring or receiving e-mail to and from the ISP. **B** is incorrect because this is a feature of a mirrored server. A mirrored server contains an exact duplicate of the primary server's transactions and configurations so that it can take over and maintain the network even if the primary server fails. **D** is incorrect because this is the job of a cache server. When a user requests a Web page, a copy of the page is retained in the cache. When another user requests the same page, the server finds it in the cache, and then delivers it without having to download it again from the Internet (which is much slower).

20. ☑ **A.** The most important thing you can recommend is a list server. The only thing you can assume from the information given is that Blitz plans to automatically send large numbers of e-mail messages to users who visit their Web site. A list server can be configured to automatically add new users to the mailing list and send messages to large groups of users. In practical terms, the large number of users (20,000) prevents manual maintenance of the list and transmission of e-mail.

☒ **B** is incorrect. FTP stands for File Transfer Protocol, and offers a faster method of file transfer than downloading from a Web site. However, in this scenario, users are expected to download files from the Web site, not a separate FTP site (the line "Thank you for visiting blitz.com…" indicates a Web site, not an FTP site). Furthermore, using an FTP site for downloads benefits the user, not the company hosting the site. From the information given, you can assume that the main issue is maintenance of the Web site, not the speed at which users can download information. **C** is also incorrect because this can improve downloading speed for the user, but does not help in maintaining the Web site. A mirrored site is an exact replica of a main Web site. It is usually placed in a different geographical location in order to server users in different areas. For example, an American company may place a mirrored site in Europe to provide faster access to European users. **D** is incorrect. Cache servers retain frequently accessed Web sites in order to speed up Internet access for end users on a network. There is no need for a cache server on the Web site end unless the Web site is also part of a network that provides Internet access for internal users of the company.

**21.** ☑   **B.** You should use at least two servers—the Web server should be placed closest to the Internet, and the firewall/proxy server should be placed between the Web server and the network. Because external Internet users will be accessing the Web site, the Web server should be close to the Internet and easy to access. The firewall server will block access from the outside. This configuration ensures easy access to the Web site, which is outside the protected area, and blocks access to the internal network, which is protected by the firewall.

☒   **A** and **D** are incorrect because they both suggest using only one server. However, the Web server is designed to provide easy access, and the firewall is designed to prevent access. Therefore, you should separate these functions across machines to minimize the chances of access to the network from outside. **C** is incorrect because it suggests placing the Web server inside the firewall. The firewall is designed to prevent access from the outside. If users must first encounter the firewall, they will not be allowed to access the Web server. Any users who can access beyond the firewall will also be able to access all computers inside the firewall, including the internal network.

**22.** ☑   **A.** This newsgroup uses the NNTP protocol. NNTP stands for Network News Transfer Protocol, and it used in maintaining USENET discussion forums, where users can read messages from other users and add their own messages. USENET itself is one of the largest bulletin board (news) systems on the Internet, with over 14,000 forums (discussion topics).

☒ **B** is incorrect because SMTP is a protocol used by mail servers to address, sort, and deliver e-mail to the proper users. **C** is incorrect because FTP is a method of downloading files from the Internet. Many organizations offer FTP sites as a faster, but less visual alternative to HTTP (Web) sites. **D** is incorrect because HTTP is the protocol used to transfer and view Web pages on the Internet.

23. ☑ **A.** A certificate server is responsible for maintaining the confidentiality and security of this Web site. Before users can access a secure Web site, they must obtain a digital certificate by registering their personal information with a certificate authority, such as telephone number, employee ID, credit card number, etc. The certificate authority is hosted by the certificate server, which may be located at the Web site itself, or may be hosted by a third party. When the user attempts to access the secure site, the certificate server uses the user's digital certificate to allow, reject, or restrict access to the Web site.
☒ **B** and **C** are both incorrect because they are not legitimate terms. **D** is incorrect because this type of server is used to host Web sites. Although a Web server may also have certificate server software installed on it, the two functions are separate, and the Web server itself cannot manage digital certificate security.

24. ☑ **B.** The credit card company is most likely hosting the certificate authentication. In this scenario, Blitz needs to ensure your credit card is valid, and that you are authorized to make a purchase. They do this by checking your status with the credit card company's records. If your credit card is valid for the purchase you are making, Blitz's certificate server will authorize the purchase.
☒ **A** and **D** are incorrect. In this case, Blitz is checking on your personal information, not the other way around. You do not have the authority to verify your own credit record with a company, and they would be unlikely to take your word for it. **C.** is also incorrect. Your credit information is of interest to Blitz itself. Blitz will check your credit record with the credit card company, then the Blitz certificate server will use that information to either accept or reject your purchase.

**25.** ☑ **B.** The function of LDAP is to enable users to locate resources on the network. LDAP stands for Lightweight Directory Access Protocol, and is a directory service used to provide the locations of users and resources on a network. When a user tries to access a network resource such as a printer, LDAP is responsible for locating it and providing the user's computer with the printer's location. This prevents the user from having to search through or enter long network pathnames to find or access a resource on the network.

☒ **A** is incorrect because this is the function of a list server. **C** is incorrect because this is the job of the network's client/server software. Each user in a client/server environment is granted particular rights by the network's administrator. It is the responsibility of the network server itself to enforce these rights. LDAP typically works in conjunction with the network server to ensure that users only see resources for which they have been given rights. **D** is incorrect because this is the responsibility of a firewall.

**26.** ☑ **C.** This company is using a Telnet server. Telnet is a service that allows users to access a remote network over the Internet, and use the network as if they were actually at that location. In this scenario, employees access the Internet from home, and go to the company's Telnet site. The Telnet site will prompt users for their network username and password. Once verified, users will have access to the same resources as they would if they logged on to the network from an office computer.

☒ **A** is incorrect because it is used to host a Web site. Web sites do not allow users to log in and access the internal network. In fact, many networks that host Web sites use firewall security specifically to prohibit external access to the internal network. **B** is incorrect because this type of server is used to host FTP sites, not Telnet sites. FTP sites are used strictly for downloading files. They are not part of the World Wide Web, and they do not allow Internet users to access the internal network, if there is one. **D** is incorrect because this is not a valid term.

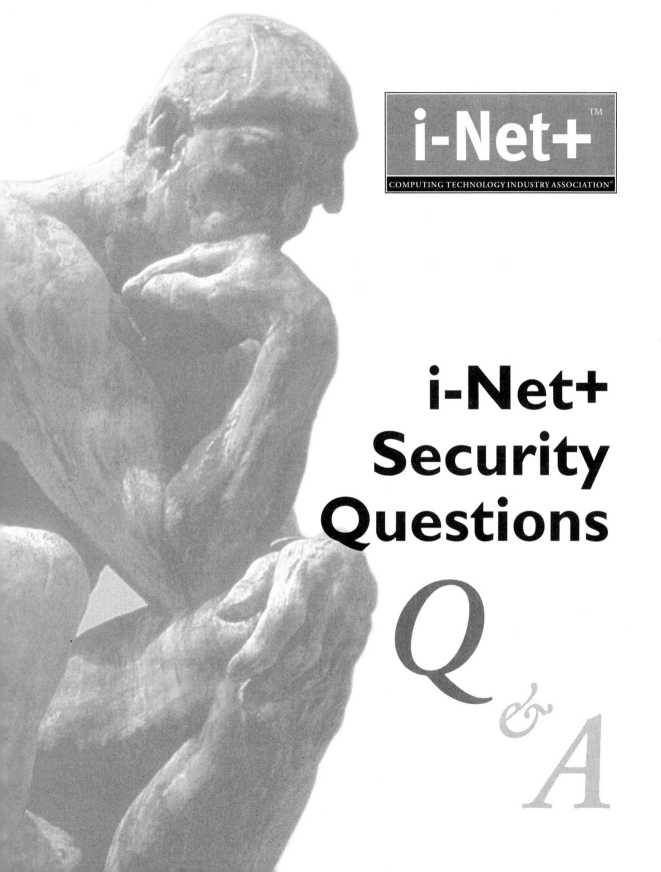

i-Net+
Security
Questions

*Q & A*

# i-Net+ Security

1. You suspect that your network has been compromised by attacks from the outside or even from malicious attacks within. Where are the best places to start looking for evidence?

   A. E-mail messages that have been sent
   B. Log files
   C. ARP table entries
   D. Network analyzers

2. Which of the following is an example of nonrepudiation?

   A. A PPTP
   B. Encryption
   C. Digital signature
   D. E-mail read receipt

3. You need to transmit sensitive data stored in an electronic form from your office in San Francisco to your corporate office in Washington, D.C. If this data should fall into the wrong hands, it would mean the end of your company. What might be the best way to transmit the data?

   A. Put the data on a floppy disk and send it via overnight express. The employees are all security conscious and packages are guaranteed to reach their destination.
   B. Use data encryption on the information and send it as an attachment to an e-mail message that is digitally signed so that the end user can verify the integrity of the e-mail.
   C. Turn on auditing on your FTP server, place the file in the public folder on your FTP server, and allow someone from HQ to FTP into your system to retrieve it. You can use anonymous for the access since only you and the other person know the file is there.
   D. Send the information in the form of an attachment to an e-mail message. E-mail is the most secured form of transfer since it cannot be intercepted.

4. You manage a group of lab assistants who perform labs and put the results in a directory. You want each of the lab assistants to be able to place his or her reports in a directory called results but not be able to read any file there or look at the directory. The users are using Windows NT 4.0 systems and NTFS drives. What privileges do you need to assign to the users?

   A. Read and write
   B. Execute
   C. Write only
   D. Read only

5. Many times a company has a need for someone from the "outside" to connect to a system on the inside. When using a VPN, at what point is the data encrypted during transfer?

   A. As soon as the outsider makes contact with the firewall, all data from that point on is encrypted.
   B. The outsider encrypts all data before sending anything. This is even done for the connection to the firewall and initial authentication.
   C. Encryption starts after the initial authentication at the firewall.
   D. After the initial authentication with the firewall, the outsider establishes a second authentication using an assigned "key" that will start the encryption.

6. You manage the information systems department of your company. One of your network administrators sends you an e-mail stating that systems are crashing randomly, and his best guess is that it's a Ping of Death attack. The vice president wants to know what is causing the problem. How do you define a Ping of Death attack?

   A. A Ping of Death attack is when users or hackers send thousands and thousands of Internet Control Message Protocol (ICMP) requests to a system and have the reply packet sent to another system, thereby using up CPU cycles and eventually causing the system to crash.
   B. A Ping of Death attack is when users initiate a TCP handshake process, but do not respond to the system's Acknowledgment (ACK) packets. The system keeps the connection open until it times out, and after receiving thousands of these TCP handshake requests and no response, the system eventually crashes.

C. A Ping of Death attack is when users or hackers send ICMP packets that are over 65,535 bytes long; some systems cannot handle a ICMP packet this large and they consequently crash.

D. A Ping of Death attack is when a user or hacker sends hundreds of e-mails to a given e-mail account with large attachments, causing the e-mail account to fill. Once it does, that user can no longer accept mail.

7. You are experiencing a server that randomly reboots. You can find no reason for this to be happening, and you believe that someone is rebooting the system. You suspect that several of your systems have been compromised. You saw a user logged in to one of your NT systems who you are sure no longer works at the company, but before you could check on the name again to make sure, he had logged off. How could you best troubleshoot this problem?

A. Change the passwords to all accounts immediately and give them out only if the users call you to complain that they can't get in. This would eliminate the users who no longer work for the company.

B. Turn on auditing and monitor who logs in to a system and what that person does. You can turn on several different auditing features, such as logins, disk access, and reboot.

C. Take away all users rights except to read and write files to the systems. This way, no one would be able to reboot the system unless he or she has the rights.

D. With all the hackers and other problems that exist today, there is very little that can be done to prevent unauthorized access to a system— it is a fact of life.

8. Your company has offices in the U.S. and in the U.K. You are working on a new prototype computer chip that would allow for over 10GB of data to be stored on a single chip the size of our standard SIMM today. You have been corresponding with your coworkers in the U.K. and now need to send them the plans for the chip so that a prototype can be built in their new lab. You both have decided on encryption as the best means of making sure that the plans are not intercepted. What level or number of bits of encryption can you use to transmit the document?

A. 64-bit

B. 128-bit

C. 256-bit

D. 512-bit

**9.** You are an employee of a research company and work from home. You currently have an ISDN data line from your home to your company's network. With the downsizing of your company, you are being asked to disconnect the ISDN line to help save money. You must come up with a solution on how to work from home and maintain security on information you transmit to the company, or you and all the other work-from-home employees will be forced to move back to the office. Your company wants to spend as little money as possible in doing this. What is your best option?

A. Use SLIP and dial in to the company.

B. Use PPP and dial in to the company network.

C. Subscribe to an ISP and use the Internet to telnet into your company. Have the network administrator open the telnet ports on the firewall that will allow you and your teammates to work from home.

D. Subscribe to an ISP and use Virtual Private Network (VPN) to access your network from the Internet.

**10.** You have about 300 users in five departments attached to your local network who need to access the Internet. You have assigned all the users a private address space address as your company cannot afford to purchase valid TCP/IP addresses for all the systems on your network. You do, however, have five TCP/IP addresses assigned to you by your ISP. How can you best use these five addresses so that your users can access the Internet?

A. Install a firewall with the five TCP/IP addresses from your ISP and allow data going out of the network to use those IP addresses.

B. Install one system in each department with a valid IP address from the ISP and allow only that system to connect to the Internet.

C. Install a Proxy server and assign it the five TCP/IP addresses from your ISP.

D. Assign the valid IP addresses on a rotating basis; each department gets them for one day each week. Use DHCP to assign them automatically. This will give five systems in each department access to the Internet once a week.

**11.** There is an industry standard for encrypting your e-mail messages. What is it, and how does it work?

    A. It is PGP and it encrypts the data at the transport layer.

    B. It is S/MIME and it encrypts the data at the Network layer.

    C. It is PGP and it encrypts the data at the Application layer.

    D. It is S/MIME and it encrypts the data at the application layer.

**12.** What are some of your options when setting up an Internet server to help keep attacks down and to assist in finding attacks?

    A. Encrypt transmissions.

    B. Use authentication such as usernames and passwords.

    C. Log all users.

    D. Enforce strong authentication.

    E. All of the above.

**13.** What is the most restrictive level of security you can apply on an NT system?

    A. Drive/Share level.

    B. Directory level.

    C. File level.

    D. All of the above are the same; when you assign one, you assign all.

**14.** You are setting up a new Web page that will require some type of authentication for access. What is the best way to make sure that only authorized users gain access?

    A. Set up a database with each authorized user's MAC address, and check it for access.

    B. Set up a database with each authorized user's TCP/IP address, and check it for access.

    C. Use usernames and passwords to gain access to the Web page.

    D. Web pages are unable to distinguish a user; all users with the TCP/IP address for the Web page domain name will be granted access to the page.

**15.** You are the network administrator of a network that is ready to be connected to the Internet. You are concerned with users on the Internet being able to access your network from the outside. You feel that you need to have a network connection so that your users can access the Internet for their daily duties. How could you give your users access to the Internet while keeping others out of your network?

A. Install a Proxy server.

B. Install a firewall.

C. Install a Web server.

D. Use a private address scheme on your network so that the TCP/IP address being sent out of your network cannot be used to gain access to your network.

**16.** You are having a serious problem on your network. Systems are crashing for no apparent reason. You have studied the problem and see no reason—hardware or software—for the systems to crash. The only thing you find out of the ordinary is when you attach a sniffer to the network, you notice hundreds of thousands of ICMP requests going across your network. What is the problem?

A. Syn floods

B. E-mail bombing

C. Spamming

D. Ping floods

**17.** You are the Webmaster for your company. You take orders from your online catalog via your Web page. Customers are concerned with other companies hacking your site and changing the link to the order page from your company to theirs. You too are concerned and want to make sure that the customers know that your site is yours and they are not being redirected someplace else where their personal information may be stolen. What measures can you take to help your customers feel more secure about your site?

A. Install encryption tools on your site and have your customers encrypt any data they send to you.

B. Request and install a certificate from a certificate authority.

C. Request a username and password from the customers before they enter their information.

D. Put your Web server behind your firewall so hackers cannot reach it.

18. What is the difference between an intranet and the Internet?

A. The Internet is the public network that users use for Web browsing, e-mail, and such; it has no security to speak of. An intranet is what a company uses among offices. Intranets still use the Internet cabling, but they have added security to insure authenticity of the data.

B. The Internet is the public network that users use for Web browsing, e-mail and such; it has no security to speak of. An intranet is what is inside a company or a local area network that also offers Web browsing and services such as e-mail only to people who are inside a company or on the LAN. This has the addition of security.

C. An intranet is the public network that users use for Web browsing, e-mail and such; it has no security to speak of. The Internet is what a company uses between offices where they use the intranet cabling, except it adds security to ensure authenticity of the data.

D. An intranet is the public network that users use for Web browsing, e-mail and such; it has no security to speak of. The Internet is what is inside a company or a local area network that also offers Web browsing and services such as e-mail only to people inside a company or on the LAN. This has the addition of security.

19. There are currently over 46,000 known computer viruses. Many are just variations of others, but each one must be checked independently. Of the different types of viruses, what is the most common?

A. Boot Sector.

B. Worm.

C. Macro.

D. All three are seen just about the same amount.

**20.** Ping floods, syn floods, and UDP attacks are all what type of attack?

   A. Smurf attack

   B. Denial of service

   C. Hijacking

   D. Back door

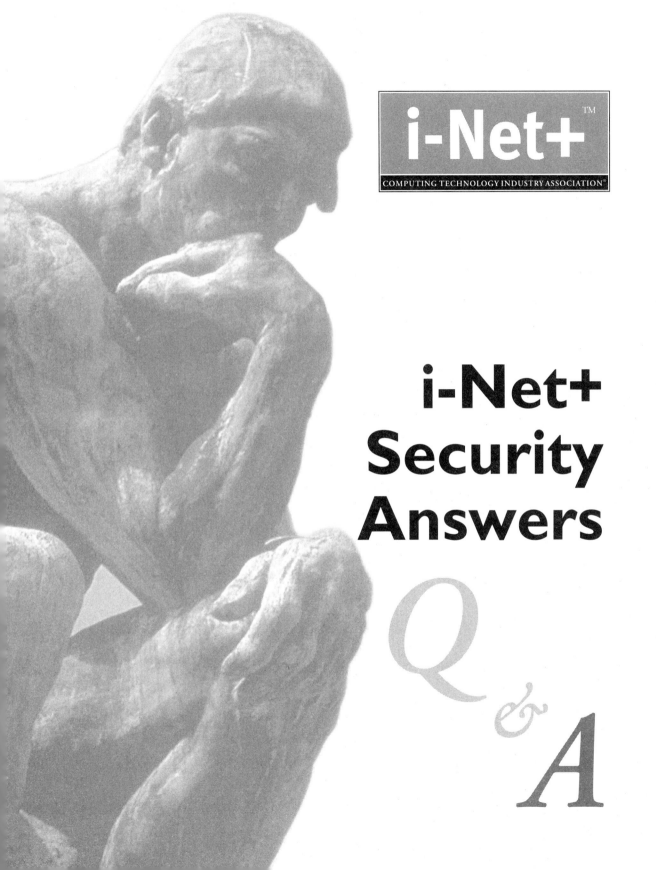

# i-Net+ Security

1. ☑ **B** and **D.** The first place to start looking for evidence of an attack or hack is to look in the log files on your systems. These log files keep lists of logins both denied and authorized and other important information. You can turn on different levels of logging depending on your operating system. Even some network equipment such as routers maintains log files to help determine where or when an attack took place.

   Network analyzers such as MS NetMon can be used for monitoring certain types of attacks that a log file just can't provide: syn floods, pings, stuff like that. You can also filter requests and log network activity. Usually a hacker will cover his tracks by deleting the server logs because they are usually located in a common place. Network analyzers take a bit more effort to cover up because they don't necessarily have to be loaded on the machine that is attacked.

   ☒ **A** is incorrect. E-mail messages might give you some indication of an attack if it's an e-mail bomb, but usually hackers creating e-mail bombs use a fake or anonymous e-mail system so that the e-mails cannot be traced. **C** is incorrect. ARP table entries will only show where a system has been transmitting data recently. ARP tables expire rather fast.

2. ☑ **C** and **D.** Nonrepudiation means to be able to verify that a transaction took place or occurred. For example, sending an e-mail and receiving a read receipt is proof that the transaction—the e-mail message—had occurred. The digital signature is another form of nonrepudiation.

   ☒ **A** is incorrect. A PPTP connection is a virtual private network; it is a protocol to access a network from the Internet in a secured manner. **B** is incorrect. Encryption by itself would not be considered nonrepudiation because unless performed with a public/private key combination, you have no proof that the transaction took place.

3. ☑ **B.** You can encrypt the data using an encryption algorithm and then attach the data to an e-mail message. Electronically sign the e-mail with a certificate and the end user will be able to determine if the e-mail was tampered with during the transfer. Encrypting the data adds an additional security step in the process. E-mail is very quick; you can call the person and be on the phone for the few minutes that it takes for the e-mail to traverse the Internet and reach the other party.

☒   **A** is incorrect. Placing the data that is vital to the life of the company in a raw form on a diskette is risky, and sending it via overnight express where it could be lost, stolen, or copied is a very poor choice. **C** is an option, but do not use the anonymous access method. Create a user and password for the person who is fetching the information. **D** is another option; e-mail is a semi-secure system, but can still be compromised easily. If you are sending sensitive data, use electronic signatures and data encryption even with e-mail.

**4.** ☑   **C.** You need to give the users write-only access to the drive. Anything more would allow them to either read the files or execute a program that is there.
☒   **A** would allow the assistants to both read and write to the directory. **B** would not allow them to write their results to the directory. **D** would allow them to read the results but not write to them.

**5.** ☑   **D.** The outsider makes an initial connection to the firewall and gains authorization. After authentication is made, the outsider then initiates a second connection, this time using a key or encryption sequence that must match up with the system that the outsider needs to communicate with. This is done all "behind the scenes"—the outsider usually does not know about the two connections; all he or she does is generally enter a password to activate the connection.
☒   **A.** The firewall has no encryption built in. The first contact is to allow connection through the firewall. **B** is incorrect. If all data was encrypted from the first packet being sent, there would need to be a system outside the firewall that would decipher the data before sending it to the firewall. This would 1) allow hackers to gain access to this system, and 2) accomplish nothing in encrypting data and deciphering it before it enters the network. **C** is also incorrect. After the initial contact with the firewall, some form of contact must be made to initiate the encryption. The firewall has no built-in encryption, so once this connection is made, the outsider's system would not know it needed to encrypt the data.

6. ☑ **C.** A Ping of Death attack is ICMP packets over 65K bytes being sent to a system that cannot handle packets that size. It will eventually cause the system to crash.

 ☒ **A** is a Ping flood, **B** is a syn_flood, and **D** is an e-mail bombing.

7. ☑ **B.** If you start auditing on your systems, you can determine who logs in and does what to each system. On the system that is rebooting, turn on auditing for login and system reboots. This way, after the system comes back up you can determine who was logged in at the time and if someone forced the reboot. This would also give you a permanent record of access to your systems for checking for unauthorized access.

 ☒ **A** would stop only people who have left the company from using accounts of employees. If someone is rebooting the system after his password was changed, he would be able to reboot the system again. **C** might fix the problem of someone rebooting the system, but it would not fix the problem of people using unauthorized accounts to access the system. This would only limit what these accounts could do. **D** is becoming a fact of life, but no one should stand by and let it happen. Security on a network is a full-time job and should be taken very seriously. As employees leave the company, their accounts should be deleted. If they are away for extended periods of time, disable their accounts until they return. The fewer accounts that you have active to access a system, the less chance that someone will be able to use one.

8. ☑ **B.** Currently, 128-bit encryption is the highest level of encryption that you can use when exporting information outside the U.S.

 ☒ **A** is a legal level of encryption to export data, but the question asked what was the highest level to transmit the data. **C** and **D** are both illegal to use when transmitting the data outside the U.S.

9. ☑ **D.** Using a VPN to access your company is the best option. The VPN uses PPTP (Point-to-Point Tunneling Protocol) to encapsulate your data inside an encrypted data packet and transmits it to a PPTP server where the data is deciphered and put onto the private network. This would cost a little up front for the software, but no ongoing fees are required.

☒   **A** and **B** would require phone lines to be added to the company, modem purchases, and a dial-in server to connect the user to the network. **C** is a security risk; opening the telnet port on the firewall is inviting hackers to walk in.

**10.** ☑   **C.** Install a Proxy server and assign it the five TCP/IP addresses from your ISP. Then configure the users' systems to use the Proxy server for Web browsing. This will allow each of the systems on your network to access the Internet any time it needs to by sending the request to the Proxy server with its private address attached. The Proxy server will take the request, attach one of the five valid IP addresses, and send it off to the Internet. When the Web page is returned to the Proxy server, it will forward it to the requesting system.
☒   **A.** A firewall will not help; it is purely there for security. If you open Port 80, the systems inside the firewall will attempt to transmit their Internet request with their private IP address and will be denied. **B** would work, but with 300 users, that averages out to 60 per department; therefore, trying to access one system is not a workable option. **D** would work, but giving each department access to the Internet only once a week is really as bad as not giving them access at all.

**11.** ☑   **D.** The industry standard for encrypting e-mail messages is S/MIME. It operates at layer 7 of the OSI model, so it encrypts the e-mail message, not the data stream. It uses a series of public and private keys for encrypting and deciphering, but what sets it off from other encryption programs is that it's done at the App layer, not at a lower layer where most other encryption programs work.
☒   **A** and **C** are excellent encryption algorithms and can be added to some e-mail packages, but they do not operate on the Application layer, they operate on the Transport layer. They are not an industry standard for encryption. You also must be aware of your encryption key length when you use PGP. Each country has laws regulating the length of the key used for data to be transmitted inside and outside the country. The U.S. allows 128-bit encryption. **B** works on the Application layer, not the Network layer.

12. ☑ **E.** All of the above are ways to help assist in fighting attacks from the outside. Encrypting transmissions makes it harder for hackers to capture and decode the data being transferred. Using strong authentication such as usernames and passwords and logging users helps you track down unauthorized access.

13. ☑ **C.** You can assign security down to the file level. You can grant a user rights to one file in the directory while denying them rights to another file in a directory.
    ☒ **A** is incorrect. If you assigned security at the drive level or share level, the user would either have rights to everything on the share/drive, or not have rights to anything on the share/drive. **B** is also incorrect. If you assigned rights to the directory, users would either be granted or denied rights to everything on the directory. **D** is incorrect. The above are very different. They all are security levels, but they are all-or-none items.

14. ☑ **C.** Using usernames and passwords are your best options. You can keep better control over who has access to the Web page.
    ☒ **A, B,** and **D** are not valid options.

15. ☑ **B.** By installing a firewall between your network and the Internet, you can control what data passes into and out of your network. You can control if e-mail is sent in or out, Web browsing, FTP, and Telnet. You can set up the firewall so that users can telnet out of your network, but outsiders cannot telnet in.
    ☒ **A** is incorrect. A Proxy server is used to serve Web pages from the Internet to users on a LAN. It is not meant or designed to keep users out of your network. **C** is also incorrect. A Web server has no security ability to keep users off your network; it houses your Web pages and transmits them as requested by a user. **D** is incorrect. If you used a private address space everywhere on your network, your users would be unable to access the Internet because routers do not route packets with private address space IP addresses.

16. ☑ **D.** This is a ping flood. Users will send thousands of ICMP requests to a system and cause the system to send the ICMP results to another system. This will eventually cause the system to crash as the ICMP requests and results take up the CPU cycles. This is called SMURFing a network.

&#9746; **A** is incorrect. A syn flood occurs when a hacker initiates a TCP handshake thousands of times. Your system never receives a response back after it sends the ACK packet, so it keeps the connection open for a set amount of time until it times out. As your system receives thousands of these TCP handshakes and no response from the ACK packet, it will eventually crash. **B** is incorrect. E-mail bombing is when a user/hacker sends large amounts of e-mail messages to a server with e-mail attachments. These attachments and e-mails fill a user's "inbox" and keep valid e-mail from being received. **C** is also incorrect. Spamming is the act of sending unsolicited e-mail to people, similar to junk mail.

**17.** &#9745; **B.** Request and receive a certificate from a certificate authority and install it on the Web page. This tells customers' browsers that you are who you claim to be. Customers can manually check the certificate from a site if they so choose, but it is generally done automatically. If customers access your site and the certificate is expired or revoked, they know that they should not use that page as it might have been compromised.

 &#9746; **A** would require your customers to have encryption software and know how to properly install and run it. This also would add additional overhead that a customer might not be willing to incur to do business with your company. **C** is incorrect. Even a bogus Web page could request a username and password. Hackers can compare them to the real database; they accept anything that you enter, and this way not only do they have the information you give them, because you believe them to be the real site, but they also have your username and password for the real site. **D** is incorrect. Placing the Web server behind your firewall will not stop a good hacker.

**18.** &#9745; **B.** The Internet is what's outside a company and is made up of cabling and routers connected together. There is very little to no security in place on the Internet. An intranet is internal to a company. It can do everything the Internet can do, but is on a LAN. It also adds many security features to help with authentication.

 &#9746; **A, C,** and **D** are all incorrect.

19. ☑  **A.** The Boot Sector viruses are the most common, not the most numerous. There are approximately 800 known Boot Sector viruses running rampant on the Internet. What makes these the most common is that they are very easy to transmit. They like to reside in memory and are copied to every diskette, hard drive, removable and network drive that comes in contact with the system.

    ☒  **B.** Worm viruses are more plentiful, but not the most common. They move on their own. Once activated, they move throughout the system infecting just about everything they touch. **C** is incorrect. Macro viruses are also plentiful, but require a program to be attached to. They run in programs such MS Word and Excel. **D** is also incorrect. Boot Sector viruses are the most common, then Worm, followed by Macro.

20. ☑  **B.** These are all types of denial of service attacks. They are meant to cause a system or host to crash due to the overwhelming amount of processing that takes place on the host when under attack.

    ☒  **A** is incorrect. A Smurf is another name for a ping flood. **C** is also incorrect. Hijacking is where a hacker pulls a datastream off the wire, changes it for his purpose, and then transmits it back on the wire. **D** is incorrect. Back doors are holes in code that allow a person to enter the system undetected. Some of these are placed on purpose, but the majority are by accident.

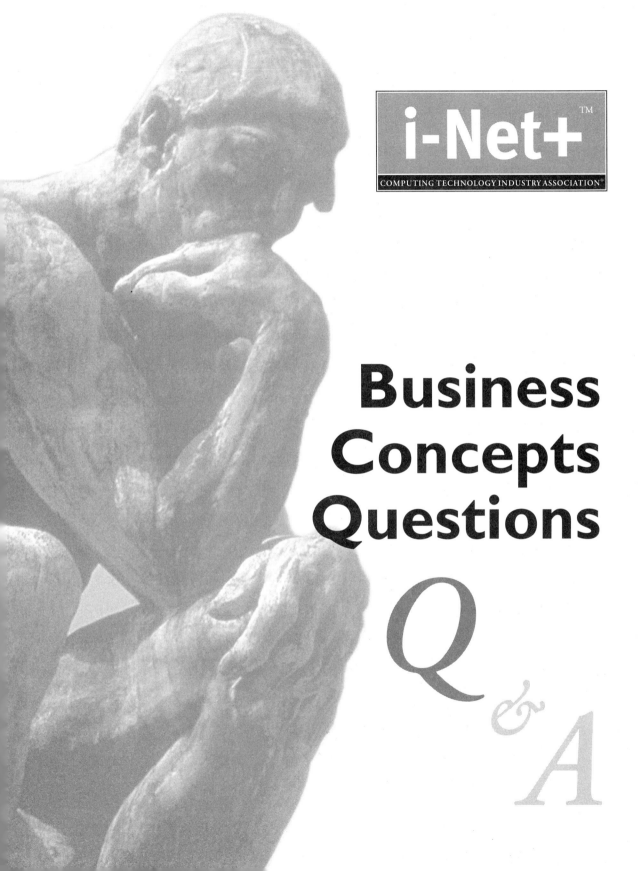

# i-Net+™
COMPUTING TECHNOLOGY INDUSTRY ASSOCIATION®

# Business
# Concepts
# Questions

Q&A

# Business Concepts

1. You have contracted out the development of your e-commerce site to a Web consulting firm. Which statement(s) are true?

    A. Since you are paying the contractors under a work-for-hire agreement, your company automatically owns your content.

    B. Since the contractor is creating the works, he owns all rights to them, and you must license the content.

    C. Since you are paying the contractors to produce a commissioned work, the creator must sign a written agreement stating that the work is for hire, before commencing development of the product, to retain all rights to your works.

    D. Since this is a Web site, the content is not protected by copyright.

2. You have an Adobe PDF file on your Web site. Many of your customers have sent you e-mail requesting a copy of the Adobe Acrobat Reader application. Since the reader itself can be freely distributed, you decide to make a copy available for download from your Web page. What do you need to do?

    A. Contact Adobe and inform the vendor that you are distributing PDF files.

    B. You need do nothing, since the Acrobat reader is freely distributable.

    C. Seek permission from the vendor through a license.

    D. Seek permission from the vendor through an assignment.

3. You are incorporating documents from the Engineering department to post on your e-business extranet. Which of the following types of documents can be copyrighted?

    A. Factual information or ideas

    B. Schematics and drawings

    C. Computer-related software code

    D. All of the above

**4.** You are creating a not-for-profit Web site that highlights U.S. Government affairs and publishes official U.S. Government documents. You are not sure whether you need to license or seek approval before publishing these works. A call to the Copyright Office informs you that (select all that apply):

   A. You are free to publish these works since they are owned by the Government and cannot be copyrighted.
   B. Since the material is being published as not-for-profit, you are free to publish the works.
   C. You may not publish these works without the express approval of the Copyright Office.
   D. You may not publish these works without paying a transaction-based licensing tax.

**5.** Which of the following is true about domain names? (Select all that apply.)

   A. Domain names can be copyrighted.
   B. Domain names cannot be copyrighted.
   C. Domain names can be trademarked.
   D. Domain names cannot be trademarked.

**6.** Which of the following government agencies grant trademark protection? (Select all that apply.)

   A. Copyright Office
   B. Patent and Trademark Office
   C. Patent and Commerce Department
   D. None of the above

**7.** What is the correct definition of a trademark? (Select all that apply.)

   A. A trademark can be a word, phrase, symbol, or design.
   B. A trademark identifies and distinguishes the source of the goods or services of one party from those of others.
   C. A trademark can be a combination of a word, phrase, symbol, or design.
   D. All of the above.

**8.** The registration symbol, ®, designates (select all that apply):

    A. That a copyright is registered at the Copyright Office.

    B. That a trademark is registered at the Copyright Office.

    C. That a trademark is registered at the Patent and Trademark Office.

    D. That a copyright has been trademarked.

**9.** Is it true that any information posted on a Web server is in the public domain and can be freely copied? (Select all that apply.)

    A. Yes, but only if the information is not registered.

    B. Yes, since the Web is on the public Internet.

    C. Yes, but only if the Web site is nonprofit.

    D. No, you still need permission to be able to copy the information.

**10.** To best anticipate customer demand on your global e-commerce site, applications should be designed to scale. This means? (Select all that apply.)

    A. Developing applications in cross-platform languages such as Java

    B. Reusing and repurposing components and software across your global systems

    C. Developing code based on component reuse and modular design

    D. All of the above

**11.** Which of the following attributes are important for global e-commerce solutions?

    A. Applications built to leverage proprietary solutions

    B. Applications built on open standards

    C. Applications built to run on multiple platforms

    D. All of the above

**12.** Your company is replacing its legacy and mainframe systems with a Web-based architecture. Some of the advantages to customers, users, and partners include (select all that apply):

A. Applications can run in any standards-based Web browser.

B. Applications and systems are accessible to a wider audience of users.

C. Enhanced interoperability between platforms and applications.

D. All of the above.

13. Supply chain management is best defined as? (Select all that apply.)

   A. A process for enhancing networking technology

   B. A process using the low cost of the Internet to leverage B2B commerce and tighter integration across suppliers, manufacturers, and distributors

   C. A management process for creating online shopping malls for conducting B2C commerce

   D. All of the above

14. Your CEO gives a briefing on the goals of transforming your company into an e-business. A key target area discussed is optimizing your supply chain. Some of the benefits include? (Select all that apply.)

   A. All players in the global supply chain, from raw material providers to final point of distribution, are linked.

   B. Real-time market and process information will be distributed to all players, allowing them to anticipate and adjust their operations in response to market conditions.

   C. Operating costs are lowered through reduced inventory requirements, which will help to eliminate costly stockpiling.

   D. All of the above.

15. You are a project manager tasked with localizing the corporate e-commerce site for France. Besides translating the content into French, you must also perform which of the following tasks? (Select all that apply.)

   A. Develop an understanding of the cultural issues relating to France.

   B. Use JavaScript to code your Web site in French.

   C. Determine which e-commerce strategies work in the French marketplace.

   D. All of the above.

**16.** Unicode is best described as? (Select all that apply.)

A.  A vendor-neutral programming language for global e-commerce sites
B.  A standard developed to support global currency transactions
C.  A standard to internationalize content so that the code never needs modification
D.  A and C

**17.** One of the costs of doing business in a global marketplace is understanding legal and regulatory issues of the local market. Which of the following statement(s) is accurate? (Select all that apply.)

A.  Since foreign governments create their own laws, U.S. laws are irrelevant.
B.  Understanding and complying with U.S. laws on copyright, trademarks, and service marks serves as a natural starting point.
C.  In many countries, bribes are the only acceptable way of conducting business and laws do not matter.
D.  Strategically select the countries in which you want to conduct business and avoid countries that are considered too risky.

# i-Net+™

COMPUTING TECHNOLOGY INDUSTRY ASSOCIATION®

# Business
# Concepts
# Answers

## Q & A

# Business Concepts

**1.** ☑ **C.** Generally, the person (or persons) who creates the work owns the copyright. However, if the work is signed over by the creator as a "work for hire," you retain all rights to the content.
☒ **A** is incorrect because work-for-hire arrangements do not automatically afford protection. **B** is incorrect because you should have the contractor sign a work-for-hire agreement, so your company retains all rights. **D** is incorrect because original works including Web sites are protected by copyrights.

**2.** ☑ **B.** Since Adobe has allowed their product to be freely distributed, you are free to distribute Acrobat.
☒ **A** is incorrect because you do not need to gain permission to distribute Adobe files. **C** and **D** are incorrect because you can freely distribute PDF files without a license. A license is required when copyrighted works require payment of specified royalties and compliance with statutory conditions. Using copyrighted material without getting permission can have disastrous consequences. An assignment is generally understood to transfer all of the intellectual property rights in a particular work. A license provides the right to use a work and is generally quite limited.

**3.** ☑ **D.** All of the above document types are copyrightable. Original works include literary works of text; architectural works, including drawings; Web sites; software source code; musical works and sound recordings; pictorial, graphic, and sculptural works; dramatic works; motion pictures; and other audiovisual works.

**4.** ☑ **A.** Documents and publications authored by the federal government are not copyrighted, and therefore are considered to be in the public domain. Consequently, if you obtain a government document from the Internet, such as a law, statute, agency circular, federal report, or any other document published or generated by the federal government, you are free to copy or distribute the document.

☒   **B** is incorrect because even if you do not plan to resell the works, you must still abide by copyright law. **C** and **D** are incorrect because copyright law does not protect government documents.

**5.** ☑   **B** and **C**. Domain names cannot be copyrighted. If an Internet domain name is used to identify and distinguish the goods and/or services, it may be registered as a trademark.
☒   **A** is incorrect. Copyright laws do not protect domain names. **D** is incorrect because domain names can be trademarked.

**6.** ☑   **B**. Trademarks are granted by filing an application to register a mark at the Patent and Trademark Office (PTO).
☒   **A** is incorrect because the Copyright Office deals with copyrights, not trademarks. **C** is incorrect because this is an invalid government agency.

**7.** ☑   **D**. A *trademark* is either a word, phrase, symbol, or design, or combination of words, phrases, symbols, or designs, which identifies and distinguishes the source of the goods or services of one party from those of others. Trademarks are used by manufacturers to distinguish their goods from goods manufactured and sold by others. For example, Netscape and Netscape Navigator are registered trademarks of Netscape Communications Corporation used to identify that company's Web browser and distinguish that software from other vendors' Web browsers.

**8.** ☑   **C**. The registration symbol, ®, is used when a trademark is registered in the PTO. It is improper to use this symbol at any point before the registration issues. You should omit all symbols from the mark in the drawing you submit with your application; the symbols are not considered part of the mark.
☒   **A** and **D** are incorrect because ® designates a trademark, not a copyright. **B** is incorrect because trademarks are registered at the PTO, not the Copyright Office.

**9.** ☑ **D.** Most of the digital works on the Internet are not in the public domain and are eligible for copyright protection, including the text of Web pages, ASCII text documents, contents of e-mail and Usenet messages, sound, graphics, executable computer programs, source code, and other multimedia objects.

☒ **A** is incorrect because copyright protection is afforded even if the works are not registered. **B** is incorrect because although information is on the Internet or a public Web server, it does not mean that the creators give up their copyright. **C** is incorrect because copyright is independent of being for profit.

**10.** ☑ **D.** Scalability allows your environment and platform to adjust to meet a dramatic surge in demand once you have deployed your e-business infrastructure. If an e-business fails to predict demand when deploying applications, it risks losing potential online sales, making customers and suppliers frustrated or dissatisfied when system response time increases and performance decreases. Developing applications in cross-platform languages such as Java makes it easy to deploy the same applications across multiple operating systems, Web browsers, and hardware platforms. Further, developing object-oriented Java applications that are modular enables objects to be repurposed for other applications across your enterprise.

**11.** ☑ **B** and **C.** Using open standards technologies, cross-platform applications will run on platforms and operating systems from multiple vendors (for example, IBM, Microsoft, Netscape, Oracle, Sun, Apple) by using standard protocols such as TCP/IP, HTTP, and HTML, Java, SSL and Java.

☒ **A** and **D** are incorrect. E-business applications are designed to run on multiple hardware platforms, operating systems, and vendor tools and applications not proprietary or product-specific solutions.

**12.** ☑ **D.** E-business solutions by their very nature support distributed computing solutions and multiple hardware/software vendors, cross-platform applications, and open scalable solutions that are standards based. A Web-enabled e-business infrastructure supports the use of Web browsers as a universal interface to access legacy systems. This ensures that your data is available to the wider population of users irrespective of the type of PC or operating system they are using.

13. ☑ **B.** Supply Chain Management (SCM) uses the low cost of the Internet to leverage tighter integration across suppliers, manufacturers, and distributors. SCM is about optimizing business processes and business value in every corner of the extended enterprise, from your supplier's supplier to your customer's customer.

    ☒ **A** is incorrect because it is not a network technology. **C** is incorrect because SCM is not focused on B2C e-commerce.

14. ☑ **D.** SCM uses e-business concepts and Web technologies to manage beyond the organization, both upstream and downstream. Manufacturers and vendors can share sales forecasts, manage inventories, schedule labor, optimize deliveries, and improve productivity. Suppliers need to be able to provide their business partners with secure access to their existing Web site and maintain product catalogs when they are making pricing and/or inventory changes.

15. ☑ **A** and **C.** Creating e-commerce sites as part of a global strategy involves more than delivering content that has been translated and localized for the native audience. It also requires an understanding of the cultural issues relating to a specific continent, country, or region. Before you enter a new market, you must do your homework in that specific country.

    ☒ **B** is incorrect because the selection of a scripting language is unrelated to localization.

16. ☑ **C.** The Unicode Worldwide Character Standard is a character coding system developed for computers to support the interchange, processing, and display of written texts of the languages of the modern world. Unicode provides the foundation for internationalization and localization of content for e-commerce and Web sites and computer software.

    ☒ **A** is incorrect because Unicode is not a programming language. **B** is incorrect because Unicode is not a standard to support currency transactions.

17. ☑    **B** and **D**. With the explosion in e-commerce, one of the costs of doing business internationally is the necessity to abide by foreign laws, rules, and regulations. Since many of the progressive nations around the world are modeling their trade and commerce laws after U.S. laws and regulations that may become part of an international standard, the natural starting point for any company is to make sure that it is in total compliance with domestic laws. Check with Forrester Research to get reports on the best countries for conducting e-commerce and e-business.

   ☒    **A** is incorrect because many countries are using U.S. laws as a standard for modeling their own laws. **C** is incorrect because laws are always important in any country.

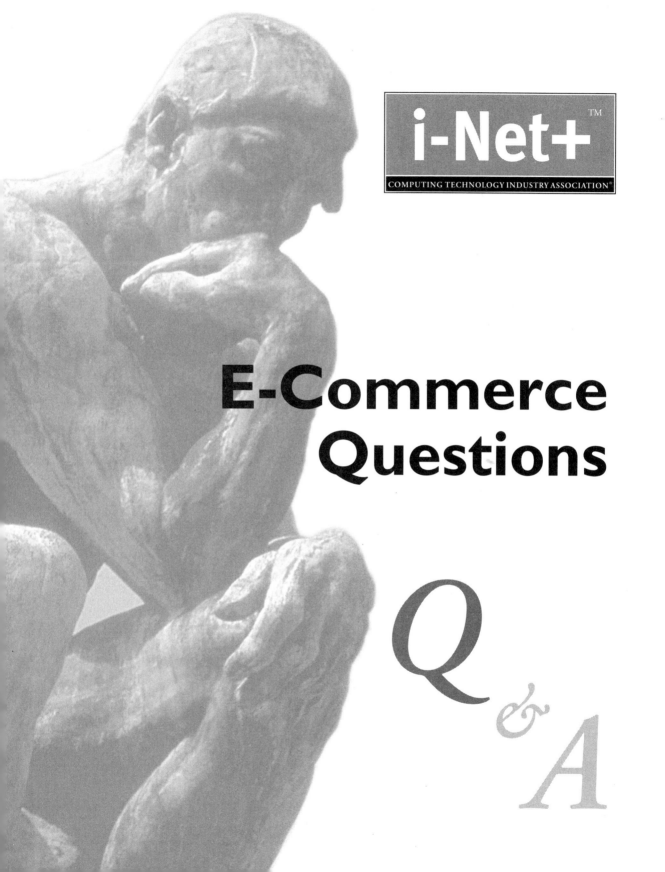

# E-Commerce and Your Internet Audience

**1.** You want to simplify the process for repeat customers to make return visits to your e-commerce site. One of the techniques is to automatically log them in. Which technique(s) should you use?

A. Use a client-pull model to automate the login process.
B. Use cookies to store name/password information.
C. Use the <META> tag store name/password information.
D. All of the above.

**2.** You are developing an online e-catalog for selling sporting goods and uniforms. You have selected an e-catalog system that uses cookies with a shopping cart metaphor to allow customers to shop on your site, save their order, and return later. Which statement most accurately describes the HTTP protocol?

A. HTTP stores session information in CGI gateways.
B. Since HTTP is a state-based protocol, cookies can be used to store session information.
C. Since HTTP is a stateless protocol, cookies can be used to store session information.
D. None of the above.

**3.** To improve security on your e-commerce site, you decide to prompt users every 15 minutes informing them they will be logged off unless there is further activity. What are the possible method(s) for accomplishing this goal?

A. Use cookies in Web pages.
B. Use client-pull statements in Web pages.
C. Use server-push technologies.
D. None of the above.

**4.** Which tag is used to implement a client pull statement?

    A. Client pull is implemented using the <META PULL> tag.

    B. Client pull is implemented using the <META> tag.

    C. Client pull is implemented using the <PULL> tag.

    D. Client pull is implemented using the <http-equiv> tag.

**5.** Internet List Servers control which of the following services?

    A. The management of access control lists

    B. The management of routing tables

    C. The management and distribution of mailing lists

    D. All of the above

**6.** List servers are most commonly used in which of the following applications? (Select all that apply.)

    A. CRC error-correction algorithms

    B. Distribution of mailing lists and newsletters

    C. Web Portals sites

    D. Client-pull technology

**7.** Web sites that organize information into topical hierarchical lists are called what?

    A. Extranets

    B. Search engines

    C. Directories

    D. None of the above

**8.** Your e-commerce site includes a Web form for customers to enter billing and shipping information. As a Web developer, in order to insure all information is entered correctly into the form, you decide to add an error-checking capability. How can you implement this? (Select all that apply.)

A. Server-side scripting and CGI

B. HTML and XML

C. Secure Socket Layer

D. Client-side scripting

**9.** Which of the following are some of the most common applications of push technology? (Select all that apply.)

A. Relational database technology

B. Automated data retrieval

C. B2B solutions tool for data encryption

D. List Server mailing lists

**10.** What are some major functions provided by an intranet? (Select all that apply.)

A. Supply chain management

B. Online publishing and sharing of documents and files

C. Real-time transaction processing for bill payment

D. Groupware applications such as calendars and online directories

**11.** You are part of a team designing the next-generation e-commerce site for your company. Management has decided to expand the site to business partners and suppliers in your supply chain. What type of network is designed for this purpose?

A. Local area networks (LANs)

B. Corporate intranets

C. Extranets

D. None of the above

**12.** Your company has decided to deploy an e-commerce site to promote direct sales to your customer base. Which of the following business objectives map to an e-business strategy? (Select all that apply.)

A. Increased market share and greater profit margins
B. Less control over the supply chain
C. Instant communications with customers and clients
D. None of the above

13. What are the essential differences between B2B and B2C e-commerce? (Select all that apply.)

   A. B2C e-commerce emphasizes transactions between a consumer and a business.
   B. B2B e-commerce emphasizes transactions between a consumer and a business.
   C. B2B e-business emphasizes trading between partners in the supply chain.
   D. B2C e-business emphasizes trading between partners in the supply chain.

14. You are implementing a B2B extranet site to link your company with its supply chain. You have decided to use EDI to interface to your business partner systems. Which of the following is a benefit of EDI? (Select all that apply.)

   A. Data only needs to be entered once into an electronic format, thereby saving time.
   B. Data entry errors are minimized.
   C. Data entry errors are propagated down the supply chain.
   D. All of the above.

15. Open Buying on the Internet is best described as? (Select all that apply.)

   A. A client-pull technology
   B. A vendor-neutral standard that has emerged for electronic catalog systems
   C. A server-push technology
   D. All of the above

**16.** Merchant systems include which of the following types of systems? (Select all that apply.)

    A. Groupware applications

    B. Electronic malls and collections of online catalogs from different merchants

    C. Stand-alone Web sites built for the explicit purpose of B2C e-commerce

    D. None of the above

**17.** Web-based Customer Relationship Management is best defined as?

    A. A process to identify, develop, and retain your best and most profitable customers

    B. An extension of help desk and technical support functions

    C. A cost-effective approach to providing 24-7 online support

    D. All of the above

**18.** Sales Automation tools that leverage Web-based e-commerce include? (Select all that apply.)

    A. Contact management

    B. EDI systems

    C. Automatic quote generators

    D. None of the above

**19.** You are the Webmaster in a large Fortune 1000 company. The marketing department has come to you for suggestions on how your company can market its products on the Internet. Which of the following statements are accurate? (Select all that apply.)

    A. Targeted e-mail advertising is effective for alerting customers to upcoming sales.

    B. Banner ads on high-profile Web sites are an excellent way to attract new customers.

    C. Personalize the user experience to increase repeat business to your e-commerce site.

    D. All of the above.

**20.** Internet marketing techniques used to attract customers to your e-commence site should include which of the following? (Select all that apply.)

    A. Web-based banner advertisements

    B. EDI and OBI systems

    C. E-mail newsletters and list servers

    D. All of the above

**21.** You are a Web developer heading up the steering committee at your company investigating trends in e-commerce. Based on your research, some of the future trends for e-commerce include? (Select all that apply.)

    A. Personalization and customization of site for customers

    B. Instant order fulfillment

    C. Intelligent agent software

    D. All of the above

# E-Commerce
# Answers

*Q & A*

# E-Commerce and Your Internet Audience

1. ☑   **B.** Cookies help to save information about customers such as their username and password. Each time a user logs in to a site, they do not need to reenter that information. Cookies also provide Web developers with a means of keeping site content updated and relevant to customers' interests, as well as providing information about the type of Web browser used to access a site.

    ☒   **A** is incorrect because client pull is not used to create an automatic login process. **C** is incorrect because the <META> tag is used for creating client-pull statements, not for storing name and password information.

2. ☑   **C.** Cookies are very useful for maintaining "state" information. Since HTTP is a "stateless" protocol, it is impossible to differentiate between user visits to a Web site. To enable this, Web servers mark a visitor by storing a piece of information about the visitor in a cookie. This allows customers to shop on your site, save their order, and return later to modify or place their order.

    ☒   **A** is incorrect because stateless protocols such as HTTP do not store state information in CGI gateways. **B** is incorrect; HTTP is a stateless protocol.

3. ☑   **B and C.** Both client-pull and server-push approaches can be used to prompt users by presenting a dialog box or another event to attract their attention.

    ☒   **A** is incorrect because cookies do not provide the functionality to prompt users at predetermined intervals.

4. ☑   **B.** Client-pull is implemented using the <META> tag. By using client-pull, you can update pages in both Netscape and Microsoft browsers using the <META> tag in the header of an HTML document. There is a special HTTP header field called "Refresh" that reloads the document at a preset interval. The content being updated can be the same HTML document, or another HTML document as defined in the URL parameter.

    ☒   **A, C,** and **D** are incorrect because these are not valid tags.

5. ☑ **C.** Electronic mailing lists provide forums for Internet users to participate in discussions or to receive e-mail messages sent in "bulk." The software responsible for the management and distribution of these mailing lists to thousands of subscribers is commonly called *list server*. A list server automatically distributes an e-mail message from one member of a list to all other members on that list.

☒ **A** is incorrect because list servers are not responsible for updating ACLs. **B** is incorrect because list servers are not responsible for updating routing tables.

6. ☑ **B.** List servers provide the software responsible for the management and distribution of mailing lists and newsletters. A list server automatically distributes an e-mail message from one member of a list to all other members on that list.

☒ **A** is incorrect because error-correction algorithms are used for data communications. **C** is incorrect because Web Portals are Web based, not e-mail based as are list servers. **D** is incorrect because list servers are a push technology, not a pull technology.

7. ☑ **C.** Directories organize information about sites into hierarchical lists, beginning with a topic, and descending through the layers of subtopics. Some directories, such as Excite, have self-service submission policies. Others directories, such as About.com and Magellan, rely on experts to report and review new sites.

☒ **A** is incorrect because extranets are networks designed for B2B e-commerce. **B** is incorrect because search engines are used to retrieve information from the Web.

8. ☑ **A and D.** Both client-pull and server-side scripting with CGI can implement error-checking. The trade-off is that server-side solutions place a heavy burden on the server and the network due to the need for additional transactions. Each time an error is detected, the user must be informed, which generates a client-server transaction. Client-side solutions minimize the transactions between the client and server.

⊠ **B** is incorrect because HTML and XML do not have logic to perform error checking without using a scripting language. **C** is incorrect because Secure Socket Layer, or SSL, is a method for data encryption and security.

9. ☑ **D.** The most common method of *push publishing* is to send users and customers information about services, products, or news.
⊠ **A** is incorrect because push is not a database technology. **B** is incorrect because push technology is not a retrieval process. **C** is incorrect because push technology is not used for data encryption. Data encryption technologies include Secure Socket Layer, public and private key encryption, and HTTPS.

10. ☑ **B and D.** Intranets are best defined as collections of Web sites belonging to an organization that are usually only accessible by members of that organization. Intranets can also be thought of as extensions of local area networks (LANs) that are Web enabled and facilitate the sharing of documents and files. Groupware applications are often part of intranet solutions.
⊠ **A** is incorrect because intranets are for internal use. Extranets link your supply chain with trading partners. **C** is incorrect because intranets do not provide real-time transaction processing for bill payment. Merchant servers perform this function.

11. ☑ **C.** Extranets connect an intranet site to the Internet to allow your suppliers and business partners to gain access to your site in order to share information, data, and applications. Extranets provide secure links between business partners and organizations in the supply chain.
⊠ **A and B** are incorrect because LANs and intranets are designed for internal use by an organization, and are not designed for sharing data and applications with business partners. Often times, an intranet is located behind a firewall to prevent unauthorized access from outside the intranet. Intranets can also be thought of as extensions of LANs that are Web enabled. Extranets are outside of a firewall.

12. ☑ A and C are correct.

☒ B is incorrect because the goals of e-commerce are to improve the control in your supply chain, thereby reducing inventory size, shipping and manufacturing delays, and increasing overall customer satisfaction and loyalty.

13. ☑ A and C. B2C e-commerce is based on transactions conducted between a consumer and a business, and is characterized by low-volume, low-dollar transactions (e.g., ordering a book or CD over the Internet). This is quickly changing as more expensive items, such as automobiles, are being sold directly from the manufacturer to the consumer. B2B e-commerce is based on transactions between partners in the supply chain.

☒ B and D are incorrect because B2B commerce is between business partners in the supply chain and B2C commerce is between a business and a consumer as opposed to between trading partners.

14. ☑ A and B. A great advantage of EDI is that data must only be entered once into an electronic format. This saves time and money by reducing redundancy in the data entry process and reducing the chances for data entry error. Once in EDI, data is in an electronic format that is easily transferred across the supply chain.

☒ C is incorrect because if data is entered incorrectly, it is passed down the supply chain to business partners downstream.

15. ☑ B. Open Buying on the Internet (OBI) is a vendor-neutral standard that has emerged for electronic catalog systems. OBI defines the rules for conducting B2B commerce over the Internet. Most Internet-based procurement software relies on a proprietary system for exchanging transactions between companies. Some require both ends of a transaction to have the same software. Others take old EDI formats directly to the Web. As a result, many B2B systems are built using customized links between trading partners. This approach is expensive and labor intensive. As OBI becomes more widely adopted, B2B e-commerce will become an easier and more affordable option.

☒ **A** and **C** are incorrect because OBI is not a client-pull or server-push type of technology.

16. ☑ **B** and **C**. Merchant systems can be stand-alone Web sites built for the explicit purpose of B2C e-commerce (e.g., Amazon.com). Electronic malls are collections of online catalogs from different merchants integrated into a central B2C e-commerce site. The Internet Shopping Network is a good example of an electronic mall.

☒ **A** and **D** are incorrect because groupware applications are used on intranets rather than merchant systems.

17. ☑ **D**. Customer Relationship Management (CRM) is the business process of identifying, selecting, acquiring, developing, and retaining your most profitable customers. CRM helps companies cultivate a one-to-one customer service relationship with the customer over time, while providing 24-7 access to customer support 365 days a year. CRM solutions may include help desk and technical support functions.

18. ☑ **A** and **C**. Sales automation tools offer salespeople applications for managing their contact lists and configuring complex price quotes while on the road using Web-based applications they access via a browser.

☒ **B** is incorrect. EDI is a system for electronic transaction processing, not sales automation.

19. ☑ **D**. E-mail newsletters are one of the least expensive means for Internet marketing to lure customers to Web sites, introduce new products, offer special promotions targeted at specific audiences, and collect customer feedback. Web banner ads are a popular way to advertise and attract business to your Web site. Banner ads are placed on popular Web sites and allow customers to "click-thru" the banner ad and be connected directly to your e-commerce site. The days of the mass-marketing campaign aimed at anonymous customers are coming to an end. Internet marketing allows companies to personalize their marketing messages based on the various needs of distinct customers. Through the use of personalized targeted advertising, the most appropriate messages can be targeted at the right customer at the right time.

**20.** ☑ A and C. Web banner ads are a popular way to advertise and attract new business to your Web site. E-mail newsletters and list servers are being used to carefully target users.

    ☒ B is incorrect. EDI and OBI systems are not methods for attracting users to e-commerce sites.

**21.** ☑ D. In the future, e-commerce merchants will be required to know their customers, not just by name, but also by buying habits. By understanding consumer behavior and preferences, merchants can provide each customer with a personalized, interactive experience. Future e-commerce companies may use local affiliate stores. After customers buy a product online, the site will direct them to stores closest to the their home or office to pick the product up. Intelligent software agents will find the best products and best prices for customers. These autonomous intelligent agents will be able to be personalized and run 24 hours a day. Consumers will use agents to find the best prices for products and services.

# Part 2

## Test Yourself: i-Net+ Certification Practice Exams

# i-Net+
# Certification
# Practice Exam I

Q & A

# Practice Exam Questions

1. A company often uses videoconferencing to conduct meetings with its four branches. Which of the following types of Internet service should they use to get the best results?

   A. Frame Relay

   B. X.25

   C. ATM

   D. Any of the above

2. A user with an analog modem complains that the Internet connection is often unexpectedly dropped. The problem always occurs when a telephone call comes in on the same line. Which of the following will fix this problem?

   A. ATDT5551234

   B. ATDT*70,5551234

   C. ATDT9,5551234

   D. Unplug all telephones connected to the same telephone line.

3. Your company is developing a Web site with the objective to sell it to car dealers. The Web site provides many personalized services to their customers such as service reminders, online service scheduling, etc. Since this is a package, it needs to be tailored to each dealer, especially the appearance of the pages. More specifically, the background image, background color, the color of the text, table attributes such as header background, and hyperlink colors should be customized. This is a complete turnkey Web site that will be adapted to the dealer on very short notice once the dealer makes the purchase. You want to design it to be as flexible as possible, yet the effort to change the appearance should be minimal. What technique in HTML (4.0) should you use?

A. Use appropriate attributes for appearance control such as BGCOLOR, BACKGROUND, TEXT, FONT, etc. When a new dealer signs up, just do a global "change" in the editor of choice.

B. Store the elements that can be customized and the corresponding values in the database by dealer. Change the values for each dealer in the database and programmatically change the page when it loads.

C. Use linked external Cascading Style Sheets to define all the elements that can be customized on all HTML pages. Load the customized Cascading Style Sheets into the dealer's specific Web folder.

D. None of the above.

4. You have been hired to update a company's internal Web server and page. You design a new page with the latest software and then upgrade the server to a new version of Web server software. After the upgrades and changes, you receive numerous support calls from the company's employees stating that they can no longer access the Web pages. What is likely the problem?

A. When you updated the server, you deleted the user database, and now the users' usernames and passwords no longer work.

B. The IP address of the site must have been changed during the install, and that is why they can't reach the site.

C. The NIC card in the server is not compatible with the Web server software.

D. The version of browser the users are running is out of date and can't access the page now that you've added new features that require a newer version of their browser.

5. You copied a program from the Internet to your system at work and installed it. During the process, you scanned the file for viruses and none were found. After running the program, you decided that you would like to use it at home and at work. When you go to install the program at home, your virus software kicks in and warns you that the file is infected. You take the diskette back to work, scan it on your system again, and it shows nothing. Why is it infected when you install it at home but not when you check it at work?

A. The diskette you placed it on was infected and the virus was copied to your home system, thus removing it from your floppy. When you checked it at work, it showed clean.

B. The virus software you are running at work is older than what you have at home.

C. The virus software you are running at home is older than what you are running at work.

D. It is a false alarm from the virus software at home. If there were a virus, both systems would have found it.

**6.** You find a Web site that contains a nonstreaming video file. What advantage does this file have over a streaming file?

A. It can be downloaded.

B. It will play only once, so it won't slow the loading of the Web page.

C. It will fade in gradually, allowing you to see the image before it has finished loading.

D. It is capable of greater compression than streaming media.

**7.** In the late 1970s, IBM created a common communication between databases called what?

A. Common Gateway Interface

B. American National Standards Institute

C. Internet Service Application Program Interface

D. Structured Query Language

**8.** There are several segments of cable within a company that have systems and other network equipment attached to them. Each segment contains the data transmitted on that segment and the data destined for that segment via another segment. All the segments come together at a location to join another larger segment called _____?

A. The routers

B. The bridges

C. The NICs

D. The backbone

**9.** You have users who are local 100% of the time, some who are remote 100% of the time, and others who work both from the local office and home offices and sometimes travel. All of your users need access to a directory listing of users for e-mail addresses and other vital information for contact. You have been requested to set up a central information depository so that updates only need to be made in one location. How could you go about setting this up?

A. Install a TFTP server and have users download the database each time they need it to make sure it is up to date.

B. Install a LDAP server so that users can access the info from wherever they might be at the time. Updates would be made directly to the database and users would have up-to-the-minute correct information at all times.

C. Install an Archie server and let the users access it to search for the information they need.

D. Install an LPR server to allow users to gain access to the information they request.

**10.** You look at your logs on your UNIX system and notice that one username has 423 denied logins, and the user logged in over 20 times within a few hours. You look further and notice that several usernames have four or five denied logins, and a few have over 200 each with no logins granted. What do you gather from this observation?

A. You have a few users who can't remember their passwords and have to try numerous times to log in.

B. Your network is under attack from a hacker using a password-cracking program.

C. Your UNIX system is stuck in a loop on these names and just keeps entering denied login entries for them.

D. A hacker is running a mail bomb program to crash your system.

**11.** What type of law protects original works of authorship?

A. Work for Hire law

B. Trademark law

C. Copyright law

D. B and C

**12.** A client is planning to connect a North American server with a European server, and plans to use T1 line for one leg of the connection, and E1 line for the final leg of the connection. What advice should you give this client?

   A. Obtain a flow controller to even out the speed differences between the two lines.

   B. Use a line interpreter at the junction of the two lines to interpret the digital signal between them.

   C. You cannot connect a T1 line to an E1 line.

   D. None of the above.

**13.** You are using a particular word processor to create an important document. However, the person you are e-mailing the document to uses a word processor that is not compatible with yours. What should you do to ensure the recipient can open and read the content of the document in his word processor?

   A. Nothing—the recipient's e-mail program will convert the document.

   B. Save the document as a PDF file.

   C. Nothing—the recipient's Web browser will convert the document.

   D. Save the document as an RTF file.

**14.** You are working for a company that wants you to design a Web page for them that will allow their customers to be able to enter a request such as a part number and have it return the results quickly. The data is stored in a plain text file. You need a language that is good at quickly scanning a text file and returning results. Which would you use?

   A. Java

   B. C++

   C. VBScript

   D. Perl

**15.** When converting an IP address from decimal to binary, the first octet in a Class C address will always begin with?

    A. 100

    B. 101

    C. 010

    D. 110

**16.** You are working for an ISP and part of your weekly job is to update the DNS server with any new domain names your ISP is housing for its clients. You have a request to enter the domain greatfood.com for a new company. What type of record will you need to enter?

    A. A

    B. HINFO

    C. CNAME

    D. NS

**17.** The majority of bandwidth used on the Internet is packets containing what type of information?

    A. E-mail

    B. HTTP

    C. FTP

    D. Telnet

**18.** When a station wants to send a packet to another station, it must first determine the other station's MAC address. What utility in the TCP/IP suite is used to accomplish this?

    A. You would issue a PING to the IP address and then follow that path to the other station.

    B. You would issue a TRACE Route to find the best path to the station.

    C. You would send a request to the DNS for the MAC address.

    D. You would use ARP to send out a broadcast asking for the MAC address of the station you want to talk to.

**19.** The ability to verify the identity of a user or system process is?

   A. Access control

   B. Auditing

   C. Authentication

   D. Encryption

**20.** You have just put up a new firewall for your company. You attached the network cables to the NICs on the server and brought it online. You have turned on ports 25 and 80. The next business day, you start to receive reports that users are not receiving e-mails from their customers. What is the problem?

   A. You have not opened any mail ports.

   B. You have opened the port for POP3 only and need to open the port for SMTP.

   C. You have opened the port for SMTP only and need to open the port for POP3.

   D. The software on the firewall is not functioning correctly and needs to be reinstalled.

**21.** You are a new company and transmit data to many companies throughout the world. You just started to use encryption and decided to find out what the global standard for encryption is so that you are not in violation of any government laws. What body or group should you contact for the global standards for encryption?

   A. The Internet Engineering Task Force (IETF).

   B. The World Wide Web Consortium (W3C).

   C. The Standardizing Information and Communication System (ECMA).

   D. There is no global standard.

**22.** Your company is having problems with viruses being downloaded not only from files off the Internet but also from e-mail attachments. It seems that you spend most of your time fighting viruses on the servers. What can be done to help stop viruses from infecting your systems?

A. Install virus software on the servers only. This will protect them; the users' systems are not that big of a concern.

B. Install virus software on the end users' systems only; if you catch the virus before it gets to the server, there is no need to spend the money to put the software on the servers also.

C. Install virus software on the end users' systems and the servers.

D. Block all TCP/IP packets from entering your company.

**23.** You have taken over a project and you are now the Webmaster for your company. You are concerned with security about the data on your Web pages, not only those who can access it but also the transmission of the data from the Web page across the network or Internet. What are valid options that can be put into place on an HTTP server?

A. Encrypt data being transferred from the page to the user such as files.

B. Maintain logs of all access, both authorized and denied.

C. Use usernames and passwords for authentication.

D. Encrypt transmission of data back and forth such as with secured servers.

E. All of the above.

**24.** While on your break at work, you connect to http://www.dressclothes.com, and decide to make a purchase. You choose the dress shirts you wish to buy, and when you proceed to check out, you notice that the URL has changed to HTTPS://www.dressclothes.com. For some reason, you get an error when trying to attach to the page. When you get home, you try it again and are able to complete the transaction. The next day at work, you decide to check and see if you are able to access the page, and you again receive an error. You are running IE 5.0 in both places. What is likely the problem?

A. You are using a Proxy server and it doesn't understand HTTPS://.

B. You are behind a firewall and Port 8080 is not open.

C. You are behind a firewall and Port 443 is not open.

D. There is some configuration difference between the browser on your work system and the browser on your home system preventing you from accessing the page.

**25.** A computer on a network has proxy software installed on it. What is the function of this computer?

A. To prevent access of the internal network by external Internet users

B. To speed up Internet access by retaining recently used Web pages

C. To manage and filter users' Internet requests

D. All of the above

**26.** A business is planning to set up an online shopping Web site. Which types of software are they most likely to use?

A. Web server, FTP server, list server, and e-commerce server

B. Web server, e-commerce server, list server, and certificate server

C. Web server, authentication server, and purchase server

D. E-commerce server, list server, and inventory server

**27.** You use Dynamic HTML to build a Web page for the users to view the orders they have placed with your company. Since the payment part involves different types of payment and the information varies depending on the payment type, you want to dynamically show the information on the page. The Web page must support Netscape 4 and later and Internet Explorer 4 and later. Therefore, some portions of JavaScript are written specifically for Netscape and some others are written for Internet Explorer to accommodate different implementations of the Document Object Model. To dynamically test the browser name and version, which object can be used?

A. browser

B. document

C. frame

D. navigator

**28.** You are building a data entry page that shows many HTML controls such as text boxes and select boxes. The page has a button labeled "UPDATE DATA" that allows users to submit the form to the server for processing. This page needs validation on the client side by JavaScript before the form is sent to the server for maximum network efficiency. The form is called form1 in HTML code. What technique(s) can be used? (Choose two.)

A. Use a "submit" button. Write code for the event onsubmit of the <FORM> tag as follows:

```
<FORM NAME=form1 ACTION="processdata.asp" METHOD=POST
onsubmit="ValidatePage()".
```

In the function ValidatePage, use the statement "return" if all controls pass validation and "return false" if one control fails.

B. Write code for the event onsubmit of the <INPUT> tag corresponding to the button as follows:

```
<INPUT TYPE=submit NAME=btnsubmit
ONSUBMIT="ValidatePage()" VALUE="Update Data">.
```

In the function ValidatePage, use the statement "return" if all controls pass validation and "return false" if one control fails.

C. Use a "submit" button. Write code for the event ONSUBMIT of the <FORM> tag as follows:

```
<FORM NAME=form1 ACTION="processdata.asp" METHOD=POST
onsubmit=
"return ValidatePage()".
```

In the function ValidatePage, use the statement "return true" if all controls pass validation and "return false" if one control fails.

D. Write code for the event ONCLICK of the <INPUT> tag
corresponding to the button as follows:

```
<INPUT TYPE=button ONCLICK="ValidatePage() VALUE="Update
Data"".
```

In the function ValidatePage, use the statement
"document.form1.submit()" if all controls pass validation and "return"
if one control fails.

29. You are part of a Web Development team and are asked to produce a Web
page for the Quarterly Sales Report for your company's intranet. See the
illustration for the layout of the report. Which HTML code is most
appropriate?

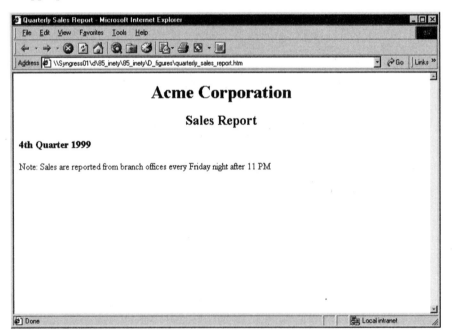

A. ```
<html>
<head>
<title>Quarterly Sales Report</title>
</head>
```
```

```
<body>
<h1 align="middle">Acme Corporation</h1>
<h2 align="middle">Sales Report</h2>
<h3 align="left">4th Quarter 1999</h3>
<p>Note: Sales are reported from branch offices every
Friday night after 11 PM</p>
</body>
</html>
```

B.
```
<html>
<head>
<title>Quarterly Sales Report</title>
</head>
<body>
<h3 align="center">Acme Corporation</h1>
<h2 align="center">Sales Report</h2>
<h1 align="left">4th Quarter 1999</h3>
<p>Note:
Sales are reported from branch offices every Friday night
after 11 PM</p>
</body>
</html>
```

C.
```
<html>
<head>
<title>Quarterly Sales Report</title>
</head>
<body>
<h1 align="center">Acme Corporation</h1>
<h2 align="center">Sales Report</h2>
<h3 align="left">4th Quarter 1999</h3>
<p>Note:
Sales are reported from branch offices every Friday night
after 11 PM</p>
</body>
</html>
```

D.
```
<html>
<head>
<title>Quarterly Sales Report</title>
</head>
<body>
```

```
<h1 align="center">Acme Corporation</h1>
<h2 align="center">Sales Report</h2>
<h3 align="left">4th Quarter 1999</h3>
<br>Note:
Sales are reported from branch offices every Friday night
after 11 PM
</body>
</html>
```

**30.** You are part of a Web Development team and are asked to produce a Web page for the Sales By Region Search for your company's intranet. Part of the search form contains option buttons as shown in the following illustration. Which code is appropriate? (Choose all that apply.)

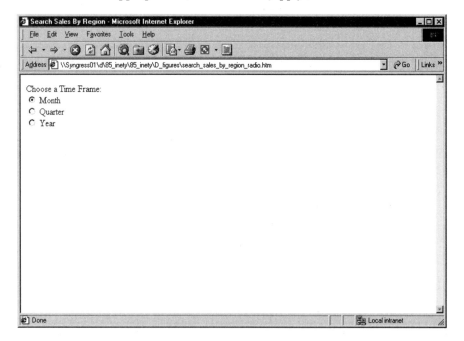

A. 
```
<html>
<head>
<title>Search Sales By Region</title>
</head>
<body>
```

```
<form name=form1 action="salesbyregion.asp"
method="post">
        Choose a Time Frame:<br>
        <input type=radio name=Month value="M" checked>
Month<br>
        <input type=radio name=Quarter value="Q">
Quarter<br>
        <input type=radio name=Year value="Y" > Year<br>
</form>
</body>
</html>
```

B.
```
<html>
<head>
<title>Search Sales By Region</title>
</head>
<body>
<form name=form1 action="salesbyregion.asp"
method="post">
        Choose a Time Frame:<br>
        <input type=radio name=TimeFrame value="M" checked>
Month<br>
        <input type=radio name=TimeFrame value="Q">
Quarter<br>
        <input type=radio name=TimeFrame value="Y" >
Year<br>
</form>
</body>
</html>
```

C.
```
<html>
<head>
<title>Search Sales By Region</title>
</head>
<body>
<form name=form1 action="salesbyregion.asp"
method="post">
        Choose a Time Frame:<br>
        <input type=radio name=TimeFrame> Month<br>
        <input type=radio name=TimeFrame> Quarter<br>
        <input type=radio name=TimeFrame> Year<br>
</form>
</body>
</html>
```

D. 
```
<html>
<head>
<title>Search Sales By Region</title>
</head>
<body>
<form name=form1 action="salesbyregion.asp"
method="post">
      Choose a Time Frame:<br>
      <radio name=TimeFrame value="M" checked> Month<br>
      <radio name=TimeFrame value="Q"> Quarter<br>
      <radio name=TimeFrame value="Y" > Year<br>
</form>
</body>
</html>
```

**31.** In 1969, the Department of Defense commissioned the ARPA to do some computer network research. They placed computers on several university campuses to create the first WAN connected network. These universities consisted of Stanford, University of Utah, University of California at Santa Barbara, and _____?

A. Harvard

B. Princeton

C. UCLA

D. Berkeley

**32.** You are using your browser and need to access a file located on the c:\ drive of your local system. You do not want to have to open another application such as Windows Explorer to view this file, so you decide to just use your browser. To access a local file from a browser window, you would do what?

A. You need to have a Web server running on the local system, and issue the command HTTP://local/"file name".

B. You issue the command File://local/c:/filename, or another drive if the file is not on C.

C. You issue the command File://c:/filename, or another drive and filename if the file is on another drive.

D. You cannot access a file on the local system from a browser window.

**33.** The FCC currently puts a maximum speed on the use of analog modems. What is the top speed for a standard analog dial-up modem connection?

A. 33.6K

B. 56K

C. 64K

D. 128K

**34.** Which of the following is not a valid transport protocol?

A. https://

B. ftp://

C. mail://

D. File://

**35.** You have set up your browser as your primary e-mail application. You know that when you surf with your browser, you are using an HTTP transport. What protocol are you using when you use your browser to send e-mail to a friend?

A. HTTP

B. POP3

C. SMTP

D. SNMP

**36.** In the following URL, what is the directory path?
HTTP:\\www.mypage.org\pictures\family.html

A. HTTP:\\

B. WWW.mypage.org

C. Pictures

D. Family.html

**37.** A Web server is defined as _____?

A. A system designed to maintain database information for quick retrieval

B. A system used to browse the Internet

C. A system designed to maintain documents and other information to be served to and by the request of a Web browser

D. None of the above

**38.** Your department has an intranet Web application that allows employees to learn about the progress of various projects. Only the employees use this application. The department manager now wants to give Internet access to all employees of the department, and gives you the following objectives:
a) Secure the intranet application. Only employees of the department can access it.
b) Establish access to the Internet for all employees quickly and easily.
c) Block access to some Internet sites.
d) Improve performance and access for Internet-based services on the internal network.
You decide to put a proxy server (firewall) between your internal network and the Internet and set appropriate configuration options. If the options are used properly, what objectives would you achieve?

A. Secure the intranet application, only employees of the department can access it, block access to some Internet sites (objectives a and c).

B. Establish access to the Internet for all of the internal network clients quickly and easily (objective b).

C. Improve performance and access for Internet-based services on the internal network (objective d).

D. Secure the intranet application, only employees of the department can access it, establish access to the Internet for all of the internal network clients quickly and easily, block access to some Internet sites, improve performance and access for Internet-based services on the internal network (objectives a, b, c, and d).

**39.** You have to travel to meet with prospective clients and show many statistics about the industry your company is in. The industry statistics you use to show your clients change every week, and you notice that they are updated on Saturday, not during business hours on weekdays. You are not sure you can have modem connection everywhere you go, but you still want to show the statistics figures to your clients during your meetings. You do not want to use a slow connection but still want to show the Web pages as they are shown on the Internet so the clients can check the source of the information. What would be the best solution? (Choose all that apply.)

A. You need a wireless connection to get the pages when you go to the meeting.

B. Set the browser cache option to "Check for new version when the browser is open." Make sure the browser cache is large enough, browse to the pages you need to show every night before going to the meeting, and use the cache without being connected during the meeting.

C. Make sure the hard disk is large enough, save all the necessary pages on hard disk on Sunday night, and show them from the hard disk during the meeting.

D. Set the browser cache option to something other than "Check for new version when the browser is open." Make sure the browser cache is large enough, browse to the pages you need to show on Sunday before going to the meeting, and use the cache without being connected during the meeting.

**40.** You are the Webmaster and you maintain a Web site that has a large number of static pages containing legal data about superior court cases around the country. The Web site is a major source of information for law firms, and your site is very well known in the legal field. The number of legal terms is very large, as well as the number of pages. You want the public to access specific terms contained in the pages of your site as quickly as possible when they visit your site. What would be the best solution?

A. Build indexes on all the legal terms on your pages, store them with the page's URL in a database, and offer the users a Search page that runs the search against the database.

B. Use the <META> tag and use the attributes NAME and CONTENT to specify the description and keywords of all the HTML pages of your site.

C. Submit your pages to all the search engines and take advantage of their full-text index engine.

D. You have nothing to do. The search engine's robots can find your pages and index them.

**41.** To publish works held in the public domain you must (select all that apply):

A. License the works from the author.

B. Apply for trademark or copyright protection.

C. Register the works for copyright protection.

D. You are free to publish those works without a license.

**42.** Which of the following issues are important when dealing with international currency conversion? (Select all that apply.)

   A. Systems designed to deal with currency conversion between the consumer and the banking and merchant organizations
   B. Deciding whether to take credit card transactions
   C. Online transaction payment software able to translate your customers' currency into the your preferred currency
   D. Systems designed to collect taxes

**43.** Unicode provides the following benefit(s) (select all that apply):

   A. You can replace multiple scripting languages with Unicode.
   B. You have a standard format for document and data interchange that is language independent.
   C. You no longer have to manage multiple language versions of your Web sites.
   D. You no longer need to use HTML to author Web pages.

**44.** While developing a global presence does not change the principles of your overall business strategy, it does require a change in your thinking toward? (Select all that apply.)

   A. Your business processes and procedures
   B. The relationships in the supply chain between your company, suppliers, distributors, and business partners
   C. The relationship with your customers
   D. All of the above

**45.** What is required to log on to an IBM mainframe using Internet Explorer or Netscape?

   A. You must have an external SNA Telnet application that the browser will call.
   B. You must install IBM's SNA extensions.
   C. You must install IBM's Host on Demand.
   D. You cannot log on to an IBM system via a Web browser.

**46.** When searching a company's Web site for updates on its programs or applications, what is the most important piece of information to have to ensure you get the correct update?

A. The version number

B. The programmer's name

C. The type of OS you are running

D. The error message

**47.** What information must be provided no matter what options your e-mail application has?

A. IP address or Fully Qualified Domain Name of the POP3 server

B. Address book location on your system

C. Telephone number of your ISP

D. Username of e-mail account

**48.** How many cookies can a system running Netscape Communicator 4.5 maintain?

A. 150

B. 300

C. 500

D. Limited only by the amount of free space on the system

**49.** You have decided to create vector graphics on a Web page. Which of the following file formats can you use?

A. GIF

B. Flash

C. JPEG

D. PDF

**50.** Employees in your company want to be able to get news, sports, and entertainment information over the Internet. They also want to be able to view televised conferences with a branch in another area. Which program should you recommend?

A. Flash

B. Shockwave

C. RealPlayer

D. MP3

**51.** You are considering the use of JPEG graphics in your Web page. Which of the following will these files not be capable of?

A. Slowly fading into view rather than loading from the top down

B. Supporting 32-bit color

C. Animation

D. Compression

**52.** The PostScript language contains commands that will print a document with high resolution and object-oriented graphics and fonts. How can you see what the document will look like once it has been converted to PostScript?

A. Open the PostScript file by double-clicking on it.

B. Open the associated EPS file.

C. Open the PostScript file in a word processor.

D. None of the above.

**53.** You are using a Windows 98 computer to access the Internet. You find a Web site with the file movie.mov, which displays a video clip that runs once. Your browser has no additional plug-ins. Of the following, which application is running the movie?

A. Windows 98 media player

B. QuickTime movie player

C. The browser

D. None of the above

**54.** Many Internet languages require special add-ons or require a particular browser to use them. Which of the following does not have these requirements, as it runs on the Web server and not in the browser at the end-user side?

A. API

B. Java

C. JScript

D. CGI

**55** When an analog modem dials up another modem, you can hear a series of tones and some buzzing. What is the name for the source of this noise?

A. Guard sequence

B. Equalization tone

C. Handshake

D. Carrier protocol

**56.** A computer has been configured for Internet access using asymmetric analog communications. Which type of Internet access is being used?

A. Analog

B. DSL

C. Cable

D. There is not enough information to determine the answer.

**57.** Which of the following statements most accurately reflects the difference between an active hub and a passive hub?

A. An active hub sends data to other computers on the network, and a passive hub holds all data until it is picked up by the destination computer.

B. An active hub repeats data signals, and a passive hub does not.

C. An active hub can periodically check the network cable for noise, and a passive hub does not.

D. An active hub can screen out messages to and from computers that do not have user privileges to each other, and a passive hub will send data between any two users, regardless of user restrictions.

**58.** A network is divided into four segments using three routers and a switch. Two segments use TCP/IP, and one segment uses IPX/SPX. It is a server-based network with ISDN Internet access. What is the role of a gateway on this network?

A. To enable the switch to use segments of the routers' routing tables

B. To enforce user restrictions and access rights on the network

C. To allow the TCP/IP networks to communicate with the IPX/SPX networks

D. To prevent outside Internet users from accessing the internal network

**59.** Your network's firewall provides the network with security by screening out incoming data from unrecognized external IP addresses. Which type of firewall is this network using?

A. Application level

B. Packet level

C. Circuit level

D. Dual-homed host

**60.** You are designing an HTML page that contains a form. The form is used to get a User ID and Password. The form is submitted to a server script to be processed. You do not want the User ID and Password to be seen as part of the URL (Uniform Resource Locator) of the new script page in the URL address box of the browser. How would you do that?

A. Use the appropriate <!DOCTYPE > to block out the URL.

B. Set the attribute METHOD=GET for the <FORM> tag.

C. Set the attribute METHOD=POST for the <FORM> tag.

D. None of the above.

**61.** You need at least 3150 users per subnet, but can only get a Class B network address range because all Class As have been assigned to larger companies. A normal Class B address does not allow for the number of users you need per subnet, so you decide to use VLSM to gain the needed number of host addresses. What subnet mask would you need to assign?

A. 255.255.192.0

B. 255.255.240.0

C. 255.255.252.0

D. 255.255.255.0

**62.** A client has asked you to design a Web site that will contain many pictures of the items they sell. Assuming that each file type is supported by the Web browser, should you consider using BMP or GIF files?

A. Use BMPs because GIFs are not supported by older browsers.

B. Use GIFs because BMPs can cause the Web site to load slowly.

C. Use BMPs because GIFs require a browser plug-in.

D. Use BMP because GIFs can lose data during compression.

**63.** The following display is of what?

```
Active Connections
Proto  Local Address        Foreign Address                              State
TCP    SALESPC:nbsession    imcalftun1-27-104.mycompany.com:1534         ESTABLISHED
TCP    SALESPC:1189         sales1.mycompany.com:2516                    ESTABLISHED
TCP    SALESPC:1203         sales1.mycompany.com:1053                    ESTABLISHED
TCP    SALESPC:1207         sales1.mycompany.com:1053                    ESTABLISHED
TCP    SALESPC:1512         payroll.mycompany.com:nbsession              ESTABLISHED
TCP    SALESPC:1534         imcalftun1-27-104.mycompany.com:nbsession    ESTABLISHED
TCP    SALESPC:4876         mail.mycompany.com:telnet                    ESTABLISHED
TCP    SALESPC:4887         sales1.mycompany.com:2516                    ESTABLISHED
TCP    SALESPC:1433         web5.thatplace.com:80                        CLOSE_WAIT
TCP    SALESPC:1434         web5.thatpalce.com:80                        CLOSE_WAIT
TCP    SALESPC:1105         localhost:1106                               ESTABLISHED
TCP    SALESPC:1106         localhost:1105                               ESTABLISHED
TCP    SALESPC:1125         localhost:1139                               ESTABLISHED
TCP    SALESPC:1139         localhost:1125                               ESTABLISHED
```

A. NETSTAT table

B. ARP table

C. WINIPCONFIG

D. PING response

**64.** What is the definition of a Network Access Point?

A. A NAP is the point where the phone companies' wiring ends at a given location. This point is the box usually located on the outside of a building that houses both the telephone companies' wiring and the local wiring.

B. The NAP is a high-speed network or switch in which several routers are attached. NAPs run at speeds of 100Mbps or higher.

C. The NAP is the equipment that runs at level 3 of the OSI model and determines where packets will be transmitted as they enter.

D. The NAP is the point where all the local phone wires meet and phone calls are routed.

# Practice Exam Answers

1. ☑ **C.** ATM. This technology supports transmission speeds up to 622 Mbps, and creates a dedicated route for data from the source to the destination until the data transfer is complete. This means no other transmissions will share the line, so video data can be sent and received in a fast, steady stream.

   ☒ **A** is incorrect because this Frame Relay is a "shared line" technology in which several data streams from different sources can occupy the same line. This can lead to an uneven flow of data from source to destination, which can make video data appear choppy. **B** is incorrect because X.25 supports a maximum of 64 Kbps, which is only slightly faster than analog telephone line communications. Video data typically requires a much higher transmission speed than X.25 services can provide. **D** is incorrect because it suggests that all of the answers given are equally suitable.

2. ☑ **B.** ATDT*70,5551234. If the Internet connection is dropped when a telephone call comes in, it is because the line has call waiting, and the modem drops the connection in order to answer the telephone. To temporarily disable the call waiting feature while accessing the Internet, use the *70, command. Any callers will get a busy signal as long as you're on the Internet. *The code to disable call waiting may be slightly different in your area. Check the syntax of this command with your TELEPHONE ISP.*

   ☒ **A** is incorrect because this is the command for performing a regular tone dial-up. It does not instruct the modem to disable call waiting. **C** is incorrect because 9 is the command used to get an outside line when you're dialing from an internal phone system (like in an office that uses phone extension numbers). **D** is incorrect because this will not stop calls from coming in on the line. Try it—if you unplug your telephone from the wall, callers will still hear ringing. The line is still available, your phone just can't pick up the signal until it's plugged back in.

**3.** ☑ C. Style Sheets simplify HTML markup and largely relieve HTML of the responsibilities of presentation. They give control over the presentation of documents: font information, alignment, colors, etc. Some elements or attributes that deal with presentation used today may be obsolete in the future as new versions of HTML are proposed. Style Sheets are by far more powerful and more flexible and are very appropriate in this scenario. This approach also adheres to the W3C (World Wide Web Consortium) recommendation of "separating structure and representation."

☒ A is incorrect because although it is possible, this approach represents tedious conversion and is still limited in functionality. Changing text through a text editor also represents some maintenance risk since you have to test all the pages again when they are modified. **B** is incorrect because this approach represents a workload for the server. You have to access the database and load the data for each page (or go through some caching mechanism that may affect scalability). Besides, if the elements and attributes used are from standard HTML (before version 4.0), then we have the same problem as in answer A. **D** is incorrect because the appropriate approach is Style Sheets.

**4.** ☑ D. The best and most likely reason is that their browser is now out of revision. If you coded the Web page with JavaScript or ActiveX codes, and their browser was not able to use them, they could have problems with the page.

☒ A is incorrect because it's likely that since it was an internal site, there was no authentication needed. If there was, you would have been aware of it when looking at the old Web page. **B** is incorrect. More than likely you as the designer checked the connection from another station—probably a laptop—which would have the latest version of code on it. **C** is incorrect because the NIC would have no compatibility issues with the software on the system.

**5.** ☑ B. Most likely, the virus software you are running at work is older than the version you are running at home. Many times companies do not have the manpower to keep the virus signature or definitions up to date. Contact your system administrator and ask him or her for the current signature files for your virus protection software.

☒   **A** is possible, but not probable. Most virus software products copy themselves from a diskette to the hard drive, leaving a copy on the floppy for the next system that it encounters. **C** is incorrect. If the virus software at work is newer than that at home, the virus would have been detected at work and not at home. If the software is newer at work, the software at home needs to be replaced or upgraded to a better virus software package. **D** is possible, but not probable. Virus software packages do not generally give false positive alarms. They are searching for particular definitions or signatures of a virus.

6.  ☑   **A.** The streaming file can be downloaded. Nonstreaming media does not run within the browser when you are online. In order to run the file you must download it, then run it within a separate application. The advantage to this is that you can use the file within other applications, and you can run it whenever you want to, without having to go online to do so. Streaming files run directly from the Web site, so they cannot be downloaded.

☒   **B** is incorrect because nonstreaming media does not run within the browser when you are online. Only streaming media is capable of this. The number of times a video clip is repeated online is a characteristic of streaming media called "looping." **C** is incorrect because this is a method of image loading called "interlacing" (called "progressive" in JPEG files). The term "streaming" refers to the ability of a file to run while you are visiting that particular Web site. It is unrelated to whether an image gradually fades in or loads one line at a time. **D** is incorrect because it refers to the amount of compression of nonstreaming media. Streaming files are simply files that have the "streaming" option enabled. Their degree of compression depends on the file type itself (e.g., MOV, AVI, GIF), rather than the presence or absence of the streaming attribute.

7.  ☑   **D.** IBM created SQL in the 1970s to create a common communicator between databases. SQL is a programming language that can be used to replace the slower CGI scripting language.

☒  **A** is incorrect. CGI is a scripting tool used on Web servers. **B** is incorrect. ANSI is the institute that is responsible for creating standards for many things associated with computers and networks. **C** is also incorrect. ISAPI is a set of program calls that allows you to create a Windows Web-based application that will run faster than a CGI application.

**8.** ☑  **D.** The backbone of a network is what handles the majority of the information on the network. Each segment feeds into a backbone segment that is usually a high-speed segment of 100Mbps minimum. This segment could be a back plane in a gigaswitch, and FDDI ring or high-speed copper.
☒  **A** is incorrect. Routers route the packets from network to network. The routers work on level 3 of the OSI model and create a collision domain. **B** is incorrect. Bridges are used to join two or more segments. Bridges operate at layer 2 of the OSI model. A bridge will propagate a collision. **C** is also incorrect. The NIC is the network interface card that is in your system and network equipment. The NIC is the adapter that transmits and receives packets on the network.

**9.** ☑  **B.** By installing an LDAP server, you fulfill the requirements for the problem. An LDAP server would allow a central location for the information to be maintained, and allow all users to access it either via the local LAN or via the Internet. You can set up security so that only authorized users can access it from the Internet.
☒  **A** is not a feasible plan. It would cause a lot of overhead having to download a new copy of the database every time users needed to make sure it was correct. As the database grew, the download time would increase. There is also very little security built into a TFTP server, so anyone knowing the filename and server address would be able to access the information. **C** would not work because Archie is an FTP search engine. Archie servers are used to search the FTP databases for a particular file and return its location. **D** is incorrect because an LPR server is a print server. This would not fit the requirements.

10. ☑ **B.** Users may forget their passwords, and some make several attempts to determine what their password is. This would account for the users who had four or five errors in the log file. The users who have several hundred entries in the log file with either a valid entry or no valid entry would indicate an attack from a hacker wishing to gain entry to your system. Also, if you notice that one account is being accessed numerous times in a short period or at odd hours (e.g., a secretary who only works in the office shows a login in at 3 A.M. on Sunday), you may possibly be under attack.
    ☒ **A** is incorrect. No user would need 423 retries at logging in to gain access to a system. **C** is incorrect; if the system were having problems, all users would probably show up the same way. **D** is incorrect; a mail bomb has nothing to do with incorrect logins; it's purely a mailbox filling attack.

11. ☑ **C.** Copyright law protects original works of authorship. The philosophy behind copyright protection was to encourage individuals to create literary works and works of art by ensuring economic gain. In 1996, Congress enacted the Copyright Act, which protects "original works of ownership," including literary and other original works.
    ☒ **A** is incorrect because Work for Hire is a form of protection that captures ownership from independent contractors. **B** is incorrect because Trademark law protects words, names, and symbols used by manufacturers and businesses to identify their goods and services.

12. ☑ **D.** None of the above. T1 lines can be connected to E1 lines without causing any of the obstacles listed. T1 and E1 lines are both based on the same technology, so they are fully compatible with each other.
    ☒ **A** is incorrect because it suggests using a flow controller to even out the speed differences between the two lines. An E1 line is faster than a T1 line, so there may be a slight bottleneck between the two, but there is no such thing as a "flow controller." **B** is incorrect because it suggests the use of an interpretation device to allow the two lines to communicate. T1 and E1 lines use compatible technology, so they may be interconnected without additional translation or conversion hardware. **C** is incorrect because E1 is simply the European version of a T1 line. Although their specifications are slightly different, they are compatible with each other.

13. ☑ **D.** Save the document as an RTF file. RTF files contain commands about the layout and fonts used in a document. The commands appear in such a way that they are interpreted by whichever program is being used to open the document. This allows files to be opened and formatted by programs that are incompatible with the program used to create the document. However, the document may have a slightly different layout and use different fonts than the original.

☒ **A** and **C** are both incorrect because they suggest you should do nothing because the e-mail or browser program will automatically convert the document. This is incorrect because although they are capable of downloading different file types, neither of these programs can convert or alter the contents of a document. **B** is incorrect because it suggests sending a PDF file. Although this will allow the reader to view your document in its original formatting and layout, it will not allow the reader to open the document in his word processing program. PDF files are opened using a separate reader program. One requirement in this scenario is that the reader will open the file in his word processor (perhaps to do some editing of the document).

14. ☑ **D.** For quick searches of text files, Perl is your answer. It is easy to learn, is based on C++, and runs cleanly and quickly. Perl can also be compiled into C code or cross-platform byte-code to be used on other operating systems.

☒ **A, B,** and **C** are incorrect. They all can be used to retrieve information from a text document, but none are streamlined to do it quickly. Perl was developed to search and return results.

15. ☑ **D.** 110 is the lowest number a Class C address can have. 110 translates to 128 in decimal. You can tell the class of an IP address in binary by looking at the first three bits in the first octet of an address. Class A will start with 0, Class B will start with 101, and Class C will start with 110.

☒ **A** is a Class B address space that translates to 128. **B** translates to 160, also a Class B address. **C** translates to 64, a Class A address.

16. ☑ **A.** You will need to enter an A type record. An A type record is a host entry. It is the primary entry for all domains in a DNS. After an A record is entered, other records in regard to the domain can be entered.

    ☒ **B** is incorrect. HINFO is an entry that allows other hosts on the network to find out information about a host, such as operating system type. **C** is incorrect. CNAME are the Canonical names associated with the domain, such as www and ftp. **D** is also incorrect. NS records are name server records. These are used by name servers to locate other name servers on a network.

17. ☑ **A.** E-mail makes up the majority of bandwidth usage on the Internet.

    ☒ **B, C,** and **D** are all types of information passed across the Internet, but use less bandwidth than e-mail.

18. ☑ **D.** When you send packets to a station that you have not spoken to before, or to a station you do not speak to very often, you must first ARP for the MAC of that station. Your system does this for you. When you ARP, you are asking if anyone on your network knows the MAC of the station you are trying to reach. Once you obtain that MAC, you then send your packets directly to that MAC address.

    ☒ **A** and **B** are both troubleshooting utilities to determine if a station is up and running, and determine the path you are taking to that station and the time it takes to reach it. **C** is used when you need to convert an FQDN such as www.mycompany.com to an IP address to send over the network.

19. ☑ **C.** The ability to verify the identity of a user or system process is called authentication.

    ☒ **A** is incorrect. Access control is defined as the ability to determine who is and who is not allowed access to a computer or network. **B** is also incorrect. Auditing is a feature that can be turned on so you can keep a running log of processes that have run or users who have accessed the system. You can audit many different things depending on the operating system. **D** is incorrect. Encryption is the scrambling of data with the use of a set algorithm so that anyone intercepting the data will be unable to read it. The intended receiver of the data will have the algorithm and run it again to unscramble the data.

**20.** ☑ **C.** Port 25 is for SMTP; this means that mail can be sent out, but that's it. For e-mail to be received, you must have Port 110 open for POP3.
☒ **A** is incorrect. You have turned on one-half of the e-mail ports; otherwise, your users would also notice that they cannot send e-mail to their customers. **B** is incorrect. If POP3 was turned on and SMTP was not, you would be able to receive e-mail, but not send it. **D** is also incorrect; the firewall is working properly. Firewalls are set up so that all traffic is denied unless specifically granted. Therefore, when you first bring a firewall online, all traffic is denied both in and out of the firewall.

**21.** ☑ **D.** At the current time, there is no global standard for encryption; each country has its own standard. Hopefully, in the next few years a global standard will be in place.
☒ **A**, **B**, and **C** are all groups or bodies that are working on a standard, but as of yet none has been created.

**22.** ☑ **C.** By installing virus software on both the end users' systems and the servers, you are attacking the problem at more than one entry point. The end users' systems will catch the majority of the viruses downloaded in programs and files from the Internet, and e-mail attachment viruses. The server will catch the viruses embedded in compressed files that are uncompressed on the server. Some virus software when placed on the e-mail server will scan the e-mail attachments before they reach the end user.
☒ **A** is incorrect. If you only put the virus software on the servers, the viruses will spread from user to user via file copy and e-mail. **B** is also incorrect. If you only put the virus software on the end users' systems, you will not catch the viruses that infect the servers via files being copied from the end users' systems to the servers. **D** is incorrect. Blocking all TCP/IP packets from entering your company will only stop viruses from entering via the Internet—what about viruses from users bringing diskettes from home?

**23.** ☑ E. All of the above are valid options for securing a Web page. You must take into account the Web server; if it is a slower system or small hard drive, you will bog down the system's resources when keeping logs and authenticating users. A small hard drive will cause the system to crash as the log files fill quickly. If you choose to encrypt data, the user must also have the ability to de-encrypt it once he or she receives the download.

**24.** ☑ C. To access a Secured Socket Layer (SSL) page, you must be able to connect to Port 443 through the firewall.

☒ A is incorrect. A Proxy server will be able to send and receive HTTPS:// requests. B is incorrect. Port 8080 is generally used for HTTP connections. D is also incorrect. Configurations in the browser would not keep you from accessing an SSL location.

**25.** ☑ C. The function of the proxy server is to manage and filter users' Internet requests. Proxy servers intercept Internet requests from the internal network, apply filtering rules to them, and then make the request on behalf of the user. Requests can be filtered to prevent user access to particular Web sites, and the proxy server can provide minimal security by masking the user's IP address with its own.

☒ A is incorrect because this is the function of a firewall. Although a single computer may contain firewall and proxy software, each service is separate, and proxy software cannot do the job of a firewall. B is incorrect because this is the function of a cache service. A cache server is able to remember recently accessed Web sites. If that site is requested at a later time, it is delivered from the server's cache, rather than from the Internet itself. Although proxy and cache services can exist on the same computer, they are separate functions, and proxy software does not inherently include cache services. D is incorrect because it states that proxy software is able to perform all of the functions listed. Again, one *computer* may be able to perform all of these functions, but only if separate proxy, cache, and firewall software is installed.

26. ☑ **B.** The company is most likely to use a Web server, e-commerce server, list server, and certificate server. A Web server is required to host any type of Web site. E-commerce servers are used to take customer orders, keep track of inventory, and organize customer profiles. Although a list server is not required on an e-commerce site, it may be used to organize the e-mail addresses of customers, and automatically send out product or price information to groups of users. Finally, it is likely that this business will make use of their own, or a third-party certificate server. The function of a certificate server is to authorize user transactions, such as credit card purchases, on the Internet.

    ☒ **A** is incorrect because it suggests the company is likely to use an FTP server. FTP servers host FTP sites for file downloads only, and do not play a role in e-commerce sites (unless the business is actually selling downloadable files). **C** is incorrect because it suggests using an authentication server and purchase server. Neither of these are valid terms. A server that authenticates users is called a certificate server, and a server that allows you to make purchases is called an e-commerce server. **D** is incorrect because it suggests using an inventory server. There is no such thing as an inventory server, as e-commerce software typically includes the ability to track and order inventory.

27. ☑ **D.** The properties *appName* and *appVersion* of the *navigator* object return the name of the browser and the version, respectively.

    ☒ **A** is incorrect because there is no *browser* object. **B** is incorrect because the *document* object represents the content viewed in the browser window or frame and the other content of the HTML document such as the <HEAD> section including the <TITLE>. It does not contain information about the browser. **C** is incorrect because the *frame* object reflects the <FRAME> element and does not contain information about the browser.

28. ☑ **C, D.** When the form is submitted, the event ONSUBMIT for the <FORM> tag fires and runs the code. The event handler for the <FORM> tag must contain the keyword return and if the event procedure returns false, the submit action is canceled. The other technique is to write code for the event ONCLICK for the tag <INPUT TYPE=BUTTON> corresponding to the button, and in the procedure, invoke the method submit of the form like document.form1.submit() when validation suceeds and simply exit the procedure if validation fails.

☒  **A** is incorrect because even if the procedure returns false, without the keyword return in the <FORM> tag, the form is still submitted when validation fails. **B** is incorrect because there is no event *onsubmit* for a button of type SUBMIT.

29. ☑  **C**. This code is well structured (notice the start-tag, end-tag pairs) and produces the expected result.

☒  **A** is incorrect because the correct value of the attribute ALIGN of the tag <H1>, <H2> is "center," not "middle." **B** is incorrect because the order of the header tags <H1>, <H2>, <H3> is wrong. **D** is incorrect because the "line break" tag <br> will cause an additional line break. The end tag </h3> already signals the start of a new paragraph, so in this case we have an extra blank line between the header "4ᵗʰ Quarter 1999" and the last line.

30. ☑  **B**. The tag <input type=radio ...> is used to present to the users a group of choices where only one is selected at a time. To group related radio buttons together so only one can be selected, give them the same name as in answer B. To select one of them by default, use the attribute CHECKED.

☒  **A** is incorrect. The radio buttons must have the same name so only one of them can be selected. **C** is incorrect. The attribute CHECKED must be used to select one of the radio buttons by default as in the exhibit. **D** is incorrect. There is no tag called <radio ...>.

31. ☑  **C**. UCLA was the other university to receive one of the first computers; in fact, it was the first university to get one of the computers.

☒  **A**, **B**, and **D** are incorrect; they received computers at a later time.

32. ☑  **C**. You would issue the transfer type of file:// followed by the location of the file.

☒  **A**, **B**, and **D** are all incorrect. You cannot use HTTP://local if you have a Web server running on the system. You would have to give it a domain name, not the word "local." The word "local" in answer B is incorrect, as it has no meaning.

**33.** ☑ **B.** 56K is the fastest speed at which a dial-up modem using POTS (plain old telephone system) can connect. The actual connection is usually somewhere around 53K.

☒ **A** is incorrect; 33.6 is a slower connection speed than the maximum available. In some areas of the country, even with a 56K modem, 33.6K might be your best connection. **C** and **D** are also incorrect, as these are connection speeds of ISDN connections.

**34.** ☑ **C.** mail:// is not a transport protocol. mailto:// is the correct transport to use. This is a cause for many support calls from users who try to use mail:// and receive an error.

☒ **A**, **B**, and **D** are all incorrect. These are all valid transport protocols.

**35.** ☑ **C.** It does not matter what application you use to create the e-mail message, it is still sent to the mail server via the SMTP protocol.

☒ **A** is incorrect. HTTP is used for browsing. You may create and read your e-mail in a browser, but SMTP is used to send the e-mail. **B** is incorrect. POP3 is used to retrieve the e-mail from the server regardless of which application is used to read it. **D** is also incorrect. SNMP is a protocol used to manage network equipment such as switches and hubs.

**36.** ☑ **C.** The "pictures" is the directory path. This path may be just one or many directories deep; each \ is another directory.

☒ **A** is incorrect. The HTTP:\\ is the transfer protocol, and could be FTP:\\, HTTPS:\\, or a few others. **B** is incorrect. The www.mypage.org is the domain name of the site. **D** is also incorrect. Family.html is the page name or filename located in the pictures directory.

**37.** ☑ **C.** A Web server serves Web pages at the request of a user or proxy server via a Web or http request.

☒ **A** is incorrect. This would be a database server. **B** is also incorrect. This would be an end-user system, not a web server.

38. ☑ **D.** The proxy server can secure access to an Internet, block access to specified Internet Web sites, allow for quick Internet access to all clients of an internal network, and improve performance through its own cache. The proxy cache holds frequently accessed Web pages so all clients can benefit from a faster network cache, therefore reducing the need for Internet access and improving performance for internal clients.
☒ **A, B,** and **C** are incorrect because they are incomplete.

39. ☑ **D.** With most major browsers, you can work offline, and the browser can get the pages saved in the cache. This requires that we refresh the cache by browsing (on Sunday or before the meeting).
☒ **A** is incorrect because if the pages are updated weekly, there is no need to refresh the pages during the week. **B** is incorrect because there is no need to refresh every day if the pages change only on Saturday. **C** is incorrect because when we show the pages from the hard disk, the URL address will contain the name of the file and the location on the hard disk; it does not reflect the original address. The prospective customers cannot see the source of the data on the browser.

40. ☑ **A.** This solution offers the fastest access to the pages for the users. This usually means we have to use specific software for indexing and a database as development tools.
☒ **B, C,** and **D** are incorrect because we will use the search engines for indexing. This will happen as the robots visit the pages; the legal terms will be indexed and can be found by users running search engines. However, this is not the fastest and most convenient way for users to search for specific legal terms on the Web site once they are on your Web site. The result of a search (through search engines) usually contains all Web sites that are indexed by the search engine, and is not appropriate since the users want to search this Web site.

41. ☑ **D.** A license is not required to use a work in the public domain. Such a work, one that is not protected by copyright, can be used by anyone. Because it is not protected by copyright, no one can claim the exclusive rights of copyright for such a work.

☒ **A**, **B**, and **C** are incorrect because a license is not required to use pubic domain works, nor do you need to apply or register for copyright protection since the works are not created by you.

42. ☑ **A** and **C**. E-commerce transactions often involve multiple currencies from countries all around the world, and systems must be built to deal with currency conversion between the consumer and the banking and merchant organizations in real time.
☒ **B** is incorrect because determining the form of payment is not the same as converting between foreign and domestic currency. **D** is incorrect because tax collection is an issue independent of currency conversion.

43. ☑ **B**. Unicode is a general technique used to internationalize content, to prepare it so that the code never needs modification. The actual content is separated from the rules of translation. The formatting then becomes language independent, meaning that dates, times, numbers, and currencies all call up logic that provides the formatting based on local language and country code requirements.
☒ **A**, **C**, and **D** are incorrect because Unicode does not replace scripting or authoring languages. Rather, it's a standard used to code characters used in modern spoken languages.

44. ☑ **D**. There's more to developing a global e-business presence than deploying a company intranet and Internet site. You need a plan to craft your business into a global e-business that crosses barriers of currency, language, time, and geography. The Internet does not change the principles of your business strategy. A company should begin by selecting one application or business process to transform that will have the greatest impact on its business. Critical business processes that provide the highest return on investment (ROI) include customer relationship management, supply chain management, e-commerce, knowledge management, and e-learning.

45. ☑ **C**. IBM mainframes use a program called Host on Demand that can be installed on a system that has IE or Netscape. Once it's installed, you can connect to the IBM mainframe just as you would any other Web page and be greeted with a logon prompt.

☒    A, B, and D are all incorrect. SNA stands for Systems Network Architecture, which is what IBM mainframes are also called; Host on Demand is the extension or program that must be installed. You do not require an external Telnet application to connect to an IBM system once the program is installed.

**46.** ☑    A. You need to make sure you have the version number of the application or program you need updates for. No matter what the error message is, the version number is the most important. If you are running a newer version than what is listed on the Web site, you might cause problems by installing a patch or update for a program. For example, if you are running, say, version 1.2, and there are versions 1.3, 1.5, 2.0, and 2.5, the update for version 2.5 might not work with the version you are running. ☒    B is incorrect; the programmer's name is not important. C is incorrect. The OS is important when searching for an update or fix, but the version number is the main information needed. D is also incorrect. There may not be an error message, or the same error message might mean different things depending on the version of code you are running. Always have the version number of the product you are searching on.

**47.** ☑    A and D. The application will need to know the username and location of the POP3 server. It will also need to know the password of the account and the location of the SMTP server to send outgoing mail. ☒    B is incorrect. You are not required to have an address book to run an e-mail client. C is incorrect. A telephone number is only required if you are using a dial-up connection. If you are on a LAN, there is no need for a telephone number.

**48.** ☑    B. Netscape 4.5 will keep up to 300 cookies on the system, after which it will work on a first-in first-out basis, replacing the oldest cookies with newer ones. ☒    A and C are incorrect; see the explanation for B. D is also incorrect. An unlimited number of cookies would cause a bottleneck on your system while you are browsing. If there were thousands of cookies on your system, it would take extra time in searching to see if it had a cookie from this site.

49. ☑ **B.** Flash. Flash files contain vector graphics, which are images created using a series of lines rather than dots. Vector graphics can be resized without a loss of resolution, and they support better overall resolution than their bitmapped counterparts.

☒ **A** and **C** are incorrect because these are both types of bitmapped image formats. Bitmapped images are made up of a series of independent dots on the screen. They are generally unaffected by increased monitor resolution, and appear grainy when enlarged. **D** is incorrect because this is a text file format, not a graphic file format.

50. ☑ **C.** RealPlayer. This media format is designed to deliver streaming, real-time audio and video over the Internet. It is ideal for viewing live or previous television broadcasts. RealPlayer also provides users with "channels" for up-to-date news, sports, and entertainment information.

☒ **A** and **B** are incorrect because these programs are designed to display still or animated graphics. They do not offer channels for news or other media broadcasts. **D** is incorrect because this is an audio file format. MP3 files do not support video content of any type.

51. ☑ **C.** JPEG graphics are not capable of animation. JPEGs offer photo-like images. Each file holds only one image, so you cannot create the illusion of animation by running a series of slightly different images, like you can with GIF89a files.

☒ **A** is incorrect because it states that the JPEG files will not be able to slowly fade into view. This is untrue because that is exactly what progressive JPEG files do. Rather than load with full clarity one line at a time, progressive JPEGs load colors over the whole area of the object. With each pass, the object becomes clearer and more defined until full clarity is achieved. This is similar to the action of interlaced GIFs. **B** is incorrect because this is a characteristic of JPEG files. They support many more colors than GIFs, and this is what makes them ideal for displaying digital or scanned photos. **D** is incorrect because JPEG files are capable of compression. They use lossy compression, meaning that redundant parts of the image are removed. Although this can lead to grainy images at very high compression, it makes JPEG files easy to download because of their reduced size.

52. ☑   **B.** Open the associated EPS file. The PostScript file itself contains only commands for printing a document. If you viewed a PostScript file, you would see line after line of commands, not the actual image to be printed. Because of this, EPS (Encapsulated PostScript) files are created that display how the printer will interpret the PostScript commands. In essence, EPS provides a sort of "print preview" of the PostScripted document.

☒   **A** and **C** are both incorrect because they suggest opening the PostScript file itself to see how the printout will look. However, the PostScript file itself contains only commands, not a representation of the actual document. **D** is incorrect because it is possible to view PostScript documents using EPS.

53. ☑   **A.** Windows 98 Media Player. The Windows 98 Media Player comes with Windows 98 and supports .mov, .avi, midi, and .wav files. *Note: The Windows 98 ActiveMovie application will also run these files.*

☒   **B** is incorrect because although this program will run .mov files, it is a separate plug-in program. In this scenario, there are no additional browser plug-ins. **C** is incorrect because the browser itself cannot interpret .mov files; it requires the aid of an external plug-in or application, such as Windows Media Player or QuickTime. **D** is incorrect because it states that no answer given is correct.

54. ☑   **D.** CGI applications run directly on the Web server system. The results are then displayed on the end-users' systems via their browser. No additional hardware or software requirements are needed on the end-user side to view CGI applications. One big CGI application in use today is the counters on many Web sites. CGI runs under UNIX.

☒   **A, B,** and **C** are incorrect, as they require either a specific browser or some type of add-on or plug-in to be compatible with the browser.

55. ☑   **C.** Handshake. When one modem dials another, the answering modem picks up and sends out a guard tone to indicate its presence on the line. The answering modem then sends a carrier tone to establish the connection speed with the sending modem. Finally, both modems perform equalization, where they test the line for noise.

☒   **A** is incorrect. Although a modem may send a *guard tone* to another, there is no such term as *guard sequence* in modem communications. **B** is incorrect because the term *equalization* is used to describe both modems testing the line for noise. This is not called an equalization tone, because it actually sounds more like static. **D** is also incorrect. A *carrier tone* is used to establish a communication speed, but there is no such term as *carrier protocol.*

**56.** ☑   **C. Cable.** Cable modems plug into a regular TV cable outlet. Cable uses radio frequencies, which are analog, and cable is available in symmetric and asymmetric. Symmetric cable devotes equal bandwidth to upstream and downstream data, and asymmetric cable allocates more bandwidth to downstream data.
☒   **A** is incorrect because although this type of modem uses analog communication, it is not asymmetric. When using an analog modem, upstream data is given as much bandwidth as downstream data. **B** is incorrect because although it may be symmetric or asymmetric, it uses digital rather than analog communication. **D** is incorrect because it states there is not enough information to determine the access type. This is untrue because cable (and only cable) access fits the description given.

**57.** ☑   **B.** An active hub repeats data signals, and a passive hub does not. Computer signals can degrade (attenuate) over distance. An active hub is capable of repeating (boosting) the signal so that it arrives at its destination at the proper strength. A passive hub simply resends data from one computer to the others on a network without changing the signal strength.
☒   **A** is incorrect because it states that an active hub *sends* data, while a passive hub *holds* data until the destination computer picks it up. This is untrue because all hubs resend data to all other computers. **C** is incorrect. Hubs do not check the status of the network cable, and are not intelligent enough to make adjustment for noise if it exists. **D** is incorrect because it refers to an active hub's ability to enforce network restrictions. This is the job of network software and routers. Hubs do not read destination addresses or the content of data packets, so they are unable to make decisions about data access.

**58.** ☑    **C.** To allow the TCP/IP networks to communicate with the IPX/SPX networks. The function of a gateway in any network is to translate data between networks using dissimilar protocols. All data between the networks passes through the gateway where it is examined, translated, and then passed along to its destination.

☒    **A** is incorrect because it suggests the gateway allows the switch to use portions of the routers' routing tables. The switch has a routing table of its own, and although it is not as sophisticated as a router's routing table, there is no device that allows the gateway use of another device's routing table. **B** is incorrect because this is the responsibility of the network server. **D** is incorrect because this is the job of a security firewall.

**59.** ☑    **B.** Packet level. Packet-level firewalls (usually built into a router) are programmed by the network administrator to recognize certain external IP addresses. Data from all other IP addresses are screened out by the router, so they never enter the internal network.

☒    **A** is incorrect because this is a more sophisticated type of firewall that uses a proxy server to make data requests on behalf of the network's users. The proxy provides the user with the appropriate interface, and examines all incoming and outgoing data. The proxy makes decisions about whether to allow data in or out based on the content of the data packet, or the data's application type. **C** is also incorrect because it works in a manner similar to that of an application level firewall. **D** is incorrect because this is a type of application-level architecture (physical setup). In a dual-homed host setup, the proxy server is located between the network and the Internet connection so that data can be screened before it reaches the network.

**60.** ☑    **C.** With the HTTP "get" method, the form data set is appended to the URL (Uniform Resource Locator, also known as URI for Uniform Resource Identifier) specified by the action attribute (with a question-mark (?) as separator), and this new URL is sent to the processing agent. With the HTTP "post" method, the form data set is included in the body of the form and sent to the processing agent. This way, the URL does not contain the value of the controls contained in the form.

☒   **A** is incorrect because the <!DOCTYPE statement is for version information, not for controlling form data submission. **B** is incorrect because with the HTTP "get" method, the form data set is appended to the URL specified by the action attribute (with a question-mark (?) as separator), and this new URL is sent to the processing agent. This means that the User ID and Password values will be seen in the URL address box of the browser; this is not the desired result. **D** is incorrect because the appropriate method is the POST method.

**61.**   ☑   **B.** 255.255.240.0 would allow for 4094 users per subnet, but only allows for 14 subnets.

☒   **A** is incorrect because 255.255.192.0 would allow for 16,382 users per subnet. This would be serious overkill and would allow for two subnets. **C** is incorrect because 255.255.252.0 would only allow for 1022 users per subnet, much lower than you require. **D** is incorrect because 255.255.255.0 would allow for the standard 254 users per subnet; again, much lower than needed.

**62.**   ☑   **B.** Use GIFs because BMPs can cause the Web site to load slowly. GIF files are capable of compression, but BMP files are not. Therefore, the same image can be twice as large as a BMP as it would be as a GIF. Larger images load into the browser more slowly, and take longer to download.

☒   **A** is incorrect because it suggests that GIF files are not supported by older browsers. In fact, GIF is a very common image format that is supported by almost all browsers and graphics programs. **C** is incorrect because it suggests that GIFs require a browser plug-in. This is untrue because almost all browsers support the GIF format, so no external plug-in is required. **D** is incorrect because it states that GIF files can lose data during compression. GIF files use lossless compression, meaning no parts of the image are removed (as in lossy compression). A GIF image looks the same with or without compression.

**63.**   ☑   **A.** This is a display of a NETSTAT command from the command prompt. This shows all the active TCP connections from the system. There are several switches you can use to gain more or less information.

☒   **B** is incorrect. An ARP table would look something like this:

Interface: 16.72.27.104 on Interface 3

| Internet Address | Physical Address | Type |
|---|---|---|
| 43.55.98.123 | 08-00-2b-45-11-00 | dynamic |

**C** is incorrect. WINIPCONFIG would show the IP address, gateway, and other information concerning the local system's IP stack. **D** would display information regarding whether a site or system is alive and responding.

**64.** ☑   **B.** The NAP is a high-speed network in which routers are attached. Per Cisco, a NAP must run at speeds of at least 100Mbps. The NAP is also a logical point for congestion and therefore should be upgradable as needed.
☒   **A** is the definition of a Demark. **C** is the definition of a router. Routers operate at level 3 of the OSI model, and as packets enter, they are transmitted out the appropriate interface to reach the destination. **D** is the definition of the CO, or Central Office, of the telephone company.

# i-Net+
# Certification
# Practice Exam II

Q&A

# Practice Exam Questions

**1.** Cookies are used to store which type of information? (Select all that apply.)

A. Information about the user

B. Information about the browser

C. Information about the network

D. All of the above

**2.** Your company is considering deploying an online catalog system. What are the benefits of doing so? (Select all that apply.)

A. E-catalogs are online versions of printed catalogs that are much easier to update.

B. E-catalogs are useful for B2C and B2B e-commerce applications.

C. Electronic malls can be created to support multiple e-catalog merchants.

D. All of the above.

**3.** A customer wants high-speed Internet access, and is considering ISDN. The customer wants more information about whether to get an internal or external modem. What is your recommendation?

A. Internal—they do not cause bottlenecks.

B. External—they are less susceptible to line noise.

C. Internal—they are less susceptible to line noise.

D. External—they are much cheaper.

**4.** You want to host a news forum that will allow users to participate in a discussion by reading and replying to each other's messages. What is the proper term for the computer you should use to host the discussion forum?

A. A news server

B. A list server

C. A forum server

D. An FTP server

**5.** Customers have requested self-service functions from your Web site. Which of the following applications lend themselves to self-service? (Select all that apply.)

A. Technical support and help desk functions

B. Online FAQs and software distribution

C. Planning business travel, ordering supplies, and managing medical benefits

D. All of the above

**6.** When connecting to a Web site, your screen downloads the image, but you notice a generic icon-looking graphic instead of the graphic that should be there. You can assume what from this?

A. Your connection to the Web server is too slow, so the file was not downloaded.

B. The file has been removed from where the HTTP document believes it is.

C. The graphic is located in your browser's cache.

D. The page is being retrieved from cache, and if you click Refresh, you will get the graphics.

**7.** Your company wants to do e-commerce. You have to build Web pages (called Catalog pages) that show the products your company is selling. Around 500 products can be bought online. Most of them are fashion related. From your preliminary interviews with a panel of customers, you know that they want to see the products before they decide to buy. You already have in the company's archive all pictures of all products in JPG format, and the average size is 100K bytes. How would you design the catalog page(s) for performance and user comfort?

A. Design a search page to narrow down the list of products to be displayed. Display the products found one by one (one page for one product) with the product picture and put a hyperlink to the next product on the next page.

B. Design a search page to narrow down the list of products to be displayed. Display a small number of products on a page with hyperlinks to the next page. Display only the thumbnail pictures. Each thumbnail picture is a hyperlink to the full-size picture.

C. Design a search page to narrow down the list of products to be displayed. Display all the products with a text hyperlink "Click to view picture." The hyperlink points to the full-size picture of the product.

D. Design a search page to narrow down the list of products to be displayed. Display a small number of products on a page with hyperlinks to the next page. For each product, a text hyperlink "Click to view picture" points to the full-size picture of the product.

8. Multitiered applications are used all the time on networks. Which of the following is an example of a tiered application?

A. A game played on a single system, such as Solitaire.

B. A user using a application to access a database of customer information.

C. A Web browser connecting to a Web server where it calls for information contained in a database on another server.

D. A user playing a multiplayer game such as Doom attached to a game server.

9. You work for a public library. The library has an intranet Web site available to the public for document and books searching. The workstations are scattered around on all floors and run Internet Explorer 4. You have a page that presents hyperlinks to educational books; each link points to a description page of the book. You want young children to be able to read the page easily and want the links' background color to change and the font to be bigger when the mouse pointer is over the hyperlink text. The links look like this currently:

```
<A HREF="PoohFriends.htm">Pooh bear makes new friends</A>
```

How would you do this? (Choose all that apply.)

A.  Use Cascading Style Sheets or inline style to specify the background and font size of the anchor tag (<A>). Write script to handle the event ONMOUSEOVER of the <A> tag and change the background color and font of the <A> tag. Write script to handle the event ONMOUSEOUT of the <A> tag and change the background color and font of the <A> tag back to what it was.

B.  Write script to handle the event ONMOUSEOVER of the <A> tag and change the background color and font of the text of the link. Write script to handle the event ONMOUSEOVER of the <A> tag and change the background color and font of the text of the link back to what it was.

C.  Put the hyperlink block (<A...> through </A>) inside a <DIV> block. Assign to the <DIV> a style with a background color and font. Write script to handle the event ONMOUSEOVER of the <A> tag and change the style of the <DIV> tag to a new one with a different color and bigger font. Write script to handle the event ONMOUSEOUT of the <A> tag and change the style of the <DIV> tag back to the previous one.

D.  Put the hyperlink text inside a <SPAN> block. Assign to the <SPAN> a style with a background color and font. Write script to handle the event ONMOUSEOVER of the <A> tag and change the style of the <SPAN> tag to a new one with a different color and bigger font. Write script to handle the event ONMOUSEOUT of the <A> tag and change the style of the <SPAN> tag back to the previous one.

**10.** When entering new global markets, it is a good idea to seek counseling from? (Select all that apply.)

A.  International attorneys, and accountants experienced in global e-business

B.  The U.S. State Department

C.  Foreign governments

D.  Your competitors

**11.** A software company hosts a Web site from which users can download updates and patches. Users have been complaining that downloads from the site are very slow. What can this company do to speed up download time for users?

A. Set up a Telnet site to allow access to the company's network file server

B. Increase firewall restrictions to limit the number of concurrent accesses to the Web site

C. Set up an FTP site that contains the downloadable files

D. Restrict downloads to users who have 1.5 Mbps access or faster

**12.** You have successfully deployed localized versions of your e-commerce sites in Spain and Mexico. Your IT department is finding it very labor intensive to maintain all these sites. What are some of the possible reason(s)?

A. Managing updates to multiple Web sites around the world can be burdensome.

B. It is difficult to manage human and technical resources around the globe.

C. Dealing with differences in technology infrastructures in different countries can be complicated.

D. All of the above.

**13.** A client uses a line service in which they are only billed for the time they actually use. The line is analog, and can transmit up to 64 Kbps. What type of service is this?

A. Frame Relay

B. X.25

C. ATM

D. ADSL

**14.** You have a Web site containing pictures of exotic indoor plants that your company is selling. The plants are ordered by specialists such as interior designers or sometimes by university researchers, and the plants have very rare names (scientific names usually). You have a large number of pages and over a thousand species of plants. The pages are designed as catalog pages that contain pictures of the plants in a table sorted by plant names, and each page has an average of 50 pictures. You know that if the users use a search engine and put in the name of the plant, your Web site would be found easily given the rareness of the names. How should you design your pages to take advantage of the full-text index used by the search engines? (Choose two.)

A. Use the META tag to specify the names of the plants as keywords.

B. Put the plant name below each picture.

C. Put the name of the plants at the top of the page inside COMMENT tags.

D. Name the picture file after the plant name; for example, "BirdOfParadise.jpg."

**15.** You connect to a work system from home. You notice that at times it seems like it just hangs. You complain to your helpdesk, but they claim the problem is with your ISP. You call your ISP and they say they do not have any problems and that the problem is on your company's network. What would be the best utility to use to determine where the slowdown is occurring?

A. WINIPCONFG

B. PING Utility

C. TRACE Routing Utility

D. Network Analyzer

**16.** You maintain an intranet Web site that allows Product Managers of your company to update the catalog of products. They can select the set of products by entering selection criteria and get a list of products that satisfy the selection criteria. The products are displayed in a tabular format. Each line on the page contains the picture of the product displayed as a thumbnail picture, the name, and the price. The users can select a specific product on that list and bring up the data entry page to modify the characteristics of the products. When the users are finished entering data, they click on a hyperlink to go back to the list of products. You want the list of products to show the new data and use the HTTP Expires header to specify that the Product List page expires immediately. What is the appropriate HTML element and attributes?

A. Element <HEAD>, attribute EXPIRES set to yesterday's date and time

B. Element <META>, attribute EXPIRES set to yesterday's date and time

C. Element <META>, attribute HTTP_EQUIV="EXPIRES", attribute CONTENT set to yesterday's date and time

D. Element <BODY>, attributes HTTP-EQUIV="EXPIRES", attribute CONTENT set to yesterday's date and time

17. To publish works held in the public domain you must (select all that apply):

A. License the works from the author.

B. Apply for trademark or copyright protection.

C. Register the works for copyright protection.

D. You are free to publish those works without a license.

18. You want to offer your online catalog to your suppliers and distributors to reproduce and/or print as they see fit, without allowing them to change any of the content. The best course of action is (select all that apply):

A. You put the information in the public domain.

B. You authorize your business partners to copy, duplicate, and print the product catalog.

C. You register the works for copyright protection to ensure that no changes are made.

D. All of the above.

19. Before Internet search engines, the only way to find files you were looking for was to use an Archie server. When connecting to the server you would generally enter Archie as the username so that the server would recognize

you as an anonymous user and log you in to the account and start the Archie search engine. What service was used to connect to the Archie servers?

A. FTP

B. Telnet

C. Gopher

D. HTTP

**20.** While developing a global presence does not change the principles of your overall business strategy, it does require a change in your thinking toward? (Select all that apply.)

A. Your business processes and procedures

B. The relationships in the supply chain between your company, suppliers, distributors, and business partners

C. The relationship with your customers

D. All of the above

**21.** You are a manager in a large organization. You send out memos from your e-mail system to many of your users, and have noticed that people have memos with your e-mail address on them that you never sent. These memos are authorizing pay increases, vacation authorization, and other important issues. You also notice that you sent an e-mail informing a user that his pay raise is 15%, and when he received the e-mail, it said 25%. What is an easy-to-add option that you can use to guarantee your e-mail is only from you and is unaltered when it arrives?

A. Use data encryption to send the information.

B. Quit using e-mail and just post memos or hand deliver information pertaining to one person.

C. Change your e-mail address; it seems that someone else has the identical e-mail address and is sending data out to his users and your users seem to be receiving it.

D. Use a digital signature on your e-mail.

**22.** The points where a local ISP joins other larger ISPs or phone companies that transmit their packets over the Internet are called what?

A. Backbone connections

B. Network Access Point

C. Demark

D. Central office connection

**23.** Unicode provides the following benefit(s) (select all that apply):

A. You can replace multiple scripting languages with Unicode.

B. You have a standard format for document and data interchange that is language independent.

C. You no longer have to manage multiple language versions of your Web sites.

D. You no longer need to use HTML to author Web pages.

**24.** Which of the dial-up connection types offers CRC checking?

A. SLIP

B. PPP

C. PPTP

D. HTTP

**25.** You maintain a Web server that hosts a public Web site. The site allows users to view technical documentation on various FAX machines that your company manufactures. The number of documents has been increasing steadily, and you received recently through the Help Desk feedback from the users that the site performance is degrading. You investigated and used a performance-monitoring tool to monitor the Web server on a daily basis for about a week. You noticed that there is a ratio called "Cache Hit" that is decreasing over time. What course of action should you take?

A. Increase the cache size on the Web server.

B. Increase network bandwidth.

C. Upgrade the Web server processor.

D. Increase the memory on the server.

**26.** You need to get some price quotes to a customer in France quickly. The customer does not have a FAX machine, so faxing is not an option. What would be your best option in getting the needed information to the customer quickly?

A. FTP the document to the customer's FTP server.

B. Send an e-mail with the information included.

C. Telnet to the customer's site and leave him a note on this system.

D. Send the information by Airmail.

**27.** The correct syntax for the <META> tag is?

A. `<META http equiv="Refresh" content="field value">`

B. `<META http="Refresh" content="field value">`

C. `<META http-equiv="Refresh" content="field value">`

D. `<META httpequiv ="Refresh" content="field value">`

**28.** Which of the following addresses would you use to reach the White House's Washington, D.C., main Web page?

A. http://www.white-house.com

B. http://www.whitehouse.org

C. http://www.whitehouse.mil

D. http://www.whitehouse.gov

**29.** When optimizing your HTML coding, it is always a good idea to follow some simple rules. These rules include:

A. Keep database connections to a minimum.

B. Keep your servers close to your end users no matter how spread out they are.

C. Once an object is called or opened, do not release or close it until the program has completed, to reduce CPU requirements to reopen it.

D. Avoid multiple transfers; do as many data transfers as possible at the same time to reduce network bandwidth requirements.

30. You have received your public and private keys from an encryption key organization. What do you do with these keys so that you can send encrypted data and your receiver can read the data?

A. You install the public key and encrypt all data being sent out with it. The private key should be given to anyone who will receive your encrypted data. This private key will prove that you are the person sending the data.

B. You install the private key and encrypt all data being sent out with it. You then give the public key to anyone who will be receiving data from you. This public key will prove that the data sent is from you and will allow the user to decipher it.

C. You install both the public and private keys. Any data sent out will be encrypted using a mixture of both keys. The receiver will use his or her public and private keys to decipher the data.

D. You send your public key to the general public who will be receiving your encrypted data and send your private key to those who are close to you or are in need of higher security. For general mailing, you would encrypt the data with the public key; for high-security data, you would encrypt it with your private key.

31. IPCONFIG is to Windows NT as _____ is to UNIX.

A. NETSTAT

B. GETIP

C. IPC CONFIG

D. ARP

**32.** You are building a Web site for your company to allow your customers to get vehicle owner manuals online. The manuals are rarely updated, but the pages are rather lengthy and take a while to download the first time. What features of the Web server can you use, and/or what features of the browser can you recommend to your users to improve the users' experience when they browse the owner manual pages of your Web site? (Choose all that apply.)

    A. Use the caching mechanism of the Web server.

    B. Use the browser cache.

    C. Shorten the pages and use navigation buttons to allow users to move back and forth between pages.

    D. Recommend that users use the cache of the proxy server.

**33.** You are a developer and have installed the Java Development Kit. What else is installed with the JDK?

    A. ODBC

    B. JDBC

    C. DHTML

    D. C++ Compiler

**34.** You are building a Web page for the product manager of your company so she can maintain the catalog of your company's online e-commerce store. She has to assign pictures to the products. She wants to be able to pick a picture from the list of thumbnail pictures of all products. Since she needs to see the product characteristics while selecting the picture, the thumbnail list must be in another browser window so she can move it around and see the product page. Which JavaScript snippet is appropriate?

    A. `Picwin = window.new ("thumbprod.asp", "prodpic", "width=150")`

    B. `Picwin = window.open ("thumbprod.asp", "prodpic", "width=150")`

    C. `Picwin = screen.open ("thumbprod.asp", "prodpic", "width=150")`

    D. `Picwin = screen.new ("thumbprod.asp", "prodpic", "width=150")`

**35.** In defining an extranet, which of the following statement(s) is true?

A. Extranets are derived from Internet-based technologies and standards.

B. Extranets enable secure communications to link your supply chain.

C. Extranets are often connected to internal corporate intranets.

D. All of the above.

**36.** Some of the advantages of Visual Basic are:

A. Easy to learn

B. Can write C++ code

C. Is great for Rapid Application Development

D. Can directly access hardware on a system

**37.** You are planning to use a single computer to host a Web site. What type of software will you need?

A. List server

B. FTP server

C. Certificate server

D. Web server

**38.** Which of the following choices represents a line from the ping display shown below?

```
Reply from 134.55.33.66: bytes=32 time=110ms TTL=124
TCP    MartinS:4875         inside.sales.company.com:6667
ESTABLISHED
Description . . . . . . . . : DEC EtherWORKS Turbo PCI 10
(DE450-CA)
Physical Address. . . . . . : 00-00-F8-07-36-0A
DHCP Enabled. . . . . . . . : No
```

A. `IP Address. . . . . . . . . : 134.55.33.66`

B. `Subnet Mask . . . . . . . . : 255.255.255.0`

C. `Default Gateway . . . . . . : 134.55.33.66`

D. `16.72.27.103       08-00-2b-00-00-02      dynamic`

**39.** You receive a call from a user who says that after downloading and running some files from the Internet, he noticed that his disk access light was blinking continuously. Upon questioning him further, you determine that he no longer has any .doc files on his system. What is the most likely problem?

   A. Someone has hacked into the system and deleted the .doc files, which is why the disk access light is on all the time.

   B. The user deleted the files, and the problem has nothing to do with the disk light or the files downloaded from the Internet.

   C. The user downloaded a file infected with a virus, and upon activation, it deleted all the .doc files on the system.

   D. Nothing is wrong. The user uses a word processing system that stores the documents with a different extension than Word does.

**40.** A streaming animation on a Web site uses bitmapped graphics and appears to fade into view when the Web page first loads. Which of the following file types is this animation?

   A. BMP

   B. GIF

   C. JPEG

   D. PNG

**41.** Server-push technology is often used for which of the following application(s)?

   A. Web site portals

   B. To deliver information and news

   C. To distribute product information

   D. All of the above

**42.** You have many static pages on your Web site and you already use the META element to facilitate search engine indexing. You have a specific part of the site that stores sales information. These pages are recreated every night as the sales figures are consolidated. You do not want these pages to be indexed by search engines since the content may change significantly. What can you do? (Choose two.)

A. Empty the content of the META tag on these pages.

B. Create the file robots.txt in the top-level directory of the Web site.

C. Use the keyword ROBOTS for the attribute NAME and keyword NOINDEX for the META tag.

D. Use the keyword NOROBOTS for the attribute NAME and keyword ALL for the META tag.

**43.** Which of the following issues are important when dealing with international currency conversion? (Select all that apply.)

A. Systems designed to deal with currency conversion between the consumer and the banking and merchant organizations

B. Deciding whether to take credit card transactions

C. Online transaction payment software able to translate your customers' currency into the your preferred currency

D. Systems designed to collect taxes

**44.** Your marketing department has decided to follow your suggestion and list your e-commerce site in popular search engines and directories such as Yahoo! and Excite. What techniques can you use to rank high in searches when a user queries on keywords that are related to your products?

A. Embed keyword scripting tags

B. License use of keywords that are close matches to your products or services

C. Use cookies to increase hit counts

D. Use descriptive and precise keywords in your <TITLE> and <META> statements

**45.** Which of the following elements are essential to operating in a global e-commerce environment? (Select all that apply.)

A. Systems designed to deal with international currency conversion

B. Content that has been localized for specific markets

C. Credit card processing capability

D. All of the above

**46.** You receive a call from a user stating that, since changing e-mail packages yesterday, she has been unable to access e-mail. It turns out that the user is able to send e-mail, but is unable to retrieve e-mails sent to her. You Telnet to the mail node and notice the user has 12 unread e-mails. What is most likely the reason that she is unable to retrieve e-mail?

    A. Her POP3 socket settings need to be set to port 25.

    B. Her SMTP socket settings need to be set to port 110.

    C. Her POP3 socket settings need to be set to port 110.

    D. She is entering the incorrect username and password when connecting to the server.

**47.** You are a Web page designer, and the company you are designing for wants to keep track of customers' return visits to their site. They don't, however, want to force customers to give their e-mail address each time they arrive in order to track them. What could you do as a designer to assist the company in this?

    A. Code a JavaScript that will ask for the customers' names, so you can track them that way.

    B. There is no way to do this, so you inform the company of this and continue with your designing.

    C. Code a cookie into the Web page and allow it to collect the data for you.

    D. Inform the company that the only way to do this is to have some type of authentication on the Web site. They agree, and you implement a username and password sign-on to access the site.

**48.** Examples of popular list server software include? (Select all that apply.)

    A. LISTING_SERVICE

    B. MajorListserv

    C. LISTSERVE

    D. All of the above

**49.** Your company sells custom investigation information. To fulfill a request, a dozen of your employees have to conduct extensive searches through many government agencies' Web sites and FTP sites. There are a limited number of these public sources, and they are accessed frequently by the employees. Since response time is a competitive factor, you would like to speed up access to these Web and FTP sites. What solution can you implement?

A. Increase browser cache size to hold more information.

B. Write a batch program that downloads frequently used pages and files during off-hours and makes them available for the employees.

C. Set up a proxy server to benefit from its caching mechanism.

D. Set up a Web server to benefit from its caching mechanism.

**50.** You are the network administrator of a large company that has over 200 servers running UNIX and NT 4.0. You have approximately 3000 users all using Windows NT workstations to access your network. You have had problems in the past with systems crashing from denial of service attacks from the outside. You have activated logging on all your servers but do not have the time to search each log on a regular basis to check for problems. Unfortunately, you end up using the logs to try to figure out who attacked the system and how. You know you have a problem, but you can't get your managers to give you additional headcount. What is a good option?

A. Remove your network from the Internet.

B. Purchase a Intrusion Detection System.

C. Demand additional people or advise them that these attacks will go on.

D. Continue as usual. Hackers are usually better than most administrators, so even with additional personnel, you will always be a step behind the hacker.

**51.** You are implementing a B2B link between your company and its distributors. You have decided to use an EDI solution to match your business partner systems. Which statement(s) is true about EDI? (Select all that apply.)

A. EDI is exclusively for Electronic Funds Transfers between banks.

B. EDI is a process and a standard for the electronic exchange of data across networks.

C. EDI can be costly and complex to implement.

D. None of the above.

52. You are coding Web pages for your company and need to determine which language you can code the pages in. Your pages will be housed on a UNIX system. What Internet language is not usable on a UNIX system?

A. JavaScript

B. CGI

C. Perl

D. Visual Basic

53. You are planning to set up a network whose only purpose is to provide Internet and e-mail access to your company's users. Which of the following best describes the type of services you may need?

A. Proxy server, cache server, mail server, and list server

B. Cache server, list server, Web server, and mail server

C. FTP server, proxy server, list server, and cache server

D. FTP server, Web server, list server, and certificate server

54. The programming language JScript was developed by?

A. Netscape

B. Sun

C. Microsoft

D. Berkeley University

55. You are troubleshooting your network for a fault in a cable. You have determined that the problem is an AUI tap on your backbone segment. Which type of cable would have an AUI tap?

A. 10Base2

B. 10Base5

C. 10BaseT

D. 100BaseFL

**56.** Which addressing method do computers use to locate and identify other computers on the Internet?

A. MAC addresses

B. Domain names

C. IP addresses

D. Internet names

**57.** You have been hired to restructure an existing network. The customer is upgrading from 10mb/s to 100mb/s on all nodes and segments. You notice that two systems are transmitting data between themselves more than with other systems. You see an opportunity to increase the bandwidth between these two systems to 200mb/s by setting the two systems to be full duplex. What type of connection must both systems have in order to do full duplex?

A. PPTP on both sides

B. Point-to-Point

C. POP3

D. Point-to-Multi-Point

**58.** The Internet is made up of physical cables. In the following list, which one is most likely a cable used for the Internet backbone?

A. 10BaseT

B. 10Base2

C. 100BaseFL

D. 10Base5

**59.** We use e-mail daily to transmit information to others in a fast and reliable manner. Our e-mail clients use two protocols in transmitting and receiving e-mail. These protocols are?

A. SNMP

B. SMTP

C. HTTP

D. POP3

**60.** A company has asked for your advice about their network. The network is an Ethernet star with a 12-port hub. Each port on the hub is being used by the network's 12 users. Recently, users have been complaining that the network is very slow. What should you recommend?

A. Replace the hub with a router.

B. Divide the network into two different protocols and install a gateway.

C. Divide the network into two segments and use a bridge to connect them.

D. Replace the current hub with a hub that can handle more users.

**61.** What is the protocol that is used for an e-mail message that contains a MIME attachment to get the e-mail from the client to the server?

A. POP3

B. SNMP

C. SMTP

D. MIME

**62.** Your Web development team has included a Zip archive file in the distribution of your software code as well as a copy of Winzip.exe. You are in charge of making sure that all software that you use for distribution has been properly licensed. What do you need to do?

A. Contact the vendor and inform the vendor that you are distributing your software in Zip archive format.

B. You need do nothing, since you are not modifying the Zip source code.

C. Seek permission from the vendor through a license.

D. Seek permission from the vendor through an assignment.

63. Your departmental users are posting sensitive internal information to your public Web site. You send out a memo reinforcing the policies for posting information, which says:

A. It is illegal to publish copyrighted material to the company Web site.

B. Material should not be posted to the Web site if it is proprietary information without approval from an appropriate company officer or manager.

C. It is a copyright infringement to post confidential information.

D. All of the above

64. You have successfully launched a B2C e-commerce site. The management team decides next to build a B2B extranet with your suppliers and trading partners. Which of the following statement(s) is true?

A. Extranets are derived from Internet based technologies and standards.

B. Extranets enable secure communications to link your supply chain.

C. Extranets enable customers to create their own HTML pages.

D. All of the above

# Practice Exam Answers

1. ☑ **A and B.** One of the first technologies for customizing and personalizing the user experience of Web surfers was the use of "cookies." A cookie is an HTTP header that consists of a text string, and stores information about the user and the browser. This data is saved to file on the users local hard disk.
   ☒ **C** is incorrect because information about the network is not stored in the cookie.

2. ☑ **D.** Electronic catalogs, or *e-catalogs*, are online analogs of mail order or printed catalogs. As an integral part of any e-commerce site or Merchant system, e-catalogs support online shopping, ordering, and payment. Typically, e-catalogs offer more than their paper-based counterparts, such as more competitive online prices, interactive site and product exploration tools, and more detailed information on products and services. E-catalogs are useful for B2C and B2B e-commerce and e-business applications.

3. ☑ **A.** You should recommend an internal modem because they do not cause bottlenecks. External ISDN modems usually connect to the computer via a serial port, which can transmit data up to 115 Kbps. However, ISDN Internet access can reach 128 Kbps, so data transfer can slow at the point of the serial port. Internal modems use the computer's internal data bus to transfer information to and from the computer, so there is no bottleneck in the data. *Note: While not listed as an answer here, you can avoid external modem bottlenecks by attaching the modem to a computer via an internal Ethernet network card.*
   ☒ **B** is incorrect because it states that you should recommend an external ISDN modem because they are easier to install and troubleshoot. Although this is true, the customer in this case is interested in speed. External ISDN modems cannot transmit information to and from the computer as fast as internal modems. **C** and **D** are incorrect because they suggest you recommend a modem based on its susceptibility to noise. Internal and external modems do not differ in their tolerance for noise on

the line. **D**, which states that external modems are cheaper, is incorrect. Remember, speed is the issue, not cost. In any case, *internal* modems are usually cheaper than external.

4. ☑ **A.** You should use a news server. This type of software will organize newsgroup postings by category, and will update other servers that are involved in that particular discussion. Anyone can start a newsgroup simply by configuring a news server and posting the forum (discussion topic) on USENET, the Internet's largest bulletin board.

   ☒ **B** is incorrect because this type of server is used to manage e-mail addresses and organize them into groups. Although a news server may employ a list server from time to time to schedule e-mail transmissions, the list server itself cannot be used to host a newsgroup. **C** is incorrect because this is not a valid term. The term "forum" refers to a particular discussion or topic within a newsgroup. **D** is incorrect because this is a type of server used to host FTP file download sites on the Internet. It will not support newsgroups, as it is unable to track and organize message postings.

5. ☑ **D.** In an e-business world, self-service is critical. Customers expect interaction with the Web to be immediate and direct. Self-service applications include technical support and help desk functions. Online FAQs can provide users with answers for common problems. Distributing software via a Web site is a very cost-effective way to make sure users have the most frequent version of your software products. Lastly, self-service applications are gaining popularity on corporate intranets, helping to streamline procurement processes and cut down on paperwork.

6. ☑ **B.** This generally means that the file has been removed from the location where the HTTP document believes it to be. This can also happen if the graphics file has been corrupted, or never existed at the location. If the designer mistyped the location or filename, you would receive this graphic, indicating that the file cannot be found.

   ☒ **A** is incorrect. If the connection to the Web server were slow, you would get a small box with an x in it as the display. **C** is incorrect. The graphic does not need to be located in local cache to be displayed. Once it is downloaded, it will be stored there temporarily; if you return to the site, your browser can pull it from cache instead of downloading it again. **D** is also incorrect. If the page were in cache, the graphic would also be in cache.

7. ☑ **B.** The thumbnail pictures are small graphics and do not constitute a performance problem but they still give a good idea of the products. The user still has the possibility to see the full-size picture. Also, the small number of products per page makes the pages load relatively fast. The navigation hyperlinks give the user the ability to continue to browse the catalog.

☒ **A** is incorrect because the full-size picture will cause a performance problem because of its size. The users have to wait to see the product and then probably have to move on to the next product. **C** is incorrect because it is important for the users to see the products. In this case, they will have to click on the hyperlink to see the full-size picture and do this for all the products—this is not comfortable for the users. Besides, showing all the products on one page like this may not be a good approach if there are a large number of products found. **D** is incorrect because it is important for the users to see the products. In this case, they will have to click on the hyperlink to see the full-size picture.

8. ☑ **C.** This is a good representation of a three-tiered application: tier one, the user application, is the web browser; tier two, the web server; and tier three, the database server.

☒ **A** is incorrect. This would be a one-tiered application, the game on the user's system only. **B** is incorrect as this would be a two-tiered application: the application and the database server. **D** is incorrect as this would be a two-tiered application: user system and game server.

9. ☑ **A, C,** and **D.** The ONMOUSEOVER event is raised when the mouse is over the element. To change the style of the hyperlink, we can either put the whole hyperlink block (<A...> through </A>) inside a <DIV> block, or the hyperlink text (the text surrounded by the <A> and </A> tags) inside a

<SPAN> block, assign a style to the block, and use script to change the style dynamically. The ONMOUSEOUT event is raised when the mouse moves out of the element; we can put script in this event handler procedure to change the style of the block back. The difference between the two solutions is the width of the background: with <SPAN>, the background occupies the text only, whereas with <DIV>, the background is the whole <DIV> block that occupies the whole browser screen. We can also use CSS or inline style A:hover , etc. to control the background color and font attributes of the anchor tag.

☒ **B** is incorrect because if we do not put the text inside a block (or <SPAN>), we cannot control its apprearance.

10. ☑ **A, B,** and **C.** There are many ways to build a global e-business in order to enter foreign markets. To get started, seek counsel from consultants, accounting firms, and lawyers that specialize in international business. They can assist your company in evaluating and preparing for the legal and regulatory issues you will encounter abroad, to avoid costly mistakes. You may also want to consider going into partnership with a foreign company. A foreign government is less likely to harass a U.S. firm working with a respectable local company.

☒ **D** is incorrect because your competitors are unlikely to share information with you that decreases their competitive advantage.

11. ☑ **C.** The company should set up an FTP site that contains the downloadable files. FTP stands for File Transfer Protocol, and is used as a fast method for uploading and downloading files on the Internet. Web sites use Hypertext Transfer Protocol (HTTP), which is graphic, text, and multimedia intensive. This provides a user-friendly Internet interface, but can cause file transfer to be very slow. FTP sites differ from HTTP (Web) sites in that they exist only for file transferring, not for browsing. When you visit an FTP site, you will see only a list of downloadable files, without the graphics, fonts, and multimedia that typically make up a Web site.

☒ **A** is incorrect. Telnet sites allow remote users to access an internal network. However, for security reasons, most companies do not want

Internet users to access their internal networks. Although creating a Telnet site may help speed up download time, it is not a practical option. **B** is incorrect because it suggests using the firewall to limit the number of concurrent users on the Web site. It is true that fewer users means faster download time, but firewalls are located behind the Web site, not in front of it. The purpose of a firewall is to prohibit external access to an internal network; it cannot be used to restrict the number of users on a Web site. **D** is incorrect because it suggests speeding up download time by restricting access to only those who have fast connections to begin with. It is true that users will no longer complain about the slow download time, because users with slow connections will not be allowed to download at all. This would be a case of fixing a problem by removing the complainers.

12. ☑  **D.** Managing multiple Web sites around the globe creates a whole new set of challenges that include managing human and technical resources, dealing with variability in technological infrastructure, and legal/regulatory issues in the markets where you are conducting business. Managing updates to multiple Web sites around the world is now a much more complex problem. There is a whole host of other business-related problems that must be tackled, including a brand identity strategy, trademark/copyright issues, and other business-related issues such as channel strategies of using distributors versus a direct sales model, and the like.

13. ☑  **B.** X.25. This type of service is available from many ISPs to provide customers with faster Internet access than regular phone lines, but at a price that is less expensive than leasing a dedicated ISDN or DSL line. X.25 is an analog technology capable of speeds up to 64 Kbps, and customers are only billed for the data transfers that they make (contrary to dedicated leased lines, in which customers are billed a steady amount, regardless of the number and frequency of data transfers).
☒  **A** is incorrect because, although this service offers the same "pay as you go" billing as X.25, Frame Relay uses digital T1 or T3 lines and can achieve speeds up to 1.5 Mbps. **C** is incorrect because ATM is digital and transmits

up to 622 Mbps. **D** is incorrect because ADSL is a dedicated line for which customers are billed regardless of usage. ADSL lines transmit digital computer signals up to 6 Mbps.

14. ☑ **B, and D.** If the names of the plants are on the page, they will be indexed by the search engines. Also, many search engines can index the pictures on a page; therefore, by naming the pictures after the names of the plants, we can help the search engines.
☒ **A** is incorrect. The number of names is large, and this is not an appropriate solution. **C** is incorrect because the COMMENT element is ignored by search engines.

15. ☑ **C.** The trace route utility shows you each hop that your packets are taking and the amount of time it takes for them to reach their destination. This would show you where the slowdown is and give you some solid proof to take back to your helpdesk or ISP.
☒ **A** is incorrect because the WINIPCONFG utility is used to determine IP stack information such as IP address, network mask, gateway, and other information that is needed for your PC to communicate on a network. **B** is a good option if you are wondering if a remote system is working, but it will not give you the information you need to determine where the problem is located. **D** is incorrect because a network analyzer is not what is needed for this problem yet. If you find that the problem is on your company's network and it happens at a given time each day, then your company could use an analyzer to determine the cause of the problem. The analyzer is used to locate network problems on a LAN.

16. ☑ **C.** To set a page to expire immediately, the attribute HTTP-EQUIV and CONTENT of the <META> tag can be used to set the Expires header. The values are EXPIRES and the date (in the past), respectively.
☒ **A** is incorrect because there is no attribute EXPIRES for the <HEAD> tag, and the <HEAD> tag is not used to control HTTP header. **B** is incorrect because there is no attribute EXPIRES for the <META> tag.

**D** is incorrect because there is no attribute HTTP-EQUIV for the <BODY> tag, and the <BODY> tag is not used to control HTTP header.

17. ☑ **D.** A license is not required to use a work in the public domain. Such a work, one that is not protected by copyright, can be used by anyone. Because it is not protected by copyright, no one can claim the exclusive rights of copyright for such a work.
☒ **A, B**, and **C** are incorrect because a license is not required to use pubic domain works, nor do you need to apply or register for copyright protection since the works are not created by you.

18. ☑ **B.** The owner of a copyright has the exclusive right to authorize others to copy, reproduce, duplicate, transcribe, or prepare derivative works based on the copyrighted work. By limiting your authorization to allowing your partners to copy, duplicate, or print your files, you can protect against any unauthorized changes.
☒ **A** is incorrect because if the information is in the public domain, your partners can modify the works. **C** is incorrect because you do not need to register a copyright in order to grant copyright privileges.

19. ☑ **B.** Telnet. When connecting from your local host to the Archie server, you would telnet to another host where the Archie search engine resided.
☒ **A** is incorrect because FTP was used after running the search. You would then FTP to the host that had the file you were looking for. Usually you logged in as anonymous and used your e-mail address as the password so they could log who downloaded what. **C** is incorrect because Gopher was another search engine that came along after Archie. **D** is incorrect because HTTP is used to connect to systems via the Web today. Archie was used long before browsers were even created.

20. ☑ **D.** There's more to developing a global e-business presence than deploying a company intranet and Internet site. You need a plan to craft your business into a global e-business that crosses barriers of currency,

language, time, and geography. The Internet does not change the principles of your business strategy. A company should begin by selecting one application or business process to transform that will have the greatest impact on its business. Critical business processes that provide the highest return on investment (ROI) include customer relationship management, supply chain management, e-commerce, knowledge management, and e-learning.

21. ☑ **D.** The use of a digital signature is just that: it's your signature. This is like your handwritten signature that you can look at and verify that it's yours. An electronic signature states that the e-mail was sent from you and only you. It helps provide data integrity so that end users can verify that the data reached them unaltered. It also provides proof of who sent the data.
☒ **A** is incorrect. Using encryption means that each user would have to have the encryption tool, which would defeat the problem of someone compromising the e-mail. If users had the tool to read the e-mail, they could deencrypt the data, compromise it, and then encrypt it again and send it on. **B** is not a viable option. E-mail is a vital tool in today's world, and it would be very hard, if not impossible, to stop using it. **C** is incorrect. No two people can have the same e-mail address. If someone else is sending e-mail with your e-mail address attached to it, he or she is accessing your e-mail account to do so.

22. ☑ **B.** The NAP, or Network Access Point, is where ISPs and other companies join the Internet. These points are maintained by companies such as Spring, MCI, and higher education facilities. The NAP was developed when the Internet changed from a government-financed and supported item to a commercially operated one.
☒ **A** is incorrect. The backbone connections are the fast-speed connections on a LAN; these include the FDDI, ATM, and gigaswitch connections. **C** is also incorrect. Demark is the point where the local phone companies' responsibilities end and the personal responsibility starts. This is the Network Interface box at most locations. **D** is incorrect. The central office connection is where the wiring from the Network Interface or Demark meets the switch or central office.

**23.** ☑ **B.** Unicode is a general technique used to internationalize content, to prepare it so that the code never needs modification. The actual content is separated from the rules of translation. The formatting then becomes language independent, meaning that dates, times, numbers, and currencies all call up logic that provides the formatting based on local language and country code requirements.

☒ **A, C,** and **D** are incorrect because Unicode does not replace scripting or authoring languages. Rather, it's a standard used to code characters used in modern spoken languages.

**24.** ☑ **B.** PPP offers CRC and security features.

☒ **A** is incorrect because SLIP does not offer CRC or security. SLIP allows a station to dial up and become a node on the Internet. **C** is incorrect because PPTP is used to encapsulate data into a TCP/IP packet for transmission over the Internet. PPTP is also used for creating a secured connection into a network. **D** is incorrect because HTTP is used with browsers to access Web pages.

**25.** ☑ **A.** The Cache Hit ratio measures the number of times the cache is used to retrieve an object (usually a file). On systems with many static Web pages like this one, this ratio reflects the performance of the cache. If this ratio decreases over time, this means the files are more frequently fetched from disk instead of from the cache, and that there are more files requested. Therefore, increasing the cache size would help since you will have more files in cache.

☒ **B** is incorrect because the Cache Hit ratio suggests that the cache size needs optimizing, not the network. **C** is incorrect because the Cache Hit ratio suggests that the cache size needs optimizing. There is no indication that the processor is not the bottleneck in this case. **D** is incorrect because increasing the memory would help if the cache size is proportionally increased as a consequence; it would not help if the cache size does not change.

**26.** ☑ **B.** E-mail would be the best option to get the information to the customer in a timely fashion.

☒ **A** could be used, but is not the best option. For the customer to find the information on his FTP server, he would have to know the exact filename. Also, if you forget to set the correct type when ftping the file, it might not be transmitted correctly. **C** is an option, but again not the best. You would need to have an account on a system at the location, and to leave a note would require editing a document and leaving it there, or using some sort of e-mail. **D** would not be considered an option in getting info to someone when e-mail is an option.

**27.** ☑ **C.** The http-equiv attribute notifies the HTTP server to include a Refresh field with a value specified in the content attribute field. This value is passed (in quotes) in the string of headers that is sent to the client browser. The rest of the document content is then transmitted.
☒ **A, B,** and **D** are incorrect because the http-equiv syntax is incorrect.

**28.** ☑ **D.** The White House is considered a government site; therefore, you would need to enter the address with .gov at the end.
☒ **A, B,** and **C** are incorrect. A domain name is requested and listed under its complete domain name (e.g., whitehouse.gov); therefore, these addresses might take you to other sites, but not to the President's main page.

**29.** ☑ **A** and **D.** By keeping database connection to a minimum, you can speed up the access time. Try to make all the requests at one time. By avoiding multiple transfers, you are cutting down on access time. It is recommended that you pass variables through URL instead of storing them.
☒ **B** is incorrect. Servers that interact with the Web server should all be kept close to the Web server, possibly on a separate network segment. **C** is incorrect. You should always close an object as soon as you are finished with it, so that the next time it's called, it will be a fresh running so that no previous data can corrupt the run.

**30.** ☑ **B.** You would give out your public key to anyone who will need to decipher the data you send using your private key. Your private key is kept secret and in a secured place. All data being sent out that is encrypted will use your private key. As the user receives the data, he or she will use your public key to decode it.

☒ **A**, **C**, and **D** are incorrect; they either do not work or would result in you giving your private key out. Anyone with your private key would be able to send data as you.

**31.** ☑ **C.** IPC CONFIG is the correct utility to use a UNIX box to determine IP configuration.

☒ **A** is incorrect because NETSTAT is used to show connections to other systems per protocol. **B** is an invalid response. **D** is incorrect because ARP is used by a system to determine another system's MAC address before transmitting a packet on the network.

**32.** ☑ **A**, **B**, and **C.** The Web server cache stores frequently requested pages to improve performance and is suitable for static pages. The browser cache can be used to speed up display of previously accessed pages. Users can be told to use this feature by setting the appropriate options of their browser. Also, if the pages are too lengthy, we can consider splitting them into shorter pages and linking them with navigation buttons.

☒ **D** is incorrect because the primary use of proxy server is to secure an internal network (firewall) and protect it from external access through the Internet. It is not required in this scenario where we are serving Internet users and providing Web site access through our Web server. Proxy servers do have their own cache that helps improve performance when internal clients browse external sites, but it's not appropriate to recommend clients to implement proxy servers for performance reasons.

**33.** ☑ **B.** When you install the JDK, you also get the JDBC, or Java Database Connector. This connector allows developers to access databases. The database manufacturers can provide you with the necessary drivers to access their database, but the JDK and JDBC are required prior to installing the vendor drivers.

☒ **A** is incorrect. You get ODBC with the operating system; it comes with all MS Windows based operating systems. **C** is incorrect. DHTML is a programming language. **D** is also incorrect. The C++ compiler is a purchased software that is needed to write C++ programs.

34. ☑ **B.** The method *open* of the object *window* opens a new window without closing the original one. We can specify the URL of the document to load, the name of the new window, and the window features such as MENUBAR, STATUS, etc.
☒ **A** is incorrect because the correct method is *open*, not *new*. **C** and **D** are incorrect because to open a new window, you use the *window* object. The *screen* object refers to the video display on which the browser is being viewed (the monitor screen).

35. ☑ **D.** Extranets, or External Networks, like intranets, are derived from Internet-based technologies and standards. Extranets connect an intranet site to the Internet (or intranet using the Internet). In a sense, extranets are extensions of an Internet/intranet site to another site on the Internet where information, data, applications, and resources are shared. Extranets provide secure links between business partners that need to share information between organizations in the supply chain. Extranets are the underlying technology infrastructure supporting *business-to-business* e-commerce.

36. ☑ **A** and **C.** Visual Basic is very easy to learn to program with. It is designed as a drag-and-drop language where the programmer can drag and drop items such as buttons and allow the program to write the code that is associated with it. Visual Basic is considered RAD because you can quickly write well-made programs using it. It is also used as a way to create a prototype program that can later be rewritten in another language.
☒ **B** is incorrect. You cannot write C++ code in Visual Basic, but you can write code that can be compiled into native code like C++. You can also compile objects to be used in other languages like C++. **D** is incorrect. Visual Basic cannot touch or access the hardware directly, but it can access APIs in other languages that can.

**37.** ☑ **D.** You will need Web server software. Every computer that hosts a Web site requires Web server software in order to deliver Web pages to users. This type of software uses Hypertext Transfer Protocol (HTTP), which is the basis of the World Wide Web. Users accessing your site must have HTTP client software installed, such as an Internet browser.

☒ **A** is incorrect. Although you may choose to employ a list server in order to automate e-mail transmissions to users, it is not a required component of a Web site. **B** is incorrect because FTP is an alternate method of file transfer. FTP sites use File Transfer Protocol, which is used strictly for downloading files, and cannot support HTTP Web pages. Users cannot browse through FTP sites the way they can with HTTP Web sites. Instead, they must go directly to the FTP address, then select the file they wish to download. **C** is incorrect because this type of server is used to authenticate users for access to the Web site. However, the Web site cannot exist if it is not first set up to run from a Web server.

**38.** ☑ **A.** The Ping display shows information such as Reply from or Request timed out. Bytes is how many bits were sent in the packet, Time is the total time for the packet to reach the remote station and return, and TTL = Time to live. If the packet doesn't reach the end station and return by this time, it's considered timed out.

☒ **B** is a NETSTAT request. **C** is an Ipconfig print-out. **D** is an ARP request.

**39.** ☑ **C.** The user's system is infected with a virus. Since the user had recently downloaded and installed some software from the Internet, most likely he doesn't have a virus scanner installed, or it is outdated. Recommend that the user install a virus scanner or update the one already installed and use it 100 percent of the time.

☒ **A** is incorrect. This could be the problem, but since the user downloaded and installed some files from the Internet, a virus is the first point of action. **B** is incorrect. The user could have deleted the files, but it isn't likely. **D** could be correct. If you think this could be the case, ask the user what word processing package he has on the system, and check for that package's file extension.

40. ☑ **B.** GIF. This is the only file type listed that has all of the characteristics mentioned. GIF files can be used for stationary or animated bitmapped graphics. GIF files support streaming, which means the animation will run directly on the Web site; users don't have to download the file to run it—it loads and runs automatically within the Web page. GIF files can also be interlaced, meaning they appear gradually, sharpening in image as they load. This is the opposite of noninterlaced GIFs, which are loaded from the top down.

☒ **A** is incorrect because although BMP files are bitmapped, they cannot be animated (so they cannot support streaming). BMP files are always noninterlaced, so the image appears in full clarity from the top down, not gradually throughout the entire image like interlaced images do. **C** is incorrect because although these are bitmapped images, JPEG does not support animation or streaming. However, JPEG files can be configured to gradually fade in (progressive JPEG). **D** is incorrect because although this file type is bitmapped and supports interlacing, it does not support animation or streaming.

41. ☑ **D.** Push technologies automatically deliver information such as news headlines or product updates directly to a user's computer in a customized format at designated times, without the user having to request the information updates manually. In the push-based model, information providers do not wait for visitors. The objective is to reach out to an audience by pushing content to them. This technology has had a significant impact in the field of Internet marketing and advertising. More recently, push technology has been used with Web site portals such as Excite and Yahoo!

42. ☑ **B and C.** To tell a search engine robot not to index a page, create the file robots.txt at the "root" directory of the site (the top-level directory) and specify the user-agent (robots) and the pages or directories to be excluded. Also, newer search engines look at the META tag for the name ROBOTS with the content NOINDEX (the page is not to be indexed).

☒ **A** is incorrect because emptying the META tag does not prevent the page from being visited by search engines. **D** is incorrect because there is no keyword NOROBOTS for the attribute NAME.

**43.** ☑ **A** and **C.** E-commerce transactions often involve multiple currencies from countries all around the world, and systems must be built to deal with currency conversion between the consumer and the banking and merchant organizations in real time.

☒ **B** is incorrect because determining the form of payment is not the same as converting between foreign and domestic currency. **D** is incorrect because tax collection is an issue independent of currency conversion.

**44.** ☑ **B** and **D.** Many search engines such as Yahoo! will, for a fee, allow merchants to license keywords that directly link to their Web site URL. For example, if your business sells automobile parts, you may want to license keywords such as "spark plug" and "tires." Whenever a user submits these keywords in a query, your Web site URL will be returned at the top of the hit list or in a banner display ad. By using descriptive keywords in the TITLE and META statements, search engines can be directed to your Web site.

☒ **A** is incorrect because search engines do not normally search scripting code for keywords. **C** is incorrect because cookies do not increase hit counts with search engines.

**45.** ☑ **A** and **B.** Processing international currency transactions becomes a key issue for working in a global e-business environment. E-commerce transactions often involve multiple currencies from countries all around the world, and systems must be built to deal with currency conversion between the consumer and the banking and merchant organizations. Online transaction payment software must be able to translate the client's currency into the merchant's (your organization's) preferred currency. Further, creating e-commerce sites as part of a global strategy involves translating and localizing content for specific markets.

☒ **C** is incorrect because credit card transactions may not be a primary means of currency for electronic transactions in all countries (e.g., Japan).

**46.** ☑ **C.** The POP3 socket settings on her system need to be set to port 110. POP3 and SMTP are both used when sending and retrieving e-mail. POP3 is used to retrieve e-mail from the mail server, and SMTP is used to send e-mail from the client to the mail server. POP3 uses port 110, and SMTP uses port 25. These are two of the well-known port numbers for TCP/IP.

☒ **A** is incorrect. POP3 is the correct retrieval application, but the port setting is incorrect. **B** is also incorrect. You use SMTP to send e-mail, not to receive it; in addition, the port would have to be 25 to use SMTP. **D** is incorrect because although the username and password play a major part in sending and retrieving e-mail, we have already confirmed that they are correct because the user is able to send e-mail. Both POP3 and SMTP would use the same user credentials.

47. ☑ **C.** Using a cookie would allow the site to download a cookie to the users' systems and then check for it when they return.

☒ **A** is incorrect. It should be assumed that when the company said they didn't want to ask for the users' e-mail addresses, they also didn't want to have to ask for other information either. **B** is incorrect, as you can do this with cookies. **D** is also incorrect. Cookies would gather the information requested without having to assign visitors usernames and passwords.

48. ☑ **C.** One of the most common list servers is LISTSERV. Other popular mailing list software includes "majordomo" and "listproc." Users subscribe to a list by submitting their name and e-mail address. List servers are very popular for sending electronic newsletters to customers, employees, analysts, investors, and business partners. Newsletters can help you build a strong relationship with your customers and partners and strengthen customer loyalty.

☒ **A** and **B** are incorrect because they are fictitious products.

49. ☑ **C.** The proxy server can improve performance of its client browsers through its own cache. The proxy cache holds frequently accessed Web resources so all clients can benefit from a faster network cache, therefore reducing the need for Internet access and improving performance for internal clients.

☒ **A** is incorrect because although the browser can maintain a cache for performance, this applies to only one client (employee). The proxy server can cache a page, and all browsers can get to that page very quickly across an internal network; this reduces bandwidth consumption for all clients. **B** is incorrect because this is not a realistic approach. The employees have to use different tools and, besides, the number of pages can be quite large, making the download process lengthy and difficult to maintain. This also involves the cost of developing a custom application and very likely hardware support such as application server or file server. **D** is incorrect because a Web server is used to host a Web site (Internet or intranet); although it does have its own cache to better serve the clients' requests, its use is not appropriate in this case. We do not have a need for our own Web site since we are accessing external Internet resources.

**50.** ☑ **B.** There are programs that fall under the IDS that will search log files on systems for signs of attacks. They can look for creation or deletion of large numbers of files or user accounts. They can monitor for login attempts. They can make your life much easier and give you a major tool with which to fight hacking.

☒ **A** will only work if you do not have dial-in connection and you can guarantee that your attacks come from outside your company. Many times, attacks originate from within a company by its employees. This would also cut you off from the electric world, e-mail, and Web browsing. **C** is incorrect. One Sys Admin cannot handle 200 servers and do a good job. You will always be one step behind in hardware problems, software problems, attacks, and anything else. Even with one administrator per system, you cannot guarantee that the attacks will stop. **D** is incorrect. Yes, many times hackers are a step ahead of the Sys Admins because the Sys Admins usually don't know of a hole in their software or operating system until after a hacker has exploited it. However, with the proper tools and training, a Sys Admin can at least stay right on the heels of the hackers.

**51.** ☑ **B** and **C.** Electronic Data Interchange, or EDI, is technology that has been around for over 20 years and is used for conducting electronic transactions. EDI is a process and standard for the electronic exchange of data across computer networks. EDI is the process that allows Electronic

Funds Transfers (EFT) between accounts, and was first widely used in telephone banking and Automatic Teller Machine applications.

☒    A is incorrect because EDI can be used for any type of electronic business transaction.

52. ☑    D. Visual Basic was developed by Microsoft to be used in conjunction with Internet Explorer. It does not run well with Netscape and it is very difficult, if not impossible, for VB code to run on a UNIX system. It is recommended that it be designed for pages that will be housed on an NT Web server and viewed by a system running Internet Explorer.

☒    A, B, and C are all great choices for pages designed to be run and housed on a UNIX server.

53. ☑    A. You may need to use a proxy server, cache server, mail server, and list server. The proxy server is responsible for making Internet requests on behalf of the network's users, and the cache server can speed up Internet access by remembering the information found on frequently viewed Web pages. The mail server's role is to send e-mail, and to receive mail from the ISP and distribute it to the proper users. List servers can be used by the company to manage mailing lists and automatically send e-mail to groups of users on a preconfigured schedule.

☒    B and C are both incorrect because they suggest that you may need a Web server or FTP server. Web servers are required on computers that host HTTP Web sites, and FTP servers are used to host FTP sites from which users can download files using the File Transfer Protocol. However, the only function of this network is to provide Internet and e-mail access to users. This network is not hosting any type of Internet site, FTP, or HTTP, so there is no need for either an FTP server or HTTP (Web) server. **D** is incorrect because it suggests the use of an FTP server and a certificate server. Certificate servers are used to restrict or grant user access to all or part of a Web site. Again, this particular network is not hosting a Web site, so there is no need to install a certificate server.

**54.** ☑ **C.** Microsoft wanted an easier-to-use programming language for Web pages that would be usable and viewable by both IE and Netscape users. JScript was the result. It is slower than Java, but allows IE users to use it.
☒ **A** is incorrect. Netscape developed JavaScript. **B** is incorrect. Sun developed Java. **D** is also incorrect. Berkeley University developed one of the first versions of UNIX.

**55.** ☑ **B.** 10Base5 is the thick coaxial cable used in the past as the backbone segments in a network. It is usually yellow or orange with black bands along the length. The AUI tap would be drilled into the cable at the band markers. You can only place one tap per band. After time, AUI taps can become loose and cause network problems. The AUI transceiver should have a light on it to indicate if it is passing packets. This light is the first line in troubleshooting which tap is bad.
☒ **A** is incorrect because 10Base2 cables use T connectors to create connections. **C** is incorrect because 10BaseT are two-station cables, meaning that you have one station at each end; they are not strung along like 10Base2 or 10Base5 cables. **D** is incorrect because 100BaseFL is FDDI or fiber. Connections are made at each end of a cable similar to 10BaseT. You cannot tap a 10BaseT or 100BaseFL cable.

**56.** ☑ **C.** Computers on the Internet identify each other using IP addresses. Each computer must have a unique address, such as 124.122.108.92. However, because these addresses are not easy for people to remember, you will usually see a Web site's domain name rather than its IP address.
☒ **A** is incorrect because this form of identification is based on the computer's network card. Not all computers on the Internet have a network card, so it cannot be used for identification. MAC addresses are used to identify computers on a bridged network. **B** is incorrect. People (but not computers) use domain names to identify Web sites, since names are easier to remember than numbers. Every domain name is like a nickname for that computer's IP address. **D** is incorrect because this is a bogus term.

**57.** ☑ **B.** To utilize full duplex, both systems must be connected to a switch that is a point-to-multipoint device so that data can be transmitted and received at the same time between the systems.

☒ **A** is incorrect because PPTP is used to connect to a local or private network via the Internet. **C** is used to receive mail, and **D** is a concentrator or repeater where data is received on one port and broadcasted out all other ports. This type of connection can only be half duplex, meaning a station cannot transmit while it is receiving data on the cable.

**58.** ☑ **C.** 100BaseFL would be the choice for Internet backbone connections. It runs at 100MB per second and is the most reliable for transmission from the preceding list. It is not susceptible to collisions since it is a token-type network.

☒ **A, B,** and **D** are all 10MB-per-second connections and are much too slow for a backbone connection to the Internet. 10MB is becoming very slow even on a LAN, and 100MB and 100MB networks are becoming less and less expensive.

**59.** ☑ **B** and **D** are correct. POP3 (Post Office Protocol) is used to retrieve e-mail from a mail server. SMTP (Simple Mail Transport Protocol) is used to send e-mail from our client to the server for processing.

☒ **A** is incorrect because SNMP (Simple Network Management Protocol) is used to communicate with equipment on a network for diagnosis, configuration, and monitoring of the network. It uses a series of gets and puts for acquiring information and making changes. **C** is incorrect. HTTP is used for browsing the Internet's Web pages.

**60.** ☑ **C.** Divide the network into two segments and use a bridge to connect them. Hubs transfer data by broadcasting, meaning they send all data packets to every computer on the network, and only the destination computer actually reads the packet. On this network, one computer sends a message, one computer receives it, and 10 computers get data that is not for them. This excessive amount of unnecessary traffic is probably the cause of the network slowdown. If the network is divided with a bridge between them, there will only be half the amount of traffic within each segment. Any data that is addressed within the same segment as the sender will never cross the bridge into the other segment.

☒    **A** is incorrect. Although routers are capable of sophisticated addressing, they are used to connect networks, not individual computers. While not listed as an answer here, a switching hub would also be a good solution. **B** is also incorrect. A gateway is used to translate data between networks using different protocols. This process of translation can slow network traffic, and in this case, would make the problem even worse. **D** is incorrect. The problem here isn't a lack of ports; it's that the hub broadcasts are creating unnecessary network traffic. Adding more users would compound the problem.

**61.**  ☑    **C.** No matter what is included in the e-mail message, it still uses SMTP to transport the message from the client to the server.

☒    **A** is incorrect as POP3 is used to retrieve e-mail messages from a server. **B** is incorrect as SMNP is the Simple Network Management Protocol used to manage network equipment. **D** is incorrect as MIME is used for encoding of non-ASCII messages.

**62.**  ☑    **C and D** are correct. Before using a licensed product for distribution inside or outside the company, you must first have the proper licenses and permissions from the author or company that holds the copyright for the source code.

☒    **A** is incorrect, because you must gain permission to distribute copyrighted software. **B** is incorrect, even though you are not modifying the source code you are distributing a copyrighted software.

**63.**  ☑    **B** is correct. For security purposes you need to have documentation that is clear and concise regarding what is and is not appropriate to post on a corporate Web site. Before posting any material on a company's Web site, be sure to check with the legal department or management for approval.

☒ A, C, and D are incorrect. While it is not illegal or a copyright infringement to post internal company information, it is inappropriate and may violate company policy.

64. ☑ **A and B are correct.** An extranet is nothing more then a private or virtual connection between intranets (i.e., your company and your suppliers' company or two offices of the same company) using the Internet instead of a dedicated dial-up connection. They use the same standards as the Intranet—TCP/IP. Encryption is added as an extra layer of security so that data transversing the Internet is secured in the same way that data transversing an intranet is.

☒ **C** is incorrect, because the purpose of extranets is to supply chain management, not to provide Web space for HTML pages.

**Acceptable Use Policy (AUP)**   AUP (as designed by the NSF) determined exactly how the Internet could be used by organizations and businesses.

**Access control**   Determination of who and what is allowed into an operating system or network. Access control involves the ability to grant or deny system resources to authenticated users.

**Access Control List (ACL)**   An ACL is a special file or series of values that help determine the level of access a user has to a specific resource. An operating system refers to these lists to control access to system resources. An ACL regulates a user's ability to use either an operating system, or the objects served by an operating system.

**ACL**   *See* Access Control List.

**Active caching**   Active caching takes passive caching as a foundation and builds upon it with increased performance and enhanced configuration options. Active caching helps maintain higher levels of client performance: when clients can access pages that are stored in a caching server, the transfer speed is increased, and overall session latency is reduced.

**Active hub**   An active hub performs in much the same way as a passive hub, but active hubs will also repeat (boost the signal of) the information. This is beneficial for use with long network cables, which can experience a decrease in signal strength over distance (called *signal attenuation*).

**Active Server Page (ASP)**   An ASP can be an ordinary HTML page that includes one or more scripts that are processed on the Web server before the page is sent to the user. An ASP is somewhat similar to CGI applications in that they both involve programs that run on the server.

**Active Server Page (ASP) filter**   This file-mapped filter executes script code stored in any file with an .asp extension.

**Address Resolution Protocol (ARP)**   ARP is used to obtain the hardware addresses of hosts located on the same physical network. With the ARP utility, you can find out the MAC (Media Access Channel) address of all of the machines that your computer knows about. Using ARP you can see what MAC addresses have what IP addresses.

**ADSL**   *See* Asymmetric DSL.

**Advanced Encryption Standard (AES)**   Although no encryption algorithm has been chosen as of this writing, this standard is sponsored by the U. S. government as a replacement for DES. RC6, MARS, Rijndael, Serpent, and Twofish are all finalists for this standard.

**Advanced Research Projects Agency (ARPA)**   ARPA is a U.S. government agency formed by the Eisenhower administration in 1957 with the purpose of conducting scientific research and developing advanced technologies for the U.S. military. One of ARPA's research areas was developing a large-scale computer network that could survive a serious nuclear attack. This network, ARPAnet, was to ensure reliable communications between individual computers (nodes), even in the event of massive failure. The architecture of ARPAnet provided the foundation for the Internet as we know it today.

**AES**   *See* Advanced Encryption Standard.

**All-in-one (universal) clients**   This type of client software enables users to access Web pages, FTP sites, Telnet sites, e-mail, and more through a single application. Rather than having several applications running at once, you can access diverse Internet services through a single program or suite of programs.

**Analog modems**   Analog modems connect to phone lines through a regular phone jack, using an RJ-11 connector (the same one the phone uses). Analog modems use the same frequency band on the phone line (0–4 kHz) as voice communications, which prevents their concurrent use of the line.

**AND operator**   The AND operator between two words or other values means you are searching for documents that match both the search items, not just one of them.

**Anti-virus software**   Anti-virus software searches for specific viruses, worms, and trojans, as well as other suspect executables. This type of software identifies exactly how a program behaves, and then works to inform you about the problem and effect repairs, if possible. Sometimes, an anti-virus program can only identify problems, rather than fix them. This may be because the nature of the infection is so advanced, or because an actual fix was not yet known when the vendor released the anti-virus program.

**API**   *See* Application Program Interface.

**Application gateways**   *See* Application-level firewall.

**Application layer**   Renders information for use with specific applications, such as FTP, HTTP, and so forth.

**Application Program Interface (API)**   API is the code that instructs applications to interact with the operating system by working with programming code that enables the application request services and access functionality provided by the system. This interface is the set of commands that an application uses to request and carry out lower-level services performed by a computer's operating system, or access functionality of another program.

**Application-level firewall**   Application-level firewalls (also called *application gateways*) use additional software, called a *proxy*, to filter incoming or outgoing data.

**Application-level gateway**   An application-level gateway operates at the application layer of the OSI/RM. This firewall is arguably the most thorough, because it not only can determine source and destination IP address, but it also can inspect actual data inside the packet. However, application-level gateways tend to be slower than packet filters.

**ARP**   *See* Address Resolution Protocol.

**ARPA**   *See* Advanced Research Projects Agency.

**ARPAnet**   *See* Advanced Research Projects Agency.

**AS**   *See* Autonomous System.

**ASP**   *See* Active Server Page.

**Asymmetric DSL**   An emerging technology developed by the telephone companies that transmit data at 1.5 Mbps to 9 Mbps over standard copper telephone wires and twisted-pair cabling.

**Asymmetric encryption**   This form of encryption is more complex and involves the use of a key pair. This form of encryption is much more secure. Asymmetric algorithms include ElGamal and RSA. Asymmetric encryption uses a key pair. This key pair is uniquely and mathematically related, but it is just about impossible to take advantage of this relationship.

**Asynchronous Transfer Mode (ATM)**   A transmission protocol that segments user traffic into small, fixed size cells. Cells are transmitted to their destination, where the original traffic is re-assembled. During transmission, cells from different users are intermixed asynchronously to maximize utilization of network resources.

**ATM**   *See* Asynchronous Transfer Mode.

**Attributes**   Attributes allow you to control features or characteristics of a table and caption. Attributes give you the ability to control such things as spacing, the appearance of your table, and the positioning of caption text.

**Audio Video Interleave files (AVIs)**   These movie files may contain both audio and video, and must be fully downloaded before they can be played. They are unlike RealMedia files, which provide a link to the actual file on the Web server. The benefit of having to download the entire file is that you can then play them at any time, and do not need to connect to the Internet while doing so. The quality of AVI files is similar to MPEG-1.

**Auditing**   Auditing is the ability to determine who has accessed a system and when.

**AUP**   *See* Acceptable Use Policy.

**Authentication**   Authentication is the ability to verify the identity of a particular person, network host, or system process. When authenticating users across the Internet, you generally have to use encryption in one way or another. *See also* Strong authentication.

**Autonomous System (AS)**   A service provider within a NAP.

**AVIs**   *See* Audio Video Interleave files.

**B2C**   *See* Business to Consumer.

**Back door**   A back door is a related concern to system bugs. The chief difference between a system bug and a system back door is that a system bug is generally considered to be a mistake or oversight on the part of the programmer. A back door, on the other hand, is the result of intent. The most common example of a back door is an unknown username and password that exists on the system.

**Backbone**   The high-speed infrastructure that connects the individual networks on the Internet. A backbone is a high-speed conduit for data to which hundreds and even thousands of other smaller networks are connected. Each backbone is operated and maintained by the organization that owns it.

**Back-end processing**   Refers to the integration between the e-catalog Web-based interface and the back-end systems that it is connected to, including databases, payment systems, and legacy information systems.

**BackWeb**   BackWeb provides software for e-business solutions that solve the problem of accessing timely, accurate, critical information delivery across corporate networks and the Internet.

**Basic Rate Interface (BRI)**   One-level service that is designed for home and small business users. BRI consists of two 64-Kbps bearer channels (or B channels) and one 16 Kbps delta channel (or D channel). The B channel is used for transmitting and receiving data and voice, and the D channel is used to send and receive information used for control and signaling. In North America, PRI is made up of 23 B channels and one 64 Kbps D channel.

**BinHex**    BinHex is a popular encoding method that is used to convert data from binary to ASCII. Binary is a common format for representing data, especially in executable programs, or files that use numeric data. ASCII uses numbers to represent characters. In ASCII, each letter, number, and character on a keyboard is represented as a number between 0 and 127. Because different platforms use ASCII, most computers and applications on the market can understand this format.

**Biometrics**    Biometrics is the study of authentication via physical traits, including retinal scans, fingerprints, and voice identification.

**Bitmaps (BMPs)**    *See* Raster graphics.

**Body tags**    The <BODY> ... </BODY> tags are used to define the bulk of your Web page's content. Like the body of a paragraph, it contains most of the information you want to relay to your page's reader. Text written between the <BODY> and </BODY> tags will display in the main window of a Web browser.

**Boolean operators**    Boolean statements are composed of Boolean operators such as AND, OR, and NOT. With these operators you can articulate your search to whatever degree is necessary by including and excluding relative subjects.

**Boolean queries**    Boolean queries tend to be used in simple queries to eliminate a certain property or information from a result set.

**Boolean searches**    Boolean searches are simply based upon evaluating a statement or expression for true or false. Boolean-based searches reflect logic that is typically used in programming languages, which is great for programmers, but can be too complicated for normal users.

**Boot sector virus**    The most common type, this virus infects the master boot record of a floppy or hard disk. Once the disk is activated, the virus goes into memory. If a user places an infected floppy disk into an uninfected system, the virus will then infect the uninfected system.

**BRI**    *See* Basic Rate Interface.

**Bridge**  A bridge can be used to maintain connectivity between the two (or more) network segments or Local Area Networks (LANs).

**Buffer overflow**  Whenever a programmer creates a program using C, C++, or many other languages, he or she has to create a buffer to hold information used by the program. Some of this information includes variables used by the programs. The programmer generally assigns a default size to this buffer, because he or she only expects variables of a certain size to go into the buffer. However, it is possible for a hacker to manipulate the program so that it sends information into the buffer that is too large. The result is that the buffer gets overcrowded and overflows its limits.

**Bulleted lists**  *See* Unordered lists.

**Business logic**  Refers to the functionality of the front-end systems including online search capability; online secure payment infrastructure; and online customer service, such as help-desk and customer relationship management.

**Business to Consumer (B2C) e-commerce**  B2C e-commerce is based on transactions conducted between a consumer and a business. B2C commerce is characterized by low-volume transactions (e.g., ordering a book or computer). This is quickly changing as more expensive items, such as automobiles, are being sold directly from the manufacturer to the consumer.

**Button**  A button is one of the most common elements you'll add to a form. When a button element is added to a form, it appears in the Web page as a 3-D Windows push button. The only attributes a button has are VALUE and NAME.

**Byte-code**  Byte-code is an abstraction of compiled code that serves as an instruction set.

**C++**  C++ is an object-oriented language that allows programmers to code in the style of everyday life, with interaction of one object to another. Each object has its own characteristics, properties, events, and methods of operation.

**Caching**    Caching is the process of storing requested objects at a network point closer to the client, at a location that will provide these objects for reuse as they are requested by additional clients. By doing so, we can reduce network utilization and client access times. *See also* Active caching; Distributed caching; File caching; Hierarchical caching; Parent sibling caching; Passive caching; Proxy caching; Single-server caching.

**Caching Array Protocol (CARP)**    The Caching Array Protocol (CARP) provides an alternative method to ICP to coordinate multiple caching servers. Instead of querying neighbor caches, participating CARP servers use an algorithm to label each server. This algorithm or hash provides for a deterministic way to determine the location of a requested object.

**Call Back**    *See* World Wide Web Call Back.

**Caption tags**    The <CAPTION>…</CAPTION> tags can be used to create a caption for your table. Captions are lines of text that often appear below the table, and tell the reader what information the table contains. This allows a person viewing the table to immediately recognize what data the table holds, without having to read surrounding paragraphs.

**CARP**    *See* Caching Array Protocol.

**Carrier Sense Multiple Access/Collision Avoidance (CSMA/CA)**
This type of access method is similar to CSMA/CD, except that after a collision has occurred on the network, one computer will first send out a "signal" to warn other computers that it is about to send a packet. This access method is more organized than CSMA/CD, so it may be more suitable for use on networks with a high number of Internet accesses or hits.

**Carrier Sense Multiple Access/Collision Detection (CSMA/CD)**
CSMA/CD is a type of first-come, first-served access method by which computers on the network can send packets of information at any time. If a collision between two or more computers occurs, each will resend its packet after a random amount of time.

**Cascading style sheet**   A cascading style sheet sets the style of a Web page by using multiple style sheets and/or files, and displaying them in a specific order.

**Castanet**   Castanet was a push technology used to distribute applications, including software code, content, and services, to any endpoint over a network, and to manage and maintain these applications remotely.

**CERN**   *See* Conseil European pour la Recherche Nucleaire.

**CERT**   *See* Computer Emergency Response Team.

**Certificate**   Certificates allow for enhanced authentication, as well as encryption. Once a Web server has a certificate, you can apply this certificate to certain directories. Once a user requests a specific object (i.e., a file, directory, or site), the server will then begin an SSL session before it sends information. Once a client begins an SSL session, he or she can check a server's certificate.

**CGI**   *See* Common Gateway Interface.

**Channels**   Channels are links to content that can be accessed through RealPlayer.

**Check boxes**   Check boxes are another common element in forms. When viewed through a Browser, the check box element appears as a square. When you click it, the check box will appear checked. The text appearing beside a check box is used to indicate choices for the user. When multiple check boxes appear on a form, the user can choose one or more of the check boxes.

**CICS**   *See* Customer Information Control System.

**Circuit-level firewall**   A circuit-level firewall (circuit gateway) is a type of application-based firewall that uses the same rules and principles as an application-level firewall described previously. The circuit-level firewall's security features are applied at startup; and, once an Internet connection has been made, the connection stays open and data packets are not individually examined and screened.

**Circuit-level gateway**   The chief benefit of this type of firewall is network address translation (NAT), which is the ability to use reserved IP addresses internally, and Internet-capable addresses externally. Circuit-level gateways operate at the transport layer of the OSI/RM. Circuit-level gateways are quicker than application-level gateways, although not as quick as packet-filtering firewalls. The drawback to a circuit-level gateway is that you must modify all software in order for it to communicate with the firewall. This can be very costly and prohibitive.

**Circuit-switching network**   A circuit-switching network, such as those run by telephone companies, uses dedicated connections; but a packet-switching protocol uses various programs, algorithms, and network lines to get information from the source to its destination any way it can.

**Class A networks**   Class A networks are identified by the fact that the first octet is used for network addressing, and the last three octets are used to identify the host. In decimal form, all IP addresses from 1–127.*x.x.x* are Class A networks.

**Class B networks**   Class B networks are identified by the fact that the first two octets are used for network addressing, and the last two octets are used to identify the host. In decimal form, all IP addresses from 128–192.*x.x* are Class B networks.

**Class C networks**   Class C networks are identified by the fact that the first three octets are used for network addressing, and the last octet is used to identify the host. In decimal form, all IP addresses from 193–223.*x* are Class C networks.

**Client cache**   The client cache stores these objects locally on the client computer, within memory and in an allocated section of hard disk space. The client cache is designed to reduce the load times for objects that are static in nature, or dynamic objects that have not changed since the client's last visit.

**Clusters**   Clusters are groups of systems linked or chained together that are used in the caching of information for a company or ISP. By having a cluster of cache servers you can reduce bandwidth while increasing production time of the user because the user does not have to wait for the page to be retrieved from the Internet.

**CNAME**  Allows you to provide an alternative name to a host already named in the DNS file.

**Coaxial (coax) cable**  This is a more popular choice (than twisted-pair cabling) when long distance or signal interference is an issue. Coax cable looks just like the cable used for cable TV, and uses the same BNC connector. Coax cable is able to transmit at 10 Mbps or 100 Mbps.

**Common Gateway Interface (CGI)**  Common Gateway Interface, or CGI, defines the communication link between the Web server and Web applications. CGI gives network or Internet access to specific programs of your choice.

**Compiled program**  A compiled program is converted into language that the computer can understand.

**Compound queries**  Individual queries can be combined to form a compound query. This allows for separate operators to be combined, retrieving the most accurate result set.

**Computer Emergency Response Team (CERT)**  CERT is dedicated to helping all computer users maintain security. It is not focused on any one platform. You can gain much information about past hacker attacks, including ways to protect yourself against them. You can learn more about CERT at http://www.cert.org.

**Congestion**  Congestion is a term generally used to refer to routers. When a router gets too busy breaking up packets and sending them off to other routers, it is said to be congested.

**Conseil European pour la Recherche Nucleaire (CERN)**  CERN (or, the European Laboratory for Particle Physics) is the organization based in Switzerland where the World Wide Web was started. Much of the support for the HyperText Transfer Protocol (HTTP) and the Web libraries has its origins at CERN.

**Content cache server**  A content cache server stores the Web pages most frequently accessed by the network users. This speeds up the return of Web pages to clients' browsers because they come from a local server rather than the Internet.

**Cookie**   A cookie (also known as a *Web cookie*) is a simple piece of information sent in the HTTP header during a Web transaction between a Web server and a browser. You can transmit (i.e., set) cookies using a scripting language, such as JavaScript or VBScript. The primary use of cookies is to maintain state. HTTP sessions generally "time out" quickly. In other words, the Web server normally drops the TCP connection shortly after a Web page has finished loading. Without cookies, any information entered by a user would be lost as soon as he goes to another site. If the server sets a cookie, however, this cookie store has information created during the session. The activity of using cookies to track user activity has prompted some to argue that cookie use can constitute an invasion of privacy. Although this notion is a bit extreme, you should note that Web sites do, in fact, track users all of the time. Tracking helps them tailor their site to customer interests, plan advertising campaigns, and even generate revenue through selling user profiles.

**Copyright infringement**   A violation of the exclusive rights of a copyright owner. Copyright owners can recover actual or, in some cases, statutory damages for a copyright infringement. Furthermore, courts have the power to issue injunctions to prevent or restrain copyright infringement and to order the impoundment and destruction of infringing copies.

**Copyright law**   Copyright law protects original works of authorship. Copyright is a form of legal protection provided by the laws of the United States (Title 17, U.S. Code) to the authors of "original works of authorship," including literary, dramatic, musical, artistic, and certain other intellectual works. This protection is available to both published and unpublished works. Since copyright law is federal it does not vary from state to state.

**Country-level domain**   The "int" domain is no longer common. In its place are the extremely common country codes.

**Crawling**   The process of crawling is the spider visiting your site, going through every page that is accessible via a hyperlink, and recording that information back to a database.

**CRC**   *See* Cyclic Redundancy Check.

**Cross-browser coding**   Cross-browser coding can be used to create HTML documents or parts of HTML documents that will run only in specific browsers. In other words, if users are viewing your Web page with Netscape Navigator, they will see one version of your page. Users viewing with Internet Explorer will see another version, while users with other browsers will see yet another version of your Web page. Such cross-browser coding can be added to your HTML document using any one of a number of scripting languages, such as JavaScript or VBScript.

**CSMA/CA**   *See* Carrier Sense Multiple Access/Collision Avoidance.

**CSMA/CD**   *See* Carrier Sense Multiple Access/Collision Detection.

**Customer Information Control System (CICS)**   A monitor that controls interactions between users and applications; it also provides terminal routing, transaction logging, and password security.

**Cyclic Redundancy Check (CRC)**   An automatic error-checking method used by Microsoft's Disk Operating System (MS-DOS) when writing data to a hard or floppy disk in its drive mechanism. Later, upon reading, the same error check is conducted and the results of the two checks are compared to ensure the data has not been altered.

**Daemon**   A UNIX process designed to handle a specialized function (such as handling Internet server requests) and requiring a limited user interface.

**Data confidentiality**   The use of encryption to make sure that information remains secret.

**Data Encryption Standard (DES)**   A private key encryption scheme developed by IBM in the 1970s that has been adopted by NIST as the U.S. government standard.

**Datalink layer**   This layer maps physical addresses to network addresses. Contains two sublayers: Media Access Control (MAC) and Logical Link Control (LLC). The MAC layer provides hardware addresses, whereas the LLC is responsible for how NIC drivers operate.

**Default gateway**   A default gateway is a computer or other hardware that will forward messages and data to another network. If data is meant for a computer on a remote network, it is sent to the default gateway and forwarded from there. The way that your computer knows what computer is the gateway is by configuring it with the IP address of the default gateway.

**DeMilitarized Zone (DMZ)**   It is possible to combine firewall types to create a coordinated solution. You can place a packet-filtering firewall (e.g., a packet filter) on both sides of a network. This "buffer" network is called a DMZ.

**Denial Of Service (DOS)**   A DOS attack crashes a server, or specific processes and systems that reside on a server. Sometimes, a hacker wishes to conduct a DOS attack against a server out of pure malice. Many beginning hackers enjoy the simple sense of achievement they get when they bring down their first host.

**DES**   *See* Data Encryption Standard. *See also* Triple DES.

**Desktop computers**   *See* Personal computers.

**DHCP**   *See* Dynamic Host Configuration Protocol.

**DHTML**   *See* Dynamic HyperText Markup Language.

**Dial-Up Networking (DUN)**   Where you configure settings used to connect to an ISP or a remote TCP/IP network.

**Digital certificates**   Digital certificates are the primary means of authenticating users, hosts, and servers. They use public key encryption, as well as one-way encryption. Using the information in a certificate, unknown parties can build trust with each other. Digital certificates involve the use of a trusted third party, called a Certificate Authority (CA). Arguably, the most popular CA is VeriSign.

**Digital Signal (DS)**   The Digital Signal (DS) standards provide the base for other standards, including the T and E carrier standards. The DS0 rate is 64 Kbps. The DS0 speed is fundamental for many other standards. This is because these other standards, such as the T and E rates, are multiples of 64 Kbps.

**Digital signature**   A digital signature is the electronic equivalent of your own, "real" signature that you use when signing a check. It provides proof of origin and data integrity.

**Digital Subscriber Line (DSL)**   DSL allows users to connect at speeds ranging from 512 Kbps to 8 Mbps. Theoretically, the technology provides speeds up to 8.448 Mbps (megabits per second), but typical connections are considerably lower than this. While POTS uses analog signals to transmit data, DSL uses high-bandwidth digital copper telephone lines for the transmission of data and voice. *See also* Asymmetric DSL, Symmetric DSL.

**Directories**   Directories organize information about sites into hierarchical lists, beginning with a topic, and descending through the layers of subtopics.

**Directory path**   The directory path is the name and directory path of the file on the server being requested by the browser (optional). The directory path is sometimes called the *path statement*.

**Distributed caching**   Distributed caching is much like proxy clusters. The idea is that you have several proxy servers working together to reduce the load of retrieving the information from the Internet. This also acts as a fault tolerance so that if one of the proxy servers goes offline, the others will automatically be able to respond to the requests.

**DLL**   *See* Dynamic Link Library.

**DMZ**   *See* Demilitarized Zone.

**DNS**   *See* Domain Name System.

**Domain name**   The domain name specifies the address of a specific Web server to which the browser is connecting. Similar to a telephone number, it must be unique. The first part of the domain name is usually the name of the company, person, or organization. The second part, called the *extension*, comes largely from a set of conventions adopted by the Internet community. The control and management of domain names was passed from NSF to Network Solutions, Inc. Network Solutions has had a monopoly on the distribution of domain names until 1999 when the process was opened up to other companies.

**Domain name server**   The domain name server is a dedicated computer at your ISP. This sometimes uses the acronym DNS.

**Domain Name System (DNS)**   The system designed to assign and organize addresses is called the Domain Name System (DNS). The DNS, devised in the early 1970s, is still in use today. The DNS was designed to be more user friendly than IP numbers. Because every IP address has an equivalent domain name, any server on the Internet can be specified using its IP number or domain name.

**Domains**   *See* Local domain; Remote domain.

**DOS**   *See* Denial Of Service.

**DS**   *See* Digital Signal.

**DSL**   *See* Digital Subscriber Line.

**Dual-home host firewalls**   In this setup, the proxy computer (called the *host*) is placed between the Internet and internal network, so there is no possible direct connection between Internet users and network users—all data must pass through the proxy server. The proxy server also acts as a router, so the regular network routing method must be disabled to use this architecture.

**DUN**   *See* Dial-Up Networking.

**Dynamic Host Configuration Protocol (DHCP)**   DHCP allows you to assign and configure a user's network settings dynamically as he or she logs in to your network. DHCP manages the allocation of IP addresses and eliminates many of the problems associated with manually configuring a client computer.

**Dynamic HyperText Markup Language (DHTML)**    As its name suggests, it allows a Web page to be dynamically altered once it has been loaded. While HTML allows you to format and display elements of a Web page in a static or unchanging manner, DHTML allows you to change dynamically, display, and move various elements.

**Dynamic Link Library (DLL)**    A collection of functions or a collection of programs that can be called upon by another program. The word "library" suggests that it can store a vast set of functions that can be "checked out" when they are needed. These functions are then stored in a file, usually with a .dll extension.

**Dynamic linking**    Used for program functions that are not used often in your program or are not accessed constantly.

**E1**    The European standard of T1, called E1, contains higher bandwidth (2.048 Mbps) because it is supported by 32 DS-0's. Telephone companies often refer to T1's as DS-1's, where DS stands for Digital Signal.

**E-business**    *See* Electronic business.

**E-commerce**    *See* Electronic commerce.

**Electronic business (e-business)**    E-business is about using Internet technologies to transform key business processes to capitalize on new business opportunities; strengthen relationships in the supply chain with customers, suppliers, business partners, and distributors; and become more efficient and, in the process, more profitable.

**Electronic commerce (e-commerce)**    The complete set of processes and systems that support conducting business electronically using the Internet or other private networks. E-commerce describes the business activities among consumers, vendors, distributors, suppliers, and intermediaries using computer networks such as the Internet.

**Electronic Data Interchange (EDI)**    EDI is a type of e-commerce technology that has been around for over 20 years. EDI is a process and standard for the electronic exchange of data across computer networks. EDI is the process that allows Electronic Funds Transfers (EFT) between accounts, and was first widely used in telephone banking and Automatic Teller Machine (ATM) applications.

**Electronic mail (e-mail)**    These are messages that can be sent and stored from one computer to another. Using a mail client, you can create messages, attach files to them, and transmit them over the Net. The message first goes to a mail server, and is then sent to the mail server where the receiving user's e-mail account is located. When the user connects to the mail server with his or her mail client, these messages are downloaded and can then be displayed through the mail client.

**Electronic mail (e-mail) bombing**    An e-mail bombing program generates a large number of e-mail messages, all of which contain large attachments. The result of such attacks is that they overload an account. Especially in slow network connections (less than 128 Kbps), this can effectively wipe out a user's e-mail account.

**Electronic mail (e-mail) clients**    E-mail clients are applications that enable you to send electronic messages to other users on your intranet or Internet. A number of e-mail clients are available on the market, including Eudora Pro, Outlook Express, and many others.

**Electronic mail (e-mail) reflector**    E-mail can be sent to individuals or groups of people. This is done through distribution lists and software called an e-mail reflector. This software contains a listing of users who are to receive e-mail. An e-mail message that is to be sent to those on the list is then sent to the e-mail reflector. By sending a message to an e-mail address that is assigned to the software itself, the e-mail reflector forwards a copy of the message to each person on the distribution list.

**Electronic marketing (e-marketing)**    E-marketing takes advantage of Web-based tools to enhance or broaden traditional marketing channels. Some of the functions that are easily handled include lead generation and lead qualification to consolidate and store leads and opportunities.

**E-mail**    *See* Electronic mail.

**E-marketing**   *See* Electronic marketing.

**Encapsulated PostScript (EPS)**   EPS is the file format used by PostScript to allow users to preview a PostScript font or image. PostScript files contain only the commands used to print a graphic or font. To display this font or image, an EPS file is used. Such an EPS file would contain the PostScript commands needed to print the image, and can contain a bitmapped representation, allowing the user to see what the font or image will look like. The EPS file may contain text, graphics, or both to display this representation.

**Encryption**   The use of algorithms (procedures and mathematical calculations written either by individuals or agencies) and protocols to scramble information so that users cannot engage in electronic eavesdropping or data tampering. Four levels exist: None, trivial, moderate, and strong. Some of the types are Rot13, DES, Triple DES, RSA, MD5, and SHA. *See also* Asymmetric encryption; Symmetric encryption.

**Enterprise-grade proxy server**   Enterprise-grade proxy servers, such as Linux servers with the ability to conduct proxying (called IP chaining), allow support for any protocol supported by TCP/IP. They generally do not install agent software on the clients. However, they do require software that is modified to support proxy servers.

**EPS**   *See* Encapsulated PostScript.

**Ethernet bridges**   When the modem connects to the computer's internal Ethernet network card, with 10–100 Mbps transfer rates, it is the only port on the computer capable of keeping up with the speed of the modem. For this reason, DSL modems are sometimes called Ethernet bridges.

**eXtensible Markup Language (XML)**   XML is a flexible way to define commonly used information formats. The format and the data itself may then be shared on the World Wide Web, in intranets, and even in desktop applications.

**Extensions**   *See* Plug-ins.

**External Networks (Extranets)**   An extranet involves establishing a secure network between two private networks over public lines. Generally, an extranet has the same elements as an intranet: each company is able to communicate via e-mail, and has the option of using Web sites to conduct transactions. The chief difference is that the companies communicate via encryption, which is usually enabled by two firewalls working together. An extranet provides LDAP services so that companies can exchange information quickly.

**Extranets**   *See* External Networks.

**Fair Use Doctrine**   Section 107 of the Copyright Act carves out a safe zone in which individuals can engage in the fair use of a copyrighted work and not violate the law. Specifically, Section 107 states that the fair use of a copyrighted work, including such use by reproduction in copies or by any other means specified by that section, for purposes such as criticism, comment, news reporting, teaching, scholarship, or research, is not an infringement of copyright.

**FCS**   *See* Frame Check Sequence.

**Fiber-optic cable**   This type of cable has no theoretical distance or speed limitations; and, because it transmits light instead of electrical signal, it is unaffected by electromagnetic interference. Fiber-optic cable is the most expensive type, and typically transmits at speeds of 100 Mbps to 2 Gbps.

**File caching**   Because FTP sessions tend to involve larger amounts of data than a typical HTTP session, benefits from caching FTP objects can be substantial. Using file caching for an FTP request in a large company can reduce request time and bandwidth dramatically.

**Filename**   The filename is the name of the document being requested by the Web browser. The filename is part of the directory path. The default filename when entering only the server name is usually index.htm or index.html.

**File Transfer Protocol (FTP)**   An Internet protocol allowing the exchange of files. FTP was developed to transfer files between computers on a TCP/IP network. A program enables the user to contact another computer on the Internet and exchange files.

**File Transfer Protocol (FTP) clients**   FTP clients are applications that make the FTP easy to use.

**File virus**   This type of virus attaches itself to specific files and activates once the file is put into use.

**File-based database**   A file-based database is a database that has all of the resources needed to connect to the database located within the database itself. File-based databases do not require that you install some piece of software in order to access the data contained within them.

**Firewall security**   Firewall security is software that protects the network from being accessed by other Internet users.

**Firewalls**   A firewall is a security system that prevents outside users from accessing private network resources. Firewalls can be set up between segments on a large network, but are more commonly employed for security between a network and the Internet. Firewalls can also be used to restrict which Internet resources network users can access. A firewall filters all traffic that passes between your network and the outside world. No other way should exist to enter your network. Although a firewall often does not check access from a modem bank (i.e., a collection of modems that enables network access), it is still possible to use your firewall to check such access. *See also* Application-level firewall; Circuit-level firewall; Dual-home host firewalls; Packet-level firewall; Screened-host firewalls.

**Fishwrap**   Fishwrap, under development at MIT since 1993, was one of the first experimental personalized newspaper projects.

**Fixed work**   Fixed means a work is created to be "sufficiently permanent or stable to permit it to be perceived, reproduced, or otherwise communicated for a period of more than transitory duration."

**Flash**   Flash, developed by Macromedia, Inc., is a method of creating graphic-intensive Web pages that are high performance at lower speeds. Flash files can be added to Web pages as a way of displaying animation, providing audio, and allowing interaction. They are extremely compact and stream from any Web server. It is a multimedia technology that exploits vector graphics.

**Forwarder**   *See* Forwarding server.

**Forwarding server**   Also called a *forwarder*, this type of server allows systems that cannot communicate with the root name servers on the Internet to still get information from a specific source. Pure forwarding servers do not keep their own zone databases, although it is common to have a server be both a primary and a forwarding server.

**FQDN**   *See* Fully Qualified Domain Name.

**Frame Check Sequence (FCS)**   A term corresponding to CRC; an error-checking protocol for linking modems.

**Frame Relay**   Frame Relay is a variable packet-size transport service. Frame Relay was originally designed to carry data and, therefore, uses a variable frame size. The specification allows frame sizes as large as 4096 octets. Frame Relay resides at Layer 2 in the OSI model. Frame Relay access (Layer 1 of the OSI model) may be provided over T1, E1, or ISDN digital carrier facilities.

**Framing**   Framing is an error-control procedure used to multiplex a logical data stream. In order to provide better data organization (between the bytes, so to speak), the signal is formatted using the framing process. A frame is a compilation of one byte from each of the 24 DS-0 timeslots, plus a framing bit. This makes each frame 193 bits.

**FTP**   *See* File Transfer Protocol.

**Full-text index**   A full-text index stores all the full-text words and their locations for a given table. A full-text catalog stores the full-text index of a database. The full-text service performs the full-text querying.

**Fully Qualified Domain Name (FQDN)**   An FQDN is simply a domain name that is not relative to any other domain.

**Gateway**   A gateway is a method or an on-ramp for connecting to the Internet. A gateway is often a server node with a high-speed connection to the Internet. Most individuals and smaller organizations use an ISP as their gateway to the Internet. Using a proxy server as a gateway, you can secure your network against unauthorized access. *See also* Application-level gateway; Circuit-level gateway; Default gateway.

**GIF**   *See* Graphic Interchange Format.

**Gopher**   Gopher, introduced by the University of Minnesota in 1991, is a menu-based program used as an adjunct for finding files, definitions, and resources. Gopher is a client/server software and a simple protocol that enables users to search and retrieve files from Gopher servers on the Internet. Using the Gopher service, Internet providers can create links to other servers, annotate files and directories, and create custom menus for use by Gopher clients.

**Graphic Interchange Format (GIF)**   GIF is a bitmapped graphics file format employed for graphics exchange on a BBS and networks. GIF uses a high-resolution graphics compression technique.

**Graphic Interchange Format (GIF) version 89a (GIF89a)**   The GIF89a format allows you to save images as "interlaced." When the interlaced image is viewed through a browser or graphic viewer, the picture slowly fades into view. The image first appears fuzzy. As more of the image is loaded into the browser or viewer, waves of data fill missing lines of the image. This continues until the image appears at full resolution.

**Graphical User Interface (GUI)**   An overall and consistent interface for the interactive and visual program that interacts (or interfaces) with the user. GUI can involve pull-down menus, dialog boxes, onscreen graphics, and a variety of icons.

**Hacker**   This term originally meant a technologically adept individual who explored and expanded computers to their limits. Now, the term means a person with an illegal and potentially harmful intention to slip past a computer security system or firewall in order to change data, destroy data, insert viruses, or execute other unauthorized functions.

**Handheld devices**   Handheld devices are computers and other pieces of equipment that are small enough to fit and operate in your hand.

**Hardware**   Hardware is a vital part of the infrastructure supporting an Internet client. Hardware is a blanket term for physical components on which applications run, and that they use to connect to software available on servers or to perform some specific purpose.

**HDSL**   *See* High bit-rate Digital Subscriber Line.

**Head tags**   The <HEAD> ... </HEAD> tags contain such elements as the title of your Web page and other elements that are not directly shown to the person viewing the page.

**Helper programs**   Plug-ins are different from so-called "helper programs," which are separate applications that launch in their own Window. Helper programs were common among earlier versions of Web browsers. When the browser encountered a specific file type that it wasn't able to display, it would attempt launching a separate program.

**Hierarchical caching**   Hierarchical caching is when you place a cache server at each layer of your network in a hierarchical fashion, just as you do routers. Your highest cache server would be just inside your firewall, which would be the only server responsible for retrieving information from the Internet.

**High bit-rate Digital Subscriber Line (HDSL)**   HDSL is often deployed as a substitute for T1/E1 links. HDSL is becoming popular as a way to provide symmetric data communication (data transfer rates for upstream and downstream communications are equivalent) at rates up to 1.544 Mbps (2.048 Mbps in Europe) over moderate distances via POTS connections.

**Hijacking**   Another form of attack, called "hijacking," is when a hacker successfully intercepts and controls a data stream originating from one computer and meant for another.

**HINFO**   *See* Host INFO.

**Hops**   Increased distance between client computers and the origin servers add latency and increase the risk of bottlenecks. Most connections will pass over 10 to 20 routers before end to connectivity is established. These routers along the network path are referred to as *hops*.

**Host**   *See* Server.

**Host INFO (HINFO)**   This record gives information about the system on the resolved host.

**Host on Demand**   Host on Demand keeps the session alive even if you use your browser to go to additional Web pages.

**Host-based IDS**   This form of IDS uses agents that reside on each host. In this system, centralized manager software reads the transmissions sent from agent software. The agents read the logs that reside on each system and search for suspicious activity. This form of IDS is ideal for switched networks. Once you have activated auditing for your operating system, you can install a third-party IDS to augment auditing.

**HOSTS files**   HOSTS files are static files that map host names to IP addresses. In other words, when new hosts are added to a network, the HOSTS file is not automatically updated. You need to open the HOSTS file manually, and then add the new host or domain name to the file.

**HTML**   *See* HyperText Markup Language.

**HTTP**   *See* HyperText Transfer Protocol.

**Hub**   A device with many cable ports that provides a central connection point for computers on a network. *See also* Active hub; Passive hub.

**Hyperlinks**   Hyperlinks are associated with images or text (which usually appears underlined) in a Web page. They are entered in the <BODY>...</BODY> section of your Web page. When the user clicks the hyperlinked image or text, the browser takes them to a Web page or performs an action associated with the hyperlink. To create a hyperlink, you use the anchor tags <A>...</A> combined with the hyperlink reference (HREF=) that refers to the URL or action to be performed.

**HyperText Markup Language (HTML).**    HTML is a Web-based standard that describes how HTML documents are displayed in a Web browser or thin client. HTML has three commonly used elements for textual input: text, textarea, and password.

**HyperText Transfer Protocol (HTTP)**    HTTP is the client/server protocol used by the World Wide Web. It is used by Internet browsers to retrieve HTML (HyperText Markup Language) documents from Web servers, and by Web servers to send Web pages. HTTP operates together with the TCP/IP protocol to facilitate the transfer of data in the form of text, images, audio, video, and animation. HTTP allows Web authors the ability to embed hyperlinks and also allows for transparent access to an Internet site.

**IANA**    *See* Internet Assigned Numbers Authority.

**Ibox**    *See* Internet-in-a-box.

**ICANN**    *See* Internet Corporation for Assigned Names & Numbers.

**ICMP**    *See* Internet Control Message Protocol.

**IDS**    *See* Intrusion Detection System.

**IETF**    *See* Internet Engineering Task Force.

**IGMP**    *See* Internet Group Management Protocol.

**IIS**    *See* Internet Information Server.

**Index**    *See* Full-text index; Keyword index; Static index.

**Infrastructure**    An infrastructure is the underlying features or framework of a system. In the case of a city, these features would include telephone lines for communication, roadways for transportation, and other elements that allow the city to function. For the Internet and intranets, the infrastructure consists of such things as protocols for transport of data, network connections to enable proper communication, and so on. The infrastructure is the basic systems that allow it to function. *See also* Public Key Infrastructure.

**Integrated Services Digital Network (ISDN)**    ISDN is a set of standards for transmitting data over copper wires and other media. This media allows you to transmit and receive data at speeds up to 128 Kbps. Instead of a modem, you use an ISDN adapter. The ISP also uses an ISDN adapter at their end to allow ISDN connectivity. In addition to data, ISDN allows you to communicate by voice, as you would with POTS.

**Intelligent agents**    Intelligent software agents will find the best products and best prices for customers. These autonomous intelligent agents will be able to be personalized and run 24 hours a day. Consumers will use agents to find the best prices for products and services.

**Interconnected Network (Internet)**    Perhaps best described as the world's largest *Inter*connected *Net*work of networks. Instead of a centralized control of the Internet, many millions of individual networks and individual computers interconnect throughout the world to communicate with each other. The Internet is based on Internet clients, Internet servers, and communication protocols.

**Internet**    *See* Interconnected Network.

**Internet Assigned Numbers Authority (IANA)**    The IANA is a voluntary organization that has suggested some new qualifiers (beyond the ones from the ICANN) that further differentiate hosts on the Internet.

**Internet bandwidth technologies**    Internet bandwidth technologies include various link types such as T1/E1 and T3/E3 standards for high-speed networking and data communications.

**Internet Caching Protocol (ICP)**    ICP allows several joined cache servers to communicate and share information that is cached locally among the servers. ICP is based upon the transport layer of the TCP/IP stack, utilizing a UDP or connectionless-based communication between the configured servers.

**Internet Control Message Protocol (ICMP)**    ICMP is used to send messages and report errors on the delivery of packets. These control messages and error reports are sent between the server and the gateway to the Internet or another section of a large network.

**Internet Corporation for Assigned Names & Numbers**    The group in charge of managing the Domain Name System is the Internet Corporation for Assigned Names & Numbers (ICANN). ICANN is a nonprofit organization whose purpose is to verify that no duplicate domain names are assigned. As of June 1999, ICANN accredited 42 companies from 10 countries to offer domain name assignment services. Also sometimes called International Corporation for Assigned Names and Numbers.

**Internet Engineering Task Force (IETF)**    The organization providing standard coordination and specification development for TCP/IP networking.

**Internet Group Management Protocol (IGMP)**    IGMP is used to report the memberships of computers (hosts) in a particular multicast group. The IGMP protocol is used to inform the local router that it wants to receive memberships addressed to a multicast group.

**Internet Information Server (IIS)**    Internet Information Servers are the technology used to provide access to data, resources, and information on the Internet and the World Wide Web.

**Internet Infrastructure layer**    This layer includes companies that provide products and services to network to support the Internet infrastructure. These are the "pipes" that data and content flows through. Products and services in this layer add value to the IP network infrastructure and make it possible to perform business activities online.

**Internet intermediaries**    Internet intermediaries increase the efficiency of electronic markets by facilitating the meeting and interaction of buyers and sellers over the Internet to create an e-business marketplace. They leverage investments in the infrastructure and applications layers.

**Internet Network Information Center (InterNIC)**    All Internet domain names must be registered with an organization called Internet Network Information Center (InterNIC), and your ISP can usually do this on your behalf. Your ISP will charge you a fee for hosting your own Web site through their service, and there is also a monthly fee to InterNIC for maintaining the domain name.

**Internet phone**    Internet phone is a recent innovation to the Internet, allowing users to talk verbally with one another as if they were using a normal telephone. Communication takes place over the Internet, allowing one user with an Internet phone to talk with other users with Internet phones without having to pay for long distance charges.

**Internet port number**    An Internet port number, also referred to as a *socket number* to distinguish between running applications. In some cases, a port number may be required and is appended to the server name, such as http://www.location.com:4 (80 is the port number for the Web server). The port number can usually be omitted and the server's default port will be used. The most commonly used port numbers are FTP (port 21), Telnet (port 23), SMTP (port 25), and HTTP (port 80).

**Internet Protocol (IP)**    IP has the primary responsibility for routing packets between networks and hosts on a TCP/IP network. It also specifies the format that the packet will take.

**Internet Protocol (IP) multicasting**    IP Multicasting routes data to specific computers on a network that is identified by an IP address or class.

**Internet Routing Registry (IRR)**    This registry is a central database of routes.

**Internet server**    *See* Server.

**Internet Server Application Programming Interface (ISAPI)**   A set of program calls that allows you to create a Windows Web-based application that will run faster than a CGI application.

**Internet Service Provider (ISP)**   An ISP is your gateway to the Internet. An ISP maintains a dedicated high-speed connection to the Internet 24 hours a day. In order to connect to the Internet, you must first be connected to your ISP. You can obtain a dedicated line that provides a continuous connection to your ISP (for an additional fee), or connect to the Internet only when necessary using a modem.

**Internet Society (ISOC)**   The international organization (founded 1992) supporting, enhancing, and extending the Internet via government, organizational, and public research, education, and standards development.

**Internet-in-a-box (Ibox)**   Ibox is a relatively new technology that provides networks with one-step connections to the Internet. When the Ibox is installed and properly configured, it supplies the tools necessary to connect the network to the Internet by acting as a gateway; configuring the network for Internet access; and providing Internet software tools, such as e-mail and Web browsers. Iboxes vary greatly in their features and capabilities.

**InterNIC**   *See* Internet Network Information Center.

**Interpreted program**   An interpreted program must be fed one command at a time into an interpreter.

**Intraconnected networks (Intranets)**   Intranets (internal private networks) are usually restricted to internal access only by a company's employees and workers. Often, an intranet is located behind a firewall to prevent unauthorized access from a public network. An intranet is the same thing as the Internet, except on a much less ambitious scale. An intranet offers Web sites, e-mail, and access to information relevant for a specific company. Access to an intranet is allowed only to authenticated employees. Additionally, an intranet has added authentication because information shared on an intranet is often valuable and sensitive.

**Intranets**   *See* Intraconnected networks.

**Intrusion Detection System (IDS)**   An IDS is a series of applications and services designed to detect and, if so configured, thwart illicit activity. *See also* Host-based IDS or Network-based IDS.

**IP**   *See* Internet Protocol.

**IRR**   *See* Internet Routing Registry.

**ISAPI**   *See* Internet Server Application Programming Interface.

**ISDN**   *See* Integrated Services Digital Network.

**ISOC**   *See* Internet Society.

**ISP**   *See* Internet Service Provider.

**Java**   Java is a programming language developed by Sun Microsystems (http://www.sun.com) in 1995. Java was developed specifically for use in distributed applications and, more specifically, for the Internet. Java was based on the popular C++ language. Much of the syntax and libraries created for Java was modeled after those items popular with C++.

**Java DataBase Connectivity (JDBC)**   Similar to ODBC, JDBC provides an interface for a developer to access a database. The vendor will need to provide a driver in order to access the underlying database.

**JavaScript**   JavaScript is different from the compiled language Java. JavaScript carries some of the syntax of Java and even carries some of the same functions. However, JavaScript is different in that it is interpreted rather than compiled.

**JDBC**   *See* Java DataBase Connectivity.

**Joint Photographic Experts Group (JPEG)**    The committee, under the auspices of the ISO and the CCITT, that developed the JPEG graphics standard defining how to compress still pictures. JPEG can achieve compression ratios of up to 20:1, superior to GIF ratios, without noticeable picture-quality degradation. JPEG is another popular type of graphic. Along with GIF, JPEG is one of the most common image formats you'll use and come across on the World Wide Web. Files that use this format usually have the extension .jpg, but you may also see graphic files with the extension .jpeg. One of the benefits of JPEG is its use of compression. *See also* Progressive JPEG.

**JPEG**    *See* Joint Photographic Experts Group.

**JScript**    JScript is an interpreted script language from Microsoft that is designed for use within Web pages. It adheres to the ECMAScript standard developed by Microsoft and Netscape.

**Kerberos**    Kerberos is a client/server method for controlling access to specific network resources. MIT professors originally developed the Kerberos system. It allows you to authenticate users via encryption. Once authenticated, a Kerberos server then grants "tickets" to system resources, such as printers, additional networks, databases, and file servers. These tickets exist temporarily. Kerberos has an added security feature in that it does not transport passwords over the network wire, which eliminates the threat of "sniffing" password information.

**Key escrow**    Key escrow involves the creation of powerful encryption algorithms by one body, who then reserves the right to hold all of the possible keys. The result is that, normally, a user would be able to encrypt a document that is unreadable by all but the intended recipients. However, in the case of a declared emergency, a certain body, such as the CIA or MI5 could decrypt the message immediately.

**Keyword index**    The amount of information contained on a Web site can be overwhelming. The user wishes to locate what he or she is looking for quickly. The idea of "keywords" has become a very important part of searching a Web page for content.

**Keywords**    Keywords are the basic terms that make up the functionality of the language. These terms range from instructions to initiate and end a loop to those used for simply declaring the existence of a variable.

**LAN**   *See* Local Area Network.

**Latency**   Latency is the delay experienced by a client or server that has requested information (or some sort of transaction) from a server.

**Layering**   Layering builds on the use of style sheets, enabling your page to layer one style on top of another. The content of one style sheet will replace or superimpose on sections of content that are currently visible to the user. This allows you to create dynamic presentations that change their content based on a user's interaction, or by the amount of time you've programmed to pass before the next layer appears. This can be done through the style sheets themselves, or by using the <LAYER> ... </LAYER> HTML tag set.

**LDAP**   *See* Lightweight Directory Access Protocol.

**Legacy client**   One type of legacy client is an application that was widely used before the Internet became popular. A second type of legacy client is an older application, such as the original version of Navigator or an older e-mail program. Although such applications are clearly Internet oriented, they nevertheless represent older technology. Legacy clients often impede the ability for a company to share information consistently between all workers in a company.

**Lempel-Ziv Welch (LZW) compression**   This is an older form of compression, but it continues to be used in GIFs because it works so well. The compression makes the graphic smaller, so it takes up less hard drive space, and takes less time to download.

**Lightweight Directory Access Protocol (LDAP)**   Allows e-mail clients to view remote centralized lists of employees and contacts. The LDAP is an open-industry standard that defines a method for accessing and updating information stored in directories. Since LDAP is a vendor- neutral standard, it is being widely adopted by software vendors and application developers.

**LISTSERV**   The most popular commercial list server software is LISTSERV. LISTSERV performs several functions that would otherwise have to be managed manually, as in the days before any e-mail list management software existed. LISTSERV was the first software introduced to automate the administration of e-mail lists, and currently offers a full set of features for the list member, list owner, and site maintainer to manipulate their list/site configurations.

**Load testing**   To perform load testing, you will often need to purchase software that tests your Web site. This will provide information as to probable problems encountered by users, and how fast the Web pages load. Your Web server software may also provide utilities that track the number of users, the days and times they commonly use certain Web pages, or other data.

**Local Area Network (LAN)**   A system using high-speed connections over high-performance cables to communicate among computers within a few miles of each other, allowing users to share peripherals and a massive secondary storage unit, the file server.

**Local domain**   A domain that is served by the local SMTP server. The local domain has an entry in the DNS table. When a message arrives at the SMTP server and is addressed to the local domain, the SMTP server puts the message in a local Drop folder.

**Loopback function**   A function that loops packets back to your computer.

**Lossy compression**   Lossy compression technique is one in which detail is compromised for size.

**Lynx**   The most popular text-only browser on the market is Lynx, developed at the University of Kansas for students to access UNIX servers. It has become a popular browser for accessing the Internet when only text needs to be viewed or when graphics are not required.

**LZW compression**   *See* Lempel-Ziv Welch compression.

**Macro virus**   Usually, a macro is a valuable work-saving tool. However, it is possible to create malicious programs using these powerful macro languages. Some macro viruses are capable of erasing and modifying data.

**MAE**   *See* Metropolitan Area Exchange.

**Mail eXchange (MX)**   This type of record is essential for naming the e-mail server on your domain.

**Mail Transfer Agent (MTA)**   MTAs are permanently running programs on hosts with permanent connections to the Internet. Host computers running MTA software are commonly known as mail servers. An MTA "listens" for incoming e-mail from both local and remote MTAs, examines the e-mail, and either saves it locally (in a spool file) for retrieval by the destination user, or identifies a remote MTA and transfers the e-mail to it.

**Mail User Agent (MUA)**   An MUA is a client application used to send and receive e-mail. It provides a user interface for composition and local storage of e-mail messages, and also has facilities to communicate with MTAs. There are numerous MUAs available under modern Windows-based environments; typical examples include Eudora and Microsoft Outlook.

**Markup languages**   Markup languages use symbols, characters, and statements to format a document. These are placed in the document to indicate how that area of the document should appear when viewed or printed. In HTML, the indicators that the author uses are called *tags*.

**Media Player**   Media Player allows you to view and/or listen to streaming video and audio. This allows you to watch broadcasts, listen to the radio, view video files, or listen to audio files on the Web. Like RealPlayer, Media Player also has a Web page where you can browse through different audio and video files to watch and hear.

**Meta tags**   These tags allow the developers to emphasize specific content within their page. Meta tags are added to the HTML code of your Web pages.

**Metadata**   Metadata can be added to the <HEAD> ... </HEAD> section to help define visual elements and how accessible your HTML document will be on the Web. Metadata is not a tag in itself, but is used to describe a group of tags.

**Metropolitan Area Exchange (MAE)**   An MAE is a specific example of a NAP. ISPs connect to MAEs in order to get access to the Internet. Two types of MAEs exist: tier 1 and tier 2.

**Middleware**   Software that functions as a translation or conversion layer.

**MIDI**   *See* Musical Instrumental Digital Interface.

**MIME**   *See* Multipurpose Internet Mail Extensions.

**Minus operator**   When the minus operator is present before a search item, the results will exclude all items containing that search term.

**Mirror server**   A mirror server is a backup server that duplicates all the processes and transactions of the primary server. If, for any reason, the primary server fails, the backup server can immediately take its place without losing any downtime.

**Modem**   *See* MOdulator/DEModulator.

**Moderated newsgroup**   In a moderated newsgroup, when the user posts a message, the NNTP server sends that message to the moderator. The NNTP service uses the SMTP server to send messages to the moderator.

**MOdulator/DEModulator (modem)**   The key to connecting a computer or network to the Internet lies in the ability to access the phone and cable lines that the Internet uses. This is the job of the computer's modem. Modems are responsible for creating and maintaining the computer's connection to the Internet, as well as sending and receiving data. The most common speeds of analog modems are 14.4 Kbps, 28.8 Kbps, 33.6 Kbps, and 56.6 Kbps. 56.6 Kbps is probably the fastest that analog modems will ever be able to achieve. *See also* Analog modems.

**Mosaic**   The Mosaic World Wide Web browser was developed by the National Center for Supercomputing Applications (NCSA). Mosaic was the first Web browser with a graphical user interface. It was released initially for the UNIX computer platform and later in 1993 for Macintosh and Windows computers.

**Motion Picture Experts Group (MPEG)**   MPEGs use compression to make the files smaller. They do this through a type of lossy compression, in which some redundant data is removed from the imaging. The lost data is generally unnoticeable. The way that MPEGs compress their data is interesting, since entire images are not stored. Rather than storing a movie as a series of frames, with one image following the other, MPEGs store their files by storing only the changes from one frame to the next. MPEG-1 provides a video quality that is slightly inferior to the video you'd see in a VCR. It provides a resolution of 352 by 240, and 30 frames per second (fps). MPEG-2 is the standard used by DVD-ROMs. *See also* MP3.

**MOV files**   *See* Quick Time Movie files.

**MP3**   MP3 stands for MPEG 1, Audio Layer 3. It is a standard and format that allows sound files to be compressed into a smaller size, while preserving the original sound quality.

**MPEG**   *See* Motion Picture Experts Group.

**MTA**   *See* Mail Transfer Agent.

**MUA**   *See* Mail User Agent.

**Multicasting**   Multicasting is the ability to send messages to a select group of computers. *See also* Internet Protocol multicasting.

**Multipoint technology**   Multipoint technology allows you to have multiple connections between two computers. This is used to ensure fault tolerance communications so that if one link goes down, you have another link ready to conduct the transaction.

**Multipurpose Internet Mail Extensions (MIME)**   MIME established standard ways a Web server can deliver files to a client for easy, automatic reading. The original purpose of MIME was to extend the ability for e-mail clients and servers. Most applications, however, use MIME to ensure compatibility. *See also* Secure MIME.

**Musical Instrument Digital Interface (MIDI)**   A protocol standardizing the interchange and communication between musical instruments, computers, synthesizers, and other MIDI equipment.

**MX**   *See* Mail eXchange.

**Name tag**   The NAME tag is used to provide the element with a name that can be referred to in scripts.

**NAP**   *See* Network Access Point.

**National Science Foundation (NSF)**   The NSF created NSFnet in 1986, which eventually replaces ARPAnet (1990), and substantially increases the speed of communication over the Internet.

**Natural language queries**   Natural language queries represent increased technology that allows users to search based upon naturally formed phrases, sentences, or questions. The effectiveness of searches based upon natural language becomes more reliant on the search engine technology rather that depending on the wording of the query.

**Netscape Navigator**   Netscape Navigator Web browser was introduced is 1994. Marc Andreesson left NCSA and co-founded Netscape Communications Corporation in Mountain View, California. In 1995, the Netscape Navigator Web browser quickly became the most widely used cross-platform Web browser on the market. Netscape integrated all of the features of Mosaic, and added many new features and capabilities as well.

**Network Access Point (NAP)**   A NAP is nothing more than a central point that allows Internet Service Providers (ISPs) to exchange information with each other.

**Network analyzers (also called sniffers)**   Network analyzers look at all of the packets out on the network and show you all sorts of information about them. They can be TCP/IP packets, Apple Talk packets, or IPX/SPX packets, among others. By using this utility, you can capture packets that are out on the wire and see where they came from, where they are going, and what data they have in them.

**Network connection**   A network connection consists of hardware and software working together, so that you can access network resources. In terms of hardware, your computer will need a modem or network interface card (NIC), which is used to pass data onto and pull data off of the transmission wire.

**Network Interface Card (NIC)**   NICs are often used to connect a computer to a cable or DSL modem. The network interface card may be referred to as a network adapter, or NIC. Network cards are also (and usually) used for connecting computers together in a network structure. The NIC allows a computer to see and transfer packets of information to and from other computers that are physically connected to the same network.

**Network layer**   This layer provides for actual network addresses between two systems. The Internet Protocol (IP) runs at this layer.

**Network News Transfer Protocol (NNTP)**   NNTP provides a robust and scalable service for newsgroup servers. NNTP allows you to host and participate in newsgroup-style discussion, and allows users to read articles and to post articles for others to read. NNTP service supports both client-to-server and server-to-server communication over the Internet. NNTP supports popular extensions and is fully compatible with other NNTP clients and servers.

**Network Operating System (NOS)**   An NOS, like a regular operating system, is software that controls the functions of the computer, but also includes the features required to connect to and communicate with a network. Some popular Network Operating Systems include Novell NetWare, Microsoft Windows NT, and UNIX.

**Network Virtual Terminal (NVT)**   Communication established using the TCP/IP protocols and based on a set of facilities known as an NVT. At the client end, the Telnet client program is responsible for mapping incoming NVT codes to the actual codes needed to operate the user's display device, and it is also responsible for mapping user-generated keyboard sequences into NVT sequences.

**Network-based IDS**   The simplest type of host-based IDS uses an application that scans the network wire for all hosts on a particular subnet. This type of IDS is ideal for hub-based networks, because most network switches tend to open connections in a manner that isolates an IDS from the rest of the network.

**News expiration policy**    Establishes a limit for the length of time an article may be kept. You can set this expiration limit for one or more newsgroups, and these policies can vary from newsgroup to newsgroup.

**Newsgroups**    Newsgroups are directories of messages and files available on a news server. They are similar to message groups that appear on dial-in Bulletin Board Services, where messages are posted publicly and can be viewed by everyone.

**Newshound**    Newshound service was one of the first newspapers to provide a subscription-based, e-mail–delivered, personalized news filter.

**NIC**    *See* Network Interface Card.

**NNTP**    *See* Network News Transfer Protocol.

**Nonrelational databases**    Unlike the relational databases, nonrelational systems normally contain all the data in one large file. In the early days of Web development, most of the databases were nonrelational systems.

**Nonrepudiation**    The ability to prove that a transaction has, in fact, occurred.

**Nonstreaming media**    Nonstreaming media is the opposite of streaming media. This type of multimedia covers most file formats. With nonstreaming media, you need to download a file—which may be extremely large in size—before you can play it through a browser or separate application. The benefit of this type of media is that you do not need to be connected to the Internet to view the file. All of the data is stored on your hard drive, allowing you to view it when you're not online. With streaming media, you need to be connected to the Internet, so that you can receive the streaming data from a Web server.

**NOS**    *See* Network Operating System.

**NOT operator**   The NOT operator between two words or other values means you are searching for documents that contain the first word before the NOT operator, but not the second word that follows it.

**Notebook computer**   A notebook computer is a larger handheld device that can be used to access the Internet, but is still small enough to carry around easily. It is roughly the size of a hardcover book, and has computing power comparable to desktop PCs. It can run the same applications, including operating systems and Internet client programs.

**NSFnet**   *See* National Science Foundation.

**Nuking**   Unpatched operating systems are vulnerable to attacks that send unexpected information to an open port. Doing so causes a denial of service attack called nuking.

**NVT**   *See* Network Virtual Terminal.

**OBI**   *See* Open Buying on the Internet.

**ODBC**   *See* Open Database Connectivity.

**On-demand caching**   *See* Passive caching.

**One-Time Password (OTP)**   The concept of a one-time password involves "what you know" authentication, but enhances the practice by never using the same password twice.

**Open Buying on the Internet (OBI)**   OBI is a vendor-neutral standard that has emerged for electronic catalog systems. OBI defines the rules for conducting B2B commerce over the Internet.

**Open DataBase Connectivity (ODBC)**   ODBC is an API used to connect to various databases. These datastores could be an Oracle database, SQL Server database, text database, or any other type of datastore for which an ODBC driver is available.

**Open Systems Interconnection (OSI)**    The OSI reference model is exactly what it sounds like—a networking model that we can reference so that we can see how the different protocols work. The reason you need to be aware of the OSI reference model is it is the reference point that every IT professional can go back to when discussing disparate protocols to help understand how each one works.

**Operating system**    Operating systems provide a platform on which other software can run, and provide a layer between applications and the underlying hardware. This layer is important to software developers, as it frees them from having to provide proprietary drivers for each piece of hardware.

**Operator**    *See* AND operator; Minus operator; NOT operator; OR operator; Plus operator.

**OR operator**    The OR operator between two words or other values means you are searching for items that contain one of the words.

**Orange Book**    *See* Trusted Computer System Evaluation Criteria.

**Original work**    Original means that the work is original in the copyright sense if it owes its origin to the author(s) and was not copied from a preexisting work. Only minimal creativity is required to meet the originality requirement.

**OSI**    *See* Open Systems Interconnection.

**OTP**    *See* One-Time Password.

**PAC**    *See* Proxy Auto Configuration.

**Packet filter**    A packet filter inspects source and destination IP addresses, as well as ports. This type of firewall operates at the network layer of the OSI/RM. Its chief benefit is that it inspects packets quickly, and it is quite difficult to overwhelm. However, a packet filter cannot delve as deeply into a packet as the other firewall types.

**Packet filtering**    Packet filtering is a scheme whereby certain packets are passed through to the network and others are discarded. You can block or enable reception of certain types of packets through certain ports. Ports are only opened as needed. Packets are allowed in for only the minimum duration required and only on specified ports.

**Packet INternet Groper (PING)**    A common utility program used to determine whether a computer is connected to the Internet properly. PING is a utility that operates at the IP layer sending ICMP packets from one host to another to determine if it is up.

**Packet INternet Groper (PING) floods**    Using a program called "SMURF," you can forge IP packets that send ICMP request messages to another host. Let's call this host "host B." Your SMURF program causes host B to send ICMP reply packets not to you, but to another host that we will call host C. The result is that you have sent only one ping to host B, and host B sends one ping to host C. Now, imagine what would happen if you and a bunch of your friends used your SMURF program to send thousands and even millions of ICMP packets to many different hosts, all of which then replied to host C. Host C would crash under the strain.

**Packet switching**    Packet switching provided the ability to break data into smaller chunks that are, at most, a few kilobytes in size. Each packet is transmitted separately, providing a more efficient use of the media (i.e., telephone lines or network cable). If one of these packets becomes corrupted, the entire file does not need to be resent, just that particular packet.

**Packet-level firewall**    This is a very basic type of security in which packets are allowed or denied access to the network based on source and destination IP addresses. This type of firewall is usually managed by a router, which has been configured with IP address filtering rules.

**Packet-switching protocol**    A packet-switching protocol and/or network can use a different network path to communicate each time a transaction occurs.

**Page Description Language (PDL)**    A high-level language that commands the printer's functions. Examples are PostScript and PCL.

**Palmtop**   A palmtop is an example of a handheld device that fits into the palm of your hand.

**Parent sibling caching**   The parent-sibling caching works much like the hierarchies caching except that the sibling caches are all working together. Each sibling cache is aware of what the other caches are storing and can quickly request from the correct cache server. If a new request comes in, the siblings will send the request to the "Parent" cache server, which will either return the requested information or retrieve it.

**Passive caching**   Also called *on-demand caching*. Passive caching represents the most basic form of object caching. Passive caching servers require less configuration and maintenance, but at the price of reduced performance. Passive caching, as the name implies, makes no attempt to "prefetch" Internet objects.

**Passive hub**   A passive hub receives information through one of its ports; the hub copies the information and sends it to every other port. This means that network information is broadcast to every computer on the network, but is only read by the destination computer.

**Password**   This form of authentication requires that you present a physical token of some sort. In the analog world, a key or an actual piece of paper serves as an example. As far as the Internet is concerned, digital signatures and certificates provide this service. Smart cards are the most advanced form of this kind of authentication.

**Password element**   The password element is similar to the text element, except that it hides whatever the user types by displaying asterisks instead of text. The password element appears as a box on a Web page, just like a normal text element.

**Patches**   Patches are used because (1) The product originally shipped with a flaw that could not be fixed in time; (2) A previously overlooked problem was discovered; (3) The vendor invented or adopted a new, popular technology, and wishes to update the operating system, service, or application; and (4) New hacker techniques that make existing practices untenable.

**Patent law**   Patent law protects new, useful, and "nonobvious" inventions and processes.

**Path statement**   *See* Directory path.

**PDF**   *See* Portable Document Format.

**PDL**   *See* Page Description Language.

**Peering**   The technical term for the activity of exchanging information between ISPs. Peering is the result of a special arrangement between ISPs. This activity allows any two ISPs to arrange to share traffic.

**PERL**   *See* Practical Extraction and Reporting Language.

**Permanent Virtual Circuit (PVC)**   A PVC is a connection between endpoints that is not dynamically established or removed.

**Personal computers**   Personal computers (or *desktop computers*) are designed for individual users. These computers can be placed on a desktop, and are made up of components that gather input from a user (such as through a keyboard or mouse), process data, store data on a hard disk, and output information (such as through a monitor). Other components, such as a modem or network card, enable the user to connect to other computers, like over the Internet.

**PGP**   *See* Pretty Good Privacy.

**Physical layer**   This layer sends and receives bits of data.

**PING**   *See* Packet INternet Groper.

**Ping of Death**   Some unpatched Windows NT systems are not able to accept ICMP packets over 65,535 bytes long. Using special programs, it is possible to create an ICMP packet exceeding this length, which crashes the system.

**PKI**   *See* Public Key Infrastructure.

**Plain Old Telephone Service (POTS)**    Dial-up connections that use telephone lines are a conventional method of accessing the Internet. This is often referred to as POTS, in which the media used for data transmission is also used for voice communication.

**Plug-ins (extensions)**    Plug-ins are programs that can be installed on your computer, and add their functionality to the Web browser. Another term for plug-ins is extensions, as these applications extend the capabilities of the browser. These are modules that become a part of the browser, adding new features or enabling the display of different types of multimedia.

**Plus operator**    The plus operator works in inverse manner to the minus operator. When the plus symbol is located preceding a word or search phrase, that indicates that term has to be present to match the search request.

**Point of Presence Protocol**    *See* Post Office Protocol version 3.

**PointCast**    PointCast offered a client application that any Internet user could download to gain free access news, sports results, entertainment and business information, and stock quotes. Using the PointCast application, an end user could define a profile that acted as an information filter allowing them to view only the specific type of content that they wanted to view.

**Pointer Record (PTR)**    This entry helps create reverse DNS lookup domains. PTR records go into a separate file.

**Point-to-Point Protocol (PPP)**    PPP is the primary protocol for connecting to the Internet. PPP is the replacement for SLIP. PPP supports compression and encryption. If you connect to the Internet from home over a modem, chances are you are using PPP. One of two standards for dial-up telephone connection of computers to the Internet, with better data negotiation, compression, and error corrections than the other SLIP, but costing more to transmit data and unnecessary when both sending and receiving modems can handle some of the procedures.

**Point-to-Point Tunneling Protocol (PPTP)** PPTP allows you to send information over a public network (the Internet) securely. With this protocol, you establish a PPP connection over your phone line, and then you establish another PPP connection over that connection and create the VPN.

**POP** *See* Post Office Protocol.

**POP3** *See* Post Office Protocol version 3.

**Port** Any client software that uses TCP/IP uses an identifier called a port. When FTP, Telnet, SMTP, or other software and protocols are running, they monitor this port constantly. In other words, the server listens to this port for requests for service, and the client application uses this port number to request services like Web pages, mail, and so forth.

**Port number** *See* Well-known port number.

**Portable Document Format (PDF)** PDF is an acronym for the Portable Document Format, and can usually be identified by the file extension of .pdf. This format is used to capture a document as an image, so that it can be viewed and printed exactly as intended. In other words, anyone viewing a PDF on any document will see it exactly the same way on any computer.

**Portable Network Graphics (PNG)** PNG (pronounced "ping") is expected to be the license-free answer to GIFs. If you're creating graphic software that exploits the PNG format however, there is no fee. For this reason, the World Wide Web Consortium (W3C) has approved the PNG format as a standard to replace GIFs. A disadvantage to PNG graphics is that they cannot be animated, since you cannot store multiple images in a single PNG file. However, PNG does support interlacing. With PNG files, the image is displayed faster than GIF files, which is an added benefit for those downloading and viewing the interlaced PNG file at a slower baud rate.

**Post Office Protocol (POP)** A standard that specifies how an Internet-connected computer handles electronic mail. Electronic mail programs for personal computers detect whether new mail has arrived in a user's mailbox on the service provider's computer and allows the user to read, download, reply to, print, or store it.

**Post Office Protocol version 3 (POP3)**    POP3 (also called *Point of Presence Protocol*) is a remote access protocol that allows you to receive e-mail from any server on the Internet (that you have an account on) from any computer connected to the Internet. The only requirements that you have to meet are that your computer has a POP3-compatible e-mail reader (Outlook, Netscape, and Eudora just to name a few) and that your e-mail server is configured to accept POP3 requests. POP3 is a protocol that operates at the Application layer.

**PostScript**    It is used to define the look of a page, when it is sent to an output device like a printer or plotter. PostScript fonts are also commonly referred to as outline fonts and scalable fonts.

**POTS**    *See* Plain Old Telephone Service.

**PPP**    *See* Point-to-Point Protocol.

**PPTP**    *See* Point-to-Point Tunneling Protocol.

**Practical Extraction and Reporting Language (PERL)**    Perl is an interpreted scripting language. While PERL is generally used on UNIX-platformed Web servers, it has been ported to many other operating systems as well. Since PERL is interpreted, it is compiled just before execution. It can be compiled into either C code or cross-platform byte-code.

**Pre-fetching**    Active caching servers use a proactive approach referred to as "pre-fetching" to maximize the performance of the server's cache by increasing the amount of objects that are available locally based upon several configurations and statistical analysis.

**Presentation layer**    Formats information from one language type to another.

**Pretty Good Privacy (PGP)**   Developed by Phil Zimmerman. Uses RSA methods and is available to the public for, e.g., encrypting messages.

**Primary Rate Interface (PRI)**   PRI is one level of service designed for larger user bases such as large enterprises. In Europe, PRI consists of 30 B channels and one D channel.

**Primary server**   This server contains the authoritative information for an entire zone.

**Private IP address**   A private IP address is an address that is not legal out on the Internet. It is an address that you create and assign internally within your organization to allow computers to communicate with each other over IP without using registered addresses.

**Progressive JPEG**   A progressive JPEG is similar to an interlaced GIF, in that the image slowly fades into view, as a series of lines that appear on your screen. As each wave of lines appear in the image, the graphic begins to get clearer. This allows the person viewing a JPEG on your Web page to identify what the image is as it's being downloaded, which is especially good for users accessing your site with slower modems.

**Proof of origin**   It is possible for systems to authenticate packets depending upon where they come from. Although this form of authentication is not very secure, it is still practiced by the UNIX rlogin programs.

**Protocol**   A protocol is a set of rules as to how data is packaged, transmitted, and received. It controls how data is sent over a network.

**Proxy**   A proxy mediates between one party and another. In the case of the Internet, a proxy mediates between inside users and outside traffic. A proxy receives requests from external users, investigates the nature of the request, and then passes the request on to the appropriate location.

**Proxy Auto Configuration (PAC) files**   PAC files allow the browser to reconfigure its proxy settings based on information stored within this file. During the initial client installation, a URL is supplied to direct the browser to check for updates on a periodic basis. The code is usually written in JavaScript and stored at a location within the local area network, or at the remote access point.

**Proxy caching**    Proxy caching works through a cooperative connection between the browser and the caching server, instead of the remote origin server. When a client is configured to use a particular caching proxy server (or, any proxy server for that matter), it directs all of its requests for a particular protocol (HTTP, FTP, Gopher, etc) to the port on the proxy server specified in the browser configuration. Because several different protocols can be proxied and cached, most browsers allow for different configurations for each protocol.

**Proxy server**    A proxy server is a computer that stands between the LAN and the Internet. The proxy server software on this network server allows computers on the LAN to access the Internet through the proxy server's IP address. The address consists of four sets of numbers that are three digits or less, which identify the computer on the TCP/IP network. *See also* Enterprise-grade proxy server.

**PTR**    *See* Pointer Record.

**Public Key Infrastructure (PKI)**    PKI is a term reserved for organizations and bodies that create, store, and manage digital certificates. PKI is generally a distributed system, meaning that many different hosts and servers work together to create a single solution.

**Pulse Code Modulation (PCM)**    The most common technique used to digitize an analog signal into the DS-0 format. The incoming analog signal is "sampled" at a rate of 8000 times per second and converted into subsequent pulses known as a PAM (Pulse Amplitude Modulation). Each PAM is assigned an equivalent 8-bit binary value. This provides a digital output to the analog signal.

**Push technology**    Push technology is not a specific technology solution or product, but rather a general concept to describe a way to deliver information automatically over a network. Push is actually a diverse group of companies and technologies that deliver content—either data or applications—over computer networks such as the Internet or internal corporate intranets.

**PVC**   *See* Permanent Virtual Circuit.

**QTVR**   *See* Quick Time Virtual Reality.

**Queries**   *See* Boolean queries; Compound queries; Natural language queries; Recursive queries.

**Quick Time Movie (MOV) files**   The MOV files enable you to view video and audio over the Internet, or from your hard disk. By using a browser with the QuickTime plug-in, or the QuickTime Player application, you can view a cartoon, a clip of a live-action movie, or other footage. Because MOV files have been around for a number of years, you can also view them through numerous other applications. Many image products support this file format, allowing you to play them.

**Quick Time Virtual Reality (QTVR)**   QTVR is an enhanced version of QuickTime. QuickTime is used to display different forms of multimedia on computers, including animation, audio, and video. QTVR goes beyond this, enabling browsers to display and rotate images as three-dimensional objects.

**RA**   *See* Routing Arbiter.

**Radio buttons**   Radio buttons are similar to check boxes in that they are used to gather input, by having a user click it to choose an option. Radio buttons are round, and look like an "o" in a browser. When selected, a small dot will appear in it to indicate the selection. Another difference between check boxes and radio buttons is that, while check boxes can be used to accept multiple choices, you can only click a single radio button.

**RAP**   *See* Remote Access Protocol.

**Raster graphics (bitmaps or BMPs)**   Raster graphics are sometimes referred to as *bitmaps*, as they map data directly to a grid of x and y coordinates. The display is mapped into a grid of x (horizontal) and y (vertical) coordinates. A drawback to BMP files is the lack of compression, which makes images in this format larger than many of the other types of graphics.

**Raster Image Processor (RIP)**    A hardware/software processor that prepares an image for raster display or for raster printing.

**RealPlayer**    RealPlayer is an application and plug-in that enables you to view and listen to streaming audio and streaming video over the Internet. Streaming means that you hear and/or listen to the media in real time. You can listen to a radio or TV broadcast live, or view video or audio files of previous broadcasts.

**Recursive queries**    Recursive queries occur when a resolver creates a request that requires the DNS to follow the entire request path until it is fulfilled. As you might suspect, this form of query is much more taxing on servers. Recursive queries often occur when a resolver queries a name server that is not authoritative for that domain.

**Relational database**    A database consisting of one or more related tables.

**Remote Access Protocol (RAP)**    An RAP allows you to access all of the resources on your network as if you were directly connected to it.

**Remote domain**    A remote domain is a domain that is not local. This means there is no Drop folder for that domain on the local SMTP server. Mail addressed to remote domains is forwarded to the SMTP server specified for that domain.

**Request For Comment 822 (RFC822)**    Back in 1982, RFC822 defined the standard format for text-based e-mail sent via SMTP.

**Request For Comment 1521 and 1522 (RFC1521 and RFC1522)**    These extensions allowed more freedom concerning what you can transfer via e-mail. RFC 1521 showed how users could create e-mail messages that used more sophisticated ASCII text, but were still compatible with older systems. RFC 1521 extended e-mail, yet made sure these e-mail extensions were backward compatible. RFC 1522 brought even more flexibility to e-mail by allowing users to send non-ASCII text.

**RFC**    *See* Request For Comment.

**Rich Text Format (RTF)**    A text formatting standard that enables a word processing program to create a file containing all the document's formatting instructions without using any special codes. It allows the exchange of text files between different applications and operating systems and is an almost universal file format for text files. Using this format, you can exchange text between different operating systems, word processors, and other software. For example, you could create a document using Microsoft Word on a Macintosh machine, save it as an RTF file, and then import it into an HTML editor like Microsoft FrontPage running on a Windows 98 machine. Because it is such a popular format, many of the word processors or textual readers or writers on the market support this format.

**RIP**    *See* Raster Image Processor.

**Rivest Shamir Adleman (RSA)**    A secure cryptographic system using a two-part key in which the public key is known and the private key is held by the owner.

**Root kit**    Many trojan programs have been gathered together as a root kit, which is nothing more than illicit programs that replace legitimate programs, such as ls (used to list files) su (used to become "super user," or root), and cd (used to change from one directory to another).

**Root-level domain**    The root-level domain, which is unnamed, consists of several hosts that work in tandem to form the very top of the DNS tree.

**Route Server (RS)**    These servers forward packets according to the routes in the IRR.

**Routers**    Routers (specialized hardware) intercept the packets and view the information contained in the header code. These routers use tables that provide a listing of other routers and computers on the network. Based on the destination contained in the packet's header, the router will either retransmit the packet to the destination computer or—if that computer is not part of the router's local network—retransmit the packet to another router. The router determines the best possible path for the packet to take on its way to the destination of the receiving computer.

**Routing Arbiter (RA)**    An RA is the backbone element that enacts those routing policies. The RA takes the place of the old NSFNet Acceptable Use Policy (AUP). Whenever one NAP connects to another, they use an RA. An RA is a collection of devices that provide routing maps, address resolution, and redundant connectivity. Therefore, the purpose of the RA is to make sure ISPs communicate efficiently and that packets do not get dropped (that is, lost) too often.

**RS**    *See* Route Server.

**RSA**    *See* Rivest Shamir Adleman.

**RTF**    *See* Rich Text Format.

**Safe key protocol**    Public key encryption allows you to transmit keys securely because you can embed a symmetric key within a message encrypted to someone's public key. The primary protocol for describing safe key transport is the Diffie/Hellman protocol.

**Screened-host firewalls**    This type of configuration provides more protection than a dual-homed host firewall, because it combines the use of the proxy server with a packet-filtering router. In effect, it is a combination of application and packet-level firewalls. The screening router is placed between the Internet and the proxy server. The proxy server, then, is referred to as a screened host because the router performs IP-based filtering before the packets reach the server.

**Script tags**    The <SCRIPT>…</SCRIPT> tags are used to indicate that the code appearing between these tags is a scripting language that is to execute as a program. For example, you might enter JavaScript or VBScript code that performs some action when a user clicks a button on a form.

**SDSL**    *See* Symmetric DSL.

**Searches**    *See* Boolean searches; Wildcard searches.

**Secondary server**    Also called a *slave server*, a secondary server receives its database (that is, zone file) from a primary through a zone transfer.

**Second-level domain**    Second-level domains generally include the names of organizations and companies.

**Secure Electronic Transaction (SET)**    SET is a series of procedures that enable e-commerce to conduct financial transactions sites with a secure way to exchange information with banking institutions. Although SET is not currently popular in the United States, it has been adopted by most European countries. SET uses SSL, digital certificates, and additional technologies.

**Secure Hash Algorithm (SHA)**    SHA takes a 264-bit message (maximum size) and produces a 160-bit message (maximum size). SHA is shielded against inversion attacks and brute-force collision.

**Secure MIME (S/MIME)**    S/MIME is the industry-standard method for encrypting e-mail. You should note that S/MIME is an example of encryption at the application layer of the OSI/RM, because it encrypts the actual message itself, rather than the transport stream itself. S/MIME uses public key and private key encryption. Like SSL, S/MIME is an instance of applied encryption, because it uses a combination of public key encryption, private key encryption, and one-way encryption.

**Secure Socket Layer (SSL)**    An Internet Security standard incorporated into Netscape Navigator and Netscape Commerce Server software; unlike Secure HTTP, SSL works with all the Internet tools, not just the WWW. It is a transport-layer protocol commonly used in Web-based e-commerce transactions.

**Serial Line Interface Protocol (SLIP)**    An SLIP allows you to establish a dial-up connection with a host computer over the Plain old Telephone System (POTS). SLIP operates at the Data Link layer of the OSI reference model. SLIP works by allowing you to use IP over a serial connection, in effect bringing the IP network to you.

**Server**    A server (also called a *host*) is a computer or software application that makes available (or serves the client) data and files. An Internet server works identically to a server except it does so on the Internet and makes mail, news, the Web, and other services available.

**Server-based databases**    Server-based databases are databases that require a server to be running in order to obtain the data.

**Server database**    The server database maintains status information and a record of all issued certificates. It also maintains server logs and queues. The database stores all certificates issued by the server so administrators can track, audit, and archive server activity. In addition, the server database is used by the server engine to store pending revocations prior to publishing the revocations.

**Server engine**    The server engine is the core component and acts as the data pump for the requests it receives from the users and other servers. It pushes information between the components during request processing and certificate generation. The engine monitors each request through the various processes to ensure data processing.

**Server-side scripting**    Server-side scripting allows the programmer to access server resources such as SQL Server databases, custom COM objects, MTS components, and more. Server-side scripting allows the programmer to place the business logic on the server.

**Service mark**    A service mark is the same as a trademark except that it identifies and distinguishes the source of a service rather than a product. Normally, a mark for goods appears on the product or on its packaging, while a service mark appears in advertising for the services.

**Session layer**    Establishes and maintains connections.

**SET**    *See* Secure Electronic Transaction.

**SHA**    *See* Secure Hash Algorithm.

**Shockwave**    Shockwave is another technology that was developed by Macromedia, Inc., that takes multimedia on the Web one step beyond. Using Shockwave, you can add multimedia to your Web page as objects. Not only can you view animation and video, and listen to audio, but you can actually interact with a Shockwave object. A Shockwave object that is added to a Web page has the ability to respond to mouse clicks. This means that you could create games that can be played over the Internet.

**Simple Mail Transfer Protocol (SMTP)**    A U.S. Department of Defense standard for electronic mail systems that have both host and user selections. User software is often included in TCP/IP PC packages; host software is available for exchanging SMTP mail with mail from proprietary systems. SMTP is installed on machines as part of the TCP/IP protocol suite. Because SMTP has a limited ability to queue messages on the receiving end, Post Office Protocol 3, or POP3, is the protocol often used on the receiving end of e-mail messages.

**Single-line Digital Subscriber Line (SDSL)**    This line uses a single wire pair with a maximum operating range of approximately 10,000 feet. SDSL is suitable for videoconferencing, etc.

**Single-server caching**    Single-server caching is the idea that you have one server acting as the caching server. This is generally seen primarily on a small LAN; more then 10 or 12 users will easily overrun a single cache server.

**Slave server**    *See* Secondary server.

**SLIP**    *See* Serial Line Interface Protocol.

**Smart card**    This type of card is "smart" because it has two capabilities beyond the standard credit card you probably have in your wallet: First, a smart card can store information in persistent memory. Second, a smart card can have an on-board microprocessor with volatile RAM that acts much like a mini-computer.

**S/MIME**    *See* Secure MIME.

**SMTP**    *See* Simple Mail Transfer Protocol.

**SNA**    *See* Systems Network Architecture.

**Sniffers**    *See* Network analyzers.

**SOA**    *See* Start Of Authority.

**Sockets**   An FTP port, or a socket, represents the endpoint of a network connection. Two numbers identify TCP sockets: IP address and TCP port number.

**SOCKS Proxy Service**   The SOCKS Proxy Service is a cross-platform mechanism used to establish secure communications between the server and the client. This service allows for transparent access to the Internet using Proxy Server. This service does not support applications that use UDP, nor does it support the IPX/SPX protocol.

**Spider**   A spider is simply an application running on a remote server that views raw HTML information and Meta tags and records information within the search engines database.

**SQL**   *See* Structured Query Language.

**SSL**   *See* Secure Socket Layer.

**Start of Authority (SOA)**   This identifies who/what has authoritative responsibility for a domain and also identifies the database's current version.

**Static index**   A static index allows visitors to your Web site to choose from a list of hyperlinks that will direct a visitor to the appropriate content. This is very similar to a book's table of contents. Static indexes allow us to define where content is located and assist visitors by placing these links in a readily accessible area such as the homepage.

**Static IP addresses**   Static IP addresses are IP addresses that are assigned to one—and only one—user. The IP address is manually entered into the TCP/IP configuration, and no other computer on the network is able to use that address. Static IP addresses are commonly used on networks and corporate intranets, allowing administrators to track what users are doing, control their access, and access the user's computer by connecting to the IP address of that user's computer.

**Static linking**   Static linking is used for functions that are used consistently and constantly throughout your program. Static linking is loaded at runtime and, therefore, uses more system memory (RAM).

**Streaming media**    Streaming media is a relatively new and popular method of transferring data to browsers. With this, data is sent in a continuous stream from the Web server to the browser on your computer. As the data is received, it is buffered and displayed. Streaming video involves a sequence of pictures that is compressed over the Internet, and then displayed through a plug-in or application when it arrived. Streaming audio sends sound files in a continuous stream, and then plays the sound through a plug-in or application.

**Strong authentication**    Strong authentication involves combining certificates, digital signatures, and the authentication measures of what you have, what you are, what you know, and where you are. In short, if you combine these three forms of authentication, you are able to strongly authenticate users.

**Structured Query Language (SQL)**    The common communication method between databases. The history of SQL began in the late 1970s, when IBM began developing it in a lab in San Jose, California. SQL is a nonprocedural language that will let you decide what data you want to select from a database. The term "nonprocedural" describes what data is returned as opposed to how the database performs the action.

**Style sheets**    Style sheets are embedded in HTML documents, or linked to an external file, which defines the default styles and characteristics of the Web pages used in a document or Web site. It can define how a page is laid out through the use of the <STYLE> ... </STYLE> tag set. By using style sheets, you are ensuring that each page used in your Web site has a consistent look or style. Using style sheets, you can address such issues as what the default background color or graphic will be for your pages, the size and color of text and hypertext links, fonts used, and so on.

**Subnet mask**    A subnet mask is a binary number that gets associated with the TCP/IP address. The subnet mask allows the computer to distinguish what parts of the IP address are the network ID and host ID. A subnet mask is used to block parts of the IP address to distinguish the network ID from the host ID. Like an IP address, the subnet mask is made up of four sets of 1–3 digit numbers. If a set of numbers is 255, the corresponding set in the IP address is identified as part of the network ID. If the set of numbers in the subnet mask is a zero, the corresponding set in the IP address is part of the host ID.

**Suspicious activities**    Suspicious activities include attacks waged from inside the network, as well as those that arise from outside the firewall. One of the latest suspicious activities during the network-mapping phase is for hackers to conduct scans from diverse locations.

**SVC**    *See* Switched Virtual Circuit.

**Switch**    A switch is another device that can be used to connect networks. The switch uses a specific addressing scheme for delivery of packets, much like a router does. That is, rather than broadcasting data all over the network (like a bridge), the switch is able to read the destination IP address of a packet and send it to the proper network segment.

**Switched Virtual Circuit (SVC)**    A connection set up by signaling, with the user defining the endpoints when the connection is made.

**Symmetric encryption**    The use of one key that both encrypts and decrypts information.

**Syn flood**    This form of attack takes advantage of the three-way TCP handshake process. TCP is a connection-oriented protocol. It first establishes a control connection before it transmits any information. What would happen if a hacker were to begin a TCP connection on your host by sending a SYN request, but then never replied with an ACK packet? Your computer would devote resources to keeping that connection open until it times out. This is no big deal if only one connection stays open for a little while. But what would happen if a hacker were to send thousands or millions of SYN requests? Your system will crash under the strain.

**System bug**    A system bug is when a program, application, or service contains code that results in unexpected or dangerous behavior.

**Systems Network Architecture (SNA)**    A seven-layer communications architecture developed by IBM.

**T1**    *See* Time Division Multiplexing signal number 1.

**T3 connection**   A T3 connection can range in throughput from 3 Mbps to 45 Mbps. T3 connections are used by ISPs and Telcos.

**Tagged Image File Format (TIFF)**   A bitmapped graphics format for scanned images simulating gray-scale shading with resolutions up to 300 dpi. TIFF can usually be identified by the file extension .tif or .tiff. This file format was developed in 1986 by a committee of the Aldus Corporation (which is now owned by Adobe Software), Microsoft, and Hewlett-Packard as a common format for page-layout applications. Such applications would include desktop publishing, faxing, and image-editing applications. As was the intention of this committee, TIFFs are one of the most commonly used graphic formats, and supported by
most imaging applications.

**Tags**   Tags are elements that tell a Web browser that the document uses HTML, and how information is to be formatted and displayed. A tag is a letter or statement between the < and > symbols.

**TCP**   *See* Transmission Control Protocol.

**TCP/IP**   *See* Transmission Control Protocol/Internet Protocol.

**TCSEC**   *See* Trusted Computer System Evaluation Criteria.

**Telco**   *See* Telecommunication Company.

**Telecommunication Company (Telco)**   One of the types of organizations that leases access to the Internet.

**Teletype tag**   The teletype tag, which is sometimes referred to as typewriter text, makes whatever text appears between the <TT>...</TT> tags appear as if they were typed on a typewriter. This allows you to make elements of your Web page take on a typewriter-style face.

**Telnet**   A virtual terminal protocol from the U.S. Department of Defense that interfaces terminal devices and terminal-oriented processes. Telnet is a client/server software and a simple protocol that enables users to log in to remote computers to run programs and access files. Like Gopher, Telnet goes back to the early days of the Internet and is less frequently used. It provides a user with remote access to a host using a standard terminal emulator such as a VT-100. It is described in RFC854 and was first published in 1983.

**Telnet clients**   Telnet clients are terminal emulation programs that run on TCP/IP networks. Telnet clients allow you to access information in a text-based manner.

**Terminal emulation**   Terminal emulation means that the software allows your computer to run like an older dumb terminal, and connect to mainframes, Bulletin Board Systems (BBSs), and other servers.

**Text element**   The TEXT element is used for situations when the user needs to enter a single line of text, such as name, username, age, and so forth.

**Textarea element**   The TEXTAREA element is also similar to the TEXT element, except that it can accept multiple lines of text. You often see the TEXTAREA element being used for accepting comments or feedback.

**Thin client**   A thin client may be a Web browser, network computer, personal digital assistant, or any device capable of displaying HTML. A thin client is a client that you can install and use on multiple platforms to access complex applications, services, and servers that reside on the back end (i.e., on the server side).

**Tier**   A tier in an application is where a process of an application takes place.

**TIFF**   *See* Tagged Image File Format.

**Time Division Multiplexing (TDM)**   TDM is used to transmit a number of small signals (in this case, the DS-0's) into one continuous, larger signal. TDM interleaves a piece (eight bits) of each incoming signal, one after another, into each of the T1's 24 timeslots. The compilation of these timeslots comprises one frame. Subsequent frames are then used to continue transferring the data.

**Time Division Multiplexing (TDM) signal number 1 (T1)** T1 is simply ITU-T's (International Telecommunication Union-Telecommunication Standardization Sector, formerly the CCITT) North American name for the 1.544 Mbps standard pipe that can be used to pass signal traffic. These pipes, or circuits, consist of 24 56 Kbps or 64 Kbps channels, known as DS-0's.

**Time To Live (TTL)** Set times a packet can travel through a network before being deleted.

**Trace route** The trace route utility can find a route that is being used by the Internet protocol to pass packets between two machines. The trace route utility will show us the routers that the packets had to travel over to get from one computer to another. If there are no routers that they have to travel over, the trace route will come back very quickly. If there are multiple routers that the packets have to go over, then it will show you, in reverse order, each router that the packets have to go through to get to the destination. It will do this for up to 30 routers.

**Trademark** A trademark is a word, phrase, symbol, or design, or combination of words, phrases, symbols, or designs, which identifies and distinguishes the source of the goods or services of one party from those of others.

**Trademark law** Trademark law protects words, names, and symbols used by manufacturers and businesses to identify their goods and services. Trademark law in general, whether federal or state, protects a trademark owner's commercial identity (goodwill, reputation, and investment in advertising) by giving the trademark owner the exclusive right to use the trademark on the type of goods or services for which the owner is using the trademark. Any person who uses a trademark in connection with selling goods or services in a way that is likely to cause confusion is infringing on that trademark.

**Transactional systems** Transactional systems allow you to do a full recovery in case of failure in the transaction. If a user comes in and in the process of transaction something fails, then the transaction reverts back to the beginning as if nothing has occurred—no partial or orphaned data will exist in the database.

**Transfer protocol**   The transfer protocol is the method of transferring or downloading information into a browser such as HTTP (for Web pages), FTP (for files), or NNTP (for USENET news). The transfer protocol determines the type of server being connected to, be it a Web, FTP, Gopher, mail, or news server.

**Transmission Control Protocol (TCP)**   TCP is used to provide connection-oriented, reliable sessions between computers. TCP is commonly used when large amounts of data are being sent, or acknowledgment of data being received is required.

**Transmission Control Protocol (TCP) port**   A TCP port is the address of a server on an IP network. When an application uses TCP, it calls an assigned port for access.

**Transmission Control Protocol/Internet Protocol (TCP/IP)**   The TCP/IP protocol suite is a set of protocols incorporated into software. Once installed on a computer, it can be used to communicate with other computers that also use TCP/IP. TCP/IP was established in 1982 as the data transfer protocol for ARPAnet. The Internet is based on scores of protocols that support each of the types of services and technologies deployed on the Internet. The basic suite of protocols that allow this mix of hardware and software devices to work together is called TCP/IP, which is a packet-switching system that encapsulates data transferred over the Internet into digital packets.

**Transport layer**   Provides reliable transport and error control mechanisms, including checksum and ports. TCP and UDP run at this layer.

**Triple DES**   This form of encryption is more secure and powerful than DES.

**Trojan**   A trojan is an illicit program that appears to have a legitimate function. *See also* Root kit.

**Trusted Computer System Evaluation Criteria (TCSEC)**    TCSEC, also called the Orange Book, was originally published with an orange cover. Although quite old (it was written in 1983 and revised in 1985), many security professionals still refer to this book. The Orange Book rates the security protection of various operating systems according to an alphabetical scale (D through A). Systems given a D rating are the least secure, whereas an A-grade system is specially designed to give granular control over system users and processes. The most common rating is C2, which certain Novell, UNIX, and NT systems can achieve with some work.

**TTL**    *See* Time To Live.

**Twisted-pair cable**    This is the most common (and least expensive) type of network cable. Twisted-pair cable attaches to a NIC with an RJ-45 connector, which resembles a large phone jack. Twisted pair can transmit at either 10 Mbps or 100 Mbps.

**UDP**    *See* User Datagram Protocol.

**Unicode**    The Unicode Worldwide Character Standard is a character coding system developed for computers to support the interchange, processing, and display of written texts of the languages of the modern world. Unicode provides the foundation for internationalization and localization of content for e-commerce and Web sites, and computer software.

**Uniform Resource Locator (URL)**    A unique address on the Internet, similar to an e-mail address. A URL specifies the address of a server, or a specific Web page residing on a server.

**Universal clients**    *See* All-in-one clients.

**Unordered lists (bulleted lists)**    Unordered lists are used when items in the list do not need to be listed in a set order. For this reason, in HTML, bulleted lists are more commonly referred to as unordered lists. They are created using the <UL> and </UL> tags.

**URL**    *See* Uniform Resource Locator.

**Usage tracking**   Refers to the ability of an e-catalog system to track the number of hits to a site, customer demographics, and interface with a knowledge-based system to customize the presentation to its users.

**User Datagram Protocol (UDP)**   UDP provides connectionless communication between computers. It does not guarantee that packets will be delivered, and is generally used to send small amounts of data or data that is not crucial for delivery. Any reliability of data being sent is the responsibility of the application, not this protocol.

**User Datagram Protocol (UDP) attack**   A UDP attack could involve sending many UDP packets to one host, as in a ping flood attack. However, it is also possible to attack a system by sending UDP packets that then overlap once the receiving host puts them back together again. In nonpatched Windows NT and Linux systems, this overlapping of UDP packets crashes the system, resulting in the "blue screen of death" and a kernel panic, respectively.

**VBScript**   VBScript is yet another interpreted scripting language. VBScript is provided by Microsoft and is a smaller subset of its Visual Basic programming language. VBScript is similar to other Web-based script languages like JavaScript, Tcl, PERL, and REXX.

**Vector graphics**   Vector graphics use geometrical formulas to represent images, and are the alternative method to creating images through bitmaps. While bitmaps are also called raster graphics, and represent images as a series of dots, vector graphics are distinguished as a series of lines.

**Virtual Private Network (VPN)**   A VPN allows you to encrypt all network communications. A VPN is an example of a tunneling protocol. It operates at the network layer and encrypts all transmissions, making it difficult for hackers to sniff information. A VPN is so named, because it is a protocol that allows users to communicate securely over public lines. Normally, a private network, such as one created over leased frame relay lines, is secure from outside "sniffing" attacks.

**Virtual Reality Modeling Language (VRML)**   VRML is a language used for describing three-dimensional image sequences and user interactions with them. VRML allows you to build a sequence of visual images into Web pages.

**Virtual server**    The WWW service supports the concept of virtual servers. A virtual server can be used to host multiple domain names on the same physical Web server. You need a unique IP address for each virtual server that you host. This is sometimes referred to as *multihoming.*

**Viruses**    A virus is a miniprogram specially designed to interrupt the normal workings of your computer. A virus generally has a payload. Depending upon the virus, the payload can be something annoying, such as a sound playing at a particular time, or downright destructive. The old Michelangelo virus, for example, erased entire hard drives. *See also* Boot sector virus; File virus; Macro virus.

**Visual Basic**    Visual Basic is a programming language from Microsoft. The word "visual" comes from the idea that dragging and dropping objects and controls on the form can create the program's interface.

**VPN**    *See* Virtual Private Network.

**VRML**    *See* Virtual Reality Modeling Language.

**Web**    *See* World Wide Web.

**Web Cache Communication Protocol**    The Web Cache Communication Protocol was developed by Cisco in order to provide routers with the ability to redirect specified traffic to caching servers. With WCCP version 2, the previous limitations of single routers have been replaced with support for multiple routers. This is important in environments in which the router introduced a single point of failure.

**Web caching**    Caching is the process of storing requested objects at a network point closer to the client, at a location that will provide these objects for reuse as they are requested by additional clients. Web caching allows us as Network Administrators and System Engineers to reduce bandwidth peaks during periods of high network traffic.

**Web cookie**    *See* Cookie.

**Web Proxy Automatic Discovery (WPAD) protocol**    This protocol allows a browser to automatically detect proxy settings. Web Proxy Automatic Discovery (WPAD), is supported through the use of Dynamic Host Configuration Protocol (DHCP) and Domain Name System (DNS). Once the proper settings are configured, DHCP and DNS servers can automatically find the appropriate proxy server and configure the browser's settings accordingly.

**WebTV**    WebTV is a Microsoft product that allows those without computers to access the Web through a television and a box that is similar in appearance to those used for cable TV. With these two requirements, you then sign up with a WebTV access service.

**Well-known port number**    Server applications or processes using TCP/IP have, at least, one assigned port number, which is called a well-known port number.

**Well-known ports**    Port numbers 0 through 1023 are called well-known ports because they never change. These well-known ports are preassigned by the Internet Assigned Numbers Authority (IANA). TCP ports can be numbered from 0 to 65,535. Port numbers 0 through 1023 are reserved for server-side use and never change.

**Whitespace**    Whitespace is the space between characters, where nothing has been entered. For example, when using a text editor, you may press the ENTER key several times, so that there are several spaces between lines.

**Whois**    The whois service allows you to determine information about a DNS domain.

**Wildcard character**    The asterisk wildcard will allow you to search for all items or phrases that match a particular pattern.

**Wildcard searches**    Wildcard searches allow for searches to match a certain pattern instead of a fixed word or phrase. The accepted character for wildcard searches is the asterisk. The asterisk can be placed at the beginning or the end of a search word or phrase.

**Windows Internet Name Service (WINS)**   WINS gives Windows NT Servers the ability to resolve NetBIOS computer names on a TCP/IP network. WINS keeps a database that is dynamically updated on the NT network, adding NetBIOS and IP addresses to it as new computers are found. When WINS is used on a network, client computers register their names with the WINS server as they connect to the network. The WINS server then maps the names of these computers to their IP addresses. When a WINS client requests a resource from one of these clients, the WINS server resolves the name and returns the IP address to the requesting computer.

**Windows Sockets (WinSock)**   WinSock is a set of APIs that applications can use to communicate with other applications in the network. Many applications may be running on the same computer, even though the processes are being conducted across the network.

**Work for Hire**   When a work is created by an employee within the scope of his or her employment contract, the employer owns the copyright to the works since it's a "work for hire."

**World Wide Web (WWW / Web)**   Tim Berners-Lee at CERN drafted a proposal for the Web in 1989. He conceived the architecture for the Web as a multimedia hypertext information system based on a client/server architecture. The Web was born at CERN in Geneva, Switzerland, in 1992.

**World Wide Web (WWW / Web) browser**   A Web browser is a client application that displays multimedia hypertext documents. The first-generation Web browser developed at CERN was character based. It was very primitive by today's standards and only capable of displaying text. It wasn't until the Mosaic browser became available in 1993 that the potential of the Web began to be realized. Web browsers provide the ability to interpret and display HyperText Markup Language (HTML) documents, which are documents that are written in HTML and contain indicators (called tags) that dictate how text and graphics are to be formatted. *See also* Mosaic.

**World Wide Web (WWW / Web) Call Back**   Web Call Back is a relatively new technology that further enhances CRM. Web Call Back works by allowing your customers to click a link on your e-commerce site and enter their phone number. The link immediately triggers a call to a specific phone number at your company.

**World Wide Web Consortium (W3C)**    This organization sets the standards that are to be followed in developing Web pages and the browsers that view them. Despite this, many browsers also include proprietary features. This means that in order to view a Web page that exploits these features, you must use that particular browser. These innovations occasionally become accepted standards by W3C, and are then implemented in other browser types.

**Worm**    A worm, on the other hand, is somewhat more ambitious, because it can spread by itself, given certain conditions. For example, the Melissa "virus" had many worm-like qualities, because it took advantage of Word and Excel macros.

**WPAD**    *See* Web Proxy Automatic Discovery.

**WWW**    *See* World Wide Web.

**X.25**    X.25 is similar to Frame Relay in that it is a packet-switched technology that typically operates as PVC. Since data on a packet-switched network is capable of following any available circuit path, it is usually depicted as clouds in graphical representations. X.25 was introduced at a time when WAN links, traveling through the public switched network, were primarily analog lines producing errors and poor transmissions. X.25 sought to remedy this through built-in error correction and flow control.

**XML**    *See* eXtensible Markup Language.

**Zone transfer**    In a zone transfer, the primary server gives its database (that is, its zone file) to the secondary server. It is possible to establish times and conditions under which a zone transfer will take place.

# Custom Corporate Network Training

**Train on Cutting Edge Technology**  We can bring the best in skill-based training to your facility to create a real-world hands-on training experience. Global Knowledge has invested millions of dollars in network hardware and software to train our students on the same equipment they will work with on the job. Our relationships with vendors allow us to incorporate the latest equipment and platforms into your on-site labs.

**Maximize Your Training Budget**  Global Knowledge provides experienced instructors, comprehensive course materials, and all the networking equipment needed to deliver high quality training. You provide the students; we provide the knowledge.

**Avoid Travel Expenses**  On-site courses allow you to schedule technical training at your convenience, saving time, expense, and the opportunity cost of travel away from the workplace.

**Discuss Confidential Topics**  Private on-site training permits the open discussion of sensitive issues such as security, access, and network design. We can work with your existing network's proprietary files while demonstrating the latest technologies.

**Customize Course Content**  Global Knowledge can tailor your courses to include the technologies and the topics which have the greatest impact on your business. We can complement your internal training efforts or provide a total solution to your training needs.

**Corporate Pass**  The Corporate Pass Discount Program rewards our best network training customers with preferred pricing on public courses, discounts on multimedia training packages, and an array of career planning services.

**Global Knowledge Training Lifecycle**  Supporting the Dynamic and Specialized Training Requirements of Information Technology Professionals

- Define Profile
- Assess Skills
- Design Training
- Deliver Training
- Test Knowledge
- Update Profile
- Use New Skills

**College Credit Recommendation Program**  The American Council on Education's CREDIT program recommends 53 Global Knowledge courses for college credit. Now our network training can help you earn your college degree while you learn the technical skills needed for your job. When you attend an ACE-certified Global Knowledge course and pass the associated exam, you earn college credit recommendations for that course. Global Knowledge can establish a transcript record for you with ACE, which you can use to gain credit at a college or as a written record of your professional training that you can attach to your resume.

# Registration Information

**COURSE FEE:** The fee covers course tuition, refreshments, and all course materials. Any parking expenses that may be incurred are not included. Payment or government training form must be received six business days prior to the course date. We will also accept Visa/MasterCard and American Express. For non-U.S. credit card users, charges will be in U.S. funds and will be converted by your credit card company. Checks drawn on Canadian banks in Canadian funds are acceptable.

**COURSE SCHEDULE:** Registration is at 8:00 a.m. on the first day. The program begins at 8:30 a.m. and concludes at 4:30 p.m. each day.

**CANCELLATION POLICY:** Cancellation and full refund will be allowed if written cancellation is received in our office at least six business days prior to the course start date. Registrants who do not attend the course or do not cancel more than six business days in advance are responsible for the full registration fee; you may transfer to a later date provided the course fee has been paid in full. Substitutions may be made at any time. If Global Knowledge must cancel a course for any reason, liability is limited to the registration fee only.

**GLOBAL KNOWLEDGE:** Global Knowledge programs are developed and presented by industry professionals with "real-world" experience. Designed to help professionals meet today's interconnectivity and interoperability challenges, most of our programs feature hands-on labs that incorporate state-of-the-art communication components and equipment.

**ON-SITE TEAM TRAINING:** Bring Global Knowledge's powerful training programs to your company. At Global Knowledge, we will custom design courses to meet your specific network requirements. Call 1 (919) 461-8686 for more information.

**YOUR GUARANTEE:** Global Knowledge believes its courses offer the best possible training in this field. If during the first day you are not satisfied and wish to withdraw from the course, simply notify the instructor, return all course materials, and receive a 100% refund.

## In the US:

CALL: 1 (888) 762-4442

FAX: 1 (919) 469-7070

VISIT OUR WEBSITE:

www.globalknowledge.com

MAIL CHECK AND THIS FORM TO:

Global Knowledge

Suite 200

114 Edinburgh South

P.O. Box 1187

Cary, NC 27512

## In Canada:

CALL: 1 (800) 465-2226

FAX: 1 (613) 567-3899

VISIT OUR WEBSITE:

www.globalknowledge.com.ca

MAIL CHECK AND THIS FORM TO:

Global Knowledge

Suite 1601

393 University Ave.

Toronto, ON M5G 1E6

## REGISTRATION INFORMATION:

Course title _____

Course location _____ Course date _____

Name/title _____ Company _____

Name/title _____ Company _____

Name/title _____ Company _____

Address _____ Telephone _____ Fax _____

City _____ State/Province _____ Zip/Postal Code _____

Credit card _____ Card # _____ Expiration date _____

Signature _____